Convolutional Coding:
Fundamentals and Applications

For a complete listing of the *Artech House Telecommunications Library,*
turn to the back of this book.

Convolutional Coding: Fundamentals and Applications

L. H. Charles Lee

Artech House
Boston • London

Library of Congress Cataloging-in-Publication Data
Lee, Charles, 1956-
  Convolutional coding : fundamentals and applications / Charles Lee.
    p.   cm.
  Includes bibliographical references and index.
  ISBN 0-89006-914-X (alk. paper)
    1. Digital communications—Mathematics.   2. Data protection—
Mathematics.   3. Convolutions (Mathematics)   4. Error-correcting codes
(Information theory)
    I. Title.
  TK5103.7.L433   1997
  621.382'2—dc21

                                                              97-1821
                                                               CIP

British Library Cataloguing in Publication Data
Lee, Charles
Convolutional coding: fundamentals and applications
    1. Convolutions (Mathematics)   2. Coding theory
    I. Title
    519.4

  ISBN 0-89006-914-X

Cover design by Jennifer Makower

International Standard Book Number: 0-89006-914-X
Library of Congress Catalog Card Number: 97-1821

10 9 8 7 6 5 4 3 2 1

In memory of my grandparents

Contents

Preface

Error-control coding covers a large class of codes and decoding techniques. Block codes and convolutional codes are commonly used in digital communication systems for reliable transmission of data. This book departs from the usual format in one major respect: It is devoted to the theory of error-control convolutional codes and their related topics. Emphasis is on random error-control convolutional codes. Burst error-control convolutional codes, interleaving techniques, and combined coding with precoding for bandwidth efficient channels are not discussed. Every effort has been made to explain the material as simply as possible, by examples and illustrations whenever possible. Of course, this book is by no means complete. New error-control codes and decoding methods are the result of ongoing research activities in digital communications. Naturally, completion of this book also signals and demands the beginning of new materials.

I assume that the reader is familiar with probability theory and has a sound knowledge of finite fields. I have been teaching much of the material presented here in universities over the past few years. The book can be used as a text for a final-year undergraduate or first-year graduate course on convolutional coding. It can also serve engineers who require knowledge of error-control convolutional codes.

The nine chapters each begin with an introductory section and are organized as follows.

Chapter 1 is a general review of digital communication systems. The concepts, presented at an elementary level, describe the model and elements of a digital communication system.

Chapter 2 describes the mathematical model of a convolutional encoder, followed by the polynomial matrix description of nonsystematic and systematic convolutional codes. Error-propagation effects are then presented. Simple procedures for constructing the right-inverse matrix from the generator matrix and the left-inverse matrix from the transpose of the parity-check matrix of an

$(n, n - 1, m)$ convolutional code are described for the design of noncatastrophic codes. Systematic convolutional encoders with feedback, graphical representations, distance measures, and the generating function of a code are then discussed.

Chapter 3 examines the theory of hard-decision and soft-decision suboptimum and optimum decoding processes. This is followed by a brief analysis of their performances with coherent binary phase-shifted keying signals.

Chapter 4 describes the Fano metric, the stack, and the sequential decoding processes of convolutional codes.

Chapter 5 is concerned with the encoding and decoding of punctured convolutional codes. The concepts of rate-compatible punctured convolutional codes are introduced.

Chapter 6 focuses on the hard- and soft-decision decoding of majority-logic convolutional codes.

Chapter 7 is concerned with the transmission of signals over bandwidth-constrained channels. The design theory of two-dimensional and multidimensional convolutional-coded modulation with M-ary phase-shifted keying and lattice signals are described. The design of rotationally invariant convolutional codes for bandwidth-constrained channels is also presented.

Chapter 8 describes the combined convolutional coding, modulation, and equalization technique for the transmission of signals over intersymbol interference channels.

Finally, Chapter 9 explores the application of convolutional codes to modern communication systems.

A final-year undergraduate course on convolutional coding would cover Chapters 1, 2, 3, 4, 5, and 9 and a brief introduction from the first two sections of Chapter 7. A first-year graduate course on convolutional coding would cover all the material in the book. A comprehensive reference section is included at the end of each chapter. It is hoped that the reader will benefit from the text and pursue further study on the topics of error-control coding.

I am grateful to the reviewer at Artech House, who thoroughly read the manuscript and made many valuable suggestions. I would also like to thank Professor Patrick G. Farrell, David J. Tait, and the many others who helped throughout the preparation of this book. The contributions of students who pointed out several errors are greatly appreciated.

The guidance I received from Dr. Julie Lancashire and Kate Hawes at Artech House is particularly appreciated. Finally, I thank my parents and my wife, Wendy, for their continuing support throughout the writing of this book.

L. H. Charles Lee

Introduction of Coded Digital Communication Systems

Modern digital communication systems often require error-free transmission. For example, the information transmitted and received over a banking network must not contain errors. The issue of data integrity is becoming increasingly important, and there are many more situations where error protection is required.

In 1948, the fundamental concepts and mathematical theory of information transmission were laid out by C. E. Shannon [1]. Shannon perceived that it is possible to transmit digital information over a noisy channel with an arbitrarily small error probability by proper channel encoding and decoding. The goal of approaching such error-free transmission can be achieved when the information transmission rate is less than the channel capacity, C_c, in bits per second. Since Shannon's work, a great deal of effort has been spent by many researchers to find good codes and efficient decoding methods for error control. As a result, many different types of codes, namely block codes and convolutional codes, have been found and used in modern digital communication systems. This book is mainly concerned with the structures of linear binary convolutional codes and the decoding techniques. The treatment here concentrates on the basic encoding and decoding principles of those convolutional codes.

1.1 INTRODUCTION

The development of channel coding was initiated primarily by users who wanted reliable transmission in a communication system. This chapter describes the elements that make up a reliable communication system, then examines various types of transmission channels. The mathematical models presented here give an adequate description of a communication system, because they relate to the physical reality of the transmission medium. Such mathematical models also ease the analysis of system performance. The principle concepts are presented at a basic level. For a more thorough treatment, readers should consult other, more comprehensive references [1–3].

1.2 ELEMENTS OF A DIGITAL COMMUNICATION SYSTEM

1.2.1 Data Source and Data Sink

The essential features of a digital communication system can be described in a block diagram, as shown in Figure 1.1. Binary information data are generated by the data source. The information symbols normally are sent in sequence, one after the other, to give a serial system. The key parameter here is the information rate, R_s, of the source, which is the minimum number of bits per second needed to represent the source output. Therefore, all redundancy should be removed from the data source, if possible. Details of redundancy removal from a source (source coding theory) are not discussed here. Rather, it is assumed that the binary digits generated by the data source are statistically independent and equally likely to have one of its possible values and are free of redundancy. At the receiving end, the decoded information data are delivered to the data sink (destination).

1.2.2 Channel Encoder and Channel Decoder

The information sequence generated by the data source is processed by the channel encoder, which transforms a k-symbol input sequence into an n-symbol

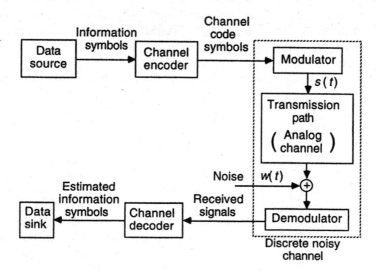

Figure 1.1 Model of a coded digital communication system.

output channel code sequence. The code sequence is a new sequence that has redundancy in it. The rate at which the transmission is performed by the encoder is defined as the code rate, R_c, where $R_c = k/n$ and $R_c \leq 1$. Two kinds of codes can be used: block codes and convolutional codes [4,5]. Block codes are implemented by combination logic circuits. Examples of block codes are *Bose-Chaudhuri-Hocquenghem* (BCH) codes, *Reed-Muller* (RM) codes, cyclic codes, array codes, *single-error-correcting* (SEC) Hamming codes, and *Reed-Solomon* (RS) codes. Convolutional codes are implemented by sequential logic circuit and are also called tree codes or trellis codes. In general, block and convolutional codes can be binary or nonbinary, linear or nonlinear, and systematic or nonsystematic. In those contexts, we do not consider block codes. At the receiving end, the channel decoder uses the redundancy in the channel code sequence to correct errors, if there are any, in the received channel sequence. The decoder then produces an estimate of the source information sequence.

1.2.3 Modulator, Transmission Path, and Demodulator

In a coded digital communication system, the modulator simply converts a block of channel code symbols to a suitable waveform, $s(t)$, of finite duration for transmission. The process is referred to as modulation. Viewed in a more general way, an M-ary modulator takes blocks of α binary digits from the channel encoder output and assigns one of the M possible waveforms to each block where $M = 2^\alpha$ and $\alpha \geq 1$. Thus, α number of binary bits are used to select a signal waveform of duration T seconds. T is referred to as the signaling interval.

Modulation can be performed by varying the amplitude, the phase, or the frequency of a high-frequency signal, called a carrier, by the input signal of the modulator. (Details of varying the frequency of a carrier signal are not discussed in this book.) If the input signal of the modulator is used to vary the amplitude of a carrier signal, the modulation is called *amplitude-shifted keying* (ASK) modulation. For example, an M-ary *amplitude-shifted keying* (M-ASK) signal can be defined by

$$s(t) = \begin{cases} A_i \cos(2\pi f_c t), & 0 \leq t \leq T \\ 0, & \text{elsewhere} \end{cases} \tag{1.1}$$

where

$$A_i = A[2i - (M - 1)] \tag{1.2}$$

for $i = 0, 1, \ldots, M - 1$. Here, A is a constant and f_c is the carrier frequency. Figure 1.2 shows the 4-ASK signal sequence generated by the binary sequence

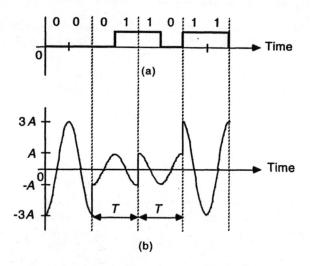

Figure 1.2 4-ASK modulation: (a) binary signal and (b) 4-ASK signal.

00 01 10 11. It can be seen that the modulated signal requires a bandwidth of $f_c = 1/T$ Hz. The signal bandwidth is obviously inversely proportional to T.

If the input signal of the modulator is used to vary the phase of a carrier signal, the modulation is called *phase-shifted keying* (PSK) modulation. An *M-ary phase-shifted keying* (*M*-PSK) signal can be defined by

$$s(t) = \begin{cases} A \cos(2\pi f_c t + \theta_i + \theta'), & 0 \leq t \leq T \\ 0, & \text{elsewhere} \end{cases} \quad (1.3)$$

where

$$\theta_i = \frac{2\pi}{M} i \quad (1.4)$$

for $i = 0, 1, \ldots, M - 1$. Here, A is the amplitude constant and θ' is an arbitrary phase angle. For convenience, the arbitrary phase angle θ' is taken to be zero. Figure 1.3 shows the *binary phase-shifted keying* (BPSK) signal sequence generated by the binary sequence 0110. Figure 1.4 shows the *4-ary phase-shifted keying* (4-PSK) signal sequence generated by the binary sequence 00 01 10 11.

Also, we can used the input signal of the modulator to vary the amplitude and the phase of a carrier signal. If the input signal is used to vary the amplitude and the phase of a carrier signal, the modulation is called *quadrature-amplitude-modulation* (QAM). An *M-ary quadrature-amplitude-modulation* (*M*-QAM) signal can be defined by

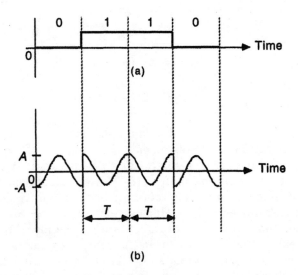

Figure 1.3 BPSK modulation: (a) binary signal and (b) BPSK signal.

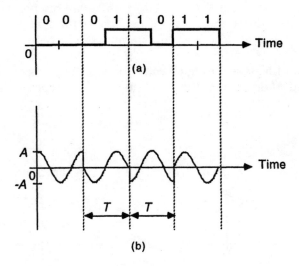

Figure 1.4 4-PSK modulation: (a) binary signal and (b) 4-PSK signal.

$$s(t) = \begin{cases} A_i \cos(2\pi f_c t) + B_j \sin(2\pi f_c t), & 0 \le t \le T \\ 0, & \text{elsewhere} \end{cases} \qquad (1.5)$$

where

$$A_i = A[2i - (\sqrt{M} - 1)] \tag{1.6}$$

$$B_j = A[2j - (\sqrt{M} - 1)] \tag{1.7}$$

for $i, j = 0, 1, \ldots, \sqrt{M} - 1$ and A is a constant. It can be seen from (1.5) that an M-QAM signal may be viewed as a combination of two $\sqrt{M}$ – ASK signals in phase quadrature. For $M = 16$, the modulation is called a *16-ary, or 16-point, quadrature-amplitude-modulation* (16-QAM). In digital communication system design, it often is convenient to represent each signal waveform, $s(t)$, as a point in a complex-number plane. This is referred to as the signal constellation diagram, and the coordinates of each point can be found by reading the values along the real and imaginary axes in the complex-number plane. Thus, a block of α channel code symbols maps implicitly to the signal point (symbol), s_l, at time l, and there is a unique one-to-one mapping between the channel code symbols and the signal symbols in the signal constellation diagram. Each signal waveform $s(t)$ of duration $T = 1/f_c$ seconds can now be identified by a signal symbol and the signal symbol rate is $1/T$ symbols per second or bauds. The transmission rate at the input of the M-ary modulator is therefore equal to α/T bits per second, where α is the number of bits required to represent a signal symbol.

Figure 1.5 gives the signal constellation diagrams of some commonly used binary and M-ary modulation techniques. The types of signal constellations

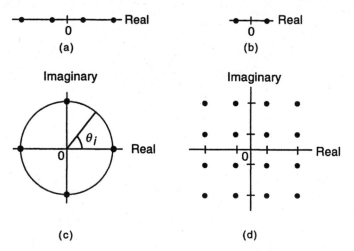

Figure 1.5 (a) 4-ASK, (b) BPSK, (c) 4-PSK, and (d) 16-QAM signal constellation diagrams.

shown in Figure 1.5(a,b) are examples of one-dimensional modulation, where all signal points lie along the real axis in the complex-number plane. Note that the BPSK signal is equivalent to the *binary amplitude-shifted keying* (BASK) signal. Figure 1.5(c,d) are examples of two-dimensional modulation, where all signal points lie along the real and imaginary axes in the complex-number plane. In all cases, it is common to set the average energy per signal symbol, E_s, to unity. For example, all the signal points are equally spaced and lie on the unit circle for the 4-PSK signals as shown in Figure 1.5(c). The average energy per signal symbol is equal to 1.

The modulator output waveform now passes into a transmission path (an analog channel), and the path may modify the waveform by introducing noise. The transmission path may take on various forms. It does not have to be a permanent hard-wired medium (e.g., a telephone line) that connects the modulator and the demodulator together. Typical transmission paths are telephone circuits, mobile radio links, satellite links, or even magnetic tapes. Each of these analog channels is subject to noise disturbance. It is assumed that *additive white Gaussian noise* (AWGN), $w(t)$, is added to the transmitted waveforms at the output of the analog channel; other types of noise have not been considered, although intersymbol interference is treated later. The received signal is

$$r(t) = s(t) + w(t) \tag{1.8}$$

The demodulator uses a process of linear coherent demodulation (matched-filter detection and sampling) to convert the received signal, $r(t)$, into its digital form. With appropriate design of the demodulator, the sampled demodulator output signal at time l is

$$r_l = s_l + w_l \tag{1.9}$$

where the real and the imaginary parts of the noise components $\{w_l\}$ are statistically independent Gaussian random variables with zero mean and fixed variance σ^2. In the case of a BPSK signaling scheme, the variance of the Gaussian noise samples is equal to the two-sided noise power spectral density $N_0/2$. The modulator together with the analog channel and the demodulator form a discrete noisy channel. The transmitter and the receiver are assumed to be held in synchronism to give a synchronous serial transmission system.

1.2.4 Channel Models

1.2.4.1 Discrete Memoryless Channel

From the viewpoint of the channel encoding and decoding operations in the digital communication system in Figure 1.1, the segment enclosed in dashed lines characterizes a discrete noisy channel. One way of realizing this channel is to use a coherent *M*-ary signaling scheme. The channel can then be characterized by a set of *M* input symbols, a set of *Q* output symbols, and a set of *M.Q* transition probabilities. The transition probabilities are time-invariant and independent from symbol to symbol. This is the *discrete memoryless channel* (DMC). In the general case, a DMC comprises an *M*-ary modulator, a transmission path, and a *Q*-ary demodulator. This channel can be represented diagrammatically as shown in Figure 1.6. $P(j/i)$ defines the transition probability of receiving the *j*th symbol given that the *i*th symbol was transmitted, where $i = 1, 2, \ldots,$ *M* and $j = 1, 2, \ldots, Q$. By making $Q > M$, the demodulator now produces soft-decision information to the channel decoder. (The advantage of using the soft-decision demodulator output in the channel decoder is discussed in Chapter 3.)

1.2.4.2 Binary Symmetric Channel

The most commonly encountered case of the DMC is the *binary symmetric channel* (BSC), where a binary modulator is used at the transmitter and the demodulator is making hard-decisions with *Q* set to 2. The schematic representation of this channel is shown in Figure 1.7, where *p* denotes the cross-over probability.

For the coherent BPSK signaling scheme, the BSC cross-over probability, *p*, and the bit error probability, P_b, are given by

$$p = P_b = Q\left(\sqrt{\frac{2E_s}{N_0}}\right) = Q\left(\sqrt{\frac{2E_b}{N_0}}\right) \tag{1.10}$$

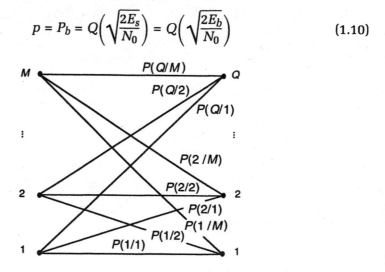

Figure 1.6 Discrete memoryless channel.

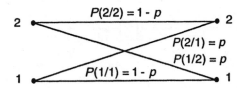

Figure 1.7 Binary symmetric channel.

where

$$Q(\alpha'') \equiv \frac{1}{\sqrt{2\pi}} \int_{\alpha''}^{\infty} e^{-\beta''^2/2} d\beta'' \tag{1.11}$$

and the average energy per signal symbol, E_s, equals the average energy per information bit, E_b. This is due to the fact that one bit is all we needed to map onto a signal symbol.

With this approach, we have combined the modulator, the transmission path, and the demodulator into a compact M-input, Q-output channel model depicted by the transition diagram.

1.2.4.3 Intersymbol Interference Channel

When the transmission path has an infinite bandwidth, the transmitted individual signal symbols will arrive at the receiver undistorted. In practice, the spectrum of the transmitted signal symbols is bandlimited by the available channel bandwidth. With insufficient channel bandwidth, each transmitted signal spreads into adjacent signal intervals, and adjacent symbols interfere with each other. The effect is termed *intersymbol interference* (ISI). In baseband, we can use a digital filter to model an ISI channel. The sampled impulse response of an ISI baseband channel is given by the $(\mu + 1)$-component complex vector

$$\mathbf{B} = [b_0 b_1 \ldots b_\mu] \tag{1.12}$$

where $b_0 \neq 0$ and $b_i = 0$ for $i < 0$ and $i > \mu$. The delay in transmission is neglected. $\mathbf{B}$ is either time-invariant or varies only slowly with time. The complex output signal at time l is

$$s_l b_0 + \sum_{h=1}^{\mu} s_{l-h} b_h \tag{1.13}$$

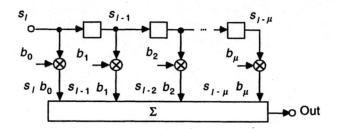

Figure 1.8 ISI channel model.

This is shown in Figure 1.8. The theory of communication over ISI channels can be found in another textbook [6]. Chapter 8 discusses the design of channel coding, modulation, and equalization for ISI channels.

References

[1] Shannon, C. E., "A Mathematical Theory of Communication," *Bell Syst. Tech. J.*, Vol. 27, No. 3, July 1948, pp. 379–423, and Vol. 27, No. 4, October 1948, pp. 623–656.

[2] Wozencraft, J. M., and I. M. Jacobs, *Principles of Communication Engineering*, New York: Wiley, 1965.

[3] Gallager, R. G., *Information Theory and Reliable Communication*, New York: Wiley, 1968.

[4] Berlekamp, E. R., "The Technology of Error-Correcting Codes," *IEEE Proc.*, Vol. 68, No. 5, May 1980, pp. 564–592.

[5] Berlekamp, E. R., R. E. Peile, and S. P. Pope, "The Application of Error Control Codes to Communications," *IEEE Commun. Mag.*, Vol. 25, No. 54, April 1987, pp. 44–57.

[6] Lucky, R. W., J. Salz, and E. J. Weldon, *Principles of Data Communication*, New York: McGraw-Hill, 1968.

Structures of Convolutional Codes 2

2.1 ENCODING AND MATHEMATICAL MODEL OF CONVOLUTIONAL CODES

An (n, k, m) binary convolutional encoder over the Galois field $GF(2)$ is a k-input, n-output, time-invariant, causal, finite-state machine of encoder memory order m [1]. The code rate is defined to be

$$R_c = k/n \tag{2.1}$$

Figure 2.1 shows the mathematical model of an (n, k, m) convolutional encoder.

The encoder can be envisaged as consisting of k shift registers where the stage inputs and outputs of the shift registers are connected in a certain pattern to n multi-input modulo-2 adders [2–4]. Since modulo-2 addition is a linear operation, the convolutional encoder is called a linear convolutional encoder. In $GF(2)$, the modulo-2 adders can be implemented as exclusive-or logic gates. The input and output sequences of the (n, k, m) convolutional encoder in the time domain can be denoted by the two row vectors

$$\mathbf{X} = [\mathbf{X}_0 \ \mathbf{X}_1 \dots \mathbf{X}_l \dots] \tag{2.2}$$

and

$$\mathbf{Y} = [\mathbf{Y}_0 \ \mathbf{Y}_1 \dots \mathbf{Y}_l \dots] \tag{2.3}$$

Here, $\mathbf{X}_l$ is the encoder input at time l and is represented by the k-component row vector

$$\mathbf{X}_l = [x_l^{(1)} \ x_l^{(2)} \dots x_l^{(k)}] \tag{2.4}$$

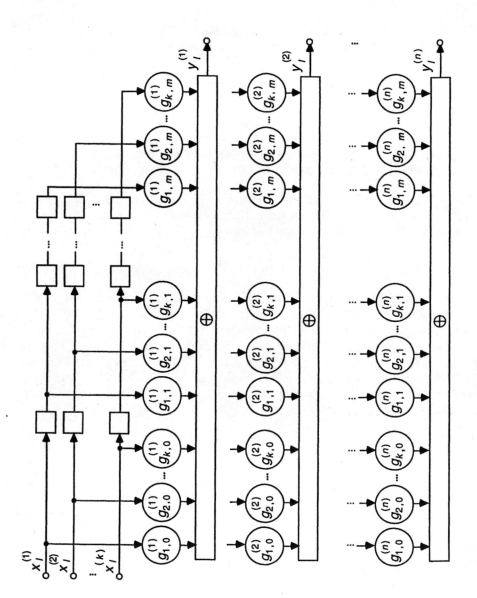

Figure 2.1 Encoder model for an (*n*, *k*, *m*) convolutional code.

Similarly, the encoder output at time l is represented by the n-component row vector

$$\mathbf{Y}_l = [y_l^{(1)} \; y_l^{(2)} \; \ldots \; y_l^{(n)}] \tag{2.5}$$

A segment of k binary information bits is shifted serially or in parallel into the shift registers, and the n-bit encoder output bits are sampled and transmitted serially. The linear relationship between the input and the output sequences can be expressed as a matrix convolutional of the form

$$\mathbf{Y} = \mathbf{X} \, \mathbf{G} \tag{2.6}$$

and

$$\mathbf{G} = \begin{bmatrix} \mathbf{G}_0 & \mathbf{G}_1 & \mathbf{G}_2 & \cdots & \mathbf{G}_m & \mathbf{0} & \mathbf{0} & \mathbf{0} & \cdots \\ \mathbf{0} & \mathbf{G}_0 & \mathbf{G}_1 & \cdots & \mathbf{G}_{m-1} & \mathbf{G}_m & \mathbf{0} & \mathbf{0} \\ \mathbf{0} & \mathbf{0} & \mathbf{G}_0 & \cdots & \mathbf{G}_{m-2} & \mathbf{G}_{m-1} & \mathbf{G}_m & \mathbf{0} \\ \vdots & & & & & & & & \ddots \end{bmatrix} \tag{2.7}$$

where $\mathbf{0}$ is the k-by-n zero matrix and each $\mathbf{G}_{l'}$, $0 \le l' \le m$, is a k-by-n submatrix

$$\mathbf{G}_{l'} = \begin{bmatrix} g_{1,l'}^{(1)} & g_{1,l'}^{(2)} & \cdots & g_{1,l'}^{(n)} \\ g_{2,l'}^{(1)} & g_{2,l'}^{(2)} & \cdots & g_{2,l'}^{(n)} \\ \vdots & \vdots & & \vdots \\ g_{k,l'}^{(1)} & g_{k,l'}^{(2)} & \cdots & g_{k,l'}^{(n)} \end{bmatrix} \tag{2.8}$$

with binary entries showing the connections from the k shift registers to the n modulo-2 adders. $\mathbf{G}$ is called the generator matrix for a convolutional encoder and is in fact a semi-infinite matrix, since the input sequence is of an arbitrary length. The output sequences are determined by n connection vectors $\mathbf{G}^{(1)}$, $\mathbf{G}^{(2)}$, $\ldots$, $\mathbf{G}^{(n)}$, where the jth connection vector $\mathbf{G}^{(j)}$ relates the stage inputs and outputs of the k shift registers to the jth output and is given by

$$\mathbf{G}^{(j)} = \left[g_{1,0}^{(j)} g_{2,0}^{(j)} \cdots g_{k,0}^{(j)} g_{1,1}^{(j)} g_{2,1}^{(j)} \cdots g_{k,1}^{(j)} \cdots g_{1,m}^{(j)} g_{2,m}^{(j)} \cdots g_{k,m}^{(j)} \right] \tag{2.9}$$

for $1 \le j \le n$. A "1" in a position of the connection vector indicates that the corresponding stage in the k shift registers is connected to the modulo-2 adder.

A "0" in a given position indicates that there is no connection between that stage of the shift registers and the modulo-2 adder. Figures 2.2 and 2.3 show the encoders for the binary (2, 1, 2) and (3, 2, 1) convolutional codes, respectively. When the length of the connection vectors become very long, they are more conveniently expressed in octal form. For instance, the connection vectors of the (2, 1, 2) convolutional code shown in Figure 2.2 are $\mathbf{G}^{(1)} = [1\ 0\ 1]$ and $\mathbf{G}^{(2)} = [1\ 1\ 1]$. In octal form, these connection vectors become $\mathbf{G}^{(1)} = (5)_8$ and $\mathbf{G}^{(2)} = (7)_8$. In general, the jth encoder output is the discrete convolution between the row vectors $\mathbf{X}$ and $\mathbf{G}^{(j)}$. For all $l \geq 0$,

$$y_l^{(j)} = \sum_{i=1}^{k} \sum_{l'=0}^{m} x_{l-l'}^{(i)} g_{i,l'}^{(j)} \tag{2.10}$$

Example 2.1

For the rate-1/2 convolutional encoder in Figure 2.2, the semi-infinite generator matrix is

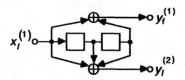

Figure 2.2 (2, 1, 2) convolutional encoder.

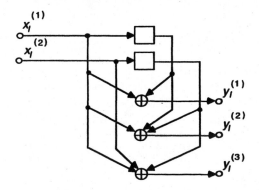

Figure 2.3 (3, 2, 1) convolutional encoder.

$$
\mathbf{G} = \begin{bmatrix} g_{1,0}^{(1)} g_{1,0}^{(2)} & g_{1,1}^{(1)} g_{1,1}^{(2)} & g_{1,2}^{(1)} g_{1,2}^{(2)} & \cdots \\ & g_{1,0}^{(1)} g_{1,0}^{(2)} & g_{1,1}^{(1)} g_{1,1}^{(2)} & g_{1,2}^{(1)} g_{1,2}^{(2)} \\ \vdots & & & \ddots \end{bmatrix}
$$

$$
= \begin{bmatrix} 1\ 1 & 0\ 1 & 1\ 1 & \cdots \\ & 1\ 1 & 0\ 1 & 1\ 1 \\ \vdots & & & \ddots \end{bmatrix}
$$

Let the encoder input sequence $\mathbf{X} = [1\ 0\ 1\ 1\ \ldots]$. Then the encoder output sequence is

$$\mathbf{Y} = \mathbf{X}\,\mathbf{G}$$

$$
= [1\ 0\ 1\ 1 \ldots] \begin{bmatrix} 1\ 1 & 0\ 1 & 1\ 1 & & & \cdots \\ & 1\ 1 & 0\ 1 & 1\ 1 \\ & & 1\ 1 & 0\ 1 & 1\ 1 \\ & & & 1\ 1 & 0\ 1 & 1\ 1 \\ \vdots & & & & & \ddots \end{bmatrix}
$$

$$= [11\ \ 01\ \ 00\ \ 10\ \ \cdots\ \cdots\ \cdots]$$

Example 2.2

For the (3, 2, 1) encoder in Figure 2.3, the semi-infinite generator matrix is

$$
\mathbf{G} = \begin{bmatrix} g_{1,0}^{(1)} g_{1,0}^{(2)} g_{1,0}^{(3)} & g_{1,1}^{(1)} g_{1,1}^{(2)} g_{1,1}^{(3)} & & \cdots \\ g_{2,0}^{(1)} g_{2,0}^{(2)} g_{2,0}^{(3)} & g_{2,1}^{(1)} g_{2,1}^{(2)} g_{2,1}^{(3)} \\ & g_{1,0}^{(1)} g_{1,0}^{(2)} g_{1,0}^{(3)} & g_{1,1}^{(1)} g_{1,1}^{(2)} g_{1,1}^{(3)} \\ & g_{2,0}^{(1)} g_{2,0}^{(2)} g_{2,0}^{(3)} & g_{2,1}^{(1)} g_{2,1}^{(2)} g_{2,1}^{(3)} \\ \vdots & & & \ddots \end{bmatrix}
$$

$$
= \begin{bmatrix} 1\ 1\ 1 & 1\ 1\ 0 & \cdots \\ 0\ 0\ 1 & 0\ 1\ 1 \\ & 1\ 1\ 1 & 1\ 1\ 0 \\ & 0\ 0\ 1 & 0\ 1\ 1 \\ \vdots & & \ddots \end{bmatrix}
$$

If the encoder input sequence $\mathbf{X} = [10 \; 11 \; \cdots \; \cdots]$, then

$$\mathbf{Y} = \mathbf{X} \mathbf{G}$$

$$= [10 \; 11 \; \cdots \; \cdots]
\begin{bmatrix}
1\,1\,1 & 1\,1\,0 & & \cdots \\
0\,0\,1 & 0\,1\,1 & & \\
 & 1\,1\,1 & 1\,1\,0 & \\
 & 0\,0\,1 & 0\,1\,1 & \\
\vdots & & & \ddots
\end{bmatrix}$$

$$= [1\,1\,1\;0\,0\,0\;\cdots\;\cdots]$$

We have seen the case where each segment of k information bits are encoded into n bits and the code rate is k/n. If the input information sequence $\mathbf{X}$ is finite, the contents of the shift registers will contain $k \cdot m$ previously transmitted information bits after the last information segment has entered the encoder. To clear the contents of the k shift registers for proper termination of the encoder, we need to input $k \cdot m$ zeros into the shift registers. The convolutional encoder now becomes a block encoder and the code rate is somewhat less than k/n.

Example 2.3

Let the encoder input sequence $\mathbf{X} = [1\,0\,1\,1]$ be terminated by two zeros. Then the encoder output sequence for the (2, 1, 2) encoder of Figure 2.2 is

$$\mathbf{Y} = \mathbf{X} \mathbf{G}$$

$$= [1\,0\;1\,1\;0\,0]
\begin{bmatrix}
1\,1 & 0\,1 & 1\,1 & & & \\
 & 1\,1 & 0\,1 & 1\,1 & & \\
 & & 1\,1 & 0\,1 & 1\,1 & \\
 & & & 1\,1 & 0\,1 & 1\,1 \\
 & & & & 1\,1 & 0\,1 & 1\,1 \\
 & & & & & 1\,1 & 0\,1 & 1\,1
\end{bmatrix}$$

$$= [11\;01\;00\;10\;10\;11\;00\;00]$$

Example 2.4

If the encoder input sequence $\mathbf{X} = [10 \; 11]$ is terminated by two zeros, then the encoder output sequence for the (3, 2, 1) encoder of Figure 2.3 is

$$\mathbf{Y} = \mathbf{X}\,\mathbf{G}$$

$$= [10 \;\; 11 \;\; 00]
\begin{bmatrix}
1\,1\,1 & 1\,1\,0 & & \\
0\,0\,1 & 0\,1\,1 & & \\
1\,1\,1 & 1\,1\,0 & & \\
0\,0\,1 & 0\,1\,1 & & \\
 & 1\,1\,1 & 1\,1\,0 & \\
 & 0\,0\,1 & 0\,1\,1 &
\end{bmatrix}$$

$$= [111 \;\; 000 \;\; 101 \;\; 000]$$

An (n, k, m) linear convolutional encoder can also be described by its semi-infinite parity-check matrix $\mathbf{H}$ with binary elements. The semi-infinite parity-check matrix of an (n, k, m) linear convolutional code satisfies

$$\mathbf{G}\,\mathbf{H}^T = \mathbf{0} \tag{2.11}$$

where $\mathbf{H}^T$ is the transpose of the matrix $\mathbf{H}$. Furthermore, the following relationship exists between $\mathbf{Y}$ and $\mathbf{H}$:

$$\mathbf{Y}\,\mathbf{H}^T = \mathbf{0} \tag{2.12}$$

We shall say no more about the semi-infinite parity-check matrix $\mathbf{H}$ until we meet the subclass of convolutional codes called systematic convolutional codes. We shall also see, in Section 2.2, that it is more useful to describe a linear convolutional code in a transform domain.

So far we have encountered only the class of convolutional codes called nonsystematic convolutional codes. Another important subclass of convolutional codes we are going to look at is the class of systematic convolutional codes. In a systematic convolutional code, all the k input information bits in $\mathbf{X}_l$ also form part of the encoder output vector $\mathbf{Y}_l$, that is,

$$y_l^{(i)} = x_l^{(i)} \tag{2.13}$$

for $i = 1, 2, \ldots, k$ and the semi-infinite generator matrix is given by

$$\mathbf{G} =
\begin{bmatrix}
\mathbf{I}\,\mathbf{P}_0 & \mathbf{0}\,\mathbf{P}_1 & \mathbf{0}\,\mathbf{P}_2 & \cdots & \mathbf{0}\,\mathbf{P}_m & & & \cdots \\
 & \mathbf{I}\,\mathbf{P}_0 & \mathbf{0}\,\mathbf{P}_1 & \cdots & \mathbf{0}\,\mathbf{P}_{m-1} & \mathbf{0}\,\mathbf{P}_m & & \\
 & & \mathbf{I}\,\mathbf{P}_0 & \cdots & \mathbf{0}\,\mathbf{P}_{m-2} & \mathbf{0}\,\mathbf{P}_{m-1} & \mathbf{0}\,\mathbf{P}_m & \\
 \vdots & & & & & & & \ddots
\end{bmatrix} \tag{2.14}$$

where $\mathbf{I}$ is the k-by-k identity matrix, $\mathbf{0}$ is the k-by-k zero matrix, and each $\mathbf{P}_{l'}$, $0 \le l' \le m$, is a k-by-$(n - k)$ submatrix

$$\mathbf{P}_{l'} = \begin{bmatrix} g_{1,l'}^{(k+1)} & g_{1,l'}^{(k+2)} & \cdots & g_{1,l'}^{(n)} \\ g_{2,l'}^{(k+1)} & g_{2,l'}^{(k+2)} & \cdots & g_{2,l'}^{(n)} \\ \vdots & \vdots & & \vdots \\ g_{k,l'}^{(k+1)} & g_{k,l'}^{(k+2)} & \cdots & g_{k,l'}^{(n)} \end{bmatrix} \tag{2.15}$$

with binary entries. Figures 2.4 and 2.5 show the encoders for the binary (2, 1, 1) and (3, 2, 1) systematic convolutional codes, respectively. For a systematic convolutional code, the semi-infinite parity-check matrix can be expressed using the elements of $\mathbf{G}$, that is,

$$\mathbf{H} = \begin{bmatrix} \mathbf{P}_0^T\mathbf{I} & & & & & & \cdots \\ \mathbf{P}_1^T\mathbf{0} & \mathbf{P}_0^T\mathbf{I} & & & & & \\ \vdots & & \ddots & & & & \\ \mathbf{P}_m^T\mathbf{0} & \mathbf{P}_{m-1}^T\mathbf{0} & \cdots & \mathbf{P}_0^T\mathbf{I} & & & \\ & \mathbf{P}_m^T\mathbf{0} & \cdots & \mathbf{P}_1^T\mathbf{0} & \mathbf{P}_0^T\mathbf{I} & & \\ & & \ddots & & & \ddots & \\ \vdots & & & \mathbf{P}_m^T\mathbf{0} & \mathbf{P}_{m-1}^T\mathbf{0} & \cdots & \mathbf{P}_0^T\mathbf{I} \\ & & & & & & & \ddots \end{bmatrix} \tag{2.16}$$

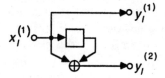

Figure 2.4 (2, 1, 1) systematic convolutional encoder.

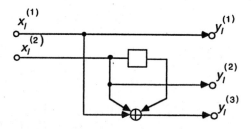

Figure 2.5 (3, 2, 1) systematic convolutional encoder.

where, in this case, I is the $(n - k)$-by-$(n - k)$ identity matrix, 0 is the $(n - k)$-by-$(n - k)$ zero matrix, and P_f^T is the transpose of P_f.

Example 2.5

Let the encoder input sequence $X = [1 \ 0 \ 1 \ 1 \ \ldots]$. Then the encoder output sequence for the $(2, 1, 1)$ systematic convolutional encoder of Figure 2.4 is

$$Y = X \, G$$

$$= [1 \ 0 \ 1 \ 1 \ldots] \begin{bmatrix} 1 \ 1 & 0 \ 1 & & & \cdots \\ & 1 \ 1 & 0 \ 1 & \\ & & 1 \ 1 & 0 \ 1 \\ & & & 1 \ 1 & 0 \ 1 \\ \vdots & & & & \ddots \end{bmatrix}$$

$$= [1 \ 1 \ 0 \ 1 \ 1 \ 1 \ 1 \ 0 \ \cdots \ \cdots \ \cdots]$$

Example 2.6

If the encoder input sequence $X = [10 \ 11 \ \cdots \ \cdots]$, then the encoder output sequence for the $(3, 2, 1)$ systematic convolutional encoder of Figure 2.5 is

$$Y = X \, G$$

$$= [10 \ 11 \ \cdots \ \cdots] \begin{bmatrix} 1 \ 0 \ 1 & 0 \ 0 \ 0 & & \cdots \\ 0 \ 1 \ 1 & 0 \ 0 \ 1 & \\ & 1 \ 0 \ 1 & 0 \ 0 \ 0 \\ & 0 \ 1 \ 1 & 0 \ 0 \ 1 \\ \vdots & & \ddots \end{bmatrix}$$

$$= [1 \ 0 \ 1 \ 1 \ 1 \ 0 \ \cdots \ \cdots]$$

2.2 POLYNOMIAL MATRIX REPRESENTATION OF CONVOLUTIONAL CODES

The description of the encoding operation can be made more precise. Specifically, convolution in the time domain can be represented as polynomial multiplication in a transform domain. Let D be the unit-delay operator. The encoder input sequences can be represented by the 1-by-k polynomial matrix in the delay operator D (D-transform)

$$\mathbf{X}(D) = [x^{(1)}(D)\ x^{(2)}(D) \cdots x^{(k)}(D)] \tag{2.17}$$

and

$$x^{(i)}(D) = x_0^{(i)} + x_1^{(i)}D + \cdots + x_l^{(i)}D^l + \cdots \tag{2.18}$$

for $1 \le i \le k$. Here, the encoder input at time l is represented by the k-component row vector $\mathbf{X}_l = [x_l^{(1)}\ x_l^{(2)} \cdots x_l^{(k)}]$. Similarly, the encoder output sequences can be represented as

$$\mathbf{Y}(D) = [y^{(1)}(D)\ y^{(2)}(D) \cdots y^{(n)}(D)] \tag{2.19}$$

where

$$y^{(j)}(D) = y_0^{(j)} + y_1^{(j)}D + \cdots + y_l^{(j)}D^l + \cdots \tag{2.20}$$

for $1 \le j \le n$ and the encoder output at time l is represented by the n-component row vector $\mathbf{Y}_l = [y_l^{(1)}\ y_l^{(2)} \cdots y_l^{(n)}]$. The input $\mathbf{X}(D)$ and the output $\mathbf{Y}(D)$ are linearly related by means of a k-by-n generator polynomial matrix $\mathbf{G}(D)$, as follows:

$$\mathbf{Y}(D) = \mathbf{X}(D)\mathbf{G}(D) \tag{2.21}$$

where

$$\mathbf{G}(D) = \begin{bmatrix} G_1^{(1)}(D) & G_1^{(2)}(D) & \cdots & G_1^{(n)}(D) \\ G_2^{(1)}(D) & G_2^{(2)}(D) & \cdots & G_2^{(n)}(D) \\ \vdots & \vdots & & \vdots \\ G_k^{(1)}(D) & G_k^{(2)}(D) & \cdots & G_k^{(n)}(D) \end{bmatrix} \tag{2.22}$$

and the element $G_i^{(j)}(D)$ is interpreted as the generator polynomial that relates the ith encoder input to the jth output and is given by

$$G_i^{(j)}(D) = g_{i,0}^{(j)} + g_{i,1}^{(j)}D + \cdots + g_{i,m}^{(j)}D^m \tag{2.23}$$

As with any k-input, n-output linear encoder, there are $k \cdot n$ generator polynomials.

Example 2.7

For the (2, 1, 2) convolutional encoder in Figure 2.2, the generator polynomials of the code are $G_1^{(1)}(D) = 1 + D^2$ and $G_1^{(2)}(D) = 1 + D + D^2$, and the generator matrix $G(D) = [1 + D^2 \quad 1 + D + D^2]$. For the (3, 2, 1) convolutional encoder in Figure 2.3, the generator polynomials of the code are $G_1^{(1)}(D) = 1 + D$, $G_1^{(2)}(D) = 1 + D$, $G_1^{(3)}(D) = 1$, $G_2^{(1)}(D) = 0$, $G_2^{(2)}(D) = D$, and $G_2^{(3)}(D) = 1 + D$, and the generator matrix $G(D)$ equals

$$\begin{bmatrix} 1 + D & 1 + D & 1 \\ 0 & D & 1 + D \end{bmatrix}$$

Example 2.8

If $X = [1\ 0\ 1\ 1]$ and $G(D) = [1 + D^2 \quad 1 + D + D^2]$, then $X(D) = [1 + D^2 + D^3]$,

$$\begin{aligned} Y(D) &= X(D)G(D) \\ &= [1 + D^2 + D^3][1 + D^2 \quad 1 + D + D^2] \\ &= [1 + D^3 + D^4 + D^5 \quad 1 + D + D^5] \\ &= [y^{(1)}(D) \quad y^{(2)}(D)] \end{aligned}$$

and $Y = [y_0^{(1)}\ y_0^{(2)}\ y_1^{(1)}\ y_1^{(2)} \dots\dots] = [11\quad 01\quad 00\quad 10\ ..\ ..\ ..]$. This agrees with the result obtained in Example 2.1.

In general, each row in $G(D)$ represents the connections from one of the shift registers to the n outputs. If the ith shift register has length L_i, the length L_i is given by

$$L_i = \max_{1 \le j \le n} [\deg G_i^{(j)}(D)] \qquad (2.24)$$

where $\deg G_i^{(j)}(D)$ is the degree of polynomial $G_i^{(j)}(D)$ and the maximum length among all k shift registers is defined as the *encoder memory order*; that is,

$$m = \max_{1 \le i \le k} L_i \qquad (2.25)$$

The total encoder memory is defined as

$$K = \sum_{i=1}^{k} L_i \qquad (2.26)$$

and the constraint length of the encoder is defined as

$$\nu = m + 1 \tag{2.27}$$

Example 2.9

If $\mathbf{G}(D) = \begin{bmatrix} 1 + D & 1 + D & 1 \\ 0 & D & 1 + D \end{bmatrix}$, then

$$L_1 = 1$$
$$L_2 = 1$$
$$m = 1$$
$$K = 2$$

and

$$\nu = 2$$

Example 2.10

If $\mathbf{G}(D) = \begin{bmatrix} 1 & D & 1 + D \\ D^2 & 1 & 1 + D + D^2 \end{bmatrix}$, then

$$L_1 = 1$$
$$L_2 = 2$$
$$m = 2$$
$$K = 3$$

and

$$\nu = 3$$

The parity-check polynomial matrix associated with $\mathbf{G}(D)$ is an $(n - k)$-by-n polynomial matrix with elements in $GF(2)$ that satisfies

$$\mathbf{G}(D)\mathbf{H}^T(D) = \mathbf{0} \tag{2.28}$$

where $\mathbf{H}^T(D)$ is the transpose of the parity-check polynomial matrix $\mathbf{H}(D)$ and is called the syndrome-former polynomial matrix of the code. For an $(n, k,$

m) convolutional encoder, the parity-check polynomial matrix $\mathbf{H}(D)$ can be represented as

$$\mathbf{H}(D) = \begin{bmatrix} H_1^{(1)}(D) & H_1^{(2)}(D) & \cdots & H_1^{(n)}(D) \\ H_2^{(1)}(D) & H_2^{(2)}(D) & \cdots & H_2^{(n)}(D) \\ \vdots & \vdots & & \vdots \\ H_{n-k}^{(1)}(D) & H_{n-k}^{(2)}(D) & \cdots & H_{n-k}^{(n)}(D) \end{bmatrix} \tag{2.29}$$

where

$$H_i^{(j)}(D) = h_{i,0}^{(j)} + h_{i,1}^{(j)}D + \cdots + h_{i,m''}^{(j)}D^{m''} \tag{2.30}$$

for $1 \leq i \leq (n - k)$, $1 \leq j \leq n$ and $m'' \geq 0$. The coefficients of $H_i^{(j)}(D)$ are binary. Similarly, the length L_i'' is given by

$$L_i'' = \max_{1 \leq j \leq n} [\deg H_i^{(j)}(D)] \tag{2.31}$$

where $\deg H_i^{(j)}(D)$ is the degree of polynomial $H_i^{(j)}(D)$ and the maximum length among all $\{H_i^{(j)}(D)\}$ is defined as

$$m'' = \max_{1 \leq i \leq (n-k)} L_i'' \tag{2.32}$$

The total parity-check memory is defined as

$$K'' = \sum_{i=1}^{n-k} L_i'' \tag{2.33}$$

Furthermore, the following relationship exists between $\mathbf{Y}(D)$ and $\mathbf{H}(D)$:

$$\mathbf{Y}(D)\mathbf{H}^T(D) = \mathbf{0} \tag{2.34}$$

$\mathbf{H}(D)$ can therefore be thought of as the generator of the dual code [5] to that generated by $\mathbf{G}(D)$.

In a systematic convolutional code, the generator matrix given in (2.22) can be written as

$$\mathbf{G}(D) = \begin{bmatrix} 1 & 0 & \cdots & 0 & G_1^{(k+1)}(D) & G_1^{(k+2)}(D) & \cdots & G_1^{(n)}(D) \\ 0 & 1 & \cdots & 0 & G_2^{(k+1)}(D) & G_2^{(k+2)}(D) & \cdots & G_2^{(n)}(D) \\ \vdots & \vdots & & \vdots & \vdots & \vdots & & \vdots \\ 0 & 0 & \cdots & 1 & G_k^{(k+1)}(D) & G_k^{(k+2)}(D) & \cdots & G_k^{(n)}(D) \end{bmatrix} \quad (2.35)$$

and the parity-check matrix can be expressed using the elements of $\mathbf{G}(D)$, that is,

$$\mathbf{H}(D) = \begin{bmatrix} G_1^{(k+1)}(D) & G_2^{(k+1)}(D) & \cdots & G_k^{(k+1)}(D) & 1 & 0 & \cdots & 0 \\ G_1^{(k+2)}(D) & G_2^{(k+2)}(D) & \cdots & G_k^{(k+2)}(D) & 0 & 1 & \cdots & 0 \\ \vdots & \vdots & & \vdots & & \vdots & \vdots & & \vdots \\ G_1^{(n)}(D) & G_2^{(n)}(D) & \cdots & G_k^{(n)}(D) & 0 & 0 & \cdots & 1 \end{bmatrix} \quad (2.36)$$

Equation (2.35) represents the necessary and sufficient condition for an (n, k, m) convolutional code to be systematic. Any convolutional code not satisfying that condition is said to be nonsystematic. In practice, nonsystematic convolutional codes normally are employed because, for the same code rate and constraint length, systematic convolutional codes do not perform as well as the nonsystematic convolutional codes [4,6,7]. However, systematic convolutional codes do possess certain advantages over nonsystematic convolutional codes. The encoding process for systematic convolutional codes uses less hardware, and the systematic convolutional codes do not require an inverter to recover the information sequence. Furthermore, systematic convolutional codes are not catastrophic [8], that is, they never possess an infinite error propagation effect whereas nonsystematic convolutional codes may. Section 2.3 discusses the error propagation effect, existence of the inverter, and its algebraic structure and construction procedures.

2.3 ERROR PROPAGATION EFFECT AND CODE DESIGN

For the encoding operation to be useful in the context of a digital communication system, the mapping of $\mathbf{X}(D)$ onto $\mathbf{Y}(D)$ should be one-to-one and reversible. Thus, the encoder must have a feedback-free inverse, that is, there exists an n-by-k polynomial matrix $\mathbf{G}^{-1}(D)$ such that

$$\mathbf{G}(D)\mathbf{G}^{-1}(D) = \mathbf{I}D^q \quad (2.37)$$

where $\mathbf{I}$ is the k-by-k identity matrix, for some values of q. $\mathbf{G}^{-1}(D)$ is denoted as the right-inverse of $\mathbf{G}(D)$ [1,8]. Recalling (2.21), this implies that

$$\mathbf{Y}(D)\mathbf{G}^{-1}(D) = \mathbf{X}(D)\mathbf{G}(D)\mathbf{G}^{-1}(D) \qquad (2.38)$$

$$= \mathbf{X}(D)D^q \qquad (2.39)$$

and the information sequence $\mathbf{X}(D)$ can now be recovered with a delay q by the above operation. Massey and Sain [8] have shown that the right-inverse of an (n, k, m) linear convolutional code exists if

$$gcd\left[\Delta_j(D) : j = 1, 2, \cdots, \binom{n}{k}\right] = D^q \qquad (2.40)$$

where $\Delta_j(D)$ represents one of the k-by-k subdeterminants of $\mathbf{G}(D)$ and gcd denotes the greatest common divisor. There are $\binom{n}{k}$ distinct ways in which the k-by-n generator matrix $\mathbf{G}(D)$ may be arranged into k-by-k sub-matrices. When (2.40) is satisfied, the right-inverse exists and the code is called a non-catastrophic convolutional code. Otherwise, the code is called a catastrophic convolutional code.

Example 2.11

Consider the (2, 1, 2) nonsystematic convolutional code with generator polynomial matrix $\mathbf{G}(D) = [1 + D^2 \quad 1 + D]$. There are two distinct ways in which $\mathbf{G}(D)$ may be arranged into 1-by-1 submatrices. The submatrices are $[1 + D^2]$ and $[1 + D]$ with subdeterminants $1 + D^2$ and $1 + D$, respectively. The greatest common divisor of the two subdeterminants is $1 + D$. Equation (2.40) is not satisfied. The code has no right-inverse and is called a catastrophic convolutional code.

All catastrophic convolutional codes suffer error propagation effect. For instance, consider the nonsystematic linear convolutional code generated by the rate-1/2 encoder shown in Figure 2.6.

The all-one information sequence is encoded into the output code sequence 11 10 00 00 .. .. If this encoded output sequence is transmitted over a discrete noisy channel and the three nonzero encoded bits are changed

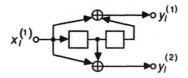

Figure 2.6 (2, 1, 2) catastrophic convolutional encoder.

to zeros as a result of transmission errors, the received sequence becomes the all-zero sequence. This is a valid code sequence. A decoder will choose the all-zero information sequence, corresponding to the all-zero code sequence, as the decoded information sequence. A finite number of channel errors causes an infinite number of decoding errors. The code suffers from catastrophic error propagation. Thus, it is important to choose good nonsystematic convolutional codes.

Example 2.12

Consider the (3, 2, 1) nonsystematic convolutional code with the generator polynomial matrix

$$\mathbf{G}(D) = \begin{bmatrix} 1 + D & 1 + D & 1 \\ 0 & D & 1 + D \end{bmatrix}$$

There are three distinct ways in which $\mathbf{G}(D)$ may be arranged into 2-by-2 submatrices. The submatrices are

$$\begin{bmatrix} 1 + D & 1 + D \\ 0 & D \end{bmatrix}, \begin{bmatrix} 1 + D & 1 \\ 0 & 1 + D \end{bmatrix} \text{ and } \begin{bmatrix} 1 + D & 1 \\ D & 1 + D \end{bmatrix}$$

with subdeterminants $D + D^2$, $1 + D^2$, and $1 + D + D^2$, respectively. The greatest common divisor of the three subdeterminants is 1. Equation (2.40) is satisfied, and $q = 0$. The code has a right-inverse and is called a noncatastrophic convolutional code.

Example 2.13

Consider the (3, 2, 1) systematic convolutional code with the generator polynomial matrix

$$\mathbf{G}(D) = \begin{bmatrix} 1 & 0 & 1 \\ 0 & 1 & 1 + D \end{bmatrix}$$

There are three distinct ways in which $\mathbf{G}(D)$ may be arranged into 2-by-2 submatrices. The submatrices are

$$\begin{bmatrix} 1 & 0 \\ 0 & 1 \end{bmatrix}, \begin{bmatrix} 1 & 1 \\ 0 & 1 + D \end{bmatrix} \text{ and } \begin{bmatrix} 0 & 1 \\ 1 & 1 + D \end{bmatrix}$$

with subdeterminants 1, 1 + D, and 1, respectively. The greatest common divisor of the three subdeterminants is 1. Equation (2.40) is satisfied, and $q = 0$. The code has a right-inverse and is called a noncatastrophic convolutional code.

It can be seen that systematic convolutional codes always satisfy (2.40) with $q = 0$. That is due to the fact that one of the submatrices is the k-by-k identity matrix with unity determinant. Therefore, all systematic convolutional encoders possess a feedback-free right-inverse and inhibit catastrophe.

In general, the right-inverse $\mathbf{G}^{-1}(D)$ is an n-by-k polynomial matrix and is denoted as

$$\mathbf{G}^{-1}(D) = \begin{bmatrix} G'^{(1)}_1(D) & G'^{(2)}_1(D) & \cdots & G'^{(k)}_1(D) \\ G'^{(1)}_2(D) & G'^{(2)}_2(D) & \cdots & G'^{(k)}_2(D) \\ \vdots & \vdots & & \vdots \\ G'^{(1)}_n(D) & G'^{(2)}_n(D) & \cdots & G'^{(k)}_n(D) \end{bmatrix} \tag{2.41}$$

for an (n, k, m) convolutional encoder, where $G'^{(i)}_j(D)$ is the inverter polynomial that relates the jth right-inverse input to the ith output, and is given by

$$G'^{(i)}_j(D) = g'^{(i)}_{j,0} + g'^{(i)}_{j,1}D + \cdots + g'^{(i)}_{j,m'}D^{m'} \tag{2.42}$$

for $1 \le i \le k$ and $1 \le j \le n$. m' is defined as the inverter memory order. There are $n \cdot k$ inverter polynomials, and the inverter can be realized as consisting of n shift registers of various length. Each row of $\mathbf{G}^{-1}(D)$ represents the connections from one of the shift registers to the k outputs. The output sequences are determined by k connection vectors $\mathbf{G}'^{(1)}, \mathbf{G}'^{(2)}, \cdots, \mathbf{G}'^{(k)}$, where the ith connection vector, $\mathbf{G}'^{(i)}$, relates the stage inputs and outputs of the n shift registers to the ith output and is given by

$$\mathbf{G}'^{(i)} = \left[g'^{(i)}_{1,0} g'^{(i)}_{2,0} \cdots g'^{(i)}_{n,0} g'^{(i)}_{1,1} g'^{(i)}_{2,1} \cdots g'^{(i)}_{n,1} \cdots g'^{(i)}_{1,m'} g'^{(i)}_{2,m'} \cdots g'^{(i)}_{n,m'} \right]$$

$$\tag{2.43}$$

for $1 \le i \le k$. Figure 2.7 shows the right-inverse circuit for an (n, k, m) linear convolutional encoder. A "1" in a position of the connection vector indicates that the corresponding stage in the n shift registers is connected to the modulo-2 adder. A "0" in a given position indicates that there is no connection between that stage of the shift registers and the modulo-2 adder. For example, Figure 2.8 shows the right-inverse circuit for the (3, 2, 1) convolutional encoder in Figure 2.3. When the length of the connection vectors become very long, they are again more conveniently expressed in octal form.

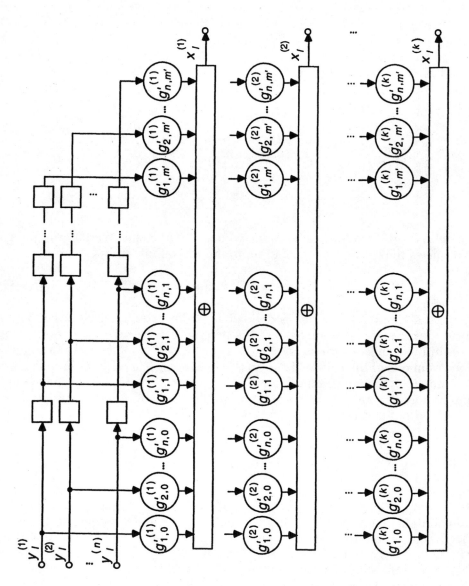

Figure 2.7 Right-inverse circuit for an (n, k, m) convolutional encoder.

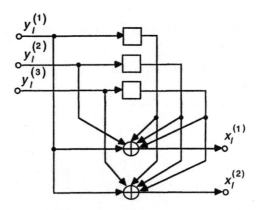

Figure 2.8 Right-inverse circuit for the (3, 2, 1) convolutional encoder of Figure 2.3.

The operation of a right-inverse for an (n, k, m) linear convolutional encoder can also be described by a polynomial matrix, $[\mathbf{H}^T(D)]^{-1}$. The matrix $[\mathbf{H}^T(D)]^{-1}$ associated with $\mathbf{G}^{-1}(D)$ is an $(n - k)$-by-n matrix with polynomial elements in $GF(2)$ that satisfies

$$[\mathbf{H}^T(D)]^{-1}\mathbf{G}^{-1}(D) = \mathbf{0} \tag{2.44}$$

where $[\mathbf{H}^T(D)]^{-1}$ is the left-inverse of $\mathbf{H}^T(D)$ and

$$[\mathbf{H}^T(D)]^{-1}\mathbf{H}^T(D) = \mathbf{I}_{n-k} \tag{2.45}$$

with $\mathbf{I}_{n-k}$, the $n - k$ identity matrix.

Before we proceed to find the right-inverse matrix $\mathbf{G}^{-1}(D)$ and the left-inverse matrix $[\mathbf{H}^T(D)]^{-1}$ for an (n, k, m) convolutional encoder, several aspects of elementary matrix operations and encoder equivalence have to be defined. The convolutional encoder is assumed to be a basic encoder [1] with matrices $\mathbf{G}(D)$ and $\mathbf{H}^T(D)$.

Definition 2.1. Elementary transformations on the polynomial matrix $\mathbf{G}(D)$ over a ring $F[D]$ include the following:

1. Interchanging the ith row (column) and the jth row (column).
2. Multiplying the ith row (column) by a nonzero element. 1 is the nonzero element in $GF(2)$.
3. Replacing the ith row (column) by itself plus (modulo-2 addition) a polynomial times the jth row (column).

Definition 2.2. Two matrices are defined as equivalent if they have the same rank.

Definition 2.3. Two encoders are equivalent if they generate the same code.

Example 2.14

Consider the matrix

$$G(D) = \begin{bmatrix} 1 & D & 1 \\ 0 & 1 & D \end{bmatrix}$$

and the matrix

$$G_{sys}(D) = \begin{bmatrix} 1 & 0 & 1 + D^2 \\ 0 & 1 & D \end{bmatrix}$$

with polynomial elements over $GF(2)$. Matrix $G_{sys}(D)$ can be obtained from $G(D)$ by a series of elementary row transformations. $G(D)$ and $G_{sys}(D)$ have the same rank and are said to be row equivalence, $G(D) \sim G_{sys}(D)$. Encoders with generator matrices $G(D)$ and $G_{sys}(D)$ generate the same set of code sequence.

Definition 2.4. An encoder $G(D)$ is called a basic encoder if there exists a $G^{-1}(D)$ such that $G(D) \, G^{-1}(D) = I$.

Definition 2.5. An (n, k, m) basic convolutional encoder is minimal if the total encoder memory K is equal to the maximum degree of the k-by-k subdeterminants of $G(D)$ [1,9–11].

2.3.1 Algebraic Structures of Generator Polynomial Matrix G(D)

To characterize the algebraic properties of the matrix $G(D)$ over a ring $F[D]$, we follow Forney's paper [1], which highlighted the important concept of the invariant-factor theorem in the analysis and design of linear convolutional codes. Forney [1] has shown that a rate-k/n linear convolutional code, $G(D)$ has the invariant-factor decomposition or Smith normal form.[1]

$$G(D) = A(D)\Gamma(D)B(D) \tag{2.46}$$

---

1. The Smith normal form was developed by the British mathematician H. R. S. Smith in the 19th century.

where $\mathbf{A}(D)$ is a k-by-k nonsingular matrix with an inverse $\mathbf{A}^{-1}(D)$; $\mathbf{B}(D)$ is an n-by-n nonsingular matrix with an inverse $\mathbf{B}^{-1}(D)$; and $\mathbf{\Gamma}(D)$ is a k-by-n matrix of the form $[\mathbf{\Gamma}_1(D),\ \mathbf{0}]$. $\mathbf{\Gamma}_1(D)$ is a k-by-k diagonal matrix and $\mathbf{0}$ is a k-by-$(n-k)$ zero matrix. The diagonal elements in $\mathbf{\Gamma}_1(D)$ are called the invariant factors of $\mathbf{G}(D)$. $\mathbf{G}(D)$ is said to be equivalent to $\mathbf{\Gamma}(D)$ if $\mathbf{G}(D) = \mathbf{A}(D)\,\mathbf{\Gamma}(D)\,\mathbf{B}(D)$. For a basic encoder, $\mathbf{G}(D) = \mathbf{A}(D)\,[\mathbf{I}_k,\ \mathbf{0}]\,\mathbf{B}(D)$, where $\mathbf{I}_k$ is the k-by-k identity matrix. The square matrix $\mathbf{B}(D)$ and its inverse can be partitioned into

$$\mathbf{B}(D) = \begin{bmatrix} \mathbf{B}_1(D) \\ \mathbf{B}_2(D) \end{bmatrix} \tag{2.47}$$

and

$$\mathbf{B}^{-1}(D) = [\mathbf{B}_1^{-1}(D)\ \ \mathbf{B}_2^{-1}(D)] \tag{2.48}$$

where $\mathbf{B}_1(D)$, $\mathbf{B}_2(D)$, $\mathbf{B}_1^{-1}(D)$, and $\mathbf{B}_2^{-1}(D)$ are k-by-n, $(n-k)$-by-n, n-by-k, and n-by-$(n-k)$ matrices, respectively. As the product of $\mathbf{B}(D)$ and $\mathbf{B}^{-1}(D)$ gives the n-by-n identity matrix, the following identities evidently hold:

$$\mathbf{B}_1(D)\mathbf{B}_1^{-1}(D) = \mathbf{I}_k \tag{2.49}$$

$$\mathbf{B}_1(D)\mathbf{B}_2^{-1}(D) = \mathbf{0} \tag{2.50}$$

$$\mathbf{B}_2(D)\mathbf{B}_1^{-1}(D) = \mathbf{0} \tag{2.51}$$

$$\mathbf{B}_2(D)\mathbf{B}_2^{-1}(D) = \mathbf{I}_{n-k} \tag{2.52}$$

The first k rows of $\mathbf{B}(D)$ constitute $\mathbf{G}(D)$, and the last $n-k$ rows constitute $[\mathbf{H}^T(D)]^{-1}$. Also, the first k columns of $\mathbf{B}^{-1}(D)$ constitute $\mathbf{G}^{-1}(D)$, and the last $n-k$ columns constitute $\mathbf{H}^T(D)$. Therefore, (2.49) to (2.52) can be rewritten as

$$\mathbf{G}(D)\mathbf{G}^{-1}(D) = \mathbf{I}_k \tag{2.53}$$

$$\mathbf{G}(D)\mathbf{H}^T(D) = \mathbf{0} \tag{2.54}$$

$$[\mathbf{H}^T(D)]^{-1}\mathbf{G}^{-1}(D) = \mathbf{0} \tag{2.55}$$

$$[\mathbf{H}^T(D)]^{-1}\mathbf{H}^T(D) = \mathbf{I}_{n-k} \tag{2.56}$$

$\mathbf{A}^{-1}(D)$ and $\mathbf{B}^{-1}(D)$ can be found from $\mathbf{G}(D)$ by performing the following operations [12]:

1. Set up k-by-k and n-by-n identity matrices $\mathbf{M}$ and $\mathbf{N}$, respectively.
2. Perform elementary row and column operations on $\mathbf{G}(D)$ to reduce it to $[\mathbf{I}_k, \mathbf{0}]$.
3. For every row and column operation on $\mathbf{G}(D)$, perform the same operation on $\mathbf{M}$ and $\mathbf{N}$, respectively.

The elementary row and column operations are defined as follows:

1. Interchange columns i and j.
2. Add to or subtract from column i column j multiplied by a polynomial $p(D)$ with coefficients over $F[D]$.
3. Interchange rows i and j.
4. Add to or subtract from row i row j multiplied by a polynomial $p(D)$ with coefficients over $F[D]$. Addition and multiplication operations are performed in $F[D]$.

After the operations, we have the identity $\mathbf{M}(D)\ \mathbf{G}(D)\ \mathbf{N}(D) = [\mathbf{I}_k, \mathbf{0}]$, where $\mathbf{M}(D) = \mathbf{A}^{-1}(D)$ and $\mathbf{N}(D) = \mathbf{B}^{-1}(D)$. $\mathbf{G}^{-1}(D)$ and $\mathbf{H}^T(D)$ are contained in $\mathbf{N}(D)$.

Since we are interested only in finding $\mathbf{G}^{-1}(D)$, $\mathbf{A}(D)$ and $\mathbf{B}_2(D)$ play no part at all. We simply can take the first k rows of $\mathbf{B}(D)$ as $\mathbf{G}(D)$, perform column transformations on the matrix $\mathbf{G}(D)$ and the identity matrix $\mathbf{N}$, which transform $\mathbf{G}(D)$ and $\mathbf{N}$ into $[\mathbf{I}_k, \mathbf{0}]$ and $\mathbf{N}(D)$, respectively. Given $\mathbf{G}(D)$, the procedure for finding $\mathbf{G}^{-1}(D)$ is reduced to the following:

1. Set up an n-by-n identity matrix $\mathbf{N}$.
2. Perform elementary column operation on $\mathbf{G}(D)$ to reduce it to $[\mathbf{I}_k, \mathbf{0}]$.
3. For every column operation on $\mathbf{G}(D)$, perform the same operation on $\mathbf{N}$.

Example 2.15

Column Operation	$\mathbf{G}(D)$ After Transformation	$\mathbf{N}$ After Transformation
No operation	$\begin{bmatrix} 1+D & 1+D & 1 \\ 0 & D & 1+D \end{bmatrix}$	$\begin{bmatrix} 1 & 0 & 0 \\ 0 & 1 & 0 \\ 0 & 0 & 1 \end{bmatrix}$
$2 := 2 + 1$	$\begin{bmatrix} 1+D & 0 & 1 \\ 0 & D & 1+D \end{bmatrix}$	$\begin{bmatrix} 1 & 1 & 0 \\ 0 & 1 & 0 \\ 0 & 0 & 1 \end{bmatrix}$

$3 := 3 + 2$ $\begin{bmatrix} 1+D & 0 & 1 \\ 0 & D & 1 \end{bmatrix}$ $\begin{bmatrix} 1 & 1 & 1 \\ 0 & 1 & 1 \\ 0 & 0 & 1 \end{bmatrix}$

$1 := 1 + 3.D$ $\begin{bmatrix} 1 & 0 & 1 \\ D & D & 1 \end{bmatrix}$ $\begin{bmatrix} 1+D & 1 & 1 \\ D & 1 & 1 \\ D & 0 & 1 \end{bmatrix}$

$1 := 1 + 2$ $\begin{bmatrix} 1 & 0 & 1 \\ 0 & D & 1 \end{bmatrix}$ $\begin{bmatrix} D & 1 & 1 \\ 1+D & 1 & 1 \\ D & 0 & 1 \end{bmatrix}$

$3 := 3 + 1$ $\begin{bmatrix} 1 & 0 & 0 \\ 0 & D & 1 \end{bmatrix}$ $\begin{bmatrix} D & 1 & 1+D \\ 1+D & 1 & D \\ D & 0 & 1+D \end{bmatrix}$

Interchange 2 and 3 $\begin{bmatrix} 1 & 0 & 0 \\ 0 & 1 & D \end{bmatrix}$ $\begin{bmatrix} D & 1+D & 1 \\ 1+D & D & 1 \\ D & 1+D & 0 \end{bmatrix}$

$3 := 3 + 2.D$ $\begin{bmatrix} 1 & 0 & 0 \\ 0 & 1 & 0 \end{bmatrix}$ $\begin{bmatrix} D & 1+D & 1+D+D^2 \\ 1+D & D & 1+D^2 \\ D & 1+D & D+D^2 \end{bmatrix}$

$$= [\mathbf{G}^{-1}(D)\ \mathbf{H}^T(D)]$$

where $:=$ is the assignment operator. The result on the right side of the assignment operator is assigned to the left. After the column operations, $\mathbf{G}^{-1}(D)$ is obtained, and $\mathbf{H}^T(D)$ drops out naturally, which is not unique at all.

2.3.2 Algebraic Structures of Syndrome-Former Polynomial Matrix $\mathbf{H}^T(D)$

For a rate-k/n linear convolutional code, $\mathbf{H}^T(D)$ has the invariant-factor decomposition or Smith normal form

$$\mathbf{H}^T(D) = \mathbf{A}'(D)\mathbf{\Gamma}'(D)\dot{\mathbf{B}}'(D) \tag{2.57}$$

where $\mathbf{A}'(D)$ is a n-by-n nonsingular matrix with an inverse $\mathbf{A}'^{-1}(D)$; $\mathbf{B}'(D)$ is a $(n$ -$k)$-by-$(n - k)$ nonsingular matrix with an inverse $\mathbf{B}'^{-1}(D)$; and $\mathbf{\Gamma}'(D)$ is a n-by-$(n - k)$ matrix of the form

$$\begin{bmatrix} \mathbf{\Gamma}'_1(D) \\ \mathbf{0} \end{bmatrix}$$

$\mathbf{\Gamma}'_1(D)$ is an $(n - k)$-by-$(n - k)$ diagonal matrix, and $\mathbf{0}$ is a k-by-$(n - k)$ zero matrix. The diagonal elements in $\mathbf{\Gamma}'_1(D)$ are called the invariant factors of $\mathbf{H}^T(D)$, and $\mathbf{H}^T(D)$ is said to be equivalent to $\mathbf{\Gamma}'(D)$ if $\mathbf{H}^T(D) = \mathbf{A}'(D) \, \mathbf{\Gamma}'(D) \, \mathbf{B}'(D)$. For a basic convolutional encoder, the syndrome-former matrix $\mathbf{H}^T(D) = \mathbf{A}'(D) \, [\mathbf{I}_{n-k}, \, \mathbf{0}]^T \mathbf{B}'(D)$, where $\mathbf{I}_{n-k}$ is the $(n - k)$-by-$(n - k)$ identity matrix. The square matrix $\mathbf{A}'(D)$ and its inverse can be partitioned into

$$\mathbf{A}'(D) = [\mathbf{A}'_1(D) \, \mathbf{A}'_2(D)] \tag{2.58}$$

and

$$\mathbf{A}'^{-1}(D) = \begin{bmatrix} \mathbf{A}'^{-1}_1(D) \\ \mathbf{A}'^{-1}_2(D) \end{bmatrix} \tag{2.59}$$

where $\mathbf{A}'_1(D)$, $\mathbf{A}'_2(D)$, $\mathbf{A}'^{-1}_1(D)$, and $\mathbf{A}'^{-1}_2(D)$ are n-by-$(n - k)$, n-by-k, $(n - k)$-by-n and k-by-n matrices, respectively. Since the product of $\mathbf{A}'^{-1}(D)$ and $\mathbf{A}'(D)$ gives the n-by-n identity matrix, the following identities evidently hold:

$$\mathbf{A}'^{-1}_1(D)\mathbf{A}'_1(D) = \mathbf{I}_{n-k} \tag{2.60}$$

$$\mathbf{A}'^{-1}_1(D)\mathbf{A}'_2(D) = \mathbf{0} \tag{2.61}$$

$$\mathbf{A}'^{-1}_2(D)\mathbf{A}'_1(D) = \mathbf{0} \tag{2.62}$$

$$\mathbf{A}'^{-1}_2(D)\mathbf{A}'_2(D) = \mathbf{I}_k \tag{2.63}$$

The first $(n - k)$ columns of $\mathbf{A}'(D)$ constitute $\mathbf{H}^T(D)$ and the last k columns constitute $\mathbf{G}^{-1}(D)$. Also, the first $n - k$ rows of $\mathbf{A}'^{-1}(D)$ constitute $[\mathbf{H}^T(D)]^{-1}$, and the last k rows constitute $\mathbf{G}(D)$. Therefore, (2.60) to (2.63) can be rewritten as

$$[\mathbf{H}^T(D)]^{-1}\mathbf{H}^T(D) = \mathbf{I}_{n-k} \tag{2.64}$$

$$[\mathbf{H}^T(D)]^{-1}\mathbf{G}^{-1}(D) = \mathbf{0} \tag{2.65}$$

$$\mathbf{G}(D)\mathbf{H}^T(D) = \mathbf{0} \tag{2.66}$$

$$\mathbf{G}(D)\mathbf{G}^{-1}(D) = \mathbf{I}_k \tag{2.67}$$

$\mathbf{A'}^{-1}(D)$ and $\mathbf{B'}^{-1}(D)$ can be found by performing the following operations [12]:

1. Set up n-by-n and $(n - k)$-by-$(n - k)$ identity matrices $\mathbf{M'}$ and $\mathbf{N'}$, respectively.
2. Perform elementary row and column operations on $\mathbf{H}^T(D)$ to reduce it to $[\mathbf{I}_{n-k}, \mathbf{0}]^T$.
3. For every row and column operation on $\mathbf{H}^T(D)$, perform the same operation on $\mathbf{M'}$ and $\mathbf{N'}$, respectively.

After the operations, we have $\mathbf{M'}(D) \, \mathbf{H}^T(D) \, \mathbf{N'}(D) = [\mathbf{I}_{n-k}, \mathbf{0}]^T$, where $\mathbf{M'}(D) = \mathbf{A'}^{-1}(D)$ and $\mathbf{N'}(D) = \mathbf{B'}^{-1}(D)$. $\mathbf{G}(D)$ and $[\mathbf{H}^T(D)]^{-1}$ are contained in $\mathbf{M'}(D)$.

Because we are interested only in finding $[\mathbf{H}^T(D)]^{-1}$, $\mathbf{A}_2'(D)$ and $\mathbf{B'}(D)$ play no part at all. We simply can take the first $(n - k)$ columns of $\mathbf{A'}(D)$ as $\mathbf{H}^T(D)$, perform elementary row transformations on the matrix $\mathbf{H}^T(D)$ and the identity matrix $\mathbf{M'}$ which transform $\mathbf{H}^T(D)$ into $[\mathbf{I}_{n-k}, \mathbf{0}]^T$ and $\mathbf{M'}$ into $\mathbf{M'}(D)$. Given $\mathbf{H}^T(D)$, the procedure for finding $[\mathbf{H}^T(D)]^{-1}$ is reduced to the following:

1. Set up an n-by-n identity matrix $\mathbf{M'}$.
2. Perform elementary row operation on $\mathbf{H}^T(D)$ to reduce it to $[\mathbf{I}_{n-k}, \mathbf{0}]^T$.
3. For every row operation on $\mathbf{H}^T(D)$, perform the same operation on $\mathbf{M'}$.

Example 2.16

Row Operation	$\mathbf{H}^T(D)$ After Transformation	$\mathbf{M'}$ After Transformation
No operation	$\begin{bmatrix} 1 \\ D \\ 1 + D \end{bmatrix}$	$\begin{bmatrix} 1 & 0 & 0 \\ 0 & 1 & 0 \\ 0 & 0 & 1 \end{bmatrix}$
$3 := 1 + 2 + 3$	$\begin{bmatrix} 1 \\ D \\ 0 \end{bmatrix}$	$\begin{bmatrix} 1 & 0 & 0 \\ 0 & 1 & 0 \\ 1 & 1 & 1 \end{bmatrix}$

$$2 := 2 + 1.D \qquad \begin{bmatrix} 1 \\ 0 \\ 0 \end{bmatrix} \qquad\qquad \begin{bmatrix} 1 & 0 & 0 \\ D & 1 & 0 \\ 1 & 1 & 1 \end{bmatrix} = \begin{bmatrix} \mathbf{H}^T (D)^{-1} \\ \mathbf{G} (D) \end{bmatrix}$$

Again, $\mathbf{G}(D)$ drops out as a by-product and is not unique.

2.3.3 Systematic Convolutional Encoder With Feedback

In this section, we return to the structure of systematic convolutional codes and introduce an alternative form of systematic convolutional encoders. In Example 2.14, we saw that the generator matrix

$$\mathbf{G}(D) = \begin{bmatrix} 1 & D & 1 \\ 0 & 1 & D \end{bmatrix}$$

is equivalent to the systematic generator matrix

$$\mathbf{G}_{sys}(D) = \begin{bmatrix} 1 & 0 & 1 + D^2 \\ 0 & 1 & D \end{bmatrix}$$

$\mathbf{G}_{sys}(D)$ is obtained by a series of elementary row transformations on the generator matrix $\mathbf{G}(D)$. Both convolutional encoders generate the same code sequence, and the encoder circuit of the systematic convolutional code is feedback free.

At first glance, a convolutional encoder may have a equivalent feedback-free systematic encoder. Unfortunately, that is not true. In general, not every convolutional encoder has a feedback-free systematic encoder. However, it can be shown that every convolutional encoder is equivalent to a systematic encoder that contains feedback [13]. Algorithms for converting convolutional codes from feedback to feedforward form and vice versa can be found in Porath [14]. When the systematic encoder contains feedback, the elements of the systematic generator polynomial matrix $\mathbf{G}_{sys}(D)$ are rational functions of the form $P(D)/Q(D)$, where

$$P(D) = p_0 + p_1 D + \cdots + p_m D^m \tag{2.68}$$

and

$$Q(D) = q_0 + q_1 D + \cdots + q_m D^m \tag{2.69}$$

respectively. A rational generator polynomial matrix with entries of the form $P(D)/Q(D)$ is realizable if $q_0 = 1$ and $Q(D)$ is now delay free. We shall not consider a non-delay-free generator polynomial matrix because it would only clutter up the analysis.

In summary, a rational systematic generator matrix can be obtained from the generator matrix $\mathbf{G}(D)$ by permutations and elementary row transformations. The systematic encoder circuit has feedback and is equivalent to the convolutional encoder. Both convolutional encoders produce identical code sequence.

Figure 2.9 shows the encoder circuit for an (n, k, m) systematic convolutional encoders with feedback. The rational generator polynomial matrix of the code is

$$
\mathbf{G}_{\text{sys}}(D) = \begin{bmatrix} 1 & 0 & \cdots & 0 & A_1^{(k+1)}(D)/Q(D) & A_1^{(k+2)}(D)/Q(D) & \cdots & A_1^{(n)}(D)/Q(D) \\ 0 & 1 & \cdots & 0 & A_2^{(k+1)}(D)/Q(D) & A_2^{(k+2)}(D)/Q(D) & \cdots & A_2^{(n)}(D)/Q(D) \\ \vdots & \vdots & & \vdots & \vdots & & & \vdots \\ 0 & 0 & \cdots & 1 & A_k^{(k+1)}(D)/Q(D) & A_k^{(k+2)}(D)/Q(D) & \cdots & A_k^{(n)}(D)/Q(D) \end{bmatrix}
$$

(2.70)

where

$$
A_i^{(j)}(D) = a_{i,0}^{(j)} + a_{i,1}^{(j)}D + \cdots + a_{i,m}^{(j)}D^m
$$

(2.71)

for $1 \le i \le k$, $(k + 1) \le j \le n$, and $Q(D)$ takes the form of equation (2.69).

We shall see in Chapters 7 and 8 that this form of encoder circuit is particularly useful for the design of $(n, n - 1, m)$ convolutional codes with 2^n-ary modulation. The encoder circuit for an $(n, n - 1, m)$ systematic convolutional codes with feedback is shown in Figure 2.10. The rational generator polynomial matrix of the code is

$$
\mathbf{G}_{\text{sys}}(D) = \begin{bmatrix} 1 & 0 & \cdots & 0 & A_1^{(n)}(D)/Q(D) \\ 0 & 1 & \cdots & 0 & A_2^{(n)}(D)/Q(D) \\ \vdots & & & \vdots & \vdots \\ 0 & 0 & \cdots & 1 & A_{n-1}^{(n)}(D)/Q(D) \end{bmatrix}
$$

(2.72)

where

$$
A_i^{(n)}(D) = a_{i,0}^{(n)} + a_{i,1}^{(n)}D + \cdots + a_{i,m}^{(n)}D^m
$$

(2.73)

for $1 \le i \le n - 1$.

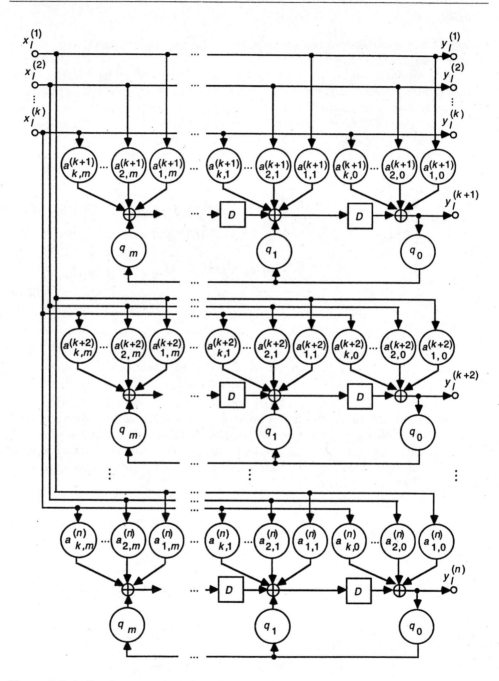

Figure 2.9 (n, k, m) systematic convolutional encoder with feedback.

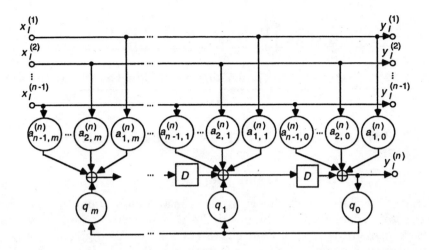

Figure 2.10 $(n, n-1, m)$ systematic convolutional encoder with feedback.

Example 2.17

The generator matrix $\mathbf{G}(D) = [1 + D^2 \; 1 + D + D^2]$ is equivalent to the systematic generator matrix $\mathbf{G}_{sys}(D) = [1 \; (1 + D + D^2)/(1 + D^2)]$. Figure 2.11 shows the $(2, 1, 2)$ systematic convolutional encoder with feedback.

Example 2.18

The generator matrix

$$\mathbf{G}(D) = \begin{bmatrix} 1 + D & D & 1 \\ 1 + D & 1 & 1 + D \end{bmatrix}$$

is equivalent to the systematic generator matrix

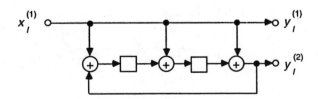

Figure 2.11 $(2, 1, 2)$ systematic convolutional encoder with feedback.

$$G_{\text{sys}}(D) = \begin{bmatrix} 1 & 0 & (1 + D + D^2)/(1 + D^2) \\ 0 & 1 & (D + D^2)/(1 + D^2) \end{bmatrix}$$

Figure 2.12 shows the (3, 2, 2) systematic convolutional encoder with feedback.

2.4 GRAPHICAL REPRESENTATIONS OF CONVOLUTIONAL CODES

2.4.1 Encoder Tree and Trellis Diagrams

So far, we have used matrix theory to describe a convolutional encoder. We can also describe a convolutional code with the aid of a tree diagram. Convolutional codes are called tree codes. Figure 2.13 shows the tree diagram of a (2, 1, 2) convolutional encoder. To obtain a sequence of the encoder output bits from the input bits, we begin at the root of the tree and follow the diagram upward if the input bit is a logic zero or downward if the input bit is a logic one, reading the corresponding encoder output bits on the branch that is reached. Assuming that the shift-register contents of the encoder are cleared initially, a particular encoder input sequence will trace out a unique path through the tree. For an example, if the 1 0 1 1 sequence is fed to the input of the encoder, then the corresponding coded output sequence is 11 01 00 10 and is traced as shown in Figure 2.13(b). It becomes clear that the tree grows exponentially as the length of the encoder input sequence increases.

In contrast to the graphical representation in Figure 2.13 of convolutional codes, there is a more compact way to visualize the code sequence. By studying the tree diagram in Figure 2.13(b), we can see that the tree begins to repeats itself after the third branch. If we stand at either node 1 or node 1', we would see identical trees growing to the right. Similarly, we can say the same thing about nodes 2, 3, 4 and 2', 3', 4', respectively. Clearly, the encoder output sequences on branches emanating from nodes 1 and 1', 2 and 2', 3 and 3', or

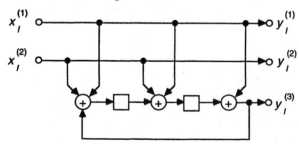

Figure 2.12 (3, 2, 2) systematic convolutional encoder with feedback.

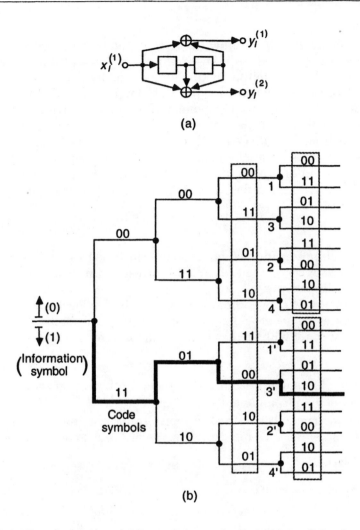

Figure 2.13 (a) Encoder circuit and (b) tree diagram of a (2, 1, 2) convolutional code.

4 and 4′ are identical. The reason is due to the fact that the convolutional encoder is a finite-state linear sequential machine. As the fourth input bit enters the shift register, the rightmost bit in the shift register drops out and no longer influences the sequential machine. Thus, nodes 1, 2, 3, 4 merged with nodes 1′, 2′, 3′, 4′, respectively, to form a more compact representation of the code. The resulting diagram takes the form of a trellis, and the number of branches over which the merging can occur corresponds to the constraint length ν of the code. The number of branches remain unchanged beyond the merging stage. The trellis diagram for the (2, 1, 2) convolutional encoder in Figure 2.13(a) is

shown in Figure 2.14. We follow the convention that a solid line denotes the coded symbols associated with the input information bit value (0) and a dashed line corresponds to the output symbols produced by the input information bit value (1). The trellis diagram contains all the information that the tree diagram does because the same input sequence of 1 0 1 1, shown in Figure 2.13(b), traces out a unique path in the trellis diagram in Figure 2.14. In the trellis diagram, each node is labeled with the state of the encoder, and the state of the encoder is defined as the contents of the shift-register elements. For an (n, k, m) convolutional code, there are 2^K possible states, where K is the total encoder memory of the code. At time l, each state corresponds to the K-tuple

$$[x_l^{(1)} x_l^{(2)} \cdots x_l^{(k)} x_{l-1}^{(1)} x_{l-1}^{(2)} \cdots x_{l-1}^{(k)} \cdots x_{l-L_1+1}^{(1)} x_{l-L_2+1}^{(2)} \cdots x_{l-L_k+1}^{(k)}]$$

Each new k-bit information block causes a transition to a new state. Thus, there are 2^k paths leaving each state, each path corresponding to one of the 2^k possible information bit patterns.

For systematic convolutional encoders with feedback, the contents of the shift-register elements are taken as the state of the machine. The next trellis state of the encoder with feedback can be determined from the current state as follows:

1. At time l, input a possible k-component information sequence $\mathbf{X}_l$.
2. Observe the n-component code sequence $\mathbf{Y}_l$.
3. Shift the contents of the shift-register elements once and take the new contents of the shift-register elements as the next state of the machine.

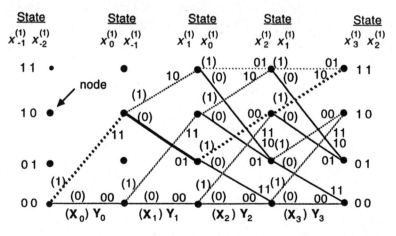

Figure 2.14 Trellis diagram for the (2, 1, 2) convolutional encoder in Figure 2.13.

Figures 2.15 and 2.16 show the encoder circuit and the trellis diagram of a (2, 1, 2) systematic convolutional code with feedback. The code is equivalent to the feedback-free convolutional encoder in Figure 2.13(a). It can be seen from their trellis diagrams that they generate the same code sequence, but the mapping between the code sequence and the information sequence are different. Because the information digits are statistically independent and equally likely to have one of its possible value, the input information sequence of the convolutional encoder with feedback is a scrambled version of the input information sequence of the feedback-free convolutional encoder.

2.4.2 Encoder State Diagram

Since the state of the encoder is defined as the contents of the shift-register elements, the entire encoding operation can be completely described by a state

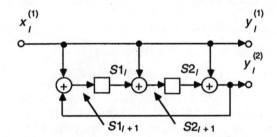

Figure 2.15 (2, 1, 2) systematic convolutional encoder with feedback.

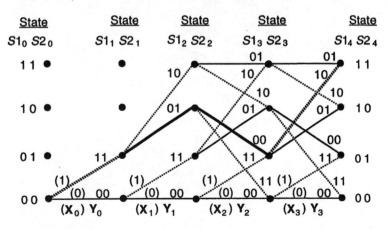

Figure 2.16 Trellis diagram for the (2, 1, 2) systematic convolutional encoder with feedback in Figure 2.15.

diagram. To make the description much simpler, the encoder shown in Figure 2.13 is taken as an example. The state diagram for the (2, 1, 2) code in Figure 2.13 is shown in Figure 2.17. The states are labeled as S_0, S_1, S_2, and S_3, where the subscript of the state corresponds to the integer representation of the contents of the shift-register elements. Each input information bit causes a transition from a state to a new state. Hence, there are two paths leaving each state, corresponding to the two possible values of information bit. Assuming that the encoder is initially in state S_0 (the all-zero state), the code sequence corresponding to the input information sequence 1 0 1 1 can be obtained by following the path through the state diagram.

In general, the states of an (n, k, m) convolutional encoder with total encoder memory K are labeled as S_0, S_1, ... , S_{2^k}. The state diagram representation of a convolutional encoder is useful to derive the generating function of the code, which is used to characterize and assess code performance and which is considered in Section 2.6.

2.4.3 Syndrome-Former Trellis Diagram

An (n, k, m) linear convolutional encoder can also be described by its $(n - k)$-by-n parity-check polynomial matrix $\mathbf{H}(D)$. Consider the syndrome-former $\mathbf{H}^T(D)$ for an (n, k, m) convolutional code, where $\mathbf{H}^T(D)$ is the transpose of $\mathbf{H}(D)$. This can be realized as a linear circuit that consists of $(n - k) \cdot m''$ memory elements and $(n - k) \cdot (m'' + 1)$ modulo-2 adders. The syndrome-former circuit for the (n, k, m) convolutional code is shown in Figure 2.18.

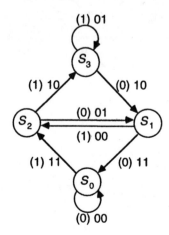

Figure 2.17 State diagram for the (2, 1, 2) convolutional encoder in Figure 2.13.

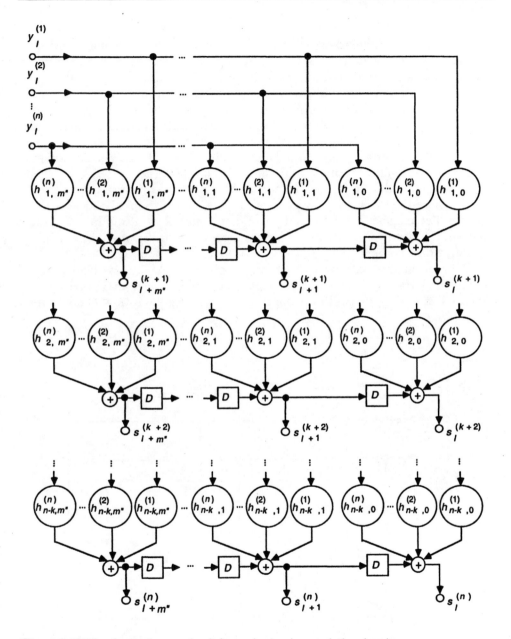

Figure 2.18 Syndrome-former circuit for an (*n, k, m*) convolutional code.

Based on the state transitions of the circuit, a $2^{(n-k) \cdot (m''+1)}$-state syndrome-former trellis can be determined. For low-rate convolutional codes ($n \gg k$), the number of trellis states is large even for a small value of m'', and the trellis is not very useful. The syndrome-former trellis is more useful for high-rate $(n, n-1, m)$ convolutional codes. Hence, we shall consider only the structures of the syndrome-former trellis for $(n, n-1, m)$ convolutional codes, in particular, the minimal convolutional codes where $m'' = K$ [15].

An $(n, n-1, m)$ linear minimal convolutional encoder can be described by its 1-by-n parity-check polynomial matrix $\mathbf{H}(D) = [H_1^{(1)}(D) \; H_1^{(2)}(D) \; \ldots \; H_1^{(n)}(D)]$. Consider the syndrome-former $\mathbf{H}^T(D)$ for an $(n, n-1, m)$ minimal convolutional code, where $\mathbf{H}^T(D)$ is the transpose of $\mathbf{H}(D)$. This can be realized as a linear circuit that consists of K memory elements and $K + 1$ modulo-2 adders. Figure 2.19 shows the syndrome-former circuit for an $(n, n-1, m)$ minimal convolutional code.

Based on the state transitions of the circuit, a 2^{K+1}-state trellis can be determined. Here, the trellis corresponding to the code vector $\mathbf{Y}_l$ consists of n stages. The state of the trellis at depth d' is expressed by a $(K + 1)$-component binary vector:

$$\mathbf{S}^{(d')} = [s_l^{(n)} \, s_{l+1}^{(n)} \, \cdots \, s_{l+K}^{(n)}] \tag{2.74}$$

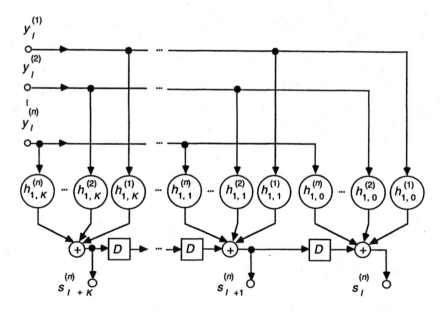

Figure 2.19 Syndrome-former circuit for a rate-$(n-1)/n$ minimal convolutional encoder.

for $0 \le d' \le n$. $\mathbf{S}^{(d')}$, $d' \ge 1$, corresponds to the state when symbols up to $y_l^{(d')}$ are input to the syndrome-former circuit. A transition then occurs when $y_l^{(d'+1)}$ is input. Initially, at depth $d' = 0$, the input code vector $\mathbf{Y}_l$ to the syndrome-former circuit is zero, and $s_{l+K}^{(n)}$ is also zero. Thus, there are 2^K possible states at depth $d' = 0$ and the state vector is

$$\mathbf{S}^{(0)} = [s_l^{(n)} s_{l+1}^{(n)} \cdots s_{l+K-1}^{(n)} 0] \tag{2.75}$$

For each possible initial state $\mathbf{S}^{(0)}$:

1. Input $y_l^{(1)} = 1$ or 0.
2. Observe the state $\mathbf{S}^{(1)}$ of the circuit and draw branch from $\mathbf{S}^{(0)}$ to $\mathbf{S}^{(1)}$.

For each intermediate initial state $\mathbf{S}^{(d')}$:

3. Input $y_l^{(d'+1)} = 1$ or 0 without altering any previous setting of the circuit.
4. Observe the state $\mathbf{S}^{(d'+1)}$ of the circuit and draw branch from $\mathbf{S}^{(d')}$ to $\mathbf{S}^{(d'+1)}$.
5. Iterate steps 3 and 4 until $y_l^{(n-1)}$ is input.
6. For the last interval ($d' = n - 1$) associated with state $\mathbf{S}^{(n-1)}$, input $y_l^{(n)} = 1$ or 0; shift all the memory contents one place to the left and reset the code vector $\mathbf{Y}_l$ to zero.
7. Observe the final state $\mathbf{S}^{(n)}$ of the circuit and draw the branch from $\mathbf{S}^{(n-1)}$ to $\mathbf{S}^{(n)}$.

Example 2.19

The syndrome-former circuit for the encoder of Figure 2.20 with $\mathbf{H}(D) = [1 \quad 1 + D \ 1 + D^2 \ 1 + D + D^2]$ is shown in Figure 2.21, and its syndrome-former trellis is given in Figure 2.22.

2.5 DISTANCE PROPERTIES OF CONVOLUTIONAL CODES

The concept of distance measure provides a way of quantitatively describing the performance of a code. This section introduces several distance measures for convolutional codes; the implications will be examined in succeeding chapters.

Definition 2.6. The Hamming weight of a binary word is defined as the number of 1s contained in the word.

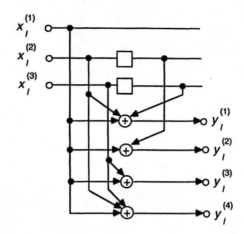

Figure 2.20 (4, 3, 1) convolutional encoder.

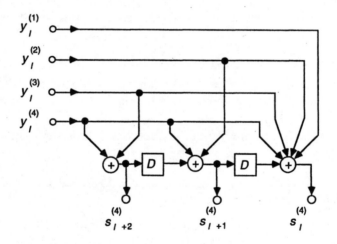

Figure 2.21 Syndrome-former circuit of Figure 2.20.

Definition 2.7. The Hamming distance between two binary words of the same length is the number of places in which their bits differ.

Definition 2.8. The smallest Hamming distance between all pairs of encoded sequences over one constraint length of a convolutional code is defined as the minimum Hamming distance of the code.

The minimum Hamming distance, d_{min}, over one constraint length of a convolutional code turns out to be an important parameter for the majority-logic

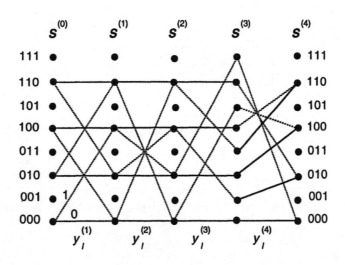

Figure 2.22 Syndrome-former trellis of Figure 2.21.

decoding of convolutional codes [16]. The theory of majority-logic decoding of convolutional codes is discussed in Chapter 6. Clearly, there is no need to constrain the minimum Hamming distance over only one constraint length of the convolutional code. By extending the distance measure beyond one constraint length of the code, the resulting distance measure d_f is the column distance function of the code, defined as the minimum Hamming distance over the first f blocks of all pairs of encoded sequences. In terms of the generator matrix of the code

$$\mathbf{Y'} = \mathbf{X'G}_f \tag{2.76}$$

where

$$\mathbf{X'} = [\mathbf{X}_0 \ \mathbf{X}_1 \ \cdots \ \mathbf{X}_f] \tag{2.77}$$

$$\mathbf{Y'} = [\mathbf{Y}_0 \ \mathbf{Y}_1 \ \cdots \ \mathbf{Y}_f] \tag{2.78}$$

and $\mathbf{G}_f$ is a $k \cdot (f + 1)$-by-$n \cdot (f + 1)$ submatrix of $\mathbf{G}$ with the form

$$\mathbf{G}_f = \begin{bmatrix} \mathbf{G}_0 & \mathbf{G}_1 & \cdots & \mathbf{G}_f \\ \mathbf{0} & \mathbf{G}_0 & \cdots & \mathbf{G}_{f-1} \\ & & \ddots & \vdots \\ & & & \mathbf{G}_0 \end{bmatrix} \tag{2.79}$$

for $f \leq m$, or

$$
G_f = \begin{bmatrix}
G_0 & G_1 & \cdots & G_{m-1} & G_m & 0 & & & \cdots \\
0 & G_0 & \cdots & G_{m-2} & G_{m-1} & G_m & 0 & & \\
\vdots & & \ddots & \vdots & \vdots & \vdots & \vdots & & \ddots \\
& & & G_0 & G_1 & \cdots & G_{m-1} & G_m \\
& & & & G_0 & \cdots & G_{m-2} & G_{m-1} \\
\vdots & & & & & \ddots & \vdots & \vdots \\
& & & & & & G_0 & G_1 \\
& & & & & & & G_0
\end{bmatrix}
\qquad (2.80)
$$

for $f > m$. The encoder input at time f is represented by the k-component row vector

$$
\mathbf{X}_f = [x_f^{(1)} x_f^{(2)} \cdots x_f^{(k)}]
\qquad (2.81)
$$

The encoder output at time f is represented by the n-component row vector

$$
\mathbf{Y}_f = [y_f^{(1)} y_f^{(2)} \cdots y_f^{(n)}]
\qquad (2.82)
$$

If $f \to \infty$, it can be shown that for noncatastrophic convolutional codes

$$
\lim_{f \to \infty} d_f = d_{\text{free}}
\qquad (2.83)
$$

where d_{free} is the minimum free Hamming distance of a convolutional code and is defined in terms of a potentially infinitely long encoded sequence. It is the minimum Hamming weight of all paths in the state diagram that diverge from a state and remerge to that state. The minimum free Hamming distance measure is important with regard to convolutional code performance with maximum-likelihood decoding. Computation of d_{free} has been developed and modified by Bahl et al. [17] and Larsen [18], respectively. Obviously, we must always have

$$
d_{\text{min}} \leq d_f \leq d_{\text{free}}
\qquad (2.84)
$$

and it is also true to say that the minimum Hamming distance, d_{min}, and the minimum free Hamming distance, d_{free}, are usually the same for many convolutional codes. For example, the minimum Hamming distance and the minimum free Hamming distance of the (2, 1, 1) convolutional code in Figure 2.4 are equal to 3. A list of good nonsystematic, noncatastrophic convolutional codes with maximal d_{free} is given in Appendix A.

2.6 GENERATING FUNCTION OF CONVOLUTIONAL CODES

The state diagram of an (n, k, m) convolutional code can be modified to provide a complete description of the weight distribution of the code. The modified state diagram can be obtained by splitting state S_0 into an initial state, S_{in}, and a final state, S_{out}, with the self-loop around S_0 being deleted. Let X be the indeterminate associated with the Hamming weight of the information vector $\mathbf{X}_l$, Y the indeterminate associated with the Hamming weight of the encoded output vector $\mathbf{Y}_l$, and L the indeterminate associated with every branch. Each path in the modified state diagram has a gain, labeled as $X^{i'} Y^{j'} L^{l'}$, where i' is the Hamming weight of the encoder input row vector $\mathbf{X}_l$; j' is the Hamming weight of the encoder output row vector $\mathbf{Y}_l$; and l' is the number of branches between two states. The modified state diagram expressed in terms of X, Y, and L is called an augmented state diagram.

Example 2.20

Consider the $(2, 1, 2)$ convolutional encoder in Figure 2.13(a) and its state diagram in Figure 2.17. The modified and the augmented state diagrams of the code are shown in Figures 2.23 and 2.24, respectively.

For the augmented state diagram, the generating function that provides the weight distribution information is given by

$$T(X, Y, L) = \sum_{i',j',l'} A_{i',j',l'} X^{i'} Y^{j'} L^{l'} \tag{2.85}$$

The coefficient $A_{i',j',l'}$ denotes the number of n encoder output bits with Hamming weight j', whose associated k input information bits have weight i' and

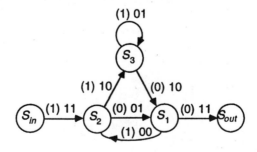

Figure 2.23 Modified state diagram of Figure 2.17.

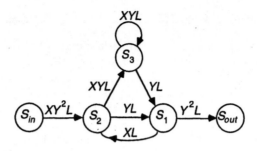

Figure 2.24 Augmented state diagram of Figure 2.17.

branch length l'. We can regard the modified state diagram as a signal flow graph and apply Mason's rule [19] to get the generating function $T(X, Y, L)$. Alternatively, we can describe the transition behavior in the augmented state diagram by a set of equations and solve those equations to obtain $T(X, Y, L)$. Consider the augmented state of the (2, 1, 2) convolutional encoder shown in Figure 2.24. The set of equations are

$$S_2 = XL\ S_1 + XY^2L\ S_{in} \tag{2.86}$$

$$S_1 = YL\ S_2 + YL\ S_3 \tag{2.87}$$

$$S_3 = XYL\ S_2 + XYL\ S_3 \tag{2.88}$$

$$S_{out} = Y^2L\ S_1 \tag{2.89}$$

From (2.88),

$$S_3 = XYL\ S_2/(1 - XYL) \tag{2.90}$$

Substituting (2.90) into (2.87), we get

$$S_1 = YL\ S_2 + XY^2L^2S_2/(1 - XYL) \tag{2.91}$$

$$S_1 = YL\ S_2/(1 - XYL) \tag{2.92}$$

Substituting (2.92) into (2.86), we get

$$S_2 = XYL^2\ S_2/(1 - XYL) + XY^2L\ S_{in} \tag{2.93}$$

$$S_2 = (1 - XYL)XY^2L\ S_{in}/(1 - XYL - XYL^2) \tag{2.94}$$

Substituting (2.92) into (2.89), we get

$$S_{out} = Y^3 L^2 S_2/(1 - XYL) \qquad (2.95)$$

Substituting (2.94) into (2.95), we get

$$S_{out} = Y^3 L^2 \{(1 - XYL)XY^2 L\, S_{in}/(1 - XYL - XYL^2)\}/(1 - XYL) \qquad (2.96)$$

$$S_{out}/S_{in} = XY^5 L^3/\{1 - XYL(1 + L)\} \qquad (2.97)$$

$$\begin{aligned}
S_{out}/S_{in} = {} & XY^5 L^3 + X^2 Y^6 L^4 (1 + L) + X^3 Y^7 L^5 (1 + L)^2 \\
& + X^4 Y^8 L^6 (1 + L)^3 + X^5 Y^9 L^7 (1 + L)^4 + X^6 Y^{10} L^8 (1 + L)^5 \\
& + X^7 Y^{11} L^9 (1 + L)^6 + \cdots
\end{aligned} \qquad (2.98)$$

$$\begin{aligned}
S_{out}/S_{in} = {} & XY^5 L^3 + X^2 Y^6 (L^4 + L^5) + X^3 Y^7 (L^5 + 2L^6 + L^7) \\
& + X^4 Y^8 (L^6 + 3L^7 + 3L^8 + L^9) \\
& + X^5 Y^9 (L^7 + 4L^8 + 6L^9 + 4L^{10} + L^{11}) \\
& + X^6 Y^{10} (L^8 + 5L^9 + 10L^{10} + 10L^{11} + 5L^{12} + L^{13}) \\
& + X^7 Y^{11} (L^9 + 6L^{10} + 15L^{11} + 20L^{12} + 15L^{13} + 6L^{14} + L^{15}) \\
& + \cdots
\end{aligned} \qquad (2.99)$$

Grouping all L terms, we get

$$\begin{aligned}
S_{out}/S_{in} = {} & XY^5 L^3 + X^2 Y^6 L^4 + (X^2 Y^6 + X^3 Y^7)L^5 \\
& + (2X^3 Y^7 + X^4 Y^8)L^6 + (X^3 Y^7 + 3X^4 Y^8 + X^5 Y^9)L^7 \\
& + (3X^4 Y^8 + 4X^5 Y^9 + X^6 Y^{10})L^8 \\
& + (X^4 Y^8 + 6X^5 Y^9 + 5X^6 Y^{10} + X^7 Y^{11})L^9 + \cdots
\end{aligned} \qquad (2.100)$$

$$S_{out}/S_{in} = T(X, Y, L) \qquad (2.101)$$

An information sequence of weight 1 and the codeword of weight 5 have length-3 branches; one information sequence of weight 2 and codeword of weight 6 have length-4 branches; another information sequence of weight 2 and codeword of weight 6 have length-5 branches; and so on. Regardless of branch length,

$$T(X, Y, L)|_{L=1} = XY^5 + 2X^2 Y^6 + 4X^3 Y^7 + 8X^4 Y^8 + \cdots \qquad (2.102)$$

Alternatively, we can formulate (2.86) to (2.89) into matrix form. Thus,

$$\mathbf{F} = \mathbf{A}\,\mathbf{F} + \mathbf{C}\, S_{in} \qquad (2.103)$$

$$S_{out} = \mathbf{L}\,\mathbf{F} \qquad (2.104)$$

where

$$
\begin{bmatrix} S_1 \\ S_2 \\ S_3 \end{bmatrix} = \begin{bmatrix} YL & 0 & YL \\ 0 & XL & 0 \\ XYL & 0 & XYL \end{bmatrix} \begin{bmatrix} S_1 \\ S_2 \\ S_3 \end{bmatrix} + \begin{bmatrix} 0 \\ X Y^2 L \\ 0 \end{bmatrix} [S_{in}]
\tag{2.105}
$$

and

$$
[S_{out}] = [Y^2 L \ 0 \ 0] \begin{bmatrix} S_1 \\ S_2 \\ S_3 \end{bmatrix}
\tag{2.106}
$$

respectively. Hence,

$$
T(X, Y, L) = \mathbf{L}[\mathbf{I} - \mathbf{A}]^{-1}\mathbf{C}
\tag{2.107}
$$

$$
T(X, Y, L) = \mathbf{LIC} + \mathbf{LAC} + \mathbf{LA}^2\mathbf{C} + \cdots
\tag{2.108}
$$

where

$$
[\mathbf{I} - \mathbf{A}]^{-1} = \mathbf{I} + \mathbf{A} + \mathbf{A}^2 + \cdots
\tag{2.109}
$$

Now,

$$
\begin{aligned}
T(X, Y, L) = {} & 0 + XY^5L^3 + X^2Y^6L^4 + (X^2Y^6 + X^3Y^7)L^5 \\
& + (2X^3Y^7 + X^4Y^8)L^6 + (X^3Y^7 + 3X^4Y^8 + X^5Y^9)L^7 \\
& + (3X^4Y^8 + 4X^5Y^9 + X^6Y^{10})L^8 \\
& + (X^4Y^8 + 6X^5Y^9 + 5X^6Y^{10} + X^7Y^{11})L^9 \\
& + \cdots
\end{aligned}
\tag{2.110}
$$

and

$$
T(X, Y, L)|_{L=1} = XY^5 + 2X^2Y^6 + 4X^3Y^7 + 8X^4Y^8 + \cdots
\tag{2.111}
$$

The total number of codeword paths of Hamming weight j' can be found by setting $X = 1$ and $L = 1$ in the transfer function $T(X, Y, L)$, that is,

$$
T(X, Y, L)|_{X=1, L=1} = Y^5 + 2Y^6 + 4Y^7 + 8Y^8 + \cdots
\tag{2.112}
$$

Furthermore, the total number of nonzero information bits on all paths of Hamming weight j' is given by the partial derivative of $T(X, Y, L)$ with respect to X, where

$$\left.\frac{\partial(X, Y, L)}{\partial X}\right|_{X=1, L=1} = Y^5 + 4Y^6 + 12Y^7 + 32Y^8 + \cdots \qquad (2.113)$$

We shall see in the next chapter that the generating function $T(X, Y, L)$ plays a vital role in evaluating the error performance of convolutional codes with maximum-likelihood decoding.

References

[1] Forney, G. D., Jr., "Convolutional Codes I: Algebraic Structure," *IEEE Trans. on Information Theory*, Vol. IT-16, No. 6, November 1970, pp. 720–738, and Vol. IT-17, No. 3, May 1971, p. 360.

[2] Viterbi, A. J., "Error Bounds for Convolutional Codes and an Asymptotically Optimum Decoding Algorithm," *IEEE Trans. on Information Theory*, Vol. IT-13, No. 2, April 1967, pp. 260–269.

[3] Peterson, W. W., and E. J. Weldon, *Error-Correcting Codes*, 2nd ed., Cambridge: MIT Press, 1972.

[4] Lin, S., and D. J. Costello, Jr., *Error Control Coding: Fundamentals and Applications*, Englewood Cliffs, NJ: Prentice-Hall, 1983.

[5] Forney, G. D., Jr., "Structural Analysis of Convolutional Codes via Dual Codes," *IEEE Trans. on Information Theory*, Vol. IT-19, No. 4, July 1973, pp. 512–518.

[6] Larsen, K. J., "Short Convolutional Codes With Maximal Free Distance for Rates 1/2, 1/3, and 3/4," *IEEE Trans. on Information Theory*, Vol. IT-19, No. 3, May 1973, pp. 371–372.

[7] Paaske, E., "Short Binary Convolutional Codes With Maximal Free Distance for Rates 2/3 and 3/4," *IEEE Trans. on Information Theory*, Vol. IT-20, No. 5, September 1974, pp. 683–689.

[8] Massey, J. L., and M. K. Sain, "Inverses of Linear Sequential Circuits," *IEEE Trans. on Computers*, Vol. C-17, No. 4, April 1968, pp. 330–337.

[9] Shusta, T. J., "Enumeration of Minimal Convolutional Encoders," *IEEE Trans. on Information Theory*, Vol. IT-23, No. 1, January 1977, pp. 127–132.

[10] Johannesson, R., and Z. X. Wan, "A Linear Algebraic Approach to Minimal Convolutional Encoders," *IEEE Trans. on Information Theory*, Vol. IT-39, No. 4, July 1993, pp. 1219–1233.

[11] Piret, P., *Convolutional Codes: An Algebraic Approach*, Cambridge: MIT Press, 1988.

[12] Lee, L. H. C., "Computation of the Right-Inverse of $G(D)$ and the Left-Inverse of $H^t(D)$," *Elect. Lett.*, Vol. 26, No. 13, June 1990, pp. 904–906.

[13] Costello, D. J., Jr., "Construction of Convolutional Codes for Sequential Decoding," Ph.D. thesis, University of Notre Dame, Notre Dame, IN, 1969.

[14] Porath, J. E., "Algorithms for Converting Convolutional Codes From Feedback to Feedforward Form and Vice Versa," *Elect. Lett.*, Vol. 25, No. 15, July 1989, pp. 1008–1009.

[15] Yamada, T., H. Harashima, and H. Miyakawa, "A New Maximum Likelihood Decoding of High Rate Convolutional Codes Using a Trellis," *Trans. Inst. Elect. & Commun. Eng. Japan*, Pt. A, Vol. J-66A, No. 7, 1983, pp. 11–16.

[16] Massey, J. L., *Threshold Decoding*, Cambridge: MIT Press, 1963.

[17] Bahl, L. R., C. D. Cullum, W. D. Frazer, and F. Jelinek, "An Efficient Algorithm for Computing Free Distance," *IEEE Trans. on Information Theory*, Vol. 19, No. 3, May 1973, pp. 437–439.

[18] Larsen, K. J., "Comments on 'An Efficient Algorithm for Computing Free Distance,'" *IEEE Trans. on Information Theory*, Vol. 19, No. 4, July 1973 , pp. 577–579.

[19] Mason, S., and H. Zimmermann, *Electronic Circuits, Signals and Systems*, New York: Wiley, 1960.

Suboptimal and Optimal Decoding of Convolutional Codes

3

3.1 INTRODUCTION

So far, we have dealt with the encoding structure of convolutional codes. This section presents three suboptimum and optimum decoding techniques for convolutional codes: (1) sliding block decoding, (2) maximum-likelihood Viterbi algorithm decoding, and (3) syndrome-former trellis decoding. Maximum-likelihood Viterbi algorithm decoding was introduced by Viterbi [1] in 1967. Active research in decoding of convolutional codes led to the discovery of sliding block decoding [2], syndrome-former trellis decoding [3], and many other decoding techniques [4–8]. For practical implementation, *scarce-state-transition* (SST) type of Viterbi and syndrome-former trellis decoding were introduced [9–13]. The principles of hard-decision and soft-decision decoding are discussed in this section. Finally, we evaluate the performance of convolutional codes with Viterbi algorithm decoding. Other techniques such as sequential decoding and majority-logic decoding are discussed in Chapters 4 and 6.

Consider the coded digital communication system model shown in Figure 3.1.

Let the input and the output of the (n, k, m) convolutional encoder of constraint length ν be represented by the k-component vector

$$\mathbf{X}_l = [x_l^{(1)} x_l^{(2)} \cdots x_l^{(k)}] \tag{3.1}$$

and the n-component vector

$$\mathbf{Y}_l = [y_l^{(1)} y_l^{(2)} \cdots y_l^{(n)}] \tag{3.2}$$

for $l \geq 0$, respectively. A binary information sequence $\{\mathbf{X}_l\}$ is encoded into a channel code sequence $\{\mathbf{Y}_l\}$ and sent to a discrete noisy channel at time l. Here, the discrete noisy channel comprises a *binary phase-shifted-keying* (BPSK)

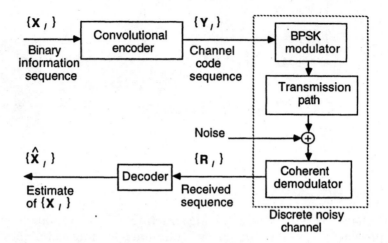

Figure 3.1 Model of a coded digital communication system.

modulator, a transmission path, and a coherent demodulator, where noise is added to the transmitted waveform at the output of the transmission path. At the receiving end, the received sequence $\{\mathbf{R}_l\}$ is fed to the input of the decoder to recover the information sequence $\{\mathbf{X}_l\}$, where

$$\mathbf{R}_l = [r_l^{(1)} r_l^{(2)} \cdots r_l^{(n)}] \tag{3.3}$$

Before we proceed to the description of suboptimum and optimum decoding for convolutional codes, let us define a useful metric measure for decoding. Let $\mathbf{Y}_0, \mathbf{Y}_1, \ldots, \mathbf{Y}_{\nu-1}$ denote the possible transmitted channel code sequence. The likelihood function associated with the code sequence is defined as

$$\prod_{l=0}^{\nu-1} P(\mathbf{R}_l/\mathbf{Y}_l)$$

$P(\mathbf{R}_l/\mathbf{Y}_l)$ is called the branch likelihood function at time l and is given as

$$P(\mathbf{R}_l/\mathbf{Y}_l) = \prod_{j=1}^{n} P(r_l^{(j)}/y_l^{(j)}) \tag{3.4}$$

where $P(r_l^{(j)}/y_l^{(j)})$ is the channel transition probability. The path metric $M_{\nu-1}$ $(\mathbf{R}_0/\mathbf{Y}_0, \mathbf{R}_1/\mathbf{Y}_1, \ldots, \mathbf{R}_{\nu-1}/\mathbf{Y}_{\nu-1})$ associated with a code sequence is defined as the logarithmic likelihood function

$$\sum_{l=0}^{\nu-1} \log P(\mathbf{R}_l/\mathbf{Y}_l)$$

and the branch metric $M(\mathbf{R}_l/\mathbf{Y}_l)$ at time l is defined as $\log P(\mathbf{R}_l/\mathbf{Y}_l)$. Furthermore, the bit metric $M(r_l^{(j)}/y_l^{(j)})$ at time l is defined as $\log P(r_l^{(j)}/y_l^{(j)})$ for $1 < j \le n$.

3.2 SLIDING BLOCK DECODING

Sliding block decoding [2] is best illustrated by describing the operation on a binary symmetric channel with the tree diagram of an (n, k, m) convolutional code of constraint length ν. Figure 3.2 shows the (n, k, m) convolutional encoder tree diagram with single path connection.

Assuming that the decoding process begins at node $0'$, there are $2^{\nu k}$ paths for the first ν branches. Let $\mathbf{Y}_0, \mathbf{Y}_1, \ldots, \mathbf{Y}_{\nu-1}$ denote the possible channel code sequence associated with the paths of the tree and set the decoding window to ν branches. Without loss of generality, the code constraint length ν is set to 2. From the received sequence $\mathbf{R}_0, \mathbf{R}_1, \ldots, \mathbf{R}_{\nu-1}$, the decoder computes all $2^{\nu k}$ likelihood functions

$$\prod_{l=0}^{\nu-1} P(\mathbf{R}_l/\mathbf{Y}_l)$$

associated with the $2^{\nu k}$ paths in sets $A_0, A_1, \ldots, A_{2^k-1}$. The largest likelihood function path from the sets is chosen, and the decoder outputs $\hat{\mathbf{X}}_0$. Suppose the decoder now chooses set A_0 and moves to node $1'$ after the preceding operation; it then uses the sets $A_0', A_1', \ldots, A_{2^k-1}'$ to find $\hat{\mathbf{X}}_1$, the estimate of $\mathbf{X}_1$. The operation is carried out after receiving $\mathbf{R}_\nu$. On receiving a new segment of the received vector $\mathbf{R}_\nu$, the decoder uses the tree and produces an estimated vector $\hat{\mathbf{Y}}_1$ of the channel code vector $\mathbf{Y}_1$. The decoder computes all $2^{\nu k}$ likelihood functions

$$\prod_{l=1}^{\nu} P(\mathbf{R}_l/\mathbf{Y}_l)$$

associated with the $2^{\nu k}$ paths in sets $A_0', A_1', \ldots, A_{2^k-1}'$ and chooses the largest-likelihood path from the sets. Thus, the decoder performs a maximum-likelihood search of the likelihood function

$$\prod_{l=1}^{\nu} P(\mathbf{R}_l/\mathbf{Y}_l)$$

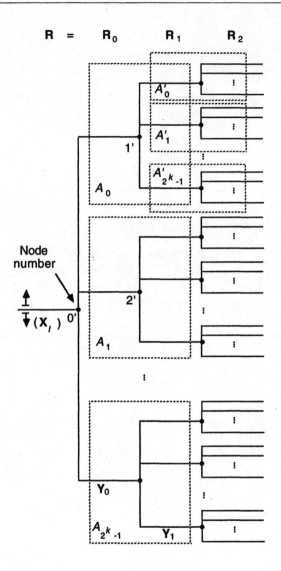

Figure 3.2 (*n, k, m*) convolutional encoder tree diagram with single path connection.

Because $\log P(\mathbf{R}_l/\mathbf{Y}_l)$ is a monotone increasing function of $(\mathbf{R}_l/\mathbf{Y}_l)$, it follows that a maximum-likelihood search of the likelihood function

$$\prod_{l=1}^{\nu} P(\mathbf{R}_l/\mathbf{Y}_l)$$

is equivalent to a search of the maximum log-likelihood function

$$\sum_{l=1}^{\nu} \log P(\mathbf{R}_l / \mathbf{Y}_l)$$

A metric can now be employed in the search. In the decoding process, the most likely path corresponds to the path with the largest metric. At each step, the decoder computes and compares the metrics of all $2^{\nu k}$ paths in the sets, chooses the path with the largest metric from the sets, and decodes. The process repeats in that way as more segments are received by the decoder. This is the sliding block decoding. The error performance of the sliding block decoding obviously depends on the decoding window size. As the decoding window size approaches infinity, the performance becomes optimum.

In hard-decision decoding, the discrete noisy channel becomes a binary symmetric channel, and the elements of $\mathbf{R}_l$ are quantized into 0 and 1. With equally likely input symbols and channel transition probability p, the hard-decision bit metrics at time l are

$$M(r_l^{(j)}/y_l^{(j)}) = \log_{10} p \tag{3.5}$$

for $r_l^{(j)} \neq y_l^{(j)}$ and

$$M(r_l^{(j)}/y_l^{(j)}) = \log_{10}(1 - p) \tag{3.6}$$

for $r_l^{(j)} = y_l^{(j)}$. Suppose the channel transition probability p is set to 0.1. We then have $M(r_l^{(j)}/y_l^{(j)}) = -1$ for $r_l^{(j)} \neq y_l^{(j)}$ and $M(r_l^{(j)}/y_l^{(j)}) = -0.05$ for $r_l^{(j)} = y_l^{(j)}$. With integer scaling, $M(r_l^{(j)}/y_l^{(j)}) = -20$ for $r_l^{(j)} \neq y_l^{(j)}$ and $M(r_l^{(j)}/y_l^{(j)}) = -1$ for $r_l^{(j)} = y_l^{(j)}$. This is shown in Table 3.1.

Example 3.1

Assuming that the all-zero code sequence is transmitted, the received sequence is $\mathbf{R} = [\mathbf{R}_0, \mathbf{R}_1, \mathbf{R}_2, \mathbf{R}_3] = [10, 00, 10, 00]$ and the decoding window size is 3.

Table 3.1
Hard-Decision Metric Table for $p = 0.1$

$y_l^{(j)}/r_l^{(j)}$	0	1
0	−1	−20
1	−20	−1

Given the hard-decision metric table in Table 3.1 and the tree diagram of a (2, 1, 2) convolutional code in Figure 3.3 with generator polynomial matrix $\mathbf{G}(D) = [1 + D^2 \quad 1 + D + D^2]$, the hard-decision sliding block decoder works as follows.

Initially, the decoder starts at node 0' (the root of the tree). When $\mathbf{R}_0$, $\mathbf{R}_1$, and $\mathbf{R}_2$ are received, it is compared to the eight possible code vectors in the set $A_0 = \{00\ 00\ 00,\ 00\ 00\ 11,\ 00\ 11\ 01,\ 00\ 11\ 10\}$ and set $A_1 = \{11\ 01\ 11,\ 11\ 01\ 00,\ 11\ 10\ 10,\ 11\ 10\ 01\}$. Their associated path metrics are quoted inside angle brackets (< >). For example, the path metric between the received vector [$\mathbf{R}_0$, $\mathbf{R}_1$, $\mathbf{R}_2$] and the all-zero code vector in set A_0 is <–20> + <–1> + <–1> + <–1> + <–20> + <–1> = <–44>. A tie exists in the sets A_0 and A_1. Because there are more of these paths with the largest metric in set A_0 than in set A_1, the decoder will favor set A_0. From set A_0, the decoder randomly selects 00 00 00 as the path with the largest metric and output $\hat{\mathbf{X}}_0 = 0$. The decoder now moves to node 1' and uses the sets A_0' and A_1' to find $\hat{\mathbf{X}}_1$, the estimate of $\mathbf{X}_1$. The operation is carried out after receiving $\mathbf{R}_3$. From our example, $\mathbf{R}_1$, $\mathbf{R}_2$, and $\mathbf{R}_3$ are compared with the eight code vectors from set $A_0' = \{00\ 00\ 00,\ 00\ 00\ 11,\ 00\ 11\ 01,\ 00\ 11\ 10\}$ and set $A_1' = \{11\ 01\ 11,\ 11\ 01\ 00,\ 11\ 10\ 10,\ 11\ 10\ 01\}$. The decoder picks 00 00 00 in set A_0' as the path with the largest metric, and output $\hat{\mathbf{X}}_1 = 0$. The next starting node is node 3' for finding $\hat{\mathbf{X}}_2$ on receipt of $\mathbf{R}_4$. The decoding

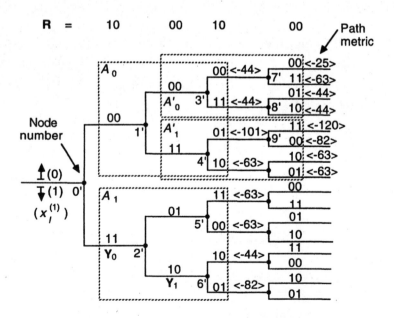

Figure 3.3 Tree diagram for the (2, 1, 2) convolutional encoder of $\mathbf{G}(D) = [1 + D^2 \quad 1 + D + D^2]$.

process continues in this way until the whole message is received and decoded. In the example, the received sequence $R_0, R_1, R_2, R_3, \ldots, = 10, 00, 10, 00, \ldots,$ is decoded to $Y_0, Y_1, \ldots = 00, 00, \ldots,$ which corresponds to the estimated information sequence $\hat{X}_0, \hat{X}_1, \ldots = 0, 0, \ldots.$

3.3 MAXIMUM-LIKELIHOOD VITERBI ALGORITHM DECODING

To perform optimum decoding, Viterbi proposed a decoding algorithm for convolutional codes in 1967 [1]. The Viterbi algorithm can achieve the maximum-likelihood decoding performance, which minimizes the probability of error in the decoding of the whole received sequence, when the binary information bits are statistically independent and equally likely to have any of their possible values [14]. The Viterbi algorithm is described next; the technique involves finding the shortest path through a weighted trellis [15].

Consider an (n, k, m) binary convolutional code with constraint length ν and total encoder memory K. There are 2^k transitions between trellis states, as shown in Figure 3.4.

Assuming that the encoder is initially in state 0, there are $2^{(\nu-1)k}$ paths for the first $\nu - 1$ branches. Let $Y_0, Y_1, \ldots, Y_{\nu-2}$ denote the possible channel code sequence associated with the paths of the trellis. From the received sequence $\{R_{\nu-2}\}$, the decoder computes all $2^{(\nu-1)k}$ path metrics $M_{\nu-2}(R_0/Y_0, R_1/Y_1, \ldots, R_{\nu-2}/Y_{\nu-2})$ associated with the $2^{(\nu-1)k}$ paths and preserves them. On receiving a new segment of the received sequence $\{R_{\nu-1}\}$, the decoder uses the trellis and produces an estimated sequence $\{\hat{Y}_{\nu-1}\}$ of the channel code sequence $\{Y_{\nu-1}\}$. The branch metrics $M(R_{\nu-1}/Y_{\nu-1})$ of 2^k paths entering a state in the trellis are computed. Each of these branch metrics is added to the corresponding path metric $M_{\nu-2}(R_0/Y_0, R_1/Y_1, \ldots, R_{\nu-2}/Y_{\nu-2})$. The path with the largest path metric

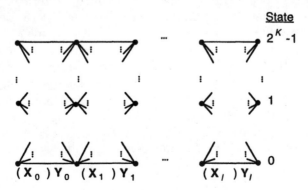

Figure 3.4 Trellis diagram for an (n, k, m) convolutional code.

entering each state is preserved, and there are a total of 2^K surviving paths. Thus, the decoder performs a maximum-likelihood search of the largest path metric $M(\mathbf{R}_{\nu-1}/\mathbf{Y}_{\nu-1}) + M_{\nu-2}(\mathbf{R}_0/\mathbf{Y}_0, \mathbf{R}_1/\mathbf{Y}_1, \ldots, \mathbf{R}_{\nu-2}/\mathbf{Y}_{\nu-2})$. The process repeats in this way as more segments are received by the decoder. This is true maximum-likelihood decoding.

Clearly, there is no firm decoding decision produced by the decoder until the whole message is received over the channel. In practice, this true maximum-likelihood decoding technique must be modified to give an implementable piece of hardware. Hard-decision and soft-decision decoding techniques are described next.

3.3.1 Hard-Decision Viterbi Algorithm Decoding

We have seen that the Viterbi algorithm decoder determines the code sequence $\{\hat{\mathbf{Y}}_l\}$ that has the largest path metric to the received sequence $\{\mathbf{R}_l\}$ at time l. The decoder recursively maximizes the path metric

$$M_l(\mathbf{R}_0/\mathbf{Y}_0, \mathbf{R}_1/\mathbf{Y}_1, \ldots, \mathbf{R}_l/\mathbf{Y}_l) = M_{l-1}(\mathbf{R}_0/\mathbf{Y}_0, \mathbf{R}_1/\mathbf{Y}_1, \ldots, \mathbf{R}_{l-1}/\mathbf{Y}_{l-1}) + M(\mathbf{R}_l/\mathbf{Y}_l)$$
$$(3.7)$$

over all code sequences $\{\mathbf{Y}_l\}$. $M(\mathbf{R}_l/\mathbf{Y}_l)$ is the branch metric between vectors $\mathbf{R}_l$ and $\mathbf{Y}_l$ at time l. In the hard-decision case, the hard-decision bit metrics at time l with equally likely input symbols and channel transition probability p are given by (3.5) and (3.6).

In this ideal hard-decision decoder, no firm decoding decision is made until the entire message is received over the channel. In practice, a decision is made when the decoder has searched approximately 6ν segments into the trellis without significant degradation in error probability performance [16]. This is exactly what a standard conventional hard-decision Viterbi decoder does. It limits the length of the path history. The decoder here holds 2^K surviving paths with fixed search length $\psi = 6\nu$ and operates iteratively on the encoder trellis by means of the Viterbi algorithm. Associated with any path is the corresponding sequences $\{\mathbf{X}_l\}$ and $\{\mathbf{Y}_l\}$. At time l, the decoder uses the metric $M(r_l^{(j)}/y_l^{(j)})$ as the bit metric and computes running metrics for all paths entering a state. That is done by adding the branch metric $M(\mathbf{R}_l/\mathbf{Y}_l)$ entering that state node to the running path metric $M_{l-1}(\mathbf{R}_0/\mathbf{Y}_0, \mathbf{R}_1/\mathbf{Y}_1, \ldots, \mathbf{R}_{l-1}/\mathbf{Y}_{l-1})$ of the associated surviving path at time $l - 1$. The decoder then selects the largest running path metric per state-node. From the 2^K surviving paths, the largest running path metric is chosen by the decoder as the final surviving path. The information symbols contained in the "oldest" segment of that path are taken as the decoded values of the information symbols that were input to the convolutional encoder. Therefore, there is a delay in decoding. Following this decoding step, the information symbols associated with all the surviving paths in that segment are discarded. The running path metrics are adjusted by normalizing the largest running path metric to zero; only the difference between the running path metrics matters. Because the values of the running path metrics are stored in finite-size semiconductor memories, the normalization process avoids any hardware memory overflow condition. From an implementation point of view, whenever a tie in running path metrics occurs, one of the paths is chosen by a random selection process. This resolution of ties has no effect on the average decoding error probability. The process repeats in that way with the receipt of the next vector, R_{l+1}.

To start the maximum-likelihood decoding process, a known training sequence of information symbols (usually zeros) is first encoded and transmitted over the channel. One of the surviving paths in the decoder is set to that transmitted sequence and the remaining surviving paths are set to arbitrary values. The running path metric associated with the correctly decoded path is set to zero, and the remaining running path metrics are set to some very small values. With correct synchronization and timing, additional received symbols will cause the decoder to determine a new set of surviving paths that are derived from the original surviving path. Correct operation is now achieved.

Example 3.2

Consider the (2, 1, 2) convolutional code with generator polynomial matrix $G(D) = [1 + D^2 \ 1 + D + D^2]$. The trellis of this code is shown in Figure 3.5(a). For simplicity, we assume that the transmitted code sequence is the all-zero codeword and employ the metric in Table 3.1 for decoding. The received sequence is 10 00 10 00 00 . . . , which has two random errors. The decoding window (search length) is set to 2ν, where $\nu = 3$. The sequence of states of the decoder is shown in Figure 3.5(b). Clearly, there are only a finite number of branches in which one can see. Inside the search window are the surviving paths. Their associated unnormalized running path metrics are quoted inside angle brackets (< >). The metric computations and the path selection mechanism can be illustrated as follows. For instance, at the end of iteration step 2, the surviving path metrics <–23>, <–42>, <–61>, and <–42> are associated with the code sequences [00 00], [11 01], [00 11], and [11 10], respectively. On receiving the vector $R_2 = 10$, we compute the branch metrics for two paths entering each trellis node. At state 0, each of the computed branch metrics entering state 0 is <–21>. The running path metric associated with the code sequence [00 00 00] is <–23> + <–21> = <–44> and the running path metric associated with the code sequence [11 01 11] is <–42> + <–21> = <–63>. The code sequence [00 00 00] has the larger running metric and is chosen as the

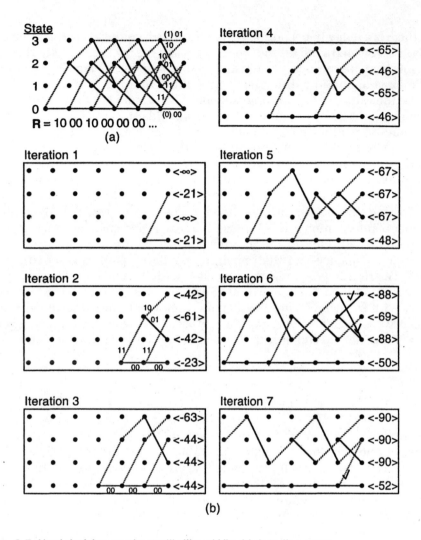

Figure 3.5 Hard-decision maximum-likelihood Viterbi decoding steps.

surviving path at state 0. These metric computations and path selection process are repeated for the remaining states in the trellis.

At the end of the fifth iteration step, the decoder has already identified the maximum-likelihood path, even though it has not reached the full decoding search length (decision). In general, the decoder determines the surviving path per node by extending all surviving paths obtained from the preceding iteration step. In the example, ties are present at iteration steps 6 and 7, and the ticked paths are randomly chosen and retained. As the decoding process continues, the earlier code symbols drop out of the window. The decoding decision is made at the far left side of the window. In the example, the decoded code sequence is 00 00 00 00 ..., and the corresponding decoded information sequence is 0 0 0 0 .... Since the code is a double error-correcting code and has a minimum free Hamming distance of 5, double errors that occur within one constraint length of the code are corrected. Since the decoder operation is constrained by the trellis, it can be seen that decoding errors occur in bursts at the output of the decoder when the channel is very noisy. Because of the channel nature, the search length has to be reasonably long for adequate decoding performance. Usually, it is set to 5ν or 6ν. Further increase in the search length does not provide significant additional coding gain because the maximum-likelihood path is almost identified by the decoder [16]. Therefore, when the search length is set to 6ν, the performance of this fixed-search-length decoder can be considered to be close to that of the true maximum-likelihood decoder. From the trellis diagram, we can see that there is a one-to-one mapping between the code symbols and the information symbol, which causes state transition. The amount of storage can be reduced by storing the information symbols rather than the code symbols.

In practice, it is common to use Hamming distance to perform metric computations. Consider the branch metric log $P(\mathbf{R}_l/\mathbf{Y}_l)$ at time l. For a binary symmetric channel, $P(r_l^{(j)}/y_l^{(j)}) = p$ for $r_l^{(j)} \neq y_l^{(j)}$ and $P(r_l^{(j)}/y_l^{(j)}) = (1 - p)$ for $r_l^{(j)} = y_l^{(j)}$. When $p < 0.5$, the branch metric can be written as

$$\log P(\mathbf{R}_l/\mathbf{Y}_l) = d(\mathbf{R}_l/\mathbf{Y}_l)\log p + [n - d(\mathbf{R}_l/\mathbf{Y}_l)]\log(1 - p) \tag{3.8}$$

$$\log P(\mathbf{R}_l/\mathbf{Y}_l) = d(\mathbf{R}_l/\mathbf{Y}_l)\log\frac{p}{1 - p} + n\log(1 - p) \tag{3.9}$$

where $d(\mathbf{R}_l/\mathbf{Y}_l)$ is the branch Hamming distance between vectors $\mathbf{R}_l$ and $\mathbf{Y}_l$. For a given value of n and p, the maximum-likelihood decoder becomes a hard-decision minimum-distance decoder, which minimizes the Hamming distance between sequences $\{\mathbf{R}_l\}$ and $\{\mathbf{Y}_l\}$.

The optimum hard-decision minimum-distance decoder determines the code sequence $\{\hat{\mathbf{Y}}_l\}$ that is closest in Hamming distance to the received sequence $\{\mathbf{R}_l\}$ at time l with elements 0 and 1. This is accomplished by the Viterbi algorithm, which recursively minimizes the Hamming metric

$$M_l(\mathbf{R}_0/\mathbf{Y}_0, \mathbf{R}_1/\mathbf{Y}_1, \cdots, \mathbf{R}_l/\mathbf{Y}_l) = M_{l-1}(\mathbf{R}_0/\mathbf{Y}_0, \mathbf{R}_1/\mathbf{Y}_1, \cdots, \mathbf{R}_{l-1}/\mathbf{Y}_{l-1}) + d(\mathbf{R}_l, \mathbf{Y}_l) \tag{3.10}$$

over all code sequences $\{\mathbf{Y}_l\}$. $d(\mathbf{R}_l, \mathbf{Y}_l)$ is the branch Hamming distance between vectors $\mathbf{R}_l$ and $\mathbf{Y}_l$ at time l.

The hard-decision minimum-distance decoder here holds 2^K surviving paths with fixed search length $\psi = 6\nu$ and operates iteratively on the encoder trellis by means of the Viterbi algorithm. Associated with any path are the corresponding sequences $\{X_l\}$ and $\{Y_l\}$. The received symbols are quantized into two levels, a "1" or a "0," and the maximization of the logarithmic likelihood function by the decoder is replaced by minimizing the Hamming distance between the received sequence, $\{R_l\}$, and the estimated code sequence, $\{Y_l\}$. At time l, the decoder uses the Hamming distance as the metric and computes running path Hamming metrics for all paths entering a state. That is done by adding the branch Hamming distance, $d(R_l, Y_l)$, entering that state node to the running path Hamming metric, $M_{l-1}(R_0/Y_0, R_1/Y_1, \ldots, R_{l-1}/Y_{l-1})$, of the associated surviving path at time $l - 1$. The decoder then selects the smallest running path Hamming metric per state-node. From the resultant 2^K surviving paths, the smallest running path Hamming metric is chosen by the decoder as the final surviving path. The information symbols contained in the "oldest" segment of that path are taken as the decoded values of the information symbols that were input to the convolutional encoder. Following this decoding step, the information symbols associated with all the surviving paths in that segment are discarded. The running path Hamming metrics are adjusted by normalizing the smallest running path Hamming metric to zero. Whenever a tie in running path Hamming metric occurs, one of the paths is chosen by a random selection process. The process repeats in this way with the receipt of the next vector, R_{l+1}.

To start the hard-decision minimum-distance decoding process, a known training sequence of information symbols (usually zeros) is again encoded and transmitted over the channel. One of the surviving paths in the decoder is set to that transmitted sequence and the remaining surviving paths are set to arbitrary values. The running path Hamming metric associated with the correctly decoded path is set to zero but the remaining running path Hamming metrics are set to some very *large* values. With correct synchronization and timing, additional received symbols will cause the decoder to determine a new set of surviving paths which are derived from the original surviving path. Correct operation is now achieved.

Example 3.3

Consider the (2, 1, 2) convolutional code with generator polynomial matrix $\mathbf{G}(D) = [1 + D^2 \quad 1 + D + D^2]$. The trellis of this code is shown in Figure 3.6(a). Again, we have assumed that the transmitted code sequence is the all-zero codeword. The received sequence is 10 00 10 00 00 . . , which has two random errors. The decoding window (search length) is set to 2ν, where $\nu = 3$. The sequence of states of the decoder is shown in Figure 3.6(b). Inside the search ·

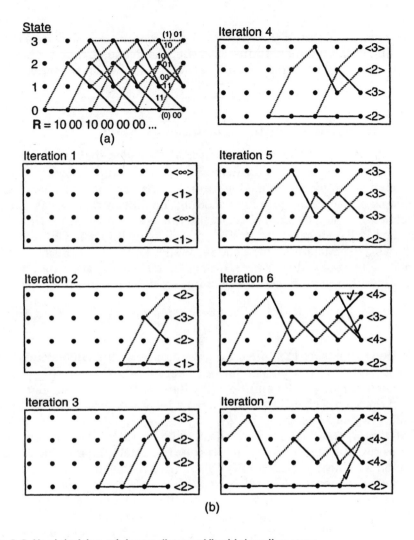

Figure 3.6 Hard-decision minimum-distance Viterbi decoding steps.

window are the surviving paths. Their associated unnormalized running path Hamming metrics are quoted inside angle brackets (< >). At the end of the fifth iteration step, the decoder has already identified the minimum Hamming distance path, even though it has not reached the full decoding search length (decision). As before, the decoder determines the surviving path per node by extending all surviving paths obtained from the preceding iteration step. In the example, ties are present at iteration steps 6 and 7, and the ticked paths are randomly chosen and retained. As the decoding process continues, the earlier code symbols drop out of the window. The decoding decision is made at the far left side of the window. In the example, the decoded code sequence is 00 00 00 00 . . . , and the corresponding decoded information sequence is 0 0 0 0 . . . .

3.3.2 Soft-Decision Viterbi Algorithm Decoding

Consider the coherent BPSK demodulator of the coded digital communication system shown in Figure 3.1. If the demodulator is left unquantized, the demodulated signal is simply in an analog form. In this case, we can use Euclidean distance as a metric measure for decoding. Euclidean distance is defined as the distance between two signal vectors in the N-dimensional Euclidean vector space. For BPSK signals, the vector space has a dimension of 1. Now, the optimum decoder determines the code sequence $\{\hat{\mathbf{Y}}_l\}$ that is closest in Euclidean distance to the received sequence, $\{\mathbf{R}_l\}$, at time l. That is accomplished by the Viterbi algorithm, which recursively minimizes the Euclidean metric

$$M_l(\mathbf{R}_0/\mathbf{Y}_0, \mathbf{R}_1/\mathbf{Y}_1, \ldots, \mathbf{R}_l/\mathbf{Y}_l) = M_{l-1}(\mathbf{R}_0/\mathbf{Y}_0, \mathbf{R}_1/\mathbf{Y}_1, \ldots, \mathbf{R}_{l-1}/\mathbf{Y}_{l-1}) + d(\mathbf{R}_l, \mathbf{Y}_l)$$

$$(3.11)$$

over all code sequences $\{\mathbf{Y}_l\}$. $d(\mathbf{R}_l, \mathbf{Y}_l)$ is the branch Euclidean distance between vectors $\mathbf{R}_l$ and $\mathbf{Y}_l$ at time l. The decoder here holds 2^K surviving paths with fixed search length $\psi = 6\nu$ and operates iteratively on the encoder trellis by means of the Viterbi algorithm. Associated with any path are the corresponding sequences $\{\mathbf{X}_l\}$ and $\{\mathbf{Y}_l\}$.

At time l, the decoder uses the Euclidean distance as the metric and computes running metrics for all paths entering a state. That is done by adding the branch Euclidean distance $d(\mathbf{R}_l, \mathbf{Y}_l)$ entering that state node to the running Euclidean path metric $M_{l-1}(\mathbf{R}_0/\mathbf{Y}_0, \mathbf{R}_1/\mathbf{Y}_1, \ldots, \mathbf{R}_{l-1}/\mathbf{Y}_{l-1})$ of the associated surviving path at time $l - 1$. The decoder then selects the smallest running Euclidean path metric per state node. From the resultant 2^K surviving paths, the lowest running Euclidean metric path is chosen by the decoder as the final surviving path. The information symbols contained in the "oldest" segment of that path are taken as the decoded values of the information symbols that were input to the convolutional encoder. Following that decoding step, the information symbols associated with all the surviving paths in that segment are discarded. The running path Euclidean metrics are adjusted by normalizing the lowest running Euclidean metric to zero. Whenever a tie in running Euclidean metric occurs, one of the paths is chosen by a random selection process. The process repeats in this way with the receipt of the next vector, $\mathbf{R}_{l+1}$. To start the decoding process, the technique employed by the hard-decision minimum-distance decoder can also be used.

In a practical implementation, each signal at the output of the coherent BPSK demodulator is often quantized to Q number of regions. Q is defined as the number of quantization levels and $Q > 2$. The demodulator is said to make soft decisions. The quantized signal, therefore, can be represented as a binary vector. In general, the binary vector is $\log_2 Q$ bits long for a Q-level quantization. Figure 3.7 shows a 3-bit natural binary quantizer with uniform quantization regions.

It can be seen that the two possible BPSK signals, –1.0 and +1.0, lie in the regions covered by the binary vectors [000] and [111], respectively. Also, the received signal that falls in the region covered by the binary vector [101] is quantized to the binary vector [101]. The leftmost bit is the hard-decision digit. From the binary vector, we can calculate the soft-decision distance between two quantized signals. To compute the soft-decision distance between two quantized signals, we simply convert the binary vectors into decimal numbers and take the absolute value of their difference. For example, the soft-decision distance between the binary vectors [101] and [111] is 2. In the decoding process, we replace the Euclidean distance by the soft-decision distance as a metric measure for decoding. The decoder is called a soft-decision minimum-distance decoder.

Example 3.4

Consider the (2, 1, 2) convolutional code with generator polynomial matrix $\mathbf{G}(D) = [1 + D^2 \ 1 + D + D^2]$. The trellis of this code is shown in Figure 3.8(a). For simplicity, we assume that the transmitted code sequence is the all-zero codeword. The received sequence is 40 00 45 00 00 ..., which has three random errors. The decoding window (search length) is set to 2ν, where $\nu = 3$. The sequence of states of the decoder is shown in Figure 3.8(b). Inside the search window are the surviving paths. Their associated unnormalized running path soft-decision metrics are quoted inside angle brackets (< >). At the end of fourth iteration step, the decoder has already identified the minimum soft-decision distance path, even though it has not reached the full decoding search

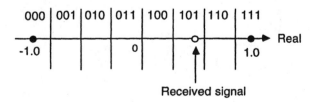

Figure 3.7 A 3-bit natural binary quantizer.

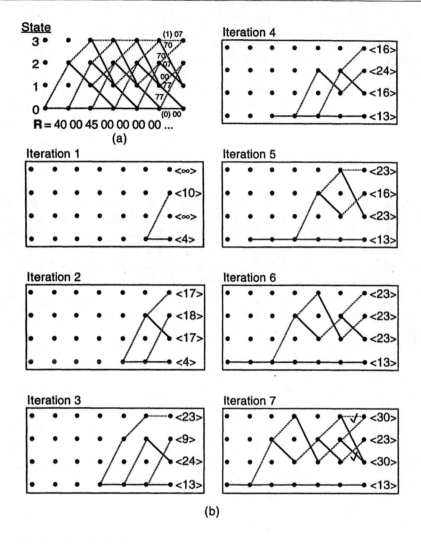

Figure 3.8 Eight-level soft-decision minimum-distance Viterbi decoding steps.

length (decision). In the example, ties are present at iteration step 7, and the ticked paths are randomly chosen and retained. As the decoding process continues, the earlier code symbols drop out of the window. The decoding decision is made at the far left side of the window. In the example, the decoded code sequence is 00 00 00 00 ..., and the corresponding decoded information sequence is 0 0 0 0 .... The triple errors that occur within one constraint length of the code are corrected with soft-decision decoding. In general, soft-decision decoding can correct more errors than hard-decision decoding for the same code.

It can be seen that the decoder stores $2^K \psi \cdot k$-component vectors, 2^K running metrics, and that there are 2^k metric computations per state node to be carried out. For a given value of K, the implementation becomes impossible as k gets large (say, greater than 10). Section 3.4 describes an alternative technique to overcome this hardware implementation problem.

3.4 SYNDROME-FORMER TRELLIS DECODING

We have seen that the Viterbi algorithm decoding is effective for low-rate convolutional codes. For high-rate convolutional codes, the implementation of the Viterbi decoder becomes very complex. The alternative decoding technique, called syndrome-former trellis decoding, is particularly effective for high-rate-k/n convolutional codes where $k = n - 1$. In the syndrome-former trellis decoding process [3], the fundamental difference from the Viterbi algorithm decoding process is that the decoder first estimates the code symbols, followed by an inverse operation. The required digital communication system model is shown in Figure 3.9.

Here, the decoder splits into two parts; a codeword estimator and an inverter. This is only a conceptual split; on average, the decoder can do no better or worse an estimation of $\{X_l\}$ than a single Viterbi decoder. In practice, the two parts are integrated as one piece of equipment. The codeword estimator uses the Viterbi algorithm and applies it to the syndrome-former trellis of the code. From the received symbols, the codeword estimator determines the maximum-likelihood sequence $\{\hat{Y}_l\}$, followed by an inverse operation that maps the decoded information sequence $\{\hat{X}_l\}$, with delay q. The actual operation of

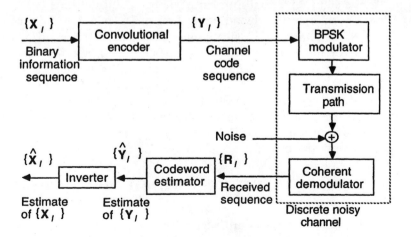

Figure 3.9 Model of a digital communication system.

the codeword estimator is exactly the same as the Viterbi decoder described in Section 3.3. At the beginning of a transmission, a known training sequence is transmitted to set up the decoder.

Example 3.5

Consider the (2, 1, 2) convolutional code with $\mathbf{G}(D) = [1 + D^2 \; 1 + D + D^2]$. Its syndrome-former trellis is shown in Figure 3.10(a). Again, we assume that the received sequence is 40 00 45 00 00 . . ., which has three random errors. The decoding window is also set to 2ν. The estimator now traces through the syndrome-former trellis and must hold 2^{K+1} surviving paths inside the search window. Their associated unnormalized running path soft-decision metrics are quoted inside angle brackets (< >). The decoded code symbols are the "oldest" symbols that drop out at the left side of the window. In delay operator form, the information sequence can be recovered from $\hat{\mathbf{X}}(\mathbf{D}) \, D^q = \hat{\mathbf{Y}}(D) \, \mathbf{G}^{-1}(D)$, where $q = 0$ for this particular convolutional encoder.

In the syndrome-former trellis decoding process, it can be seen that the decoder stores $2^{K+1} \, \psi \cdot n$-component vectors and 2^{K+1} running path metrics, but there are only one or two metric computations to be carried out at each trellis node for high rate $(n, n - 1, m)$ convolutional codes. Thus, there exist states within a syndrome-former trellis frame that do not require comparisons for the selection of surviving paths. Our example illustrates the case. This may speed up the decoding process.

In the conventional Viterbi decoding system of $(n, n - 1, m)$ convolutional codes, the decoder holds 2^K surviving paths and performs 2^{n-1} metric computations per trellis state. The total number of metric computations is $2^K(2^{n-1})$. In the syndrome-former trellis decoding system of $(n, n - 1, m)$ convolutional codes, the decoder holds 2^{K+1} surviving paths. Since the syndrome-former trellis has only one or two paths entering or leaving a node, the decoder only performs one or two metric computations per trellis node. For an n-stage syndrome-former trellis, the total number of metric computations is less than $2^{K+1} \cdot 2n$. Hence, the syndrome-former trellis decoding system reduces the total number of metric computations but doubles the storage requirement, compared with the conventional Viterbi decoding system for high rate-$(n - 1)/n$ convolutional codes.

3.5 SCARCE-STATE-TRANSITION-TYPE VITERBI ALGORITHM DECODING

In a practical realization of a Viterbi algorithm decoder, the management of the memories used in the surviving paths is a major design issue. Two commonly

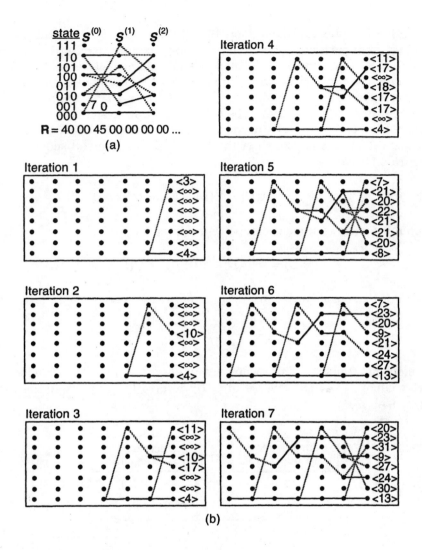

Figure 3.10 Eight-level soft-decision minimum-distance syndrome-former trellis decoding steps.

used techniques are the trace-back method and the register-exchange method [17]. In the trace-back method, pointers are used to interpret the surviving path memories. On the other hand, the contents in all the surviving paths in the register-exchanged method must be stored and exchanged at each decoding step. The register-exchange method is assumed here. Based on the register-exchange method, the SST-type Viterbi algorithm and syndrome-former trellis decoding techniques are developed [9–13]. The SST-type Viterbi algorithm decoding technique is described in this section. Section 3.6 describes the operation of the SST-type syndrome-former trellis decoding technique. Without loss of generality, a minimal convolutional encoder is assumed for all SST-type decoding systems, which implies that $\mathbf{G}(D)\,\mathbf{G}^{-1}(D) = \mathbf{I}\,D^q = \mathbf{I}$ and $q = 0$.

The scarce-state-transition type Viterbi decoding system [9–12] is a development of the conventional Viterbi decoding system in which the following modifications are made. Consider the hard-decision received sequences $\mathbf{R}(D)$ in Figure 3.11, where

$$\mathbf{R}(D) = \mathbf{Y}(D) + \mathbf{E}(D) \tag{3.12}$$

The channel error sequences can be represented as

$$\mathbf{E}(D) = [e^{(1)}(D)\, e^{(2)}(D) \cdots e^{(n)}(D)] \tag{3.13}$$

The channel errors at time l are represented by the n-component error vector

$$\mathbf{E}_l = [e_l^{(1)}\, e_l^{(2)} \cdots e_l^{(n)}] \tag{3.14}$$

with elements 0 and 1. The received sequences $\mathbf{R}(D)$ are predecoded by an inverter circuit, the right-inverse of $\mathbf{G}(D)$, to give the predecoded sequences $\mathbf{U}(D)$, where

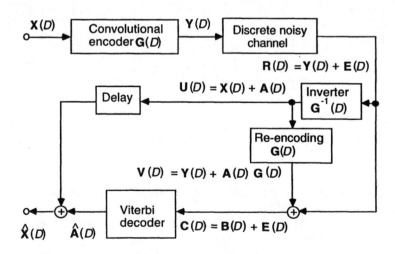

Figure 3.11 Model of a hard-decision SST-type Viterbi algorithm decoding system.

$$U(D) = R(D)G^{-1}(D) \tag{3.15}$$
$$= X(D) + A(D) \tag{3.16}$$

and $A(D) = E(D)\,G^{-1}(D)$. The predecoded error sequences $A(D)$ can be expressed as

$$A(D) = [a^{(1)}(D)\,a^{(2)}(D) \cdots a^{(k)}(D)] \tag{3.17}$$

The predecoded errors at time l are represented by the k-component vector

$$A_l = [a_l^{(1)}\,a_l^{(2)} \cdots a_l^{(k)}] \tag{3.18}$$

The predecoded sequences $U(D)$ are then re-encoded by the same convolutional encoder used in the transmitter to give the re-encoded sequences $V(D)$, where

$$V(D) = U(D)G(D) \tag{3.19}$$
$$= Y(D) + A(D)G(D) \tag{3.20}$$

The re-encoded sequences $V(D)$ are added (modulo-2 addition) to the received sequences $R(D)$, to give the received error sequences

$$C(D) = B(D) + E(D) \tag{3.21}$$

where

$$B(D) = A(D)G(D) \tag{3.22}$$

$C(D)$ can be represented as

$$C(D) = [c^{(1)}(D)\,c^{(2)}(D) \cdots c^{(n)}(D)] \tag{3.23}$$

The received errors at time l are represented by the n-component binary vector

$$C_l = [c_l^{(1)}\,c_l^{(2)} \cdots c_l^{(n)}] \tag{3.24}$$

Similarly, the re-encoded error sequences $B(D)$ can be represented as

$$B(D) = [b^{(1)}(D)\,b^{(2)}(D) \cdots b^{(n)}(D)] \tag{3.25}$$

The re-encoded errors at time l are represented by the n-component binary vector

$$\mathbf{B}_l = [b_l^{(1)} b_l^{(2)} \cdots b_l^{(n)}] \tag{3.26}$$

and

$$\mathbf{C}_l = \mathbf{B}_l + \mathbf{E}_l \tag{3.27}$$

$\mathbf{C}_l$, composed of errors only, is input into the Viterbi decoder. Comparing (3.12) with (3.21), it is clear that one can draw a 2^K-state trellis, called the error-trellis, with input $\mathbf{A}_l$ and output $\mathbf{B}_l$. For example, the error-trellis diagram has the same form as the trellis shown in Figure 3.4 for the (n, k, m) convolutional encoder with $\mathbf{X}_l$ replaced by $\mathbf{A}_l$ and $\mathbf{Y}_l$ replaced by $\mathbf{B}_l$. The decoder holds 2^K surviving paths and 2^K associated metrics and uses this error-trellis and the Viterbi algorithm to determine the sequence $\{\hat{\mathbf{B}}_l\}$ that is closest in Hamming distance to the received error sequence $\{\mathbf{C}_l\}$, bearing in mind that $\{\mathbf{A}_l\}$ is the corresponding sequence associated with the sequence $\{\mathbf{B}_l\}$. The estimated sequence $\{\hat{\mathbf{A}}_l\}$ is then added (modulo-2 addition) to the delayed (corresponding to the decoder search length) version of the pre-decoded sequence to give the estimated information sequence $\{\hat{\mathbf{X}}_l\}$.

The extension to soft-decision decoding is simple. Figure 3.12 shows the system model with eight-level soft-decision decoding, and the highlighted sig-

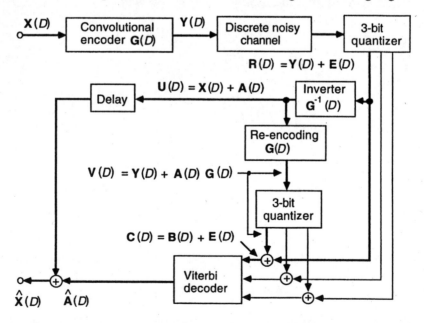

Figure 3.12 Model of an eight-level soft-decision SST-type Viterbi algorithm decoding system.

nal paths correspond to the hard-decision decoding case. The received sequence and the re-encoded sequences are quantized to eight levels by the 3-bit natural binary quantizers. They are then subtracted (bit-by-bit modulo-2 addition), and the resultant signal sequence is then decoded by the soft-decision Viterbi decoder.

The SST-type Viterbi decoder can be implemented on a single *large-scale-integration* (LSI) chip using *complementary metal-oxide semiconductor* (CMOS) technology [9,10,12]. Because the 2^K-state trellis is drawn with the input $\mathbf{A}_l$ and the transfer-function matrix $\mathbf{G}(D)$, the trellis is composed of errors only. With almost error-free transmission, the received error sequences $\mathbf{C}(D)$ to the input of the Viterbi decoder contain a large number of zeros. The decoder therefore picks the all-zero error path with high probability, and there is rarely any state change from the all-zero sequence trellis state during decoding. The CMOS on-off gates scarcely switch and consume no power at all. As a result, power consumption is significantly reduced, compared with that of the conventional Viterbi decoder. A power consumption reduction of 40% at a bit error rate of 1 in 10^4 has been reported when operating at an information rate of 25 Mbps [12].

3.6 SCARCE-STATE-TRANSITION-TYPE SYNDROME-FORMER TRELLIS DECODING

The application of the SST-type decoding technique is not limited to the encoder trellis. The technique can also be applied to the syndrome-former trellis of the code. SST-type syndrome-former trellis decoding system [13] is a development of the SST-type Viterbi decoding system in which the following modifications are made. The model for the SST-type syndrome-former error-trellis decoding system is shown in Figure 3.13.

There is no difference between the SST-type Viterbi and the new decoding system up to the received error sequences $\mathbf{C}(D)$; see (3.21). Based on (3.21) and the syndrome-former $\mathbf{H}^T(D)$ of the code with $\mathbf{G}(D)$, one can draw a 2^{K+1}-state syndrome-former trellis, called the syndrome-former error-trellis, with input $\mathbf{B}_l$. Again, the syndrome-former error-trellis diagram has the same form as the syndrome-former trellis of the code with $\mathbf{Y}_l$ replaced by $\mathbf{B}_l$. Like the error-trellis in the SST-type Viterbi algorithm decoding system, this trellis is composed of re-encoded errors $\mathbf{B}_l$ (see (3.26)) only. In hard-decision decoding, the decoder now holds 2^{K+1} surviving paths and 2^{K+1} associated metrics and uses this trellis and the Viterbi algorithm to determine the sequence $\{\hat{\mathbf{B}}_l\}$ that is closest in Hamming distance to the received error sequence $\{\mathbf{C}_l\}$, followed by an inverse operation that assigns to the estimated sequence $\{\hat{\mathbf{B}}_l\}$ the estimated sequence $\{\hat{\mathbf{A}}_l\}$. $\{\hat{\mathbf{A}}_l\}$ is then added (modulo-2 addition) to the delayed (corresponding to

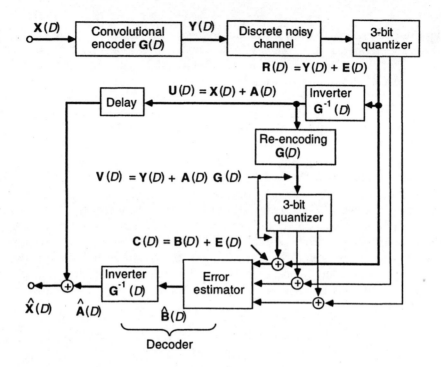

Figure 3.13 Model of an eight-level soft-decision SST-type syndrome-former error-trellis decoding system.

the decoder search length) version of the predecoded sequence to give the estimated information sequence $\{\hat{X}_l\}$.

It is clear that the SST-type syndrome-former trellis decoder can also be implemented on a single LSI chip using CMOS technology and has the following advantages:

1. At low bit-error rate (less than 1 in 10^3), it also has the advantage of consuming a similar degree of power as that of the SST-type Viterbi algorithm decoder reported in [12].
2. It reduces the number of metric computations at each node to, at most, two metric computations as in the syndrome-former trellis decoding system.

3.7 PERFORMANCE OF HARD-DECISION MAXIMUM-LIKELIHOOD DECODING

For linear convolutional codes, we can simply transmit the all-zero codeword and analyze the performance of a code without loss of generality. We saw in

Section 2.6 that the transfer function of an (n, k, m) convolutional code is given by

$$T(X, Y, L)|_{X=1,L=1} = T(Y) = \sum_{d=d_{\text{free}}}^{\infty} a_d Y^d \tag{3.28}$$

and that the total number of nonzero information bits on all paths of Hamming weight d is given by

$$\left. \frac{\partial(X, Y, L)}{\partial X} \right|_{X=1,L=1} = \sum_{d=d_{\text{free}}}^{\infty} c_d Y^d \tag{3.29}$$

where a_d is the number of incorrect paths of Hamming weight $d \geq d_{\text{free}}$ that diverge from the correct path and remerge to it at some later stage; and c_d is the total number of information bit errors produced by the incorrect paths of Hamming weight $d \geq d_{\text{free}}$ that diverge from the correct path and remerge to it at some later stage. Consider an incorrect path of Hamming weight d that diverged from the all-zero state and remerged to the all-zero state for the first time at time l. A first error event is made at time l if the Viterbi decoder favors the incorrect path. That happens when the Hamming weight between the binary received vector and the incorrect path is closer than the Hamming weight between the binary received vector and the all-zero codeword. This is shown in Figure 3.14.

Let the probability of selecting an incorrect path be P_d. For all incorrect paths of any length that diverged from the all-zero codeword path and remerged to the all-zero codeword path, the error event probability is simply upper-bounded by

$$P_e < \sum_{d=d_{\text{free}}}^{\infty} a_d P_d \tag{3.30}$$

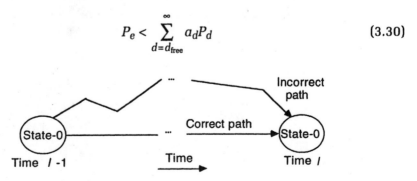

Figure 3.14 First error event at time *l*.

Comparing (3.28) with (3.30), the error event probability becomes

$$P_e < T(Y)|_{Y=[P_d]^{1/d}} \tag{3.31}$$

For the binary symmetric channel, it can be shown that

$$P_d = [2\sqrt{p(1-p)}]^d \tag{3.32}$$

and

$$P_e < \sum_{d=d_{\text{free}}}^{\infty} a_d [2\sqrt{p(1-p)}]^d \tag{3.33}$$

$$P_e < T(Y)|_{Y=2\sqrt{p(1-p)}} \tag{3.34}$$

where p is the channel transition probability.

Example 3.6

Consider the (2, 1, 2) convolutional code of $\mathbf{G}(D) = [1 + D^2 \ 1 + D + D^2]$. The transfer function of the code with $X = 1$ and $L = 1$ is

$$T(X, Y, L)|_{X=1, L=1} = Y^5 + 2Y^6 + 4Y^7 + 8Y^8 + \cdots \tag{3.35}$$

For $p = 0.01$, the error event probability on a binary symmetric channel is

$$P_e < T(X, Y, L)|_{X=1, \ Y=2\sqrt{p(1-p)}, \ L=1} \tag{3.36}$$

$$P_e < (0.199)^5 + 2(0.199)^6 + 4(0.199)^7 + \cdots \tag{3.37}$$

$$P_e < 4.858(10^{-4})$$

Because each error event causes a number of nonzero information bit errors, if we weighted each error event by the total number of nonzero information bits on all paths of Hamming weight d, the bit error probability per decoded information bit is bounded by

$$P_b < \frac{1}{k} \sum_{d=d_{\text{free}}}^{\infty} c_d P_d \tag{3.38}$$

In terms of the partial derivative of the transfer function,

$$P_b < \frac{1}{k} \left. \frac{\partial(X, Y, L)}{\partial X} \right|_{X = 1, \ Y = 2\sqrt{p(1 - p)}, \ L = 1} \tag{3.39}$$

Example 3.7

Consider the (2, 1, 2) convolutional code of $\mathbf{G}(D) = [1 + D^2 \ 1 + D + D^2]$. The partial derivative of the transfer function of the code with $X = 1$ and $L = 1$ is

$$\left. \frac{\partial(X, Y, L)}{\partial X} \right|_{X=1, L=1} = Y^5 + 4Y^6 + 12Y^7 + 32Y^8 + \cdots \tag{3.40}$$

For $p = 0.01$, the bit error probability per decoded information bit on a binary symmetric channel is

$$P_b < \left. \frac{\partial(X, Y, L)}{\partial X} \right|_{X = 1, \ Y = 2\sqrt{p(1 - p)}, \ L = 1} \tag{3.41}$$

$$P_b < (0.199)^5 + 4(0.199)^6 + 12(0.199)^7 + \cdots \tag{3.42}$$

$$P_b < 7.092(10^{-4})$$

3.8 PERFORMANCE OF SOFT-DECISION MAXIMUM-LIKELIHOOD DECODING

In general, for coherent BPSK signals with AWGN channels and unquantized received signals, it can be shown that

$$P_d = Q(\sqrt{2d(k/n)E_b/N_0}) \tag{3.43}$$

where

$$Q(\alpha'') \equiv \frac{1}{\sqrt{2\pi}} \int_{\alpha''}^{\infty} e^{-\beta''^2/2} d\beta'' \tag{3.44}$$

and E_b/N_0 is the average ratio of bit energy to noise power-spectral-density. The error event probability is

$$P_e < \sum_{d=d_{\text{free}}}^{\infty} a_d Q(\sqrt{2d(k/n)E_b/N_0}) \tag{3.45}$$

and the bit-error probability is

$$P_b < \frac{1}{k} \sum_{d=d_{\text{free}}}^{\infty} c_d Q(\sqrt{2d(k/n)E_b/N_0}) \tag{3.46}$$

With finite quantization, it is much easier to compute the error-event and bit-error probabilities from the channel transition probability and the transfer function of the code. For a binary input and Q-ary output discrete memoryless channel, the error-event probability is

$$P_e < T(X, Y, L)|_{X=1, \; Y=\sum_{j=1}^{Q}\sqrt{P(j/0)P(j/1)}, \; L=1} \tag{3.47}$$

and the bit-error probability per decoded information bit is

$$P_b < \frac{1}{k} \frac{\partial(X, Y, L)}{\partial X}\bigg|_{X=1, \; Y=\sum_{j=1}^{Q}\sqrt{P(j/0)P(j/1)}, \; L=1} \tag{3.48}$$

$P(j/i)$ is the channel transition probability between the ith input and the jth output of the discrete memoryless channel for $i = 0$ or 1.

3.9 COMPUTER SIMULATION RESULTS AND DISCUSSION

The variation of bit error rate with the E_b/N_0 ratio of the Viterbi algorithm system with coherent BPSK signals for AWGN channel has been measured by computer simulations. Here, E_b is the average transmitted bit energy, and $N_0/2$ is the two-sided power-spectral density of the noise. Three different rate-1/2 nonsystematic convolutional codes have been used in the tests. The parameters of the codes are given in Table 3.2. The code itself is determined

Table 3.2
Parameters of the Rate-1/2 Nonsystematic Convolutional Codes

K	ν	$G^{(1)}$, $G^{(2)}$	d_{free}
2	3	5, 7	5
3	4	15, 17	6
4	5	23, 35	7

by the connection vectors $\mathbf{G}^{(j)}$, for $1 \leq j \leq 2$. The connection vectors are given in octal notation and are right justified. For example, the connection vector $\mathbf{G}^{(1)} = [11101]$ becomes $[011\ 101] \underline{\underline{\Delta}} (35)_8$ after the right justification. The constraint length, ν, of a code has been selected to avoid excessive computation time. For all the simulation tests, the search length, ψ, is fixed to be six times the constraint length of the code.

The simulated error performance of the rate-1/2 nonsystematic convolutional codes with hard-decision/eight-level uniform soft-decision Viterbi algorithm decoding are shown in Figures 3.15, 3.16, and 3.17. For a certain range of low E_b/N_0 ratios, an uncoded system always appears to have a better tolerance to noise than the coded systems. It is clear that increasing the total encoder memory, K, of the code steepens the slope of the curves and shifts the curves to the left. Thus, an encoder with larger K may do better at a low error rate of 1 in 10^3. It can be seen that an improvement of about 2 dB in coding gain can be achieved with soft-decision decoding.

In a practical implementation of the coded systems, several factors must be considered. Since the decoding complexity relates to k and the total encoder memory, K, of the code, the practical limitation is therefore imposed by the values of k and K. Let us consider $(n, n - 1, m)$ convolutional codes. For the

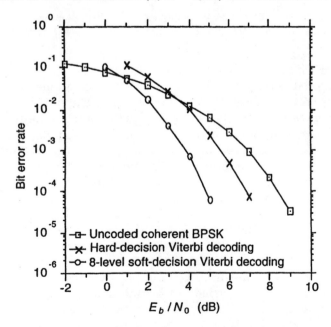

Figure 3.15 Performance of (2, 1, 2) convolutional code with hard-decision and eight-level soft-decision Viterbi decoding of search length 6ν in AWGN channels.

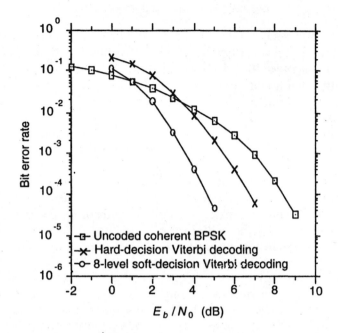

Figure 3.16 Performance of (2, 1, 3) convolutional code with hard-decision and eight-level soft-decision Viterbi decoding of search length 6ν in AWGN channels.

conventional Viterbi and the SST-type Viterbi decoding systems of $(n, n-1, m)$ convolutional codes, there are $2^K (n-1) \cdot \psi$-component storage vectors. Each vector, corresponding to a surviving path, stores information or error symbols along with the associated metric, and the storage requirements increase exponentially with K. Since there are 2^{n-1} metric computations to be carried out at each node of the trellis, the total number of metric computations is $2^K \cdot (2^{n-1})$. For the syndrome-former trellis and the SST-type syndrome-former trellis decoding systems of $(n, n-1, m)$ convolutional codes, the decoder has $2^{K+1} n \cdot \psi$-component storage vectors that hold the decoded channel error symbols. Because there are 2^{K+1} states in the trellis, the storage requirements now increases exponentially with $K + 1$. The syndrome-former trellis and the syndrome-former error-trellis have only one or two paths entering a state, rather than 2^{n-1} as the trellis in the conventional Viterbi and the SST-type Viterbi decoding systems of $(n, n-1, m)$ convolutional codes. There are at most two metric computations to be carried out at each node of the trellis, and the total number of metric computations in the syndrome-former trellis decoding system is less than $2^{K+1} \cdot 2n$. It can be seen that the syndrome-former trellis decoding system achieves no advantage in reduced equipment complexity for low rate-$(n-1)/n$ convolutional codes. This is clear from the following reduction factor,

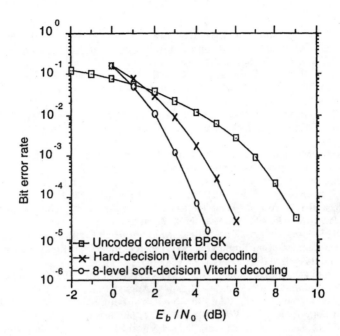

Figure 3.17 Performance of (2, 1, 4) convolutional code with hard-decision and eight-level soft-decision Viterbi decoding of search length 6ν in AWGN channels.

F, defined as the total number of metric computations in the syndrome-former trellis divided by the total number of metric computations in the encoder trellis and given by

$$F = 4n/(2^{n-1}) \tag{3.49}$$

From (3.49), it can be seen that the syndrome-former trellis and the SST-type syndrome-former trellis decoding systems can be applied and justified for rate-$(n - 1)/n$ convolutional codes with $F < 1$. Hence, maximum-likelihood Viterbi algorithm decoding is more effective for low-rate convolutional codes and the syndrome-former trellis decoding is preferred for high rate-$(n - 1)/n$ convolutional codes.

References

[1] Viterbi, A. J., "Error Bounds for Convolutional Codes and an Asymptotically Optimum Decoding Algorithm," *IEEE Trans. on Information Theory*, Vol. IT-13, No. 2, April 1967, pp. 260–269.

[2] Herro, M. A., L. Hui, and J. M. Nowach, "Bit Error Probability Calculations for Convolutional Codes With Short Constraint Length on Very Noisy Channels," *IEEE Trans. on Communications*, Vol. COM-36, No. 7, July 1988, pp. 885–888.

[3] Yamada, T., H. Harashima, and H. Miyakawa, "A New Maximum Likelihood Decoding of High Rate Convolutional Codes Using a Trellis," *Trans. Inst. Elect. & Commun. Eng. of Japan*, Pt. A, Vol. J-66A, No. 7, 1983, pp. 11–16.

[4] Schalkwijk, J. P. M., A. J. Vinck, and K. A. Post, "Syndrome Decoding of Binary Rate-1/2 Convolutional Codes," *IEEE Trans. on Communications*, Vol. COM-24, No. 9, September 1976, pp. 977–985.

[5] Schalkwijk, J. P. M., A. J. Vinck, and K. A. Post, "Syndrome Decoding of Binary Rate k/n Convolutional Codes," *IEEE Trans. on Information Theory*, Vol. IT-24, No. 5, September 1978, pp. 553–562.

[6] Clark, A. P., "Minimum Distance Decoding of Binary Convolutional Codes," *Proc. IEE—Part E*, Vol. 1, No. 4, October 1978, pp. 190–196.

[7] Reed, I. S., and T. K. Turong, "New Syndrome Decoding Techniques for the (n, k) Convolutional Codes," *Proc. IEE—Part F*, Vol. 131, No. 4, July 1984, pp. 412–416.

[8] Reed, I. S., and T. K. Turong, "Error-Trellis Syndrome Decoding Techniques for Convolutional Codes," *Proc. IEE—Part F*, Vol. 132, No. 2, April 1985, pp. 77–83.

[9] Kubota, S., K. Ohtari, and S. Kato, "High-Speed and High-Coding-Gain Viterbi Decoder With Low Power Consumption Employing SST (Scarce-State Transition) Scheme," *Elect. Lett.*, Vol. 22, No. 9 April 1986, pp. 491–493.

[10] Ishitani, T., et al., "A Scarce-State Transition Viterbi-Decoder VLSI for Bit Error Correction," *IEEE J. Solid-State Circuits*, Vol. SC-22, No. 4, August 1987, pp. 575–582.

[11] Ping, S., Y. Yan, and C. Feng, "An Effective Simplifying Scheme for Viterbi Decoder," *IEEE Trans. on Communications*, Vol. COM-39, No. 1, January 1991, pp. 1–3.

[12] Kubota, S., S. Kato, and T. Ishitani, "Novel Viterbi Decoder VLSI Implementation and Its Performance," *IEEE Trans. on Communications*, Vol. COM-41, No. 8, August 1993, pp. 1170–1178.

[13] Lee, L. H. C., Tait, D. J., and P. G. Farrell, "Scarce-State-Transition Syndrome-Former Error-Trellis Decoding of $(n, n - 1)$ Convolutional Codes," *IEEE Trans. on Communications*, Vol. 44, No. 1, January 1996, pp. 7–9.

[14] Forney, G. D., Jr., "The Viterbi Algorithm," *IEEE Proc.*, Vol. 61, No. 3, March 1973, pp. 268–278.

[15] Omura, J. K., "On the Viterbi Decoding Algorithm," *IEEE Trans. on Information Theory*, Vol. IT-15, No. 1, January 1969, pp. 177–179.

[16] Forney, G. D., Jr., "Convolutional Codes II: Maximum Likelihood Decoding," *Inf. Control*, Vol. 25, July 1974, pp. 222–266.

[17] Rader, C. M., "Memory Management in a Viterbi Decoder," *IEEE Trans. on Communications*, Vol. COM-29, No. 9, September 1981, pp. 1399–1401.

Sequential Decoding of Convolutional Codes 4

4.1 INTRODUCTION

We have seen that maximum-likelihood decoding of good convolutional codes by means of the Viterbi algorithm [1–3] can yield a useful coding gain. In applications where a high data transmission rate and good error performance are required for band-limited channels, powerful high-rate $R_c = k/n$ convolutional codes are often used. The decoding system applies the Viterbi algorithm to the encoder trellis, which corresponds to the graphical representation of the convolutional code. For a binary convolutional encoder of total encoder memory of K, the decoder holds 2^K surviving paths with fixed search length of six times the constraint length of the code. Consequently, there are 2^k paths leaving or entering each node of the trellis, and 2^k metric computations at each node must be performed for an (n, k, m) convolutional code. Clearly, the decoding complexity is proportional to the number of encoder states. The practical implementation of the maximum-likelihood decoder becomes difficult for very long constraint length convolutional codes.

To achieve arbitrarily small error probabilities, it is desirable to have a decoding procedure whose decoding effort is independent of the total encoder memory, K, of the code, so that very long constraint length convolutional codes can be used. Sequential decoding is such a decoding procedure [4–9]. Sequential decoding was first introduced by Wozencraft [4] in 1957 and a new decoding algorithm was proposed by Fano [6] in 1963. Stack algorithm was discovered by Zigangirov [8] and Jelinek [9]. The key to perform sequential decoding is based on the encoder tree diagram. This chapter discusses sequential decoding using the stack and the Fano algorithms. Hard-decision sequential decoding is assumed.

4.2 FANO METRIC

Before we proceed to the description of the stack and the Fano algorithms, we shall discuss a new metric measure for sequential decoding of convolutional codes. In Viterbi decoding, the bit metric $M(r_l^{(j)}/y_l^{(j)})$ is used at time l for $1 \le j \le n$. At any decoding step, paths of equal lengths are compared with each other, and the metric is optimum in that sense. However, paths of different lengths are compared in sequential decoding. In other words, longer paths are considered to be the most likely path at the end of the decoding process. Intuitively, longer paths should have larger metric than shorter paths. Thus, the metric measures need to be modified to give the true picture of how close the paths are to the received sequence. Massey [10] has shown that the best bit metric at time l is

$$M(r_l^{(j)}/y_l^{(j)}) = \log_2 \frac{P(r_l^{(j)}/y_l^{(j)})}{P(r_l^{(j)})} - R_c \qquad (4.1)$$

where $P(r_l^{(j)}/y_l^{(j)})$ is the transition probability of the channel, $P(r_l^{(j)})$ is the channel output symbol probability, and R_c is the rate of the code. Each branch of the code tree has n bits, and the branch metric associated with the lth branch is

$$M(\mathbf{R}_l/\mathbf{Y}_l) = \sum_{j=1}^{n} \left[\log_2 \frac{P(r_l^{(j)}/y_l^{(j)})}{P(r_l^{(j)})} - R_c \right] \qquad (4.2)$$

Suppose the decoder has searched $l' + 1$ branches. The associated path metric is

$$M_{l'}(\mathbf{R}_0/\mathbf{Y}_0, \mathbf{R}_1/\mathbf{Y}_1, \cdots, \mathbf{R}_{l'}/\mathbf{Y}_{l'}) = \sum_{l=0}^{l'} M(\mathbf{R}_l/\mathbf{Y}_l)$$

$$M_{l'}(\mathbf{R}_0/\mathbf{Y}_0, \mathbf{R}_1/\mathbf{Y}_1, \cdots, \mathbf{R}_{l'}/\mathbf{Y}_{l'}) = \sum_{l=0}^{l'} \sum_{j=1}^{n} \left[\log_2 \frac{P(r_l^{(j)}/y_l^{(j)})}{P(r_l^{(j)})} - R_c \right]$$

$$M_{l'}(\mathbf{R}_0/\mathbf{Y}_0, \mathbf{R}_1/\mathbf{Y}_1, \cdots, \mathbf{R}_{l'}/\mathbf{Y}_{l'}) = \sum_{l=0}^{l'} \sum_{j=1}^{n} \log_2 P(r_l^{(j)}/y_l^{(j)})$$

$$+ \sum_{l=0}^{l'} \sum_{j=1}^{n} \left[\log_2 \frac{1}{P(r_l^{(j)})} - R_c \right] \qquad (4.3)$$

This metric is called the Fano metric. The first term corresponds to the metric used for Viterbi decoding. The second term is always positive and increases linearly with path length. Longer paths will have a larger bias. They are closer to the end of the tree and therefore likely to be the correct path. The path with the largest Fano metric is considered as the best (most likely) path for sequential decoding. In practice, the metrics are usually scaled to integer form.

Example 4.1

For a binary-input, binary-output channel with equally likely input symbols, channel transition probability $p = 0.1$, and a code rate of 1/2, the bit metrics are

$$M(r_l^{(j)}/y_l^{(j)}) = \log_2 2p - R_c \qquad (4.4)$$

for $r_l^{(j)} \neq y_l^{(j)}$ and

$$M(r_l^{(j)}/y_l^{(j)}) = \log_2 2(1 - p) - R_c \qquad (4.5)$$

for $r_l^{(j)} = y_l^{(j)}$. Thus, $M(r_l^{(j)}/y_l^{(j)}) = -2.82$ for $r_l^{(j)} \neq y_l^{(j)}$ and $M(r_l^{(j)}/y_l^{(j)}) = 0.35$ for $r_l^{(j)} = y_l^{(j)}$. With integer scaling, $M(r_l^{(j)}/y_l^{(j)}) = -8$ for $r_l^{(j)} \neq y_l^{(j)}$ and $M(r_l^{(j)}/y_l^{(j)}) = 1$ for $r_l^{(j)} = y_l^{(j)}$. This is shown in Table 4.1.

4.3 STACK ALGORITHM DECODING

In the stack algorithm, an ordered list of previously examined paths of different lengths is kept in storage. Each stack entry contains a path along with its metric. Each decoding step consists of extending the top path in the stack by computing the branch metrics of its 2^k succeeding branches and then adding those to the metric of the top path to form 2^k new paths. Those new paths are placed at the bottom of the stack, and the top path is deleted from the stack. The stack is then rearranged in descending order of metric values. Ties in metric values can be resolved randomly. The decoding algorithm terminates when the top path in the stack reaches the end of the tree, and the top path is then taken as the decoded path. In practice, the size of the stack must be finite. Overflow may occur before the end of the decoding process. To handle that problem, we can flow away the path at the bottom of the stack. That path has the smallest metric.

Table 4.1
Metric Table for a Rate-1/2 Convolutional
Code and $p = 0.1$

$y_l^{(j)}/r_l^{(j)}$	0	1
0	1	−8
1	−8	1

For a large stack, the probability of the path being extended and reaching to the top of the stack is very small. The loss in decoding performance is negligible. In summary, the decoding steps are as follows:

1. Load the stack with the original node in the tree, whose metric is set to zero.
2. Extend the top path and compute the metrics associated with the 2^k new paths.
3. Delete the top path from the stack.
4. Put 2^k new paths to the bottom of the stack and rearrange all paths in descending order of metric values.
5. If the top path reaches the end of the tree, stop. Otherwise, go back to step 2.

A complete flow chart for the stack algorithm is shown in Figure 4.1. An example is shown with the received sequence $R = [R_0, R_1, \ldots, R_6] = [10, 00, 10, 00, 00, 00, 00]$.

Example 4.2

Consider the $(2, 1, 2)$ convolutional code in Figure 4.2 and the metric table shown in Table 4.1, where $y_l^{(j)}$ and $r_l^{(j)}$ are the jth-coded and the received bits at time l for $1 \le j \le n$, respectively.

Assume that the all-zero code sequence corresponding to the all-zero information sequence is transmitted over a BSC, and that the received sequence is $R = [R_0, R_1, \ldots, R_6] = [10, 00, 10, 00, 00, 00, 00]$. There are two channel errors. Table 4.2 shows the estimated information sequences; their metrics are quoted inside angle brackets $(< >)$ in descending order at each decoding step. The path metrics at each node of the tree are also given in Figure 4.2(b). The decoder corrects the errors, and the estimated information sequence is 0 0 0 0 0 0 0.

4.4 FANO ALGORITHM DECODING

Another approach to sequential decoding uses the Fano algorithm [6]. In the Fano algorithm, an intuitive trial-and-error technique is employed to search for the likely path in the encoder tree. The decoder always operates on a single path. It proceeds either forward or backward along a path by monitoring the path metric against a threshold. In the absence of channel errors, the running path metric of the path traced by the decoder is an increasing function. Because of the limited number of path searches in the Fano algorithm decoder, the decoded path at the end of the tree may be different from the maximum-

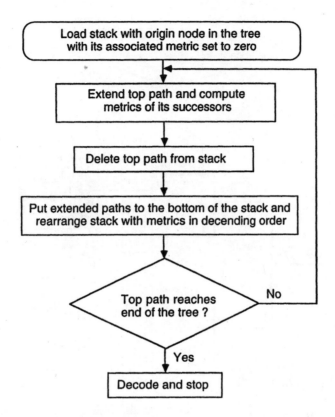

Figure 4.1 Flow chart for the stack algorithm.

likelihood path chosen by a Viterbi algorithm decoder for the same received sequence. Figure 4.3 shows the flow chart of the Fano algorithm.

The decoder begins at the origin node corresponding to the root of the encoder tree and ends at one of the nodes at the end of the tree. At every decoding stage, the decoder is located at some node, N'', in the tree. From that node, the decoder looks forward to the 2^k succeeding nodes leaving node N''. It computes the forward path metrics, $\{M_f\}$, of all paths leaving node N'' by adding the corresponding branch metric to the running path metric associated with node N''. The succeeding nodes are ranked in descending order of their metric values. The best node is associated with the largest metric value, and the worst node is associated with the smallest metric value. The decoder will move to the best node if the metric, M_f, is greater than or equal to a threshold, T_F. If the decoder reaches the end of the tree, the decoding process terminates, and the path is taken as the decoded path. If the decoder has not reached the end of the tree and the best succeeding node has not been examined before,

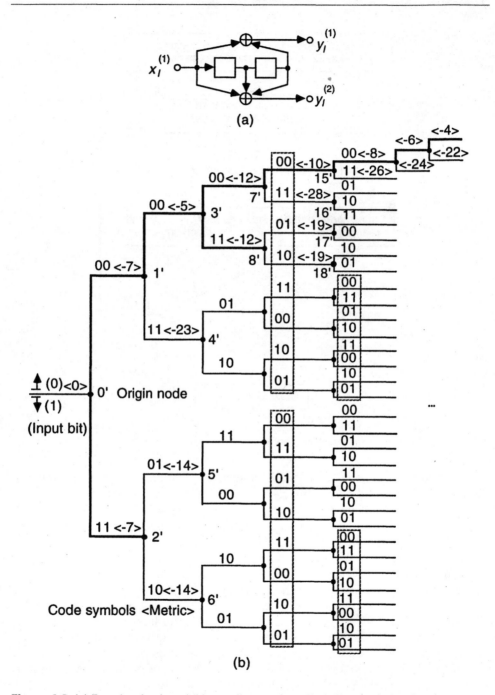

Figure 4.2 (a) Encoder circuit and (b) tree diagram for a (2, 1, 2) convolutional code.

Table 4.2
Hard-Decision Stack Algorithm Decoding Steps

Step 1	Step 2	Step 3	Step 4
0 <–7>	00 <–5>	1 <–7>	000 <–12>
1 <–7>	1 <–7>	000 <–12>	001 <–12>
	01 <–23>	001 <–12>	10 <–14>
		01 <–23>	11 <–14>
			01 <–23>

Step 5	Step 6	Step 7	Step 8
0000 <–10>	00000 <–8>	000000 <–6>	0000000 <–4>
001 <–12>	001 <–12>	001 <–12>	001 <–12>
10 <–14>	10 <–14>	10 <–14>	10 <–14>
11 <–14>	11 <–14>	11 <–14>	11 <–14>
01 <–23>	01 <–23>	01 <–23>	0000001 <–22>
0001 <–28>	00001 <–26>	000001 <–24>	01 <–23>
	0001 <–28>	00001 <–26>	000001 <–24>
		0001 <–28>	00001 <–26>
			0001 <–28>

the threshold is tightened by adding a fixed positive constant Δ to T_F before the decoder looks forward again. The tightening of T_F ensures that when the decoder moves forward and examines the node again in the future, the threshold is always lower than the current examination of the node. That prevents looping in the algorithm and ensures that the decoder will reach the end of the tree.

If the decoder cannot move forward from node N''', it looks backward to the node M''', leading to node N'''. The backward path metric, M_b, is computed by subtracting the branch metric leading to node N''' from the running path metric at node N'''. If the backward path metric is less than T_F, the decoder cannot proceed backward. The threshold is lowered by Δ, and the decoder looks forward again and attempts to move forward. If the backward path metric is greater than or equal to T_F, the decoder recognizes an unlikely path and moves backward to node M'''. If node N''' was the worst node when the decoder moved forward from node M''' to node N''' at some early decoding stage, the decoder continues to look backward. Otherwise, the decoder searches along another path by looking forward to the next best node. An example is shown next with the received sequence $\mathbf{R} = [\mathbf{R}_0, \mathbf{R}_1, \ldots, \mathbf{R}_6] = [10, 00, 10, 00, 00, 00, 00]$.

Example 4.3

Consider the (2, 1, 2) convolutional code in Figure 4.2 and the metric table shown in Table 4.1, where $y_l^{(j)}$ and $r_l^{(j)}$ are the jth-coded and the received bits

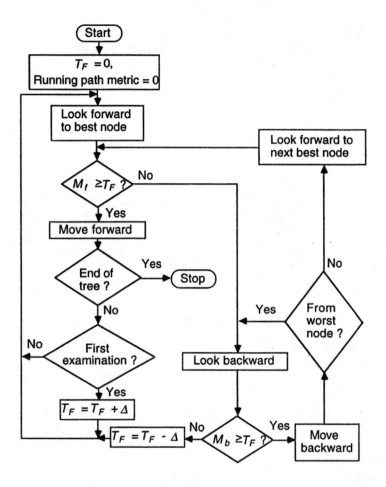

Figure 4.3 Flow chart of the Fano algorithm.

at time l for $1 \le j \le n$, respectively. Assume that the all-zero code sequence corresponding to the all-zero information sequence is transmitted over a BSC and that the received sequence $\mathbf{R} = [\mathbf{R}_0, \mathbf{R}_1, \dots, \mathbf{R}_6] = [10, 00, 10, 00, 00, 00, 00]$ has two errors. It is also assumed that when the decoder looks forward and a tie occurs in the forward path metric values, the succeeding node associated with the lower branch is always taken as the best node. Table 4.3 shows the forward path metric, the backward path metric, the estimated information sequence, the running path metric at each decoding step, and the threshold value with Δ sets to 3.

Initially, the running path metric at the origin node (node 0′) and the threshold value, T_F, are set to 0. At decoding step 1, we consider the received

Table 4.3
Hard-Decision Fano Algorithm Decoding Steps

Step	Actions	M_f	M_b	Estimated Information Sequence	Running Path Metric	T_F
1	LFB,LB	−7	−∞	X	0	−3
2	LFB,LB	−7	−∞	X	0	−6
3	LFB,LB	−7	−∞	X	0	−9
4	LFB,MF,ME	−7	−	1	−7	−9
5	LFB,LB,MB,NFW	−14	0	X	0	−9
6	LFNB,MF,1E	−7	−	0	−7	−6
7	LFB,MF,1E	−5	−	00	−5	−3
8	LFB,LB	−12	−7	00	−5	−6
9	LFB,LB	−12	−7	00	−5	−9
10	LFB,LB,MB,NFW	−12	−7	0	−7	−9
11	LFNB,LB,MB,FW,LB	−23	−∞	X	0	−12
12	LFB,MF,ME	−7	−	1	−7	−12
13	LFB,LB,MB,NFW	−14	0	X	0	−12
14	LFNB,MF,ME	−7	−	0	−7	−12
15	LFB,MF,ME	−5	−	00	−5	−12
16	LFB,MF,ME	−12	−	001	−12	−12
17	LFB,LB,MB,NFW	−19	−5	00	−5	−12
18	LFNB,MF,1E	−12	−	000	−12	−9
19	LFB,LB,MB,FW,LB,MB,NFW	−10	−7	0	−7	−9
20	LFNB,LB,MB,FW,LB	−23	−∞	X	0	−12
21	LFB,MF,ME	−7	−	1	−7	−12
22	LFB,LB,MB,NFW	−14	0	X	0	−12
23	LFNB,MF,ME	−7	−	0	−7	−12
24	LFB,MF,ME	−5	−	00	−5	−12
25	LFB,MF,ME	−12	−	001	−12	−12
26	LFB,LB,MB,NFW	−19	−5	00	−5	−12
27	LFNB,MF,ME	−12	−	000	−12	−12
28	LFB,MF,ME	−10	−	0000	−10	−12
29	LFB, MF,1E	−8	−	00000	−8	−9
30	LFB,MF,1E	−6	−	000000	−6	−6
31	LFB,MF, end	−4	−	0000000	−4	

LFB means "look forward to the best node"; LFNB, "look forward to the next best node"; LB, "look backward from a node"; MF, "move forward to a node"; MB, "move backward to a node"; FW, "from the worst node"; NFW, "not from the worst node"; ME, "a node has been examined before"; and 1E, "a first examination of a node."

vector $\mathbf{R}_0 = [1\ 0]$. The decoder looks forward from the origin node and computes the metrics of all paths leaving the origin node. The forward path metric, M_f, of the best succeeding node (node 2′) is less than the threshold value T_F. The decoder cannot proceed forward, and it looks backward from the origin node.

It is assumed that the backward path metric of the node looking backward from the origin node is $-\infty$. This is to avoid a backward move from the origin node. The backward path metric, M_b, is less than the threshold value, T_F, and it is likely that the threshold value is too high at the origin node and needed to be reduced by Δ. The decoder continues to reduce the threshold value at decoding steps 2 and 3.

At decoding step 4, the decoder looks forward again from the origin node and computes the metrics of all paths leaving the origin node. The forward path metric of the best succeeding node (node 2′) is now greater than the threshold value, T_F, and the decoder moves forward from the origin node to node 2′. The decoder has not reached the end of the tree. Node 2′ has been examined before, and the threshold value remains unchanged.

At decoding step 5, we consider the received vector $\mathbf{R}_1 = [0\ 0]$. The decoder looks forward from node 2′ and computes the metrics of all paths leaving the node. The forward path metric of the best succeeding node (node 6′) is less than the threshold value, T_F, and the decoder looks backward from node 2′ to node 0′. The backward path metric is zero and is greater than T_F, and the decoder moves backward to node 0′. This backward move is not from the worst node succeeding node 0′. The worst node is at node 1′.

At decoding step 6, the decoder looks forward to the next best succeeding node (node 1′). The forward path metric is greater than T_F, and the decoder moves forward to node 1′. The decoder has not reached the end of the tree. Node 1′ has not been examined before, and the threshold value is tightened. The decoder continues to move forward from node 1′ to the best succeeding node (node 3′) and tightens the threshold value at decoding step 7.

At decoding steps 8 and 9, we consider the received vector $\mathbf{R}_2 = [1\ 0]$. The decoder looks forward from node 3′ and computes the metrics of all paths leaving the node. The forward path metric of the best succeeding node (node 8′) is less than the threshold value, T_F. The decoder cannot proceed forward, and it looks backward from node 3′. The backward path metric is also less than T_F, and the decoder cannot proceed backward. The threshold value is lowered by Δ at decoding steps 8 and 9.

At decoding step 10, we consider the received vector $\mathbf{R}_2 = [1\ 0]$ again. The decoder looks forward from node 3′ and computes the metrics of all paths leaving the node. The forward path metric of the best succeeding node (node 8′) is again less than the threshold value, T_F. The decoder cannot proceed forward, and it looks backward from node 3′. The backward path metric is now greater than T_F, and it is likely that the decoder traced the wrong path. The decoder now moves backward to node 1′. This backward move is not from the worst node succeeding node 1′. The worst node is at node 4′.

At decoding step 11, the decoder looks forward to the next best succeeding node (node 4′). The forward path metric is less than T_F. The decoder cannot proceed forward. It looks backward from node 1'. The backward path metric is zero and is greater than T_F. The decoder moves backward from node 1' to the origin node. This backward move is from the worst node succeeding node, 0'. The best node is at node 2'. The decoder looks backward again. The backward path metric is $-\infty$ and is now less than T_F. The threshold value is lowered by Δ. Subsequent decoding steps show that the decoder proceeds to node 2' at step 12, returns to the origin node, proceeds to node 8' at step 16, returns to node 3' at step 17, proceeds to node 7' at step 18, returns to the origin node, proceeds to node 2' at step 21, returns to the origin node again, proceeds to node 8' at step 25, returns to node 3' at step 26 before it proceeds along the all-zero path. Figure 4.2(b) highlights the paths traced by the decoder.

It can be seen that the decoder looks forward and backward before moving forward and backward to search for the likely path by monitoring the path metric against the threshold value in this way. Subsequent extensions of unlikely path can be recognized by the decoder, and the decoder searches backward and tries other paths. When the decoder reaches the end of the tree, the path is taken as the decoded path. For this example, the decoder corrects the errors, and the estimated information sequence is 0 0 0 0 0 0 0.

In Example 4.3, the computed forward path metrics of the paths leaving from the origin node are identical at decoding step 1. If we choose to resolve the tie in metric values in a random manner, the decoder may pick the upper path as the likely path rather than the lower path at decoding step 1 and continue from node 1' onward. The decoder will visit different nodes but eventually find the same likely path when it reaches the end of the tree. Of course, the number of decoding steps will be different. In the Fano algorithm decoder, the number of computation steps depends on the value of Δ. Generally speaking, the number of computations decreases with a large value of Δ, because less unlikely paths can now be followed during the searching process.

It is clear that the Fano algorithm decoder does not jump from node to node during the searching process, as in the stack algorithm decoder. The Fano algorithm decoder usually explores more nodes than the stack algorithm decoder. That reduces the operation speed of the decoder. However, the Fano algorithm decoder eliminates the need for storing path metrics of previously examined nodes as required by the stack algorithm decoder. Sequential decoding can be implemented with hard or soft decisions, but the storage requirement and the number of computations of soft-decision sequential decoding become very large. Hard-decision sequential decoding is more commonly employed for very long constraint length convolutional codes. A major drawback of sequential decoding is that more path searches must be carried out at a low signal-to-noise ratio and the received sequence must therefore be stored in a buffer. The buffer holds the received sequence while trying to find the best path. If the average symbol arrival rate exceeds the average symbol decoding rate, the buffer will overflow, causing loss of data. To avoid that, the decoder will go through a recovery procedure before resuming its normal operations when the buffer overflow occurs.

To guarantee fast decoding, the initial column distance growth rate of the code should be fast. That can be found by computing the entire column distance function of the (n, k, m) convolutional code. As already defined in Section 2.5, the column distance function of the code is the minimum Hamming distance over the first f blocks of all pairs of encoded sequences. In practice, it is often easier to determine the distance growth profile over the first constraint length of the code. In other words, a code with a distance profile $d_0, d_1, \ldots, d_m$ is more favorable than another code with a distance profile $d'_0, d'_1, \ldots, d'_m$ if

$$d_l \begin{cases} = d'_l, & l = 0, 1, \cdots, l' - 1 \\ > d'_l, & l = l' \end{cases} \tag{4.6}$$

for some l', $0 \le l' \le m$. Optimum distance profile convolutional codes with larger d_{free} guarantee fast initial column distance growth and should be used for sequential decoding. A list of optimum distance profile convolutional codes for sequential decoding is given in Appendix B.

References

[1] Viterbi, A. J., "Error Bounds for Convolutional Codes and an Asymptotically Optimum Decoding Algorithm," *IEEE Trans. on Information Theory*, Vol. IT-13, No. 2, April 1967, pp. 260–269.

[2] Forney, G. D., Jr., "The Viterbi Algorithm," *IEEE Proc.*, Vol. 61, No. 3, 1973, pp. 268–278.

[3] Lin, S., and D. J. Costello, Jr., *Error Control Coding: Fundamentals and Applications*, Englewood Cliffs, NJ: Prentice-Hall, 1983.

[4] Wozencraft, J. M., "Sequential Decoding for Reliable Communication," *IRE Nat. Conv. Rec.*, Vol. 5, Pt. 2, 1957, pp. 11–25.

[5] Wozencraft, J. M., and B. Reiffen, *Sequential Decoding*, Cambridge: MIT Press, 1961.

[6] Fano, R. M., "A Heuristic Discussion of Probabilistic Decoding," *IEEE Trans. on Communications*, Vol. IT-9, No. 4, April 1963, pp. 64–74.

[7] Forney, G. D., Jr., "Convolutional Codes III: Sequential Decoding," *Inf. Control*, Vol. 25, July 1974, pp. 267–297.

[8] Zigangirov, K. S., "Some Sequential Decoding Procedures," *Problemy Peredachi Informatsii*, Vol. 2, 1966, pp. 13–25.

[9] Jelinek, F., "A Fast Sequential Decoding Algorithm Using a Stack," *IBM J. Res. and Dev.*, Vol. 13, November 1969, pp. 675–685.

[10] Massey, J. L., "Variable-Length Codes and the Fano Metric," *IEEE Trans. on Information Theory*, Vol. IT-18, No. 1, January 1972, pp. 196–198.

Encoding and Decoding of Punctured Convolutional Codes

5

5.1 INTRODUCTION

We have seen that convolutional encoding with Viterbi decoding is an attractive means to achieve significant coding gains on discrete noisy channels. In applications where a high data transmission rate and good error performance are required for bandlimited channels, powerful high-rate $R_c = k/n$ convolutional codes are needed. For an (n, k, m) convolutional code, there are 2^k paths leaving or merging at each node of the encoder trellis diagram. In the Viterbi decoder, 2^k metric computations must be carried out at each trellis node, and the most likely path is selected at each node of the trellis. This represents a practical implementation difficulty for high-rate convolutional codes. Fortunately, one can find certain codes that reduce the number of metric computations at each node of the trellis. This class of codes is called punctured convolutional codes. Punctured convolutional codes were introduced by Clark and Cain [1] in 1979. More new punctured convolutional codes have been found in recent years [2–11]. In some areas of application, different levels of error protection are desirable within an information sequence or block. A channel coding scheme with *unequal error protection* (UEP) is required. One way to achieve a UEP scheme is to group the input symbols according to their error sensitivity. A number of channel encoders and decoders are employed, in parallel, to provide the necessary error protection levels. The complexity of this scheme is high when the number of error protection levels becomes large. Alternatively, a single channel encoder and decoder structure using punctured convolutional codes can be used. Hagenauer discovered punctured convolutional codes with rate compatibility, which are well suited for this application [12]. This chapter discusses the encoding and decoding techniques of all these codes.

5.2 ENCODING OF PUNCTURED CONVOLUTIONAL CODES

Punctured convolutional codes are a subclass of the (n, k, m) convolutional codes [1–6]. They are time-varying convolutional codes. Consider the $(2, 1, 2)$

convolutional code with generator polynomial matrix $\mathbf{G}(D) = [1 + D^2 \ 1 + D + D^2]$ in Figure 5.1(a) and the encoder trellis diagram shown in Figure 5.1(b). If every third encoder output bit is deleted, the encoder produces three code bits for every two input information bits. In fact, every leading symbol of the rate-1/2 convolutional code is deleted from every other branch, and a new code is generated. The new code has rate $R_c = 2/3$, and the resulting code is identical to the rate-2/3 convolutional code with generator polynomial matrix

$$\mathbf{G}(D) = \begin{bmatrix} 1 + D & 1 + D & 1 \\ 0 & D & 1 + D \end{bmatrix} \tag{5.1}$$

The encoder circuit diagram for this code is shown in Figure 5.2(a), the encoder trellis diagram in Figure 5.2(b).

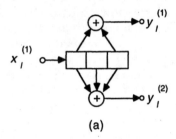

(a)

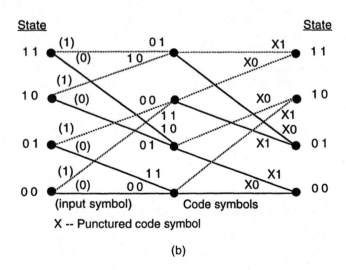

(b)

Figure 5.1 (a) Encoding circuit and (b) trellis diagrams for a (2, 1, 2) convolutional code.

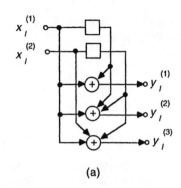

(a)

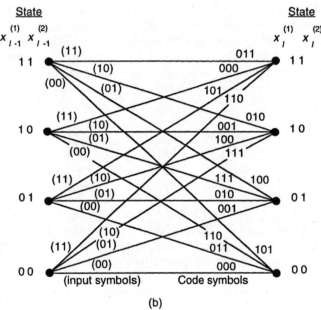

(b)

Figure 5.2 (a) Encoding circuit and (b) trellis diagrams for a (3, 2, 2) convolutional code.

For the same two input and three output symbols between two states of Figure 5.2(b), it can be seen that the transition is made within a branch of the trellis, while the transition shown in Figure 5.1(b) is made through a set of intermediate states (two branches in the example). Obviously, the same code is generated in a different manner.

In general, a rate-P/Q' punctured convolutional code can be obtained from an $(n, 1, m)$ convolutional code by deleting $n \cdot P - Q'$ code symbols from every $n \cdot P$ code symbol corresponding to the encoding of P information symbols by the $(n, 1, m)$ convolutional code. The low-rate $R_c = 1/n$ code is called the mother code, with generator polynomial matrix

$$\mathbf{G}(D) = [G_1^{(1)}(D)\, G_1^{(2)}(D) \cdots G_1^{(n)}(D)] \tag{5.2}$$

where

$$G_1^{(j)}(D) = g_{1,0}^{(j)} + g_{1,1}^{(j)}D + \cdots + g_{1,m}^{(j)}D^m \tag{5.3}$$

with elements 0 and 1. It can be seen that the rate of the punctured convolutional code is $R_c = P/(n \cdot P - \delta)$, where $\delta = n \cdot P - Q'$. The deletion of code symbols is represented by an n-by-P puncturing array $\mathbf{P}_\delta$. Each column of $\mathbf{P}_\delta$ is associated with one of the P n-component code vectors corresponding to the encoding of P information symbols by the rate-$1/n$ mother code, and each row of $\mathbf{P}_\delta$ corresponds to P code symbols at the output of the mother code. The elements of the puncturing array are zeros and ones, corresponding to the deleting or keeping of the corresponding code symbol at the output of the mother code. The puncturing array is

$$\mathbf{P}_\delta = \begin{bmatrix} p_{1,1} & p_{1,2} & \cdots & p_{1,P} \\ p_{2,1} & p_{2,2} & \cdots & p_{2,P} \\ \vdots & \vdots & & \vdots \\ p_{n,1} & p_{n,2} & \cdots & p_{n,P} \end{bmatrix} \tag{5.4}$$

with $p_{j,l'} = 0$ or 1, $1 \le j \le n$ and $1 \le l' \le P$. δ specifies the number of zeros in the array, and δ can take on values between 1 and $(n-1)P - 1$, inclusive. As the puncturing array is used periodically for every $n \cdot P$ code symbols in an encoded sequence, P is called the *puncturing period*.

Example 5.1

The rate-2/3 code in (5.1) is generated from the $(2, 1, 2)$ mother code of $\mathbf{G}(D) = [1 + D^2 \quad 1 + D + D^2]$ using the puncturing array

$$\mathbf{P}_1 = \begin{bmatrix} 1 & 0 \\ 1 & 1 \end{bmatrix} \tag{5.5}$$

The element in the first row and the second column of $\mathbf{P}_1$ is zero. Hence, every third code symbol of the four code symbols corresponding to the encoding of two information symbols by the rate-1/2 mother code is punctured. If the code sequence is 00 00 11 01 ... , the punctured code sequence is 00 X0 11 X1, ... , where X denotes the punctured symbol. The punctured symbols are not transmitted at all. In fact, the encoder for the rate-2/3 punctured convolutional code may be visualized as consisting of a rate-1/2 mother code followed by a puncturing device, as shown in Figure 5.3. The puncturing device simply deletes symbols from the code sequence according to the puncturing array $\mathbf{P}_1$.

5.3 MAXIMUM-LIKELIHOOD DECODING OF PUNCTURED CONVOLUTIONAL CODES

All punctured convolutional codes can be decoded by the Viterbi algorithm decoder [7]. Decoding of rate-$P/(n \cdot P - \delta)$ punctured convolutional codes by the Viterbi algorithm involves finding the shortest path through the punctured trellis of the $(n, 1, m)$ mother code. In the decoding process, the metric computation is prohibited corresponding to the punctured positions. The Viterbi decoder now operates on the trellis of the $(n, 1, m)$ mother code rather than the trellis of the rate-$P/(n \cdot P - \delta)$ punctured convolutional code. From the prior knowledge of the puncturing array $\mathbf{P}_\delta$, dummy data are inserted into the received sequence $\{R_l\} = \{Y_l + E_l\}$ corresponding to the positions of the punctured code symbols at the transmitter, where

$$\mathbf{R}_l = [r_l^{(1)} r_l^{(2)} \cdots r_l^{(n \cdot P - \delta)}] \tag{5.6}$$

$$\mathbf{Y}_l = [y_l^{(1)} y_l^{(2)} \cdots y_l^{(n \cdot P - \delta)}] \tag{5.7}$$

and

$$\mathbf{E}_l = [e_l^{(1)} e_l^{(2)} \cdots e_l^{(n \cdot P - \delta)}] \tag{5.8}$$

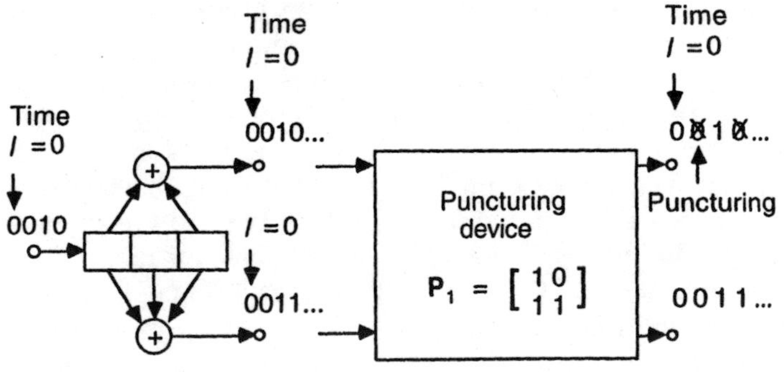

Figure 5.3 Rate-2/3 punctured convolutional encoder generated from a (2, 1, 2) mother code.

to give the modified sequence $\{R'_l\} = \{Y'_l + E'_l\}$. Vectors R'_l, Y'_l, and E'_l can be represented as the P-component vectors

$$R'_l = [R'_{l,1} R'_{l,2} \cdots R'_{l,P}] \tag{5.9}$$

$$Y'_l = [Y'_{l,1} Y'_{l,2} \cdots Y'_{l,P}] \tag{5.10}$$

and

$$E'_l = [E'_{l,1} E'_{l,2} \cdots E'_{l,P}] \tag{5.11}$$

respectively. It can be seen that each subvector in (5.10) corresponds to a trellis branch of the $(n, 1, m)$ mother code, and the output binary code symbols (punctured and nonpunctured symbols) associated with the d'th trellis branch of the mother code is

$$Y'_{l,d'} = [y'^{(1)}_{l,d'} y'^{(2)}_{l,d'} \cdots y'^{(n)}_{l,d'}] \tag{5.12}$$

for $1 \le d' \le P$. The optimum decoder determines the code sequence $\{\hat{Y}'_l\}$ that has the largest path metric to the modified sequence $\{R'_l\}$. This is accomplished by the Viterbi algorithm, which recursively maximizes the path metric

$$M_l(R'_0/Y'_0, R'_1/Y'_1, \cdots, R'_l/Y'_l) = M_{l-1}(R'_0/Y'_0, R'_1/Y'_1, \cdots,$$

$$R'_{l-1}/Y'_{l-1}) + M(R'_l, Y'_l) \tag{5.13}$$

at time l over all code sequences $\{Y'_l\}$ of the mother code. $M(R'_l, Y'_l)$ is the branch metric between vectors R'_l and Y'_l at time l.

In practice, a decision is made when the decoder has searched ψ segments into the punctured trellis of the mother code. The decoding search length ψ should be large enough to avoid significant degradation in error probability performance. At time l, the decoder holds 2^K surviving paths with fixed search length of six times the constraint length ν of the mother code and operates iteratively on P branches of the trellis of the mother code by means of the Viterbi algorithm. Associated with each path (surviving path) is the corresponding running path metric $M_{l-1}(R'_0/Y'_0, R'_1/Y'_1, \ldots, R'_{l-1}/Y'_{l-1})$. The decoder now computes the branch metrics for all the paths entering a node of the trellis at time l according to (5.13). For each trellis node of the mother code, the decoder selects the path with the largest metric. The resulting 2^K surviving paths are stored together with the associated metrics. After P trellis-branch iterations, the decoder then makes a firm decision and decodes the information bits associated with the path of maximum metric, bearing in mind that there is a unique one-to-one mapping between the information sequence of the mother code and the code sequence $\{Y'_l\}$. The process repeats in this way with the receipt of the next vector R_{l+1}. Furthermore, we would like to bring out the following features.

1. There are 2^P metric computations per trellis state to be carried out for a Viterbi decoder operating on the trellis of an rate-$P/(n \cdot P - \delta)$ nonpunctured convolutional code, while there are only two metric computations per state to be carried out for a Viterbi decoder operating on the trellis of the $(n, 1, m)$ mother code for the decoding of the rate-$P/(n \cdot P - \delta)$ punctured convolutional code.
2. For the decoding of the punctured convolutional code using the trellis of the mother code, the Viterbi decoder has to know the puncturing array P_δ, δ, the puncturing period P, and the rate of the mother code.

Example 5.2

Consider the (2, 1, 2) mother code with generator polynomial matrix $G(D) = [1 + D^2 \ \ 1 + D + D^2]$ and a puncturing array

$$P_1 = \begin{bmatrix} 1 & 0 \\ 1 & 1 \end{bmatrix}$$

The trellis of this code is shown in Figure 5.4(a). For simplicity, we have assumed a binary symmetric channel, and the transmitted code sequence is the all-zero codeword. The received sequence is 000 100 000 . . . , which has an error. Furthermore, the Hamming distance metric is used in the decoding process. The maximum-likelihood decoder now becomes a minimum-distance decoder, which minimizes the Hamming distance between sequences $\{R'_l\}$ and $\{Y'_l\}$. With dummy data X inserted into the received sequence, the received sequence becomes 00 X0 10 X0 00 X0 . . . . The decoding window (search length) is set to twice the constraint length of the mother code, where $\nu = 3$. The sequence of states of the hard-decision minimum-distance decoder is shown in Figure 5.4(b).

Clearly, there is only a finite number of branches in which one can see. Inside the search window are contained the surviving paths. Their associated unnormalized running path Hamming metrics are quoted inside angle brackets (< >). At the end of the seventh iteration step, the decoder has identified the

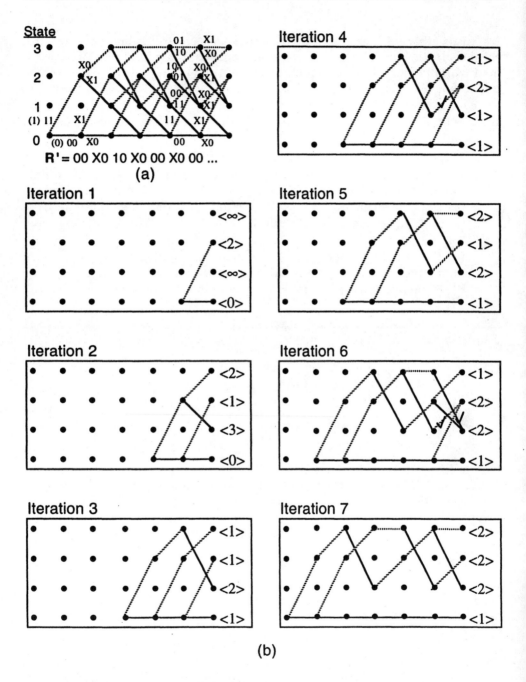

Figure 5.4 Hard-decision Viterbi decoding steps of rate-2/3 punctured convolutional code generated from a (2, 1, 2) mother code.

minimum-distance path. In general, the decoder determines the surviving path per node by extending all surviving paths obtained from the preceding iteration step. In this example, ties are present at iteration steps 4 and 6, and the ticked paths are randomly chosen and retained. As the decoding process continues, the earlier code symbols drop out of the window. The decoding decision is made at the far left side of the window. In the example, the decoded code sequence is 00 X0 00 X0 . . . , and the corresponding decoded information sequence is 0 0 0 0 . . . . Because the punctured convolutional code is a single error-correcting code and has a minimum free Hamming distance of 3, the single error, which occurs within one constraint length of the punctured convolutional code, is corrected. In practice, the search length is usually set to five or six times the constraint length of the mother code for adequate decoding performance. Further increase in the search length does not provide significant additional coding gain because the minimum-distance path is almost identified by the decoder. Therefore, when the search length is set to five or six times the constraint length of the mother code, the performance of this fixed search length decoder can be considered to be close to that of the true minimum-distance decoder.

5.4 PERFORMANCE OF PUNCTURED CONVOLUTIONAL CODES

Like any rate-k/n linear convolutional codes, the upper bound on the error-event and bit-error probabilities of rate-k/n punctured convolutional codes with Viterbi decoding on discrete memoryless channels are also given by

$$P_e \le \sum_{d=d_{\text{free}}}^{\infty} a_d P_d \qquad (5.14)$$

and

$$P_b \le \frac{1}{k} \sum_{d=d_{\text{free}}}^{\infty} c_d P_d \qquad (5.15)$$

respectively. Here, d_{free} is the minimum free Hamming distance of the code, and a_d is the number of incorrect paths of Hamming weight $d \ge d_{\text{free}}$ that diverge from the correct path and remerge with it at some later stage. c_d is the total number of information bit errors produced by the incorrect paths of Hamming weight $d \ge d_{\text{free}}$ that diverge from the correct path and remerge with it at some later stage. P_d is the probability of picking an incorrect path in the Viterbi decoding process and depends on the modulation type and channel characteristics. For coherent BPSK signals with unquantized AWGN channels

$$P_d = Q(\sqrt{2d(k/n)E_b/N_0}) \tag{5.16}$$

where

$$Q(\alpha'') \equiv \frac{1}{\sqrt{2\pi}} \int_{\alpha''}^{\infty} e^{-\beta''^2/2} d\beta'' \tag{5.17}$$

and E_b/N_0 is the average ratio of bit energy to noise-power spectral density. The weight spectra a_d and c_d can be obtainable easily from the transfer function of the code. To choose good codes, we should maximize d_{free} and minimize the terms a_d and c_d.

5.5 CONCEPT OF RATE-COMPATIBLE PUNCTURED CONVOLUTIONAL CODES

Rate-compatible punctured convolutional (RCPC) codes are a subclass of punctured convolutional codes. Consider an example where a rate-4/7 punctured code with puncturing period $P = 4$ and $\delta = 1$ is generated from the rate-1/2 mother code given in Section 5.2. The puncturing array for the rate-4/7 punctured code is

$$\mathbf{P}_1 = \begin{bmatrix} 1 & 1 & 0 & 1 \\ 1 & 1 & 1 & 1 \end{bmatrix} \tag{5.18}$$

where there is one zero element in the array $\mathbf{P}_1$. To generate a rate-4/6 punctured code with same puncturing period P from the rate-1/2 mother code, we have two zero elements in the array $\mathbf{P}_2$. For rate compatibility, the zero element in $\mathbf{P}_1$ is retained in $\mathbf{P}_2$. In general, all zero elements in $\mathbf{P}_\delta$ are retained in the subsequent arrays $\mathbf{P}_{\delta+1}$, $\mathbf{P}_{\delta+2}$, ... That restriction implies that all the code symbols of the higher rate punctured codes are required by the lower rate codes. In this example, the puncturing arrays for the rate-4/6 and rate-4/5 codes are

$$\mathbf{P}_2 = \begin{bmatrix} 1 & 0 & 0 & 1 \\ 1 & 1 & 1 & 1 \end{bmatrix} \tag{5.19}$$

and

$$\mathbf{P}_3 = \begin{bmatrix} 1 & 0 & 0 & 1 \\ 1 & 1 & 1 & 0 \end{bmatrix} \tag{5.20}$$

respectively. Thus, a family of RCPC codes can be generated in this way. RCPC codes are suitable for applications where different levels of error protection are needed within an information sequence or block. A typical information sequence or block is grouped according to the error protection requirement, and RCPC codes are assigned to the groups as shown in Figure 5.5. It can be seen that the most critical information symbols in the first group are protected by a RCPC code whose free distance is larger than or equal to the free distance of the codes for subsequent groups. The rate compatibility guarantees smooth transition between the rates [12].

5.6 MAXIMUM-LIKELIHOOD DECODING OF RATE-COMPATIBLE PUNCTURED CONVOLUTIONAL CODES

Decoding of RCPC codes is very similar to the decoding of punctured convolutional codes. For punctured convolutional codes, the Viterbi decoder operates on the trellis of the $(n, 1, m)$ mother code. From the prior knowledge of the puncturing arrays $\mathbf{P}_\delta$, dummy data are inserted into the received sequence $\{\mathbf{R}_l\}$ corresponding to the positions of the punctured code symbols at the transmitter to give the modified sequence $\{\mathbf{R}'_l\}$. In the decoding process, the metric computa-

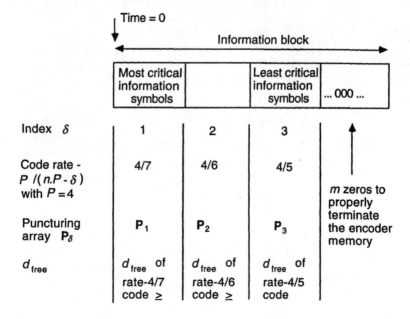

Figure 5.5 Assignments of RCPC codes to a typical information block with bits grouped according to their error sensitivity.

tion is prohibited corresponding to the punctured positions. For the decoding of RCPC codes using the trellis of the mother code, the Viterbi decoder has to know all the puncturing arrays $\mathbf{P}_\delta$, δ, the puncturing period P, and the rate of the mother code.

5.7 COMPUTER SIMULATION RESULTS AND DISCUSSION

The variation of bit error rate with the E_b/N_0 ratio of the Viterbi algorithm system with coherent BPSK signals for AWGN channels has been measured by computer simulations. The system model is shown in Figure 5.6. Here, E_b is the average transmitted bit energy, and $N_0/2$ is the two-sided power spectral density of the noise. Three different rate-2/3 punctured convolutional codes have been used in the tests. The parameters of the codes are given in Table 5.1. The constraint lengths of the mother codes have been selected to avoid excessive computation time. In each test, the average energy per information bit was fixed, and the variance of the AWGN was adjusted for a range of average bit-error rates. For all the simulation tests, the search length ψ is fixed to be six times the constraint length of the mother code.

The simulated error performance of the rate-2/3 punctured convolutional codes with hard-decision/eight-level uniform soft-decision Viterbi algorithm decoding are shown in Figures 5.7, 5.8, and 5.9. For a certain range of low E_b/N_0 ratios, an uncoded system always appears to have a better tolerance to noise than the coded systems. It is clear that increasing the total encoder memory K of the code steepens the slope of the curves and shifts the curves to the left. Thus, an encoder with larger K may do better at high signal-to-noise ratio. It

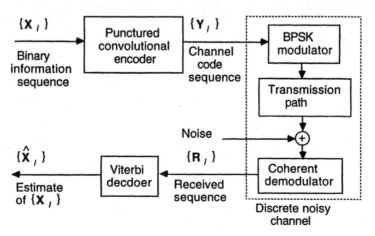

Figure 5.6 Model of a digital communication system.

Table 5.1
Parameters of Rate-2/3 Punctured Convolutional Codes

Mother Code			Punctured Convolutional Code			
K	$G^{(1)}$, $G^{(2)}$	P_δ	Punctured Rate- $P/(n \cdot P - \delta)$	d_{free}	$(a_d, d = d_{\text{free}}, d_{\text{free}} + 1, \ldots)$ $[c_d, d = d_{\text{free}}, d_{\text{free}} + 1, \ldots]$	
2	5, 7	10	2/3	3	(1, 4, 14, 40, 116)	
		11			[1, 10, 54, 226, 856]	
3	15, 17	11	2/3	4	(3, 11, 35, 114, 378)	
		01			[10, 43, 200, 826, 3314]	
4	23, 35	11	2/3	4	(1, 0, 27, 0, 345)	
		01			[1, 0, 124, 0, 2721]	

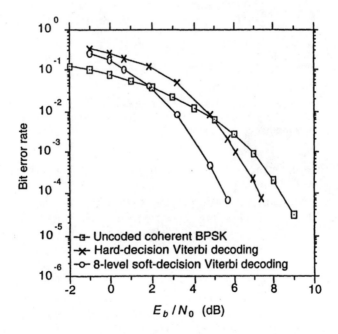

Figure 5.7 Performance of four-state, rate-2/3 punctured convolutional code with hard-decision and eight-level soft-decision Viterbi decoding in AWGN (search length = 6ν of the mother code).

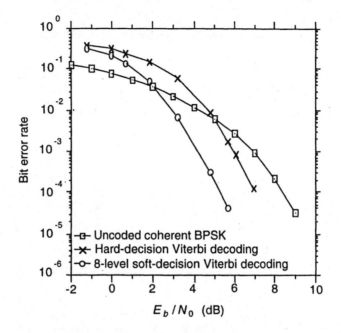

Figure 5.8 Performance of eight-state, rate-2/3 punctured convolutional code with hard-decision and eight-level soft-decision Viterbi decoding in AWGN (search length = 6ν of the mother code).

can be seen that an improvement of about 2 dB in coding gain can be achieved with soft-decision decoding.

In a practical implementation of the coded systems, several factors must be considered. Since the decoding complexity relates to the total encoder memory K of the mother code, the practical limitation is therefore imposed by the value of K. For Viterbi decoding of rate-k/n nonpunctured convolutional codes, there are 2^k metric computations to be carried out at each trellis state. For Viterbi decoding of rate-k/n punctured convolutional codes using the trellis of the rate-$1/n$ mother code, there are only two metric computations to be carried at each trellis state. In high-speed and bandwidth-efficient applications, punctured convolutional codes with Viterbi decoding are less complex than nonpunctured convolutional codes with Viterbi decoding. For applications where unequal error protection is required, rate-compatible punctured convolutional codes can be used. A list of good punctured and rate-compatible punctured convolutional codes for Viterbi decoding is given in Appendix C.

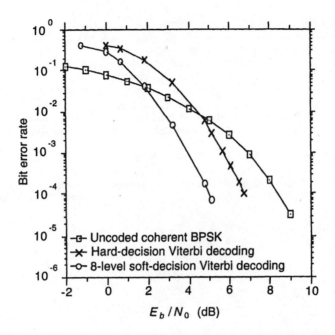

Figure 5.9 Performance of 16-state, rate-2/3 punctured convolutional code with hard-decision and eight-level soft-decision Viterbi decoding in AWGN (search length = 6ν of the mother code).

References

[1] Cain, J. B., G. C. Clark, and J. M. Geist, "Punctured Convolutional Codes of Rate $(n - 1)/n$ and Simplified Maximum Likelihood Decoding," *IEEE Trans. on Information Theory*, Vol. IT-25, No. 1, January 1979, pp. 97–100.

[2] Yasuda, Y., Y. Kashiki, and Y. Hirata, "High Rate Punctured Convolutional Codes for Soft-Decision Viterbi Decoding," *IEEE Trans. on Communications*, Vol. COM-32, No. 3, March 1984, pp. 315–319.

[3] Hole, K. J., "New Short Constraint Length Rate $(N - 1)/N$ Punctured Convolutional Codes for Soft-Decision Viterbi Decoding," *IEEE Trans. on Information Theory*, Vol. IT-34, No. 5, September 1988, pp. 1079–1081.

[4] Lee, P. J., "Construction of Rate $(n - 1)/n$ Punctured Convolutional Codes with Required SNR Criterion," *IEEE Trans. on Communications*, Vol. COM-36, No. 9, September 1988, pp. 1171–1174.

[5] Haccoun, D., and G. Begin, "High-Rate Punctured Convolutional Codes for Viterbi and Sequential Decoding," *IEEE Trans. on Communications*, Vol. COM-37, No. 11, November 1989, pp. 1113–1125.

[6] Begin, G., and D. Haccoun, "High Rate Punctured Convolutional Codes Structure Properties and Construction Techniques," *IEEE Trans. on Communications*, Vol. COM-37, No. 12, December 1989, pp. 1813–1825.

[7] Begin, G., D. Haccoun, and P. Chantal, "Further Results on High Rate Punctured Convolutional Codes for Viterbi and Sequential Decoding," *IEEE Trans. on Communications*, Vol. COM-38, No. 11, November 1990, pp. 1922–1928.

[8] Hole, K. J., "Rate k/k+1 Minimal Punctured Convolutional Encoders," *IEEE Trans. on Information Theory*, Vol. IT-37, No. 3, May 1991, pp. 653–655.

[9] Hole, K. J., "Punctured Convolutional Codes for the 1-D Partial-Response Channel," *IEEE Trans. on Information Theory*, Vol. IT-37, No. 3, May 1991, pp. 808–817.

[10] D'Sousa, J., and S. L. Maskara, "Simple Method for Constructing Equivalent Punctured Convolutional Codes for Given True High Rate Codes," *Elect. Lett.*, Vol. 30, No. 1, January 1994, pp. 24–25.

[11] Bian, Y., A. Popplewell, and J. J. O'Reilly, "New Very High Rate Punctured Convolutional Codes," *Elect. Lett.*, Vol. 30, No. 14, July 1994, pp. 1119–1120.

[12] Hagenauer, J., "Rate-Compatible Punctured Convolutional Codes (RCPC codes) and Their Applications," *IEEE Trans. on Communications*, Vol. COM-36, No. 4, April 1988, pp. 389–400.

Majority-Logic Decoding of Convolutional Codes 6

6.1 INTRODUCTION

We have seen that Viterbi decoding and sequential decoding are powerful decoding methods for convolutional codes. Suitable convolutional codes used in conjunction with Viterbi or sequential decoding yield good coding gains. However, because the number of operations required for Viterbi decoding grows exponentially with the code constraint length, its applications are limited to relatively short constraint-length codes. On the other hand, the number of operations for sequential decoding is a random variable and is almost independent of code constraint length. That makes sequential decoding very attractive in applications where long constraint-length codes are required. In each of these decoding schemes, the hardware complexity of the decoder is very high.

Majority-logic decoding [1] is an alternative decoding method for convolutional codes that is relatively simpler to implement than either Viterbi or sequential decoding. The majority-logic decoding of convolutional codes is based on the concept of orthogonal parity-check sums, and the decoder makes its decoding decision over one constraint length of the received block. That results in a suboptimum system, but the decoder implementation is much simpler and its speed of operation can be much faster than that of Viterbi or sequential decoders. Majority-logic decoders are therefore well suited to low-cost applications, where a moderate amount of coding gain is required. We shall consider only systematic convolutional codes here, since any nonsystematic convolutional code can be converted to systematic form by row transformations on the generator matrix of the nonsystematic code and the minimum Hamming distance over one constraint length of the code remains unchanged [2]. No increase in error-correcting power, therefore, can be achieved by employing nonsystematic convolutional codes with majority-logic decoding.

6.2 HARD-DECISION MAJORITY-LOGIC DECODING

For an (n, k, m) systematic convolutional code, the semi-infinite generator matrix is given by

$$
\mathbf{G} =
\begin{bmatrix}
\mathbf{I}\,\mathbf{P}_0 & \mathbf{0}\,\mathbf{P}_1 & \mathbf{0}\,\mathbf{P}_2 & \cdots & \mathbf{0}\,\mathbf{P}_m & & & \cdots \\
 & \mathbf{I}\,\mathbf{P}_0 & \mathbf{0}\,\mathbf{P}_1 & \cdots & \mathbf{0}\,\mathbf{P}_{m-1} & \mathbf{0}\,\mathbf{P}_m & & \\
 & & \mathbf{I}\,\mathbf{P}_0 & \cdots & \mathbf{0}\,\mathbf{P}_{m-2} & \mathbf{0}\,\mathbf{P}_{m-1} & \mathbf{0}\,\mathbf{P}_m & \\
\vdots & & & & & & & \ddots
\end{bmatrix}
\tag{6.1}
$$

where $\mathbf{I}$ is the k-by-k identity matrix, $\mathbf{0}$ is the k-by-k zero matrix, and each $\mathbf{P}_{l'}$, $0 \le l' \le m$, is an k-by-$(n-k)$ submatrix:

$$
\mathbf{P}_{l'} =
\begin{bmatrix}
g_{1,l'}^{(k+1)} & g_{1,l'}^{(k+2)} & \cdots & g_{1,l'}^{(n)} \\
g_{2,l'}^{(k+1)} & g_{2,l'}^{(k+2)} & \cdots & g_{2,l'}^{(n)} \\
\vdots & \vdots & & \vdots \\
g_{k,l'}^{(k+1)} & g_{k,l'}^{(k+2)} & \cdots & g_{k,l'}^{(n)}
\end{bmatrix}
\tag{6.2}
$$

with binary entries. The semi-infinite parity-check matrix of the systematic convolutional code can be expressed as the elements in $\mathbf{G}$, that is,

$$
\mathbf{H} =
\begin{bmatrix}
\mathbf{P}_0^T\mathbf{I} & & & & & & & \cdots \\
\mathbf{P}_1^T\mathbf{0} & \mathbf{P}_0^T\mathbf{I} & & & & & & \\
\vdots & & \ddots & & & & & \\
\mathbf{P}_m^T\mathbf{0} & \mathbf{P}_{m-1}^T\mathbf{0} & \cdots & \mathbf{P}_0^T\mathbf{I} & & & & \\
 & \mathbf{P}_m^T\mathbf{0} & \cdots & \mathbf{P}_1^T\mathbf{0} & \mathbf{P}_0^T\mathbf{I} & & & \\
 & & \ddots & & & \ddots & & \\
 & & & \mathbf{P}_m^T\mathbf{0} & \mathbf{P}_{m-1}^T\mathbf{0} & \cdots & \mathbf{P}_0^T\mathbf{I} & \\
\vdots & & & & & & & \ddots
\end{bmatrix}
\tag{6.3}
$$

where, in this case, $\mathbf{I}$ is the $(n-k)$-by-$(n-k)$ identity matrix, $\mathbf{0}$ is the $(n-k)$-by-$(n-k)$ zero matrix, and $\mathbf{P}_{l'}^T$ is the transpose of $\mathbf{P}_{l'}$.

Consider $\mathbf{Y}$ to be the codeword sequence that is transmitted over a noisy channel, and let $\mathbf{R}$ be the noise-corrupted sequence that is received. $\mathbf{R}$ is the sum of the channel code sequence and a channel-error sequence $\mathbf{E}$, that is,

$$
\mathbf{R} = \mathbf{Y} + \mathbf{E}
\tag{6.4}
$$

where vector (sequence) or matrix addition is modulo-2, unless the context indicates otherwise. The received and channel-error sequences can be denoted by the two row vectors

$$\mathbf{R} = [\mathbf{R}_0\ \mathbf{R}_1\ \cdots\ \mathbf{R}_l\ \cdots]$$
(6.5)

and

$$\mathbf{E} = [\mathbf{E}_0\ \mathbf{E}_1\ \cdots\ \mathbf{E}_l\ \cdots]$$
(6.6)

respectively. Here, $\mathbf{R}_l$ is the received vector at time l and is represented by the n-component row vector

$$\mathbf{R}_l = [r_l^{(1)}\ r_l^{(2)}\ \cdots\ r_l^{(n)}]$$
(6.7)

and the channel-error vector $\mathbf{E}_l$ at time l is represented by the n-component row vector

$$\mathbf{E}_l = [e_l^{(1)}\ e_l^{(2)}\ \cdots\ e_l^{(n)}]$$
(6.8)

On receiving the noise-corrupted sequence $\mathbf{R}$, the receiver determines a syndrome sequence, $\mathbf{S}$. The syndrome sequence $\mathbf{S}$ is defined as

$$\mathbf{S} = \mathbf{R}\,\mathbf{H}^T$$
(6.9)
$$= \mathbf{Y}\,\mathbf{H}^T + \mathbf{E}\,\mathbf{H}^T$$
(6.10)

where

$$\mathbf{S} = [\mathbf{S}_0\ \mathbf{S}_1\ \cdots\ \mathbf{S}_l\ \cdots]$$
(6.11)

and the syndrome vector $\mathbf{S}_l$ at time l is represented by the $(n-k)$-component row vector

$$\mathbf{S}_l = [s_l^{(k+1)}\ s_l^{(k+2)}\ \cdots\ s_l^{(n)}]$$
(6.12)

Since $\mathbf{Y}\,\mathbf{H}^T = \mathbf{0}$, we can rewrite (6.10) as

$$\mathbf{S} = \mathbf{E}\,\mathbf{H}^T \tag{6.13}$$

We can see that $\mathbf{S}$ depends on the error sequence and not on the particular codeword transmitted. Knowing $\mathbf{S}$ is equivalent to knowing $\mathbf{E}$, and the decoder can be designed to operate on $\mathbf{S}$ rather than $\mathbf{R}$. Taking the transpose of both sides of (6.9), the structure becomes

$$\mathbf{S}^T = \mathbf{H}\,\mathbf{R}^T \tag{6.14}$$

and

$$
\begin{bmatrix}
\mathbf{S}_0^T \\
\mathbf{S}_1^T \\
\vdots \\
\mathbf{S}_l^T \\
\mathbf{S}_{l+1}^T \\
\vdots \\
\mathbf{S}_{l+m}^T \\
\vdots
\end{bmatrix}
=
\begin{bmatrix}
\mathbf{P}_0^T\mathbf{I} & & & & & & & \cdots \\
\mathbf{P}_1^T\mathbf{0} & \mathbf{P}_0^T\mathbf{I} & & & & & & \\
\vdots & & \ddots & & & & & \\
\mathbf{P}_m^T\mathbf{0} & \mathbf{P}_{m-1}^T\mathbf{0} & \cdots & \mathbf{P}_0^T\mathbf{I} & & & & \\
& \mathbf{P}_m^T\mathbf{0} & \cdots & \mathbf{P}_1^T\mathbf{0} & \mathbf{P}_0^T\mathbf{I} & & & \\
& & \ddots & & & \ddots & & \\
& & & \mathbf{P}_m^T\mathbf{0} & \mathbf{P}_{m-1}^T\mathbf{0} & \cdots & \mathbf{P}_0^T\mathbf{I} & \\
\vdots & & & & & & & \ddots
\end{bmatrix}
\begin{bmatrix}
\mathbf{R}_0^T \\
\mathbf{R}_1^T \\
\vdots \\
\mathbf{R}_l^T \\
\mathbf{R}_{l+1}^T \\
\vdots \\
\mathbf{R}_{l+m}^T \\
\vdots
\end{bmatrix}
\tag{6.15}
$$

Also,

$$\mathbf{S}^T = \mathbf{H}\,\mathbf{E}^T \tag{6.16}$$

and

$$
\begin{bmatrix}
\mathbf{S}_0^T \\
\mathbf{S}_1^T \\
\vdots \\
\mathbf{S}_l^T \\
\mathbf{S}_{l+1}^T \\
\vdots \\
\mathbf{S}_{l+m}^T \\
\vdots
\end{bmatrix}
=
\begin{bmatrix}
\mathbf{P}_0^T\mathbf{I} & & & & & & & \cdots \\
\mathbf{P}_1^T\mathbf{0} & \mathbf{P}_0^T\mathbf{I} & & & & & & \\
\vdots & & \ddots & & & & & \\
\mathbf{P}_m^T\mathbf{0} & \mathbf{P}_{m-1}^T\mathbf{0} & \cdots & \mathbf{P}_0^T\mathbf{I} & & & & \\
& \mathbf{P}_m^T\mathbf{0} & \cdots & \mathbf{P}_1^T\mathbf{0} & \mathbf{P}_0^T\mathbf{I} & & & \\
& & \ddots & & & \ddots & & \\
& & & \mathbf{P}_m^T\mathbf{0} & \mathbf{P}_{m-1}^T\mathbf{0} & \cdots & \mathbf{P}_0^T\mathbf{I} & \\
\vdots & & & & & & & \ddots
\end{bmatrix}
\begin{bmatrix}
\mathbf{E}_0^T \\
\mathbf{E}_1^T \\
\vdots \\
\mathbf{E}_l^T \\
\mathbf{E}_{l+1}^T \\
\vdots \\
\mathbf{E}_{l+m}^T \\
\vdots
\end{bmatrix}
\tag{6.17}
$$

respectively. When the decoder is designed to make its decoding decision over one constraint length of an (n, k, m) systematic convolutional code, (6.15) becomes a truncated expression and is written as

$$S'^T = H'R'^T \tag{6.18}$$

and

$$
\begin{bmatrix} S_l^T \\ S_{l+1}^T \\ \vdots \\ S_{l+m}^T \end{bmatrix} =
\begin{bmatrix}
P_m^T 0 & P_{m-1}^T 0 & \cdots & P_0^T I & & & \\
 & P_m^T 0 & \cdots & P_1^T 0 & P_0^T I & & \\
 & & \ddots & & & \ddots & \\
 & & & P_m^T 0 & P_{m-1}^T 0 & \cdots & P_1^T 0 & P_0^T I
\end{bmatrix}
\begin{bmatrix} R_{l-m}^T \\ \vdots \\ R_{l-1}^T \\ R_l^T \\ R_{l+1}^T \\ \vdots \\ R_{l+m}^T \end{bmatrix}
\tag{6.19}
$$

Similarly, the truncated version of (6.16) can be written as

$$S'^T = H'E'^T \tag{6.20}$$

and

$$
\begin{bmatrix} S_l^T \\ S_{l+1}^T \\ \vdots \\ S_{l+m}^T \end{bmatrix} =
\begin{bmatrix}
P_m^T 0 & P_{m-1}^T 0 & \cdots & P_0^T I & & & \\
 & P_m^T 0 & \cdots & P_1^T 0 & P_0^T I & & \\
 & & \ddots & & & \ddots & \\
 & & & P_m^T 0 & P_{m-1}^T 0 & \cdots & P_1^T 0 & P_0^T I
\end{bmatrix}
\begin{bmatrix} E_{l-m}^T \\ \vdots \\ E_{l-1}^T \\ E_l^T \\ E_{l+1}^T \\ \vdots \\ E_{l+m}^T \end{bmatrix}
\tag{6.21}
$$

Substituting (6.2), (6.7), and (6.12) into (6.19) and (6.2), (6.8), and (6.12) into (6.21) and substantially rearranging the elements of the matrices of (6.19) and (6.21), we have

$$
\begin{bmatrix}
s_l^{(k+1)} \\
\vdots \\
s_{l+m}^{(k+1)} \\
s_l^{(k+2)} \\
\vdots \\
s_{l+m}^{(k+2)} \\
\vdots \\
s_l^{(n)} \\
\vdots \\
s_{l+m}^{(n)}
\end{bmatrix}
=
\begin{bmatrix}
g_{1,m}^{(k+1)} & \cdots & g_{1,0}^{(k+1)} & \cdots & 0 & g_{2,m}^{(k+1)} & \cdots & g_{2,0}^{(k+1)} & \cdots & 0 & \cdots & g_{k,m}^{(k+1)} & \cdots & g_{k,0}^{(k+1)} & \cdots & 0 \\
0 & \cdots & g_{1,m}^{(k+1)} & \cdots & g_{1,0}^{(k+1)} & 0 & \cdots & g_{2,m}^{(k+1)} & \cdots & g_{2,0}^{(k+1)} & \cdots & 0 & \cdots & g_{k,m}^{(k+1)} & \cdots & g_{k,0}^{(k+1)} \\
g_{1,m}^{(k+2)} & \cdots & g_{1,0}^{(k+2)} & \cdots & 0 & g_{2,m}^{(k+2)} & \cdots & g_{2,0}^{(k+2)} & \cdots & 0 & \cdots & g_{k,m}^{(k+2)} & \cdots & g_{k,0}^{(k+2)} & \cdots & 0 \\
0 & \cdots & g_{1,m}^{(k+2)} & \cdots & g_{1,0}^{(k+2)} & 0 & \cdots & g_{2,m}^{(k+2)} & \cdots & g_{2,0}^{(k+2)} & \cdots & 0 & \cdots & g_{k,m}^{(k+2)} & \cdots & g_{k,0}^{(k+2)} \\
\vdots & & \vdots & & \vdots & \vdots & & \vdots & & & & \vdots & & & & \\
g_{1,m}^{(n)} & \cdots & g_{1,0}^{(n)} & \cdots & 0 & g_{2,m}^{(n)} & \cdots & g_{2,0}^{(n)} & \cdots & 0 & \cdots & g_{k,m}^{(n)} & \cdots & g_{k,0}^{(n)} & \cdots & 0 \\
0 & \cdots & g_{1,m}^{(n)} & \cdots & g_{1,0}^{(n)} & 0 & \cdots & g_{2,m}^{(n)} & \cdots & g_{2,0}^{(n)} & \cdots & 0 & \cdots & g_{k,m}^{(n)} & \cdots & g_{k,0}^{(n)}
\end{bmatrix}
$$

$$
\begin{bmatrix}
r_{l-m}^{(1)} \\
\vdots \\
r_l^{(1)} \\
\vdots \\
r_{l+m}^{(1)} \\
r_{l-m}^{(2)} \\
\vdots \\
r_l^{(2)} \\
\vdots \\
r_{l+m}^{(2)} \\
\vdots \\
r_{l-m}^{(k)} \\
\vdots \\
r_l^{(k)} \\
\vdots \\
r_{l+m}^{(k)}
\end{bmatrix}
+
\begin{bmatrix}
r_l^{(k+1)} \\
\vdots \\
r_{l+m}^{(k+1)} \\
r_l^{(k+2)} \\
\vdots \\
r_{l+m}^{(k+2)} \\
\vdots \\
r_l^{(n)} \\
\vdots \\
r_{l+m}^{(n)}
\end{bmatrix}
\tag{6.22}
$$

and

$$
\begin{bmatrix}
s_l^{(k+1)} \\
s_{l+m}^{(k+1)} \\
s_l^{(k+2)} \\
s_{l+m}^{(k+2)} \\
\vdots \\
s_l^{(n)} \\
s_{l+m}^{(n)}
\end{bmatrix}
=
\begin{bmatrix}
g_{1,m}^{(k+1)} & \cdots & g_{1,0}^{(k+1)} & \cdots & 0 & g_{2,m}^{(k+1)} & \cdots & g_{2,0}^{(k+1)} & \cdots & 0 & \cdots & g_{k,m}^{(k+1)} & \cdots & g_{k,0}^{(k+1)} & \cdots & 0 \\
0 & \cdots & g_{1,m}^{(k+1)} & \cdots & g_{1,0}^{(k+1)} & 0 & \cdots & g_{2,m}^{(k+1)} & \cdots & g_{2,0}^{(k+1)} & \cdots & 0 & \cdots & g_{k,m}^{(k+1)} & \cdots & g_{k,0}^{(k+1)} \\
g_{1,m}^{(k+2)} & \cdots & g_{1,0}^{(k+2)} & \cdots & 0 & g_{2,m}^{(k+2)} & \cdots & g_{2,0}^{(k+2)} & \cdots & 0 & \cdots & g_{k,m}^{(k+2)} & \cdots & g_{k,0}^{(k+2)} & \cdots & 0 \\
0 & \cdots & g_{1,m}^{(k+2)} & \cdots & g_{1,0}^{(k+2)} & 0 & \cdots & g_{2,m}^{(k+2)} & \cdots & g_{2,0}^{(k+2)} & \cdots & 0 & \cdots & g_{k,m}^{(k+2)} & \cdots & g_{k,0}^{(k+2)} \\
\vdots & & & & \vdots & \vdots & & & & & & \vdots & & & & \\
g_{1,m}^{(n)} & \cdots & g_{1,0}^{(n)} & \cdots & 0 & g_{2,m}^{(n)} & \cdots & g_{2,0}^{(n)} & \cdots & 0 & \cdots & g_{k,m}^{(n)} & \cdots & g_{k,0}^{(n)} & \cdots & 0 \\
0 & \cdots & g_{1,m}^{(n)} & \cdots & g_{1,0}^{(n)} & 0 & \cdots & g_{2,m}^{(n)} & \cdots & g_{2,0}^{(n)} & \cdots & 0 & \cdots & g_{k,m}^{(n)} & \cdots & g_{k,0}^{(n)}
\end{bmatrix}
$$

$$
\begin{bmatrix}
e^{(1)}_{l-m} \\
\vdots \\
e^{(1)}_{l} \\
\vdots \\
e^{(1)}_{l+m} \\
e^{(2)}_{l-m} \\
\vdots \\
e^{(2)}_{l} \\
\vdots \\
e^{(2)}_{l+m} \\
\vdots \\
e^{(k)}_{l-m} \\
\vdots \\
e^{(k)}_{l} \\
\vdots \\
e^{(k)}_{l+m}
\end{bmatrix}
+
\begin{bmatrix}
e^{(k+1)}_{l} \\
\vdots \\
e^{(k+1)}_{l+m} \\
e^{(k+2)}_{l} \\
\vdots \\
e^{(k+2)}_{l+m} \\
\vdots \\
e^{(n)}_{l} \\
\vdots \\
e^{(n)}_{l+m}
\end{bmatrix}
\tag{6.23}
$$

respectively. It can be seen from (6.22) that each syndrome vector can be formed by re-encoding the information part of the received vector and then adding the re-encoded parity-check vector to the parity-check part of the received vector, that is,

$$
s^{(j)}_l = \left(\sum_{i-1}^{k} \sum_{l'=0}^{m} r^{(i)}_{l-l'} \, g^{(j)}_{i,l'} \right) + r^{(j)}_l
$$

for $(k + 1) \le j \le n$. Thus, (6.22) can be used to compute the syndrome bits, and (6.23) can be used to design majority-logic decoders.

6.2.1 Majority-Logic Definite Decoding

The majority-logic decoder as illustrated in Figure 6.1 is called a majority-logic definite decoder [3].

No estimated-error bit is fed back into the syndrome registers before the next error estimation. The truncated syndrome vector, $\mathbf{S'}^T$, in (6.23) needed no modification and is expressed as

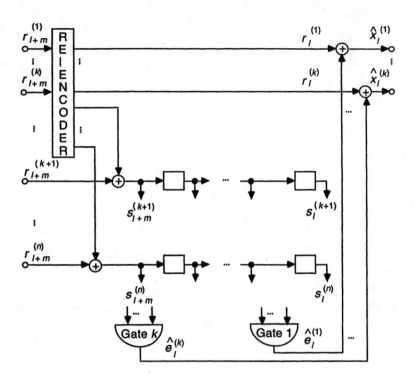

Figure 6.1 Hard-decision majority-logic definite decoding of (n, k, m) systematic convolutional codes.

$$
\begin{bmatrix}
s_l^{(k+1)} \\
\vdots \\
s_{l+m}^{(k+1)} \\
s_l^{(k+2)} \\
\vdots \\
s_{l+m}^{(k+2)} \\
\vdots \\
s_l^{(n)} \\
\vdots \\
s_{l+m}^{(n)}
\end{bmatrix}
=
\begin{bmatrix}
\mathbf{G'}_1^{(k+1)} & \mathbf{G'}_2^{(k+1)} & \cdots & \mathbf{G'}_k^{(k+1)} \\
\mathbf{G'}_1^{(k+2)} & \mathbf{G'}_2^{(k+2)} & \cdots & \mathbf{G'}_k^{(k+2)} \\
\vdots & \vdots & & \vdots \\
\mathbf{G'}_1^{(n)} & \mathbf{G'}_2^{(n)} & \cdots & \mathbf{G'}_k^{(n)}
\end{bmatrix}
\begin{bmatrix}
e_{l-m}^{(1)} \\
\vdots \\
e_l^{(1)} \\
\vdots \\
e_{l+m}^{(1)} \\
e_{l-m}^{(2)} \\
\vdots \\
e_l^{(2)} \\
\vdots \\
e_{l+m}^{(2)} \\
\vdots \\
e_{l-m}^{(k)} \\
\vdots \\
e_l^{(k)} \\
\vdots \\
e_{l+m}^{(k)}
\end{bmatrix}
+
\begin{bmatrix}
e_l^{(k+1)} \\
\vdots \\
e_{l+m}^{(k+1)} \\
e_l^{(k+2)} \\
\vdots \\
e_{l+m}^{(k+2)} \\
\vdots \\
e_l^{(n)} \\
\vdots \\
e_{l+m}^{(n)}
\end{bmatrix}
\qquad (6.24)
$$

where

$$
\mathbf{G'}_i^{(j)} = \begin{bmatrix} g_{i,m}^{(j)} & g_{i,m-1}^{(j)} & \cdots & g_{i,0}^{(j)} & & & \\ & g_{i,m}^{(j)} & \cdots & g_{i,1}^{(j)} & g_{i,0}^{(j)} & & \\ & & \ddots & \vdots & \vdots & & \ddots \\ & & & g_{i,m}^{(j)} & g_{i,m-1}^{(j)} & \cdots & g_{i,0}^{(j)} \end{bmatrix} \tag{6.25}
$$

for $1 \le i \le k$ and $(k + 1) \le j \le n$. Each submatrix $\mathbf{G}_i^{(j)}$ is called the *parity parallelogram* of the code. The channel-error sequence can be separated into an information-error sequence (errors associated with the k information bits) and a parity-error sequence (errors associated with the $n - k$ code bits). Each syndrome bit or a sum of syndrome bits represents a sum of channel-error bits and is called a parity-check sum. The total number of parity parallelograms is $(n - k) \cdot k$, and the parity parallelograms can be used to select k sets of J orthogonal check sums on $e_l^{(1)}, e_l^{(2)}, \ldots, e_l^{(k)}$. A set of J check sums is orthogonal on each of these error bits if the specific error bit $e_l^{(1)}$, $1 \le i \le k$, is checked by all the check sums in the set and no other error bit is checked by more than one check sum in the set. The total number of different error bits checked by the k sets of J orthogonal check sums is called the effective constraint length, ν_E, of the code.

It can be shown that majority-logic definite decoding of (n, k, m) systematic convolutional codes can correct $t_{ML} = J/2$ or fewer errors within the ν_E error bits checked by the k sets of J orthogonal check sums [1]. The majority-logic decoding steps are as follows:

1. Compute syndrome vector $\mathbf{S'}^T$ of length $(m + 1) \cdot (n - k)$.

2. A set of J orthogonal check sums on each $e_l^{(i)}$, for $1 \le i \le k$, is formed from the syndrome vector $\mathbf{S'}^T$.

3. Each set of J check sums is fed into the majority-logic gate. If more than half its input bits are ones, $r_l^{(i)}$ is assumed to be in error, a logic $\hat{e}_l^{(i)} = 1$ is produced for $1 \le i \le k$. If fewer than half its input bits are ones, $r_l^{(i)}$ is assumed to be error free, a logic $\hat{e}_l^{(i)} = 0$ is produced.

4. Perform error correction by adding $r_l^{(i)}$ and $\hat{e}_l^{(i)}$ to give the estimated information bits $\hat{x}_l^{(i)}$ for $1 \le i \le k$. The syndrome registers are shifted once to the right. Next, n received bits are input into the decoder. A new set of $n - k$ syndrome bits, $s_{l+m+1}^{(k+1)}, s_{l+m+1}^{(k+2)}, \ldots, s_{l+m+1}^{(n)}$, is computed and fed into the syndrome registers.

5. Steps 2, 3, and 4 are repeated to estimate the error bits $e_{l+1}^{(1)}$, $e_{l+1}^{(2)}$, ..., $e_{l+1}^{(k)}$. The process repeats in this way.

For an (n, k, m) systematic convolutional code, there are $n - k$ new syndrome bits to be formed and k error bits corresponding to the k information bits to be estimated at each time instant.

Example 6.1

Consider a $(2, 1, 1)$ systematic convolutional code of $G(D) = [1 \; 1 + D]$. On receipt of $r_{l+1}^{(j)}$, $1 \le j \le 2$, the truncated syndrome vector, $\mathbf{S}'^T$, for the code is

$$
\begin{bmatrix} s_l^{(2)} \\ s_{l+1}^{(2)} \end{bmatrix} = \begin{bmatrix} 1 & 1 & 0 \\ 0 & 1 & 1 \end{bmatrix} \begin{bmatrix} e_{l-1}^{(1)} \\ e_l^{(1)} \\ e_{l+1}^{(1)} \end{bmatrix} + \begin{bmatrix} e_l^{(2)} \\ e_{l+1}^{(2)} \end{bmatrix}
\tag{6.26}
$$

The syndrome bits $s_l^{(2)}$ and $s_{l+1}^{(2)}$ form a set of two orthogonal check sums on the information-error bit $e_l^{(2)}$. Furthermore,

$s_l^{(2)}$ checks the information-error bit $e_{l-1}^{(1)}$, and the parity-error bit $e_l^{(2)}$.
$s_{l+1}^{(2)}$ checks the information-error bit $e_{l+1}^{(1)}$, and the parity-error bit $e_{l+1}^{(2)}$.

A total of five distinct channel-error bits are checked by the two orthogonal check sums, and the effective constraint length of the code is 5. The block diagram of the encoder and hard-decision majority-logic definite decoder in the presence of channel errors is shown in Figure 6.2. Single errors can be corrected by the majority-logic definite decoder.

The orthogonal check sums for the code are

$$
\begin{aligned}
s_l^{(2)} &= e_{l-1}^{(1)} + e_l^{(1)} \qquad\qquad + e_l^{(2)} \\
s_{l+1}^{(2)} &= \qquad\quad e_l^{(1)} + e_{l+1}^{(1)} + e_{l+1}^{(2)}
\end{aligned}
$$

Clearly, in the absence of errors, both syndrome bits are always zero. In the presence of errors, the decoder now chooses the estimate $\hat{e}_l^{(1)} = 1$ if and only if both orthogonal check sums, $s_l^{(2)}$ and $s_{l+1}^{(2)}$, on $e_l^{(1)}$ have a value of 1.

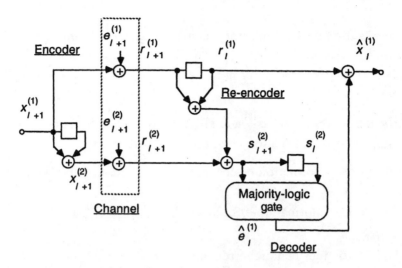

Figure 6.2 Block diagram for a (2, 1, 1) systematic convolutional code with hard-decision majority-logic definite decoding.

Example 6.2

Consider a (3, 2, 2) systematic convolutional code of

$$\mathbf{G}(D) = \begin{bmatrix} 1 & 0 & 1 + D \\ 0 & 1 & 1 + D^2 \end{bmatrix}$$

On receipt of $r_{l+2}^{(j)}$, $1 \le j \le 3$, the truncated syndrome vector, $\mathbf{S'}^T$, for the code is

$$\begin{bmatrix} s_l^{(3)} \\ s_{l+1}^{(3)} \\ s_{l+2}^{(3)} \end{bmatrix} = \begin{bmatrix} 0 & 1 & 1 & 0 & 0 \\ 0 & 0 & 1 & 1 & 0 \\ 0 & 0 & 0 & 1 & 1 \end{bmatrix} \begin{bmatrix} e_{l-2}^{(1)} \\ e_{l-1}^{(1)} \\ e_l^{(1)} \\ e_{l+1}^{(1)} \\ e_{l+2}^{(1)} \end{bmatrix} + \begin{bmatrix} 1 & 0 & 1 & 0 & 0 \\ 0 & 1 & 0 & 1 & 0 \\ 0 & 0 & 1 & 0 & 1 \end{bmatrix} \begin{bmatrix} e_{l-2}^{(2)} \\ e_{l-1}^{(2)} \\ e_l^{(2)} \\ e_{l+1}^{(2)} \\ e_{l+2}^{(2)} \end{bmatrix} + \begin{bmatrix} e_l^{(3)} \\ e_{l+1}^{(3)} \\ e_{l+2}^{(3)} \end{bmatrix} \quad (6.27)$$

Two sets of orthogonal check sums can be formed to check on the information-error bits $e_l^{(1)}$ and $e_l^{(2)}$. The syndrome bits $s_l^{(3)}$ and $s_{l+1}^{(3)}$ form the first set of two orthogonal check sums on the information-error bit $e_l^{(1)}$. Furthermore,

$s_l^{(3)}$ checks the information-error bits $e_{l-1}^{(1)}$, $e_{l-2}^{(2)}$, and $e_l^{(2)}$ and the parity-error bit $e_l^{(3)}$.

$s_{l+1}^{(3)}$ checks the information-error bits $e_{l+1}^{(1)}$, $e_{l-1}^{(2)}$, and $e_{l+1}^{(2)}$ and the parity-error bit $e_{l+1}^{(3)}$.

Similarly, the syndrome bits $s_l^{(3)}$ and $s_{l+2}^{(3)}$ form the second set of two orthogonal check sums on the information-error bit $e_l^{(2)}$. Furthermore,

$s_l^{(3)}$ checks the information-error bits $e_{l-1}^{(1)}$, $e_l^{(1)}$, and $e_{l-2}^{(2)}$ and the parity-error bit $e_l^{(3)}$.

$s_{l+2}^{(3)}$ checks the information-error bits $e_{l+1}^{(1)}$, $e_{l+2}^{(1)}$, and $e_{l+2}^{(2)}$ and the parity-error bit $e_{l+2}^{(3)}$.

A total of 12 distinct channel-error bits are checked by the two sets of two orthogonal check sums and the effective constraint length of the code is 12. The block diagram of the hard-decision majority-logic definite decoder is shown in Figure 6.3. Single errors can be corrected by the majority-logic definite decoder.

Example 6.3

Consider a (3, 1, 2) systematic convolutional code of $\mathbf{G}(D) = [1 \quad 1 + D \quad 1 + D^2]$. On receipt of $r_{l+2}^{(j)}$, $1 \leq j \leq 3$, the truncated syndrome vector, $\mathbf{S}'^T$, for the code is

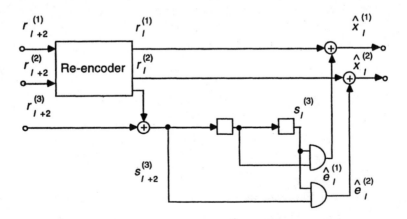

Figure 6.3 Hard-decision majority-logic definite decoding for a (3, 2, 2) systematic convolutional code.

$$
\begin{bmatrix}
s_l^{(2)} \\
s_{l+1}^{(2)} \\
s_{l+2}^{(2)} \\
\\
s_l^{(3)} \\
s_{l+1}^{(3)} \\
s_{l+2}^{(3)}
\end{bmatrix}
=
\begin{bmatrix}
0 & 1 & 1 & 0 & 0 \\
0 & 0 & 1 & 1 & 0 \\
0 & 0 & 0 & 1 & 1 \\
1 & 0 & 1 & 0 & 0 \\
0 & 1 & 0 & 1 & 0 \\
0 & 0 & 1 & 0 & 1
\end{bmatrix}
\begin{bmatrix}
e_{l-2}^{(1)} \\
e_{l-1}^{(1)} \\
e_{l}^{(1)} \\
e_{l+1}^{(1)} \\
e_{l+2}^{(1)}
\end{bmatrix}
+
\begin{bmatrix}
e_l^{(2)} \\
e_{l+1}^{(2)} \\
e_{l+2}^{(2)} \\
\\
e_l^{(3)} \\
e_{l+1}^{(3)} \\
e_{l+2}^{(3)}
\end{bmatrix}
\qquad (6.28)
$$

The syndrome bits $s_l^{(2)}$, $s_{l+1}^{(2)}$, $s_l^{(3)}$, and $s_{l+2}^{(3)}$ form a set of four orthogonal check sums on the information-error bit $e_l^{(1)}$. Furthermore,

$s_l^{(2)}$ checks the information-error bit $e_{l-1}^{(1)}$ and the parity-error bit $e_l^{(2)}$.

$s_{l+1}^{(2)}$ checks the information-error bit $e_{l+1}^{(1)}$ and the parity-error bit $e_{l+1}^{(2)}$.

$s_l^{(3)}$ checks the information-error bit $e_{l-2}^{(1)}$ and the parity-error bit $e_l^{(3)}$.

$s_{l+2}^{(3)}$ checks the information-error bit $e_{l+2}^{(1)}$ and the parity-error bit $e_{l+2}^{(3)}$.

A total of nine distinct channel-error bits are checked by the four orthogonal check sums, and the effective constraint length of the code is 9. The block diagram of the hard-decision majority-logic definite decoder is shown in Figure 6.4. In the presence of errors, the decoder chooses the estimate $\hat{e}_l^{(1)} = 1$

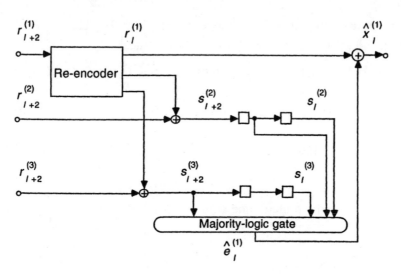

Figure 6.4 Hard-decision majority-logic definite decoding for a (3, 1, 2) systematic convolutional code.

if and only if three or more orthogonal check sums on $e_l^{(1)}$ have a value of 1. Two or fewer errors can be corrected by the majority-logic definite decoder.

Example 6.4

Consider a $(2, 1, 5)$ systematic convolutional code of $\mathbf{G}(D) = [1\ 1 + D^3 + D^4 + D^5]$. On receipt of $r_{l+5}^{(j)}$, $1 \le j \le 2$, the truncated syndrome vector, $\mathbf{S'}^T$, for the code is

$$
\begin{bmatrix}
s_l^{(2)} \\
s_{l+1}^{(2)} \\
s_{l+2}^{(2)} \\
s_{l+3}^{(2)} \\
s_{l+4}^{(2)} \\
s_{l+5}^{(2)}
\end{bmatrix}
=
\begin{bmatrix}
1\ 1\ 1\ 0\ 0\ 1\ 0\ 0\ 0\ 0\ 0\ 0 \\
0\ 1\ 1\ 1\ 0\ 0\ 1\ 0\ 0\ 0\ 0\ 0 \\
0\ 0\ 1\ 1\ 1\ 0\ 0\ 1\ 0\ 0\ 0\ 0 \\
0\ 0\ 0\ 1\ 1\ 1\ 0\ 0\ 1\ 0\ 0\ 0 \\
0\ 0\ 0\ 0\ 1\ 1\ 1\ 0\ 0\ 1\ 0\ 0 \\
0\ 0\ 0\ 0\ 0\ 1\ 1\ 1\ 0\ 0\ 1
\end{bmatrix}
\begin{bmatrix}
e_{l-5}^{(1)} \\
e_{l-4}^{(1)} \\
e_{l-3}^{(1)} \\
e_{l-2}^{(1)} \\
e_{l-1}^{(1)} \\
e_l^{(1)} \\
e_{l+1}^{(1)} \\
e_{l+2}^{(1)} \\
e_{l+3}^{(1)} \\
e_{l+4}^{(1)} \\
e_{l+5}^{(1)}
\end{bmatrix}
+
\begin{bmatrix}
e_l^{(2)} \\
e_{l+1}^{(2)} \\
e_{l+2}^{(2)} \\
e_{l+3}^{(2)} \\
e_{l+4}^{(2)} \\
e_{l+5}^{(2)}
\end{bmatrix}
\qquad (6.29)
$$

A set of three orthogonal check sums, $s_l^{(2)}$, $s_{l+3}^{(2)}$, and $s_{l+5}^{(2)}$, can be obtained to check on the information-error bit $e_l^{(1)}$. Furthermore,

$s_l^{(2)}$ checks the information-error bits $e_{l-5}^{(1)}$, $e_{l-4}^{(1)}$, and $e_{l-3}^{(1)}$ and the parity-error bit $e_l^{(2)}$.

$s_{l+3}^{(2)}$ checks the information-error bits $e_{l-2}^{(1)}$, $e_{l-1}^{(1)}$, and $e_{l+3}^{(1)}$ and the parity-error bit $e_{l+3}^{(2)}$.

$s_{l+5}^{(2)}$ checks the information-error bits $e_{l+1}^{(1)}$, $e_{l+2}^{(1)}$, and $e_{l+5}^{(1)}$ and the parity-error bit $e_{l+5}^{(2)}$.

A total of 13 distinct channel-error bits are checked by the three orthogonal check sums, and the effective constraint length of the code is 13. The block diagram of hard-decision majority-logic definite decoder is shown in Figure 6.5. In the presence of errors, the decoder chooses the estimate $\hat{e}_l^{(1)} = 1$ if and only if two or more orthogonal check sums on $e_l^{(1)}$ have a value of 1. Single errors can be corrected by the majority-logic definite decoder.

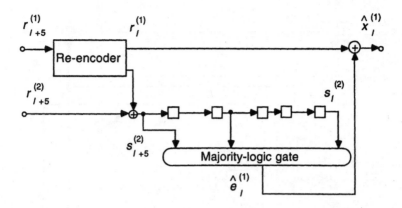

Figure 6.5 Hard-decision majority-logic definite decoding for a (2, 1, 5) systematic convolutional code.

6.2.2 Majority-Logic Feedback Decoding

We can also design a majority-logic decoder with the estimated-error bits being fed back into the syndrome registers. In general, the bit-error probability performance of majority-logic decoding with feedback usually outperforms majority-logic definite decoding for the same code. Figure 6.6 shows a complete majority-logic decoder with feedback for an (n, k, m) systematic convolutional code.

The majority-logic decoder illustrated in Figure 6.6 is called a majority-logic feedback decoder [1]. Assuming that the decoder makes correct error estimation, the truncated syndrome vector, $\mathbf{S'}^T$, of (6.23) is modified and expressed as

$$
\begin{bmatrix}
s_l^{(k+1)} \\
\vdots \\
s_{l+m}^{(k+1)} \\
s_l^{(k+2)} \\
\vdots \\
s_{l+m}^{(k+2)} \\
\vdots \\
s_l^{(n)} \\
\vdots \\
s_{l+m}^{(n)}
\end{bmatrix}
=
\begin{bmatrix}
\mathbf{G}_1^{(k+1)} & \mathbf{G}_2^{(k+1)} & \cdots & \mathbf{G}_k^{(k+1)} \\
\mathbf{G}_1^{(k+2)} & \mathbf{G}_2^{(k+2)} & \cdots & \mathbf{G}_k^{(k+2)} \\
\vdots & \vdots & & \vdots \\
\mathbf{G}_1^{(n)} & \mathbf{G}_2^{(n)} & \cdots & \mathbf{G}_k^{(n)}
\end{bmatrix}
\begin{bmatrix}
e_l^{(1)} \\
\vdots \\
e_{l+m}^{(1)} \\
e_l^{(2)} \\
\vdots \\
e_{l+m}^{(2)} \\
\vdots \\
e_l^{(k)} \\
\vdots \\
e_{l+m}^{(k)}
\end{bmatrix}
+
\begin{bmatrix}
e_l^{(k+1)} \\
\vdots \\
e_{l+m}^{(k+1)} \\
e_l^{(k+2)} \\
\vdots \\
e_{l+m}^{(k+2)} \\
\vdots \\
e_l^{(n)} \\
\vdots \\
e_{l+m}^{(n)}
\end{bmatrix}
\qquad (6.30)
$$

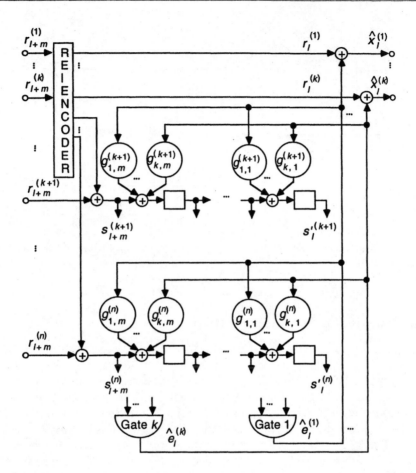

Figure 6.6 Hard-decision majority-logic feedback decoding of (n, k, m) systematic convolutional codes.

where

$$
\mathbf{G}_i^{(j)} = \begin{bmatrix} g_{i,0}^{(j)} & & & \\ g_{i,1}^{(j)} & g_{i,0}^{(j)} & & \\ \vdots & \vdots & \ddots & \\ g_{i,m}^{(j)} & g_{i,m-1}^{(j)} & \cdots & g_{i,0}^{(j)} \end{bmatrix}
\tag{6.31}
$$

for $1 \leq i \leq k$ and $(k + 1) \leq j \leq n$. Each submatrix $\mathbf{G}_i^{(j)}$ is called the parity triangle of the code. Again, the channel-error sequence can be separated into an information-error sequence (errors associated with the k information bits) and a parity-error sequence (errors associated with the $n - k$ code bits). Each syndrome bit or a sum of syndrome bits represents a sum of channel-error bits. The total number of parity triangles is $(n - k) \cdot k$ and the parity triangles can be used to select k sets of J orthogonal check sums on $e_l^{(1)}, e_l^{(2)}, \ldots, e_l^{(k)}$.

It can also be shown that majority-logic feedback decoding of (n, k, m) systematic convolutional codes can correct $t_{ML} = J/2$ or fewer errors within the ν_E error bits checked by the k sets of J orthogonal check sums [1]. The majority-logic decoding steps are as follows:

1. Compute syndrome vector $\mathbf{S}'^T$ of length $(m + 1) \cdot (n - k)$.

2. A set of J orthogonal check sums on each $e_l^{(i)}$, for $1 \le i \le k$, is formed from the syndrome vector $\mathbf{S}'^T$.

3. Each set of J check sums is fed into the majority-logic gate. If more than half of its input bits are ones, $r_l^{(i)}$ is assumed to be in error, a logic $\hat{e}_l^{(i)} = 1$ is produced for $1 \le i \le k$. If fewer than half its input bits are ones, $r_l^{(i)}$ is assumed to be error free, a logic $\hat{e}_l^{(i)} = 0$ is produced.

4. Perform error correction by adding $r_l^{(i)}$ and $\hat{e}_l^{(i)}$ to give the estimated information bits $\hat{x}_l^{(i)}$ for $1 \le i \le k$. The syndrome registers are shifted once to the right. Next, n received bits are input into the decoder. A new set of $n - k$ syndrome bits, $s_{l+m+1}^{(k+1)}, s_{l+m+1}^{(k+2)}, \ldots, s_{l+m+1}^{(n)}$, is computed and fed into the syndrome registers.

5. The syndrome registers now contain the modified syndrome bits, $s'^{(k+1)}_{l+1}, \ldots, s'^{(k+1)}_{l+m}, s'^{(k+2)}_{l+1}, \ldots, s'^{(k+2)}_{l+m}, \ldots, s'^{(n)}_{l+1}, \ldots, s'^{(n)}_{l+m}$, together with the new set of syndrome bits, $s_{l+m+1}^{(k+1)}, s_{l+m+1}^{(k+2)}, \ldots, s_{l+m+1}^{(n)}$. Steps 2, 3, and 4 are repeated to estimate the error bits, $e_{l+1}^{(1)}, e_{l+1}^{(2)}, \ldots, e_{l+1}^{(k)}$. The process repeats in this way.

For an (n, k, m) systematic convolutional code, there are $n - k$ new syndrome bits to be formed and k error bits corresponding to the k information bits to be estimated at each time instant. In step 5, estimated-error bits are fed back to modify the syndrome registers before the next error estimation.

Example 6.5

Consider a $(2, 1, 1)$ systematic convolutional code of $G(D) = [1 \ 1 + D]$. On receipt of $r_{l+1}^{(j)}$, $1 \le j \le 2$, the truncated syndrome vector, $\mathbf{S}'^T$, for the code is

$$\begin{bmatrix} s_l^{(2)} \\ s_{l+1}^{(2)} \end{bmatrix} = \begin{bmatrix} 1 & 0 \\ 1 & 1 \end{bmatrix} \begin{bmatrix} e_l^{(1)} \\ e_{l+1}^{(1)} \end{bmatrix} + \begin{bmatrix} e_l^{(2)} \\ e_{l+1}^{(2)} \end{bmatrix} \tag{6.32}$$

The syndrome bits $s_l^{(2)}$ and $s_{l+1}^{(2)}$ form a set of two orthogonal check sums on the information-error bit $e_l^{(1)}$. Furthermore,

$s_l^{(2)}$ checks the parity-error bit $e_l^{(2)}$.
$s_{l+1}^{(2)}$ checks the information-error bit $e_{l+1}^{(1)}$ and the parity-error bit $e_{l+1}^{(2)}$.

A total of four distinct channel-error bits are checked by the two orthogonal check sums, and the effective constraint length of the code is 4. It can be seen that each check sum is formed from a single syndrome bit. The systematic code is known as a self-orthogonal convolutional code [1,3–7]. The block diagram of the encoder and hard-decision majority-logic feedback decoder in the presence of channel errors is shown in Figure 6.7. Single errors can be corrected by the majority-logic feedback decoder.

The orthogonal check sums for the code are

$$s_l^{(2)} = e_l^{(1)} \qquad\quad + e_l^{(2)}$$
$$s_{l+1}^{(2)} = e_l^{(1)} + e_{l+1}^{(1)} + e_{l+1}^{(2)}$$

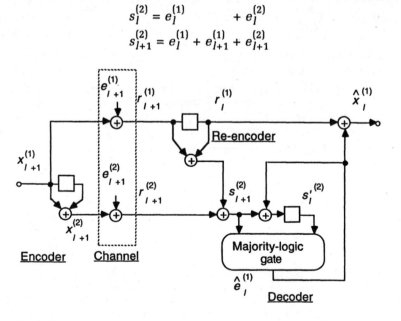

Figure 6.7 Block diagram for a (2, 1, 1) systematic convolutional code with hard-decision majority-logic feedback decoding.

Clearly, in the absence of errors, both syndrome bits are always zero. In the presence of errors, the decoder now chooses the estimate $\hat{e}_l^{(1)} = 1$ if and only if both orthogonal check sums, $s_l^{(2)}$ and $s_{l+1}^{(2)}$, on $e_l^{(1)}$ have a value of 1.

Example 6.6

Consider a (3, 2, 2) systematic convolutional code of

$$\mathbf{G}(D) = \begin{bmatrix} 1 & 0 & 1 + D \\ 0 & 1 & 1 + D^2 \end{bmatrix}$$

On receipt of $r_{l+2}^{(j)}$, $1 \leq j \leq 3$, the truncated syndrome vector, $\mathbf{S}'^T$, for the code is

$$\begin{bmatrix} s_l^{(3)} \\ s_{l+1}^{(3)} \\ s_{l+2}^{(3)} \end{bmatrix} = \begin{bmatrix} 1 & 0 & 0 \\ 1 & 1 & 0 \\ 0 & 1 & 1 \end{bmatrix} \begin{bmatrix} e_l^{(1)} \\ e_{l+1}^{(1)} \\ e_{l+2}^{(1)} \end{bmatrix} + \begin{bmatrix} 1 & 0 & 0 \\ 0 & 1 & 0 \\ 1 & 0 & 1 \end{bmatrix} \begin{bmatrix} e_l^{(2)} \\ e_{l+1}^{(2)} \\ e_{l+2}^{(2)} \end{bmatrix} + \begin{bmatrix} e_l^{(3)} \\ e_{l+1}^{(3)} \\ e_{l+2}^{(3)} \end{bmatrix} \qquad (6.33)$$

Two sets of orthogonal check sums can be formed to check on the information-error bits $e_l^{(1)}$ and $e_l^{(2)}$. The syndrome bits $s_l^{(3)}$ and $s_{l+1}^{(3)}$ form the first set of two orthogonal check sums on the information-error bit $e_l^{(1)}$. Furthermore,

$s_l^{(3)}$ checks the information-error bit $e_l^{(2)}$ and the parity-error bit $e_l^{(3)}$.
$s_{l+1}^{(3)}$ checks the information-error bits $e_{l+1}^{(1)}$ and $e_{l+1}^{(2)}$ and the parity-error bit $e_{l+1}^{(3)}$.

Similarly, the syndrome bits $s_l^{(3)}$ and $s_{l+2}^{(3)}$ form the second set of two orthogonal check sums on the information-error bit $e_l^{(2)}$. Furthermore,

$s_l^{(3)}$ checks the information-error bit $e_l^{(1)}$ and the parity-error bit $e_l^{(3)}$.
$s_{l+2}^{(3)}$ checks the information-error bits $e_{l+1}^{(1)}$, $e_{l+2}^{(1)}$, and $e_{l+2}^{(2)}$ and the parity-error bit $e_{l+2}^{(3)}$.

A total of nine distinct channel-error bits are checked by the two sets of two orthogonal check sums, and the effective constraint length of the code is 9. Each check sum is formed from a single syndrome bit, and the systematic code is again a self-orthogonal convolutional code. The block diagram of the hard-decision majority-logic feedback decoder is shown in Figure 6.8. Single errors can be corrected by the majority-logic feedback decoder.

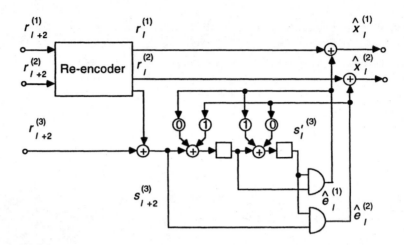

Figure 6.8 Hard-decision majority-logic feedback decoding for a (3, 2, 2) systematic convolutional code.

Example 6.7

Consider a (3, 1, 2) systematic convolutional code of $\mathbf{G}(D) = [1 \ 1 + D \ 1 + D^2]$. On receipt of $r_{l+2}^{(j)}$, $1 \le j \le 3$, the truncated syndrome vector, $\mathbf{S}'^T$, for the code is

$$
\begin{bmatrix}
s_l^{(2)} \\
s_{l+1}^{(2)} \\
s_{l+2}^{(2)} \\
\\
s_l^{(3)} \\
s_{l+1}^{(3)} \\
s_{l+2}^{(3)}
\end{bmatrix}
=
\begin{bmatrix}
1 & 0 & 0 \\
1 & 1 & 0 \\
0 & 1 & 1 \\
1 & 0 & 0 \\
0 & 1 & 0 \\
1 & 0 & 1
\end{bmatrix}
\begin{bmatrix}
e_l^{(1)} \\
e_{l+1}^{(1)} \\
e_{l+2}^{(1)}
\end{bmatrix}
+
\begin{bmatrix}
e_l^{(2)} \\
e_{l+1}^{(2)} \\
e_{l+2}^{(2)} \\
\\
e_l^{(3)} \\
e_{l+1}^{(3)} \\
e_{l+2}^{(3)}
\end{bmatrix}
\qquad (6.34)
$$

The syndrome bits $s_l^{(2)}$, $s_{l+1}^{(2)}$, $s_l^{(3)}$, and $s_{l+2}^{(3)}$ form a set of four orthogonal check sums on the information-error bit $e_l^{(1)}$. Furthermore,

$s_l^{(2)}$ checks the parity-error bit $e_l^{(2)}$.

$s_{l+1}^{(2)}$ checks the information-error bit $e_{l+1}^{(1)}$ and the parity-error bit $e_{l+1}^{(2)}$.

$s_l^{(3)}$ checks the parity-error bit $e_l^{(3)}$.

$s_{l+2}^{(3)}$ checks the information-error bit $e_{l+2}^{(1)}$ and the parity-error bit $e_{l+2}^{(3)}$.

A total of seven distinct channel-error bits are checked by the four orthogonal check sums, and the effective constraint length of the code is 7. Each check sum is formed from a single syndrome bit, and the systematic code is a self-orthogonal convolutional code. The block diagram of the hard-decision majority-logic feedback decoder is shown in Figure 6.9. In the presence of errors, the decoder chooses the estimate $\hat{e}_l^{(1)} = 1$ if and only if three or more orthogonal check sums on $e_l^{(1)}$ have a value of 1. Two or fewer errors can be corrected by the majority-logic feedback decoder. A list of good self-orthogonal systematic convolutional codes for majority-logic decoding is given in Appendix D.

Example 6.8

Consider a (2, 1, 5) systematic convolutional code of $\mathbf{G}(D) = [1 \; 1 + D^3 + D^4 + D^5]$. On receipt of $r_{l+5}^{(j)}$, $1 \le j \le 2$, the truncated syndrome vector, $\mathbf{S}'^T$, for the code is

$$
\begin{bmatrix}
s_l^{(2)} \\
s_{l+1}^{(2)} \\
s_{l+2}^{(2)} \\
s_{l+3}^{(2)} \\
s_{l+4}^{(2)} \\
s_{l+5}^{(2)}
\end{bmatrix}
=
\begin{bmatrix}
1 & 0 & 0 & 0 & 0 & 0 \\
0 & 1 & 0 & 0 & 0 & 0 \\
0 & 0 & 1 & 0 & 0 & 0 \\
1 & 0 & 0 & 1 & 0 & 0 \\
1 & 1 & 0 & 0 & 1 & 0 \\
1 & 1 & 1 & 0 & 0 & 1
\end{bmatrix}
\begin{bmatrix}
e_l^{(1)} \\
e_{l+1}^{(1)} \\
e_{l+2}^{(1)} \\
e_{l+3}^{(1)} \\
e_{l+4}^{(1)} \\
e_{l+5}^{(1)}
\end{bmatrix}
+
\begin{bmatrix}
e_l^{(2)} \\
e_{l+1}^{(2)} \\
e_{l+2}^{(2)} \\
e_{l+3}^{(2)} \\
e_{l+4}^{(2)} \\
e_{l+5}^{(2)}
\end{bmatrix}
\qquad (6.35)
$$

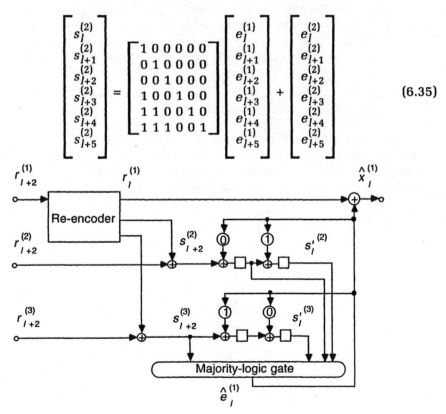

Figure 6.9 Hard-decision majority-logic feedback decoding for a (3, 1, 2) systematic convolutional code.

A set of four orthogonal check sums, $s_l^{(2)}$, $s_{l+3}^{(2)}$, $s_{l+4}^{(2)}$, and $s_{l+1}^{(2)} + s_{l+5}^{(2)}$, can be obtained to check on the information-error bit $e_l^{(1)}$. The addition of the syndrome bits $s_{l+1}^{(2)}$ and $s_{l+5}^{(2)}$ is to remove the effect of $e_{l+1}^{(1)}$, which is already checked by the syndrome bit $s_{l+4}^{(2)}$. Furthermore,

$s_l^{(2)}$ checks the parity-error bit $e_l^{(2)}$.

$s_{l+1}^{(2)} + s_{l+5}^{(2)}$ checks the information-error bits $e_{l+2}^{(1)}$ and $e_{l+5}^{(1)}$ and the parity-error bits $e_{l+1}^{(2)}$ and $e_{l+5}^{(2)}$.

$s_{l+3}^{(2)}$ checks the information-error bit $e_{l+3}^{(1)}$ and the parity-error bit $e_{l+3}^{(2)}$.

$s_{l+4}^{(2)}$ checks the information-error bits $e_{l+1}^{(1)}$ and $e_{l+4}^{(1)}$ and the parity-error bit $e_{l+4}^{(2)}$.

A total of 11 distinct channel-error bits are checked by the four orthogonal check sums, and the effective constraint length of the code is 11. It can be seen that not all the check sums are formed from a single syndrome bit. The systematic code is known as an orthogonalizable convolutional code. The block diagram of hard-decision majority-logic feedback decoder is shown in Figure 6.10. In the presence of errors, the decoder chooses the estimate $\hat{e}_l^{(1)} = 1$ if and only if three or more orthogonal check sums on $e_l^{(1)}$ have a value of 1. Two or fewer errors can be corrected by the majority-logic feedback decoder.

With majority-logic definite decoding, we have seen in Example 6.4 that a total of 13 distinct channel-error bits are checked by the three orthogonal check sums and that the effective constraint length of the code is 13. This code can correct only single errors with majority-logic definite decoding.

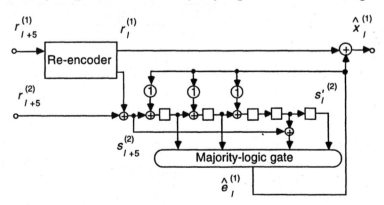

Figure 6.10 Hard-decision majority-logic feedback decoding for a (2, 1, 5) systematic convolutional code.

In general, orthogonalizable convolutional codes have the property that smaller number of orthogonal check sums can be formed with definite decoding than with feedback decoding. However, the same number of orthogonal check sums can be formed for self-orthogonal convolutional codes with definite and feedback decoding. The effective constraint length of self-orthogonal convolutional codes with definite decoding is larger than the corresponding effective constraint length of the code with feedback decoding.

We have come across the class of self-orthogonal and orthogonalizable codes for use with majority-logic decoding. Also, there exists a class of $(2^m, 1, m)$ convolutional codes, called uniform codes [8], for majority-logic decoding. The major difference between the orthogonalizable codes and the other codes is that the former do not possess automatic resychronization properties (discussed in Section 6.3), which limit error propagation in the decoder with the estimated-error bits being fed back to the syndrome register.

6.3 ERROR PROPAGATION EFFECT

We have seen that a hard-decision majority-logic feedback decoder makes a decision based only on one constraint length of the code, and the effects of previously estimated-error bits are removed by the feedback path. With an incorrect estimated-error bit being fed back to the syndrome register(s), an error-propagation effect [3, 9, 10] occurs that corresponds to an extra transmission error and can cause further decoding errors. When the incorrect estimated-error bits being fed back into the syndrome registers, the truncated syndrome vector, $\mathbf{S}'^T$, is

$$
\begin{bmatrix}
s_l^{(k+1)} \\
\vdots \\
s_{l+m}^{(k+1)} \\
s_l^{(k+2)} \\
\vdots \\
s_{l+m}^{(k+2)} \\
\vdots \\
s_l^{(n)} \\
\vdots \\
s_{l+m}^{(n)}
\end{bmatrix}
=
\begin{bmatrix}
\mathbf{G'}_1^{(k+1)} & \mathbf{G'}_2^{(k+1)} & \cdots & \mathbf{G'}_k^{(k+1)} \\
\mathbf{G'}_1^{(k+2)} & \mathbf{G'}_2^{(k+2)} & \cdots & \mathbf{G'}_k^{(k+2)} \\
\vdots & \vdots & & \vdots \\
\mathbf{G'}_1^{(n)} & \mathbf{G'}_2^{(n)} & \cdots & \mathbf{G'}_k^{(n)}
\end{bmatrix}
\begin{bmatrix}
\hat{e}_{l-m}^{(1)} \\
\vdots \\
\hat{e}_{l-1}^{(1)} \\
e_l^{(1)} \\
\vdots \\
e_{l+m}^{(1)} \\
\hat{e}_{l-m}^{(2)} \\
\vdots \\
e_l^{(2)} \\
\vdots \\
e_{l+m}^{(2)} \\
\vdots \\
\hat{e}_{l-m}^{(k)} \\
\vdots \\
\hat{e}_{l-1}^{(k)} \\
e_l^{(k)} \\
\vdots \\
e_{l+m}^{(k)}
\end{bmatrix}
+
\begin{bmatrix}
e_l^{(k+1)} \\
\vdots \\
e_{l+m}^{(k+1)} \\
e_l^{(k+2)} \\
\vdots \\
e_{l+m}^{(k+2)} \\
\vdots \\
e_l^{(n)} \\
\vdots \\
e_{l+m}^{(n)}
\end{bmatrix}
\qquad (6.36)
$$

The post-decoding error $\tilde{e}_{l-1}^{(i)} = \hat{e}_{l-1}^{(i)} + e_{l-1}^{(i)}$ is the result of adding $\hat{e}_{l-1}^{(i)}$ to the truncated syndrome equation containing $e_{l-1}^{(i)}$ for $1 \le i \le k$. Now, previously estimated-error bits are not removed from the syndrome registers. That can affect future error estimation and may cause more decoding errors.

Example 6.9

Consider the self-orthogonal convolutional code in Example 6.5 with majority-logic feedback decoding. After decoding of the error bit $e_{l-1}^{(1)}$, the modified check sums of (6.32) are:

$$s_l^{(2)} = \tilde{e}_{l-1}^{(1)} + e_l^{(1)} \qquad\quad + e_l^{(2)} \tag{6.37}$$

$$s_{l+1}^{(2)} = \qquad\quad e_l^{(1)} + e_{l+1}^{(1)} + e_{l+1}^{(2)} \tag{6.38}$$

where the post-decoding error $\tilde{e}_{l-1}^{(1)} = \hat{e}_{l-1}^{(1)} + e_{l-1}^{(1)}$ is the result of adding $\hat{e}_{l-1}^{(1)}$ to the truncated syndrome equation containing $e_{l-1}^{(1)}$. If $\tilde{e}_{l-1}^{(1)} = 1$, that corresponds to an extra transmission error and can cause error propagation. Codes, therefore, should be designed to have automatic resynchronization properties. Past errors on the syndrome can now be automatically removed when the channel is error-free over a finite length of time. Self-orthogonal and uniform convolutional codes are good examples of codes that posses automatic resynchronization properties.

If majority-logic definite decoding is used, the previous estimated-error bit, $\hat{e}_{l-1}^{(1)}$, is not fed back to the syndrome registers, and the check sums of (6.32) are

$$s_l^{(2)} = e_{l-1}^{(1)} + e_l^{(1)} \qquad\quad + e_l^{(2)} \tag{6.39}$$

$$s_{l+1}^{(2)} = \qquad\quad e_l^{(1)} + e_{l+1}^{(1)} + e_{l+1}^{(2)} \tag{6.40}$$

The number of orthogonal check sums remains unchanged. However, the effective constraint length is increased from 4 with feedback decoding to 5 with definite decoding. There are now more error bits included in the check sums. The error-correcting power of the code is reduced with majority-logic definite decoding, but the error propagation effect is eliminated.

6.4 PERFORMANCE OF HARD-DECISION MAJORITY-LOGIC DECODING

The bit-error probability performance of an (n, k, m) convolutional code with coherent BPSK signals and hard-decision majority-logic feedback decoding on AWGN channel can be upper-bounded by

$$P_b \le \frac{1}{k} \sum_{i=t_{ML}+1}^{\nu_E} \binom{\nu_E}{i} p^i (1 - p)^{\nu_E - i} \tag{6.41}$$

where p is the channel transition probability. For small values of p,

$$P_b \simeq \frac{1}{k} \binom{\nu_E}{t_{ML} + 1} p^{t_{ML}+1} \tag{6.42}$$

Equations (6.41) and (6.42) are also applicable for hard-decision definite decoding, but the effective constraint length is usually longer.

6.5 SOFT-DECISION MAJORITY-LOGIC DECODING

Massey [1] introduced a soft-decision majority-logic decoding technique, called a prior probability decoding. In 1970, Rudolph [11] proposed a generalized soft-decision majority-logic decoding. In this section, we shall assume majority-logic feedback decoding and discuss a soft-decision majority-logic feedback decoding technique, described by Goodman [12], for systematic convolutional codes. The extension to soft-decision majority-logic definite decoding is obvious and straightforward by the inclusion of extra error bits that are not feeding back into the syndrome registers.

Consider that each received signal at the output of the channel is quantized into eight levels and therefore can be expressed as a 3-bit binary vector. The leftmost bit is the hard-decision digit, and the vector gives the level value. Thus, for example, [000] = 0 and [101] = 5. The Goodman decoding system first estimates the soft-error digit, which is checked by a set of J orthogonal check sums on the assumption that the corresponding "to-be-decoded" hard-error digit is not in error. It then uses each syndrome (check sum) digit and the received digit, associated with the "worst-error" digit, to estimate the soft-decision level of each worst-error digit. The error digit that lies nearest to the hard 0/1 decision boundary is taken as the worst-error digit. When the error digits in the check sum have equal distance from the hard-decision boundary, we simply select one in random as the worst-error digit. Also, the error digit checked by the J orthogonal check sums is not included in this estimation process. An algebraic sum, A_e, of the estimated-error digit is formed, and a comparison is made against a fixed threshold level, $T_{ML} = (Q - 1)(2t_{ML} + 1)/2$, where Q is the number of quantization levels and t_{ML} is the hard-decision error-correcting power of the code. t_{ML} is, in turn, equal to $J/2$. If the algebraic sum is greater than T_{ML}, then the error digit, which is checked by all check sums, is decoded as 1. If the algebraic sum is not greater than T_{ML}, then the error digit is decoded as 0.

To estimate each worst-error digit $[e_j^{(i)}]$ in the soft-decision sense, each soft-decision error digit is derived from the corresponding soft-decision received digit $[r_j^{(i)}]$, for $1 \leq i \leq k$. When the syndrome digit is 0, the hard-decision error digit $e_j^{(i)}$ is assumed to be not in error. If the soft-decision received digit $[r_j^{(i)}] \leq 3$, the soft-decision estimate of $[e_j^{(i)}]$ is given by $[\hat{e}_j^{(i)}] = [r_j^{(i)}]$, or else $[\hat{e}_j^{(i)}] = 7 - [r_j^{(i)}]$. When the syndrome digit is 1, the hard-decision error digit $e_j^{(i)}$ is assumed to be in error. If $[r_j^{(i)}] \leq 3$, the soft-decision estimate of $[e_j^{(i)}]$ is given by $[\hat{e}_j^{(i)}] = 7 - [r_j^{(i)}]$, or else $[\hat{e}_j^{(i)}] = [r_j^{(i)}]$. The smallest sum of the estimated error digits is taken as the most likely error event, and the corresponding error digits are taken as the worst-error digits. This is the Goodman decoding system. It can be seen that the decoder initially estimates the error digit checked by the orthogonal check sums. It then uses the syndrome digits to estimate the worst-error digits before A_e is formed.

Example 6.10

Consider the case where the all-zero information sequence is transmitted via the (2, 1, 1) systematic convolutional code, as shown in Figure 6.7, where $y_j^{(1)} = x_j^{(1)}$. As described in Example 6.5, the orthogonal check sums for the code, with hard-decision majority-logic feedback decoding, are

$$s_j^{(2)} = e_j^{(1)} \qquad\quad + e_j^{(2)}$$
$$s_{j+1}^{(2)} = e_j^{(1)} + e_{j+1}^{(1)} + e_{j+1}^{(2)}$$

Assume that the soft-decision error digits are $[e_j^{(1)}] = [100]$, $[e_j^{(2)}] = [100]$, $[e_{j+1}^{(1)}] = [010]$, and $[e_{j+1}^{(2)}] = [000]$ and that the decoder has not yet made any decoding errors. In the hard-decision case, $r_j^{(1)} = y_j^{(1)} + e_j^{(1)} = 1$, $s_j^{(2)} = 0$, $s_{j+1}^{(2)} = 1$, and the estimated hard-decision error digit $\hat{e}_j^{(1)} = 0$. A hard-decision majority-logic feedback decoder with no post-decoding error would decode $\hat{x}_j^{(1)} = 1$. That gives a decoding error.

In the soft-decision case with eight-level uniform quantization, the algebraic sum, A_e, of the estimated error is performed as follows:

1. Assume the hard-decision error digit $\hat{e}_l^{(1)} = 0$. The soft-decision received digit $[r_l^{(1)}] = [y_l^{(1)}] + [e_l^{(1)}] = 0 + 4 = 4$ and $[r_l^{(1)}] \geq 4$. The estimated soft-decision error level $[\hat{e}_l^{(1)}] = 7 - [r_l^{(1)}] = 7 - 4 = 3$.

2. The syndrome digit $s_l^{(2)} = 1 + 1 = 0$ (modulo-2 addition). As the hard-decision error digit $\hat{e}_l^{(1)}$ is assumed to be not in error, $\hat{e}_l^{(2)}$ is, therefore, assumed to be not in error. Since $[r_l^{(2)}] = [y_l^{(2)}] + [e_l^{(2)}] = 0 + 4 = 4$ and $[r_l^{(2)}] \geq 4$, the estimated soft-decision error level $[\hat{e}_l^{(2)}] = 7 - [r_l^{(2)}] = 7 - 4 = 3$.

3. The syndrome digit $s_{l+1}^{(2)} = 1 + 0 + 0 = 1$ (modulo-2 addition). Because the hard-decision error digit $\hat{e}_l^{(1)}$ is assumed to be not in error, the worst-error digit $\hat{e}_{l+1}^{(1)}$ is assumed to be in error. For $\hat{e}_{l+1}^{(1)} = 1$, the soft-decision received digit $[r_{l+1}^{(1)}] = [y_{l+1}^{(1)}] + [e_{l+1}^{(1)}] = 0 + 2 = 2$ and $[r_{l+1}^{(1)}] \leq 3$. The estimated soft-decision error level $[\hat{e}_{l+1}^{(1)}] = 7 - [r_{l+1}^{(1)}] = 7 - 2 = 5$.

4. The algebraic sum $A_e = [\hat{e}_l^{(1)}] + [\hat{e}_l^{(2)}] + [\hat{e}_{l+1}^{(1)}] = 3 + 3 + 5 = 11$. For this single-error-correcting code with eight-level soft-decision decoding, $Q_L = 8$ and $T_{ML} = 10.5$, where $T_{ML} = (Q - 1)(2t_{ML} + 1)/2$. A_e is larger than the fixed threshold level T_{ML}, and the hard-decision error digit $\hat{e}_l^{(1)} = 0$ is not correctly assumed. The estimated hard-decision error digit $\hat{e}_l^{(1)}$ should be 1. Now, $\hat{x}_l^{(1)} = r_l^{(1)} + e_l^{(1)} = 0$, and the soft-decision majority-logic feedback decoder corrects the error.

6.6 COMPUTER SIMULATION RESULTS

The variation of bit-error rate with the E_b/N_0 ratio of the Goodman decoding system with coherent BPSK signals for AWGN channel has been measured by computer simulations. Here, E_b is the average transmitted bit energy and $N_0/2$ is the two-sided power-spectral density of the noise. Three rate-$(n - 1)/n$ self-orthogonal systematic convolutional codes have been used in the tests. The code rate; the error-correcting power, t_{ML}; the encoder memory order, m; and the generator polynomial matrix are given in Table 6.1.

Self-orthogonal convolutional codes are used to reduce the effect of error propagation in the feedback decoder when incorrect estimated-error digits are fed back to the decoder. The simulated-error performance of the (2, 1, 6), (3, 2, 2), and (4, 3, 3) self-orthogonal systematic convolutional codes with hard-decision/eight-level uniform soft-decision definite and feedback decoding are shown in Figures 6.11, 6.12, and 6.13, respectively. It can be seen that an

Table 6.1
Parameters of the (2, 1, 6), (3, 2, 2), and (4, 3, 3) Self-Orthogonal Systematic
Convolutional Codes

Code Rate	t_{ML}	m	$G(D)$
1/2	2	6	$[1 \ 1 + D^2 + D^5 + D^6]$
2/3	1	2	$\begin{bmatrix} 1 \ 0 \ 1 + D \\ 0 \ 1 \ 1 + D^2 \end{bmatrix}$
3/4	1	3	$\begin{bmatrix} 1 \ 0 \ 0 \ 1 + D \\ 0 \ 1 \ 0 \ 1 + D^2 \\ 0 \ 0 \ 1 \ 1 + D^3 \end{bmatrix}$

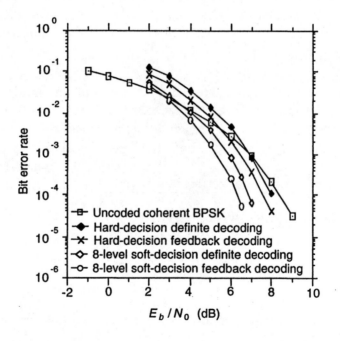

Figure 6.11 Performance of (2, 1, 6) self-orthogonal systematic convolutional code with hard-decision and eight-level soft-decision definite and feedback decoding in AWGN channels.

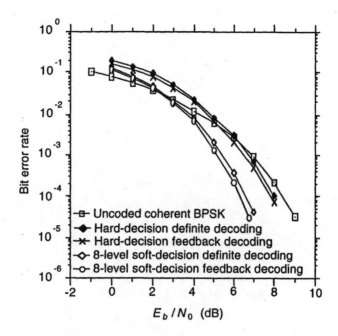

Figure 6.12 Performance of (3, 2, 2) self-orthogonal systematic convolutional code with hard-decision and eight-level soft-decision definite and feedback decoding in AWGN channels.

improvement of about 2 dB in coding gain can be achieved with soft-decision decoding. Furthermore, the bit-error probability performance of feedback decoders also outperforms definite decoders. In low-cost applications, majority-logic decoding is less complex than maximum-likelihood decoding.

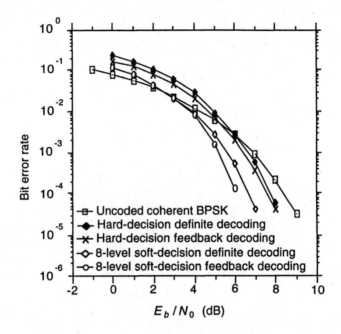

Figure 6.13 Performance of (4, 3, 3) self-orthogonal systematic convolutional code with hard-decision and eight-level soft-decision definite and feedback decoding in AWGN channels.

References

[1] Massey, J. L., *Threshold Decoding*, Cambridge: MIT Press, 1963.

[2] Bussgang, J. J., "Some Properties of Binary Convolutional Code Generators," *IEEE Trans. on Information Theory*, Vol. IT-11, No. 1, January 1965, pp. 90–100.

[3] Robinson, J. P., "Error Propagation and Definite Decoding of Convolutional Codes," *IEEE Trans. on Information Theory*, Vol. IT-14, No. 1, January 1968, pp. 121–128.

[4] Robinson, J. P., and A. J. Bernstein, "A Class of Binary Recurrent Codes With Limited Error Propagation," *IEEE Trans. on Information Theory*, Vol. IT-13, No. 1, January 1967, pp. 106–113.

[5] Wu, W. W., "New Convolutional Codes—Part I," *IEEE Trans. on Communications*, Vol. COM-23, No. 9, September 1975, pp. 942–956.

[6] Wu, W. W., "New Convolutional Codes—Part II," *IEEE Trans. on Communications*, Vol. COM-24, No. 1, January 1976, pp. 19–33.

[7] Wu, W. W., "New Convolutional Codes—Part III," *IEEE Trans. on Communications*, Vol. COM-24, No. 9, September 1976, pp. 946–955.

[8] Massey, J. L., "Uniform Codes," *IEEE Trans. on Information Theory*, Vol. IT-12, No. 2, April 1966, pp. 132–134.

[9] Massey, J. L., and R. W. Liu, "Application of Lyapunov's Directed Method to the Error-Propagation Effect in Convolutional Codes," *IEEE Trans. on Information Theory*, Vol. IT-10, No. 3, July 1964, pp. 248–250.

[10] Sullivan, D. D., "Error-Propagation Properties of Uniform Codes," *IEEE Trans. on Information Theory*, Vol. IT-15, No. 1, January 1969, pp. 152–161.

[11] Rudolph, L. D., "Generalized Threshold Decoding of Convolutional Codes," *IEEE Trans. on Information Theory*, Vol. IT-16, No. 6, November 1970, pp. 739–745.

[12] Goodman, R. M. F., and W. H. Ng, "Soft-Decision Threshold Decoding of Convolutional Codes," *Proc. IERE Conf. on Digital Signal Process. in Commun.*, University of Technology, Loughborough, UK, No. 37, September 6–9, 1977, pp. 535–546.

Combined Convolutional Coding and Modulation

7

7.1 INTRODUCTION

We have seen that in classical digital communication systems with coding, the channel encoder and the modulator design are considered as separate entities. This is shown in Figure 7.1.

The modem (*mo*dulator-*dem*odulator) transforms the analog channel into a discrete channel and the channel codec (en*co*der-*dec*oder) corrects errors that may appear on the channel. The ability to detect or correct errors is achieved by adding redundancy to the information bits. Due to channel coding, the effective information rate for a given transmission rate at the encoder output is reduced.

Example 7.1

It can be seen from Figure 7.2 that the information rate with channel coding is reduced for the same transmission rate at locations 2′ and 4′. If we increase the information rate with coding from 1 bps to 2 bps, the transmission rate at the encoder output increases to 4 bps.

In modem design, we can employ bandwidth efficient multilevel modulation to increase spectral efficiency. For 2^γ-ary modulation, γ number of bits are used to specify a signal symbol which, in turn, selects a signal waveform for transmission. If the signaling interval is T seconds, the symbol rate is $1/T$ symbol/s and the transmission rate at the input of the modulator is γ/T bps. Also, the signal bandwidth is inversely proportional to the signaling interval if the carrier signal frequency $f_c = 1/T$.

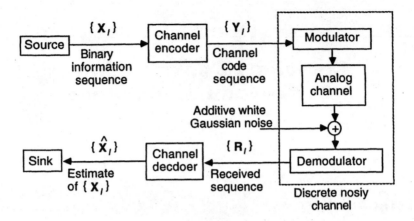

Figure 7.1 Model of a coded digital communication system.

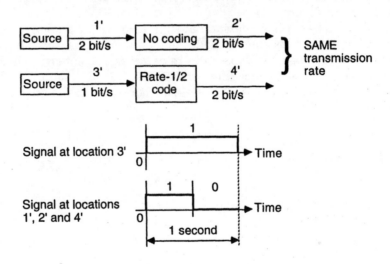

Figure 7.2 Comparison of coded and uncoded signaling schemes.

Example 7.2

Consider Figure 7.3.

For BPSK ($\gamma = 1$):   symbol rate, $1/T = 2$ symbol/s.

                                 information rate, $\gamma/T = 2$ bps.

For 4-PSK ($\gamma = 2$): symbol rate, $1/T = 1$ symbol/s.

                                 information rate, $\gamma/T = 2$ bps.

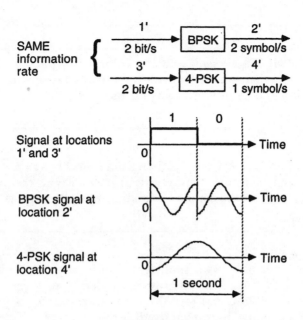

Figure 7.3 Comparison of uncoded BPSK and 4-PSK modulation schemes at same information rate.

It can be seen from Figure 7.3 that 4-PSK (1 symbol/s) requires less bandwidth than BPSK (2 symbol/s) for the same information rate of 2 bps. Suppose the following:

For BPSK ($\gamma = 1$): symbol rate, $1/T = 2$ symbol/s.
  information rate, $\gamma/T = 2$ bps.

For 4-PSK ($\gamma = 2$): symbol rate, $1/T = 2$ symbol/s.
  information rate, $\gamma/T = 4$ bps.

4-PSK (4 bps) now has a higher information rate than BPSK (2 bps) for the same bandwidth requirement.

From our early example, we know that channel coding reduces the information rate for the same symbol rate. To compensate for the loss of information rate, two methods can be employed. In the first method, if the type of modulation is fixed and the bandwidth is expandable (i.e., to increase the symbol rate), we simply increase the information rate from the output of the source for the coded system.

In the second method, if the bandwidth is not fixed, we increase the modulation level of the coded system. That increases the information rate of the coded system.

Example 7.3

From Figure 7.4, it can be seen that the information rate at location 4' with coding is reduced when compared with the uncoded case at location 1' for the same modulation and bandwidth constraints.

Example 7.4

The information rate at location 4' is increased from 1 bps to 2 bps. From Figure 7.5, it can be seen that more bandwidth is needed with coding for the same type of modulation and the same information rate at locations 1' and 4'.

Example 7.5

The information rate of 1 bps is maintained at location 4'. From Figure 7.6, it can be seen that for the same information rate at locations 1' and 4' with different modulation level (BPSK and 4-PSK), the uncoded BPSK and the coded 4-PSK require no change in the bandwidth requirement.

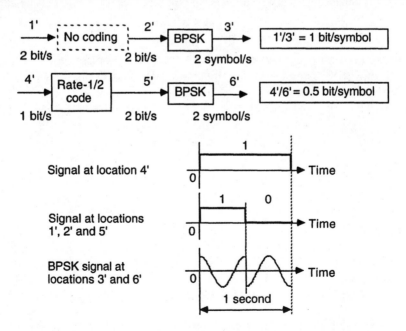

Figure 7.4 Comparison of uncoded and coded BPSK modulation schemes at same symbol rate.

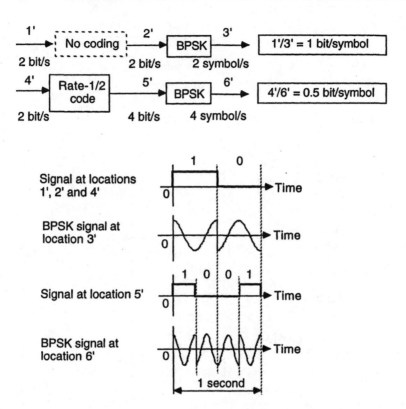

Figure 7.5 Comparison of uncoded and coded BPSK modulation schemes at same information rate.

The following discussion is concerned with bandwidth-constrained channels. We have already seen that if we double the modulation level with coding, the uncoded and the coded modulation schemes have the same information rate and the bandwidth requirement remains unchanged. We now ask ourselves some questions. Can we simply pick any well-known codes from a textbook? Will the coded modulation scheme be an optimum scheme? The answer is definitely no! Because of the independent design of coding and modulation, that approach gives disappointing performance, due to the fact that the codes were optimized for the minimum free Hamming distance and no consideration given to the importance of the Euclidean distance between signal symbols in the modulation process.

The mapping of the coded sequence onto the 2^γ-ary modulation signal symbol sequence does not guarantee a good free Euclidean distance measure. Hence, a completely new set of error-control codes has to be found using the

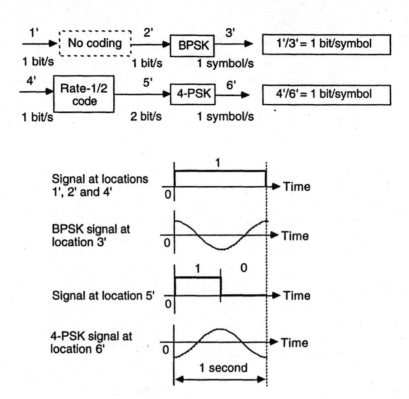

Figure 7.6 Comparison of uncoded BPSK and coded 4-PSK modulation schemes at same information and symbol rates.

new measure. We shall restrict ourselves to a particular kind of combined coding and modulation design, namely, *trellis-coded modulation* (TCM). Bandwidth-efficient modulation with coding has been studied by many researchers [1–4], but TCM was first introduced and documented by Ungerboeck [5] in 1982. Since his publication, active research works have been carried out by others in the development of *one-dimensional* (1-D), *two-dimensional* (2-D), and *multi-dimensional* (multi-D) combined coding and modulation techniques [6–66]. This chapter discusses the principles of 2-D TCM and multi-D TCM. We shall illustrate the design procedure of 2-D TCM with *M*-PSK signals. The design procedure is also valid for TCM schemes with 1-D or other 2-D signal constellations.

7.2 TWO-DIMENSIONAL TRELLIS-CODED MODULATION

In the past, channel coding design and modulation design were treated as separate entities. Hamming distance was considered an appropriate measure for system design. In the case of coding with multilevel modulation design, we simply select a conventional $(\gamma, \gamma - 1, m)$ convolutional encoder or a $(\gamma, \gamma - 1)$ block encoder. At time l, the encoder output code vector $\mathbf{Y}_l = [y_l^{(1)}\ y_l^{(2)} \ldots y_l^{(\gamma)}]$ is mapped to a signal symbol, s_l, and the corresponding modulated signal waveform is generated by a 2^γ-ary modulator for transmission. This does not correspond to the optimum matching between the channel encoder and the modulator for $\gamma > 1$. This is due to the fact that early channel encoders were found or designed on the minimum free Hamming distance criterion.

TCM design, due to Ungerboeck [5], offers the optimum matching between the channel encoder output code vector and the modulator using a special signal mapping. Ungerboeck has shown that encoders should be designed in accordance to this mapping and a new distance criterion, namely, the minimum free Euclidean distance,

$$d_{\text{fed}} = \min\left[\sum_l d^2(s_l, s_l')\right]^{1/2} \tag{7.1}$$

between all pairs of channel signal symbol sequences that diverge from one state and merge to another state in the encoder trellis where $d(s_l, s_l')$ is the Euclidean distance between two channel signal symbols at time l. The mapping is based on the concept of signal set partitioning. A signal set is partitioned into subsets with increasing intrasubset distance. Figures 7.7 and 7.8 show the

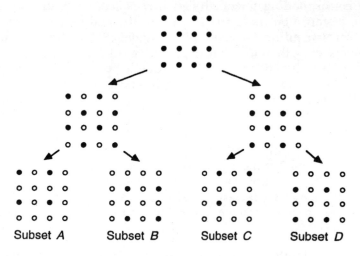

Figure 7.7 Set-partitioning of a 16-QAM constellation.

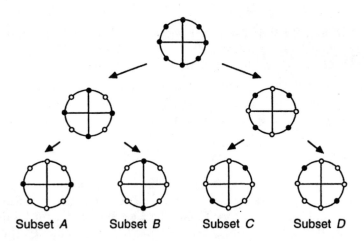

Figure 7.8 Set-partitioning of an 8-PSK constellation.

set partitioning of 16-QAM and 8-PSK signal constellations, respectively. Each signal set is partitioned into four subsets with equal number of elements and an increasing intrasubset distance.

Consider the uncoded 4-PSK and rate-2/3 trellis-coded 8-PSK signals shown in Figure 7.9(a,c), respectively. It is assumed that all the signal points are equally spaced and lie on the unit circle. The average signal symbol energy is equal to 1. The information rates of both signaling schemes are the same, but the coded signaling scheme requires more signal points for transmission than the corresponding uncoded signaling scheme. It can be seen that the Euclidean distance between any two nearest coded 8-PSK signals is smaller than the corresponding uncoded 4-PSK signals. The gain from coding with 8-PSK signals must, therefore, outweigh the loss of distance due to signal expansion. Otherwise, the coded 8-PSK signaling scheme will not outperform the corresponding uncoded 4-PSK signaling scheme.

For the uncoded 4-PSK signals, the Euclidean distance between two closest signals is $\Delta_1 = \sqrt{2}$. If we partition the coded 8-PSK signals in a natural way, as shown in Figure 7.9(c), we can see that the Euclidean distance between two closest signal points in the subset {0, 2, 4, 6} is $\Delta_1 = \sqrt{2}$, whereas the smallest subset, {0, 4}, formed from the subset {0, 2, 4, 6}, has the Euclidean distance $\Delta_2 = 2$. Hence, this set partitioning divides a signal set successively into smaller subsets with increasing intrasubset distance Δ_i for $i = 0, 1, \ldots$. The coded 8-PSK signals are then assigned to the 4-state trellis with the following Unger-boeck rules [5]:

1. All signal points are used in the trellis with equal frequency.
2. Transitions originating from or merging to one state are assigned to signals from the same subset.

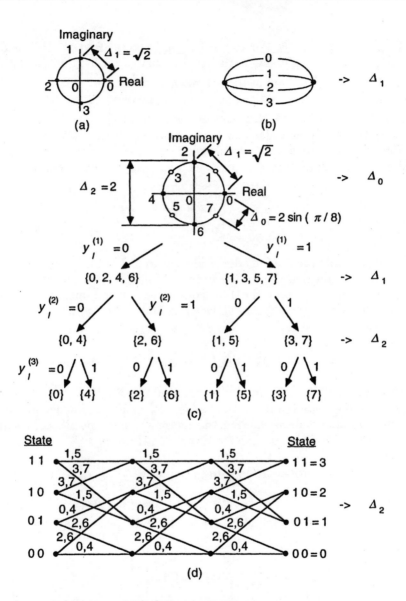

Figure 7.9 (a) 4-PSK signals, (b) trellis diagram of (a), (c) partition of redundant 8-PSK signals, and (d) assigned 4-state trellis diagram of (c).

3. Parallel transitions originating or terminating in the same state are assigned to signals from the next smaller subset.

In the 4-state trellis, any two nonparallel signal paths that diverge from a state and merge to another state have at least a squared free Euclidean distance of $(\Delta_1^2 + \Delta_0^2 + \Delta_1^2) = 4.586$. For example, the squared free Euclidean distance between the path associated with the state sequence 0-2-1-0 and the path associated with the all-zero state sequence shown in Figure 7.9(d) is $\Delta_1^2 + \Delta_0^2 + \Delta_1^2$. The squared free Euclidean distance between any two paths with parallel transitions in the trellis is $\Delta_2^2 = 4$. It can be seen that $(\Delta_1^2 + \Delta_0^2 + \Delta_1^2) > \Delta_2^2$ and the minimum free Euclidean distance in the 4-state trellis is, therefore, equal to 2.

Figure 7.10 shows one possible realization of the rate-2/3 convolutional encoder for the coded 8-PSK signals. The generator polynomial matrix of the code is

$$G(D) = \begin{bmatrix} D & 1 + D^2 & 0 \\ 0 & 0 & 1 \end{bmatrix}$$

and the truth table for the encoder is shown in Table 7.1.

It can be seen that the binary form of the signal symbol value (e.g., 100 for signal 4) corresponds to the 3-bit code vector at the output of the encoder and is a natural binary mapping. The *asymptotic coding gain* (ACG) of the TCM scheme is defined as

$$ACG = 10 \log_{10}(d_{\text{fed}}^2/P_{\text{av}})_{\text{coded}}/(d_{\text{fed}}^2/P_{\text{av}})_{\text{uncoded}} \tag{7.2}$$

in decibels, where d_{fed}^2 is the minimum squared free Euclidean distance between two paths in the coded and uncoded cases. P_{av} is the average signal power in the coded and uncoded cases. When the average signal power becomes identical in both cases for a direct comparison, the ACG becomes

$$ACG = 10 \log_{10}(d_{\text{fed}}^2)_{\text{coded}}/(d_{\text{fed}}^2)_{\text{uncoded}} \tag{7.3}$$

For our example, the ACG of this hand-designed code with 8-PSK signals is equal to $10 \log_{10}(\Delta_2^2/\Delta_1^2)$, that is, a gain of 3.0 dB. More powerful codes have

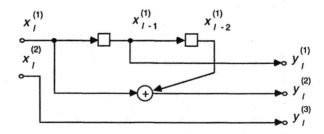

Figure 7.10 (3, 2, 2) convolutional encoder.

Table 7.1
Trellis Truth-Table of the Encoder in Figure 7.10

Signal Symbol	$y_l^{(3)} y_l^{(2)} y_l^{(1)}$	$x_l^{(1)} x_l^{(2)}$	Present State $x_{l-1}^{(1)} x_{l-2}^{(1)} (BCD)^*$	Next State $x_l^{(1)} x_{l-1}^{(1)} (BCD)$
0	0 0 0	0 0	0 0 (0)	0 0 (0)
4	1 0 0	0 1	0 0 (0)	0 0 (0)
2	0 1 0	0 0	0 1 (1)	0 0 (0)
6	1 1 0	0 1	0 1 (1)	0 0 (0)
1	0 0 1	0 0	1 0 (2)	0 1 (1)
5	1 0 1	0 1	1 0 (2)	0 1 (1)
3	0 1 1	0 0	1 1 (3)	0 1 (1)
7	1 1 1	0 1	1 1 (3)	0 1 (1)
2	0 1 0	1 0	0 0 (0)	1 0 (2)
6	1 1 0	1 1	0 0 (0)	1 0 (2)
0	0 0 0	1 0	0 1 (1)	1 0 (2)
4	1 0 0	1 1	0 1 (1)	1 0 (2)
3	0 1 1	1 0	1 0 (2)	1 1 (3)
7	1 1 1	1 1	1 0 (2)	1 1 (3)
1	0 0 1	1 0	1 1 (3)	1 1 (3)
5	1 0 1	1 1	1 1 (3)	1 1 (3)

*Binary-coded decimal (BCD) value of a binary vector.

been found by exhaustive computer search based on the set-partitioning rules [5,17,20,42,52]. A list of codes with various types of modulation signals is shown in Appendix E. In general, the channel encoder and modulator structure is shown in Figure 7.11.

$n - 1$ bits enter the rate-$(n - 1)/n$ convolutional encoder, and the resulting n coded bits specify which subset is to be used. The remaining uncoded bits

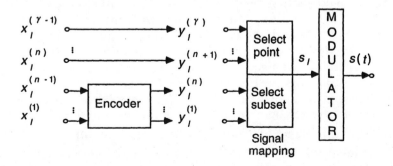

Figure 7.11 General transmitter structure of trellis-coded modulation.

specify which point from the selected subset is used to generate the correspond-ing modulated signal for transmission. For our example, $y_l^{(2)} y_l^{(1)}$ selects a subset, and $y_l^{(3)}$ selects a point from that subset. Uncoded bits correspond to parallel transitions in the trellis diagram. When $n = \gamma$, the point and the subset are selected simultaneously.

We can use the conventional Viterbi trellis decoding algorithm to recover the information symbols, bearing in mind that there is a one-to-one correspon-dence between the transmitted signal symbol sequence and the channel code sequence. If the received signal symbol at time l is r_l, the squared Euclidean distance between the received signal symbol r_l and the possible channel signal symbol s_l can be used as the branch metric for decoding. The decoder simply recursively minimizes the Euclidean metric

$$M_l(r_0/s_0, r_1/s_1, \ldots, r_l/s_l) = M_{l-1}(r_0/s_0, r_1/s_1, \ldots, r_{l-1}/s_{l-1}) + d^2(r_l, s_l)$$

(7.4)

over all channel signal symbol sequences $\{s_l\}$. $d^2(r_l, s_l)$ is the branch squared Euclidean distance between signals r_l and s_l at time l.

7.2.1 Phase-Invariant Convolutional Codes

This section addresses the problem that arises when the carrier-modulated TCM signal is demodulated with a phase offset, that is, the demodulated signal is rotated by a fixed amount in either direction. The phase offset could be caused by the carrier-recovery circuit in the demodulator. For example, when the recovered carrier signal in coherent BPSK demodulation is 180 deg out of phase to the transmitted carrier signal, the demodulated signal sequence is an inverted version of the signal sequence at the input of the modulator. A 100% error is obtained. We can insert a differential encoder at the transmitter and a differential decoder at the receiver to remove those errors. The differential encoding opera-tion can be viewed as a rotation of the previous differential encoder output signals in accordance with the current differential encoder input signals. The differential decoder is performing the reverse operation. Figure 7.12 shows the differential encoder and decoder circuits. The truth table of the differential encoder and decoder is shown in Table 7.2. Figure 7.12 illustrates how differen-tial encoding and decoding can remove those errors. It is assumed that the previous differential encoder output and the previous differential decoder out-put signals are initialized to 0 and 1, respectively. The input sequence $\{x_l^{(1)}\}$ = 10110 is differentially encoded to the sequence $\{x'^{(1)}_l\}$ = 11011. If that sequence, $\{x'^{(1)}_l\}$, is inverted to 00100, the differential decoder output sequence is $\{x_l^{(1)}\}$ = 10110. Errors have been removed.

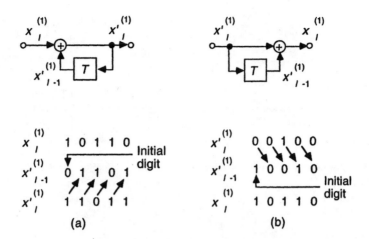

Figure 7.12 (a) Differential encoder and (b) differential decoder. Note: T = signaling interval.

Table 7.2
Truth Table for One-Bit Differential Encoding and Decoding

One-Bit Differential Encoding			One-Bit Differential Decoding		
Previous Output $x'^{(1)}_{l-1}$	*Current Input* $x^{(1)}_l$	*Current Output* $x'^{(1)}_l$	*Previous Input* $x'^{(1)}_{l-1}$	*Current Input* $x'^{(1)}_l$	*Current Output* $x^{(1)}_l$
0	0	0	0	0	0
1	0	1	1	1	0
0	1	1	0	1	1
1	1	0	1	0	1

In a TCM system, codes should, therefore, be made transparent to signal rotations. In the presence of a phase offset, a rotated signal sequence at the output of the channel decoder can be corrected by the differential decoder [7,8,19,29,65]. The system block diagram is shown in Figure 7.13.

Consider the rate-1/2 convolutional code in Figure 7.14, whose output bits are mapped onto a 4-PSK signal in Figure 7.15. The assigned encoder trellis diagram is shown in Figure 7.16.

Each transition is associated with a signal symbol from the set {0, 1, 2, 3}. The signal symbols in the subset {0, 2} are 180 deg out of phase. Similarly, there is also a 180 deg phase difference between the signal symbols in the

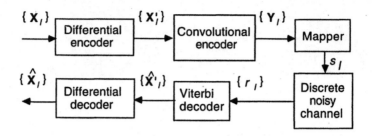

Figure 7.13 Model of a differentially coded digital communication system.

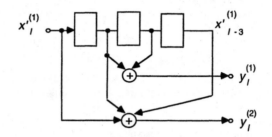

Figure 7.14 (2, 1, 3) convolutional encoder.

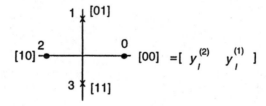

Figure 7.15 4-PSK signal constellation diagram.

subset {1, 3}. If we invert the information sequence to the encoder shown in Figure 7.14, the channel signal symbol sequence is rotated by 180 deg. Referring to the trellis diagram in Figure 7.16, it can be seen that an inverted version of the present state and the next state associated with a signal symbol results in another signal symbol, which is 180 deg out of phase from that signal symbol. For example, signal 0 is associated with the path between the present state, 001, and the next state, 100. The inverted version of the present and the next states are 110 and 011, respectively, and signal 2 is associated with the transition path. In fact, signal 2 is obtained by rotating signal 0 by 180 deg, as shown in Figure 7.15. That rotation can, therefore, be corrected by employing the

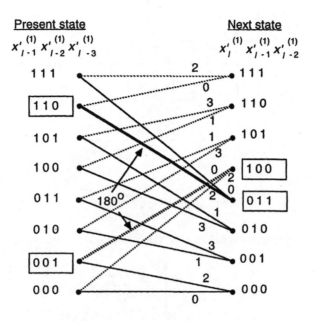

Figure 7.16 Trellis diagram of eight-state, rate-1/2 convolutional encoder of Figure 7.14.

differential encoding and decoding circuits shown in Figure 7.12. The code is called 180 deg phase-invariant or transparent code, and the code is linear.

7.2.2 90 Degree Phase-Invariant Convolutional Codes

Consider the rate-2/3 convolutional code in Figure 7.17, whose output bits are mapped onto an 8-PSK signal in Figure 7.18. The assigned trellis diagram is shown in Figure 7.19.

There are two paths (parallel paths) between trellis states. If we change the contents in the encoder shift register according to Table 7.3, the signal symbol sequence is rotated.

This is shown as below:

- Let the shift register contains all-zero bits. For a 90 deg rotation, the all-zero sequence {00, 00, 00, 00} changes to the sequence {01, 01, 01, 01} = $\{x'^{(2)}_l x'^{(1)}_l, x'^{(2)}_{l-1} x'^{(1)}_{l-1}, \ldots\}$. In terms of the trellis diagram, we have signal 0 associated with the present state 000 and the next state 000. After a 90 deg rotation, signal 2 is obtained, which is associated with the present state 111 and the next state 111. Hence, the 90 deg rotation of signal 0 is signal 2.

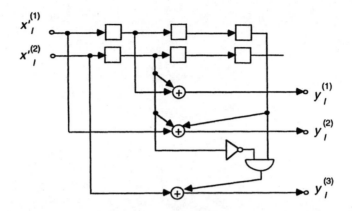

Figure 7.17 90 deg phase-invariant, rate-2/3 nonlinear convolutional encoder.

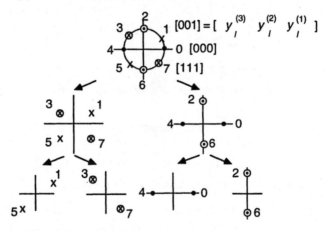

Figure 7.18 8-PSK signal set-partitioning.

- For a 180 deg rotation, the all-zero sequence {00, 00, 00, 00} changes to the sequence {10, 10, 10, 10}. Signal 4 is then obtained, which is associated with the present state 000 and the next state 000. Hence, the 180 deg rotation of signal 0 is signal 4.
- For a 270 deg rotation, the all-zero sequence {00, 00, 00, 00} changes to the sequence {11, 11, 11, 11}. Signal 6 is then obtained, which is associated with the present state 111 and the next state 111. Hence, the 270 deg rotation of signal 0 is signal 6.

It can be seen that the code is transparent to multiples of 90 deg rotation and is called a 90 deg phase-invariant or transparent code. Note that the code

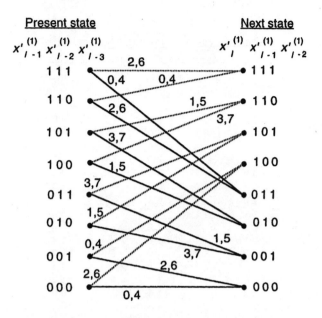

Figure 7.19 Trellis diagram of eight-state, 90 deg phase-invariant, rate-2/3 nonlinear convolutional encoder in Figure 7.17.

Table 7.3

Effect on Input Information Bits $x'^{(1)}_{p'} x'^{(2)}_{p'}$
After Rotation

		For $x'^{(2)}_{p'} x'^{(1)}_{p'}$		
Rotation	00	01	10	11
0°	00	01	10	11
90°	01	10	11	00
180°	10	11	00	01
270°	11	00	01	10

Note: $p' = l, l + 1, l + 2, l + 3$

is a nonlinear code due to the AND and inverting operations in the encoding process. Differential encoding and decoding can now be employed to correct those rotations. The differential encoding and decoding operations are modulo-4$_{base\,2}$. Tables 7.4 and 7.5 show the differential encoding and decoding operations.

Of course, we can go even one step further to find and design codes that are invariant to multiples of the smallest phase difference between signals in

Table 7.4
Truth Table for Two-Bit Differential Encoding

Previous Output $x'^{(2)}_{l-1} x'^{(1)}_{l-1}$	Current Input $x^{(2)}_l x^{(1)}_l$	Current Output $x'^{(2)}_l x'^{(1)}_l$
0 0	0 0	0 0
0 1	0 0	0 1
1 0	0 0	1 0
1 1	0 0	1 1
0 0	0 1	0 1
0 1	0 1	1 0
1 0	0 1	1 1
1 1	0 1	0 0
0 0	1 0	1 0
0 1	1 0	1 1
1 0	1 0	0 0
1 1	1 0	0 1
0 0	1 1	1 1
0 1	1 1	0 0
1 0	1 1	0 1
1 1	1 1	1 0

Table 7.5
Truth Table for Two-Bit Differential Decoding

Previous Output $x'^{(2)}_{l-1} x'^{(1)}_{l-1}$	Current Input $x'^{(2)}_l x'^{(1)}_l$	Current Output $x^{(2)}_l x^{(1)}_l$
0 0	0 0	0 0
0 1	0 1	0 0
1 0	1 0	0 0
1 1	1 1	0 0
0 0	0 1	0 1
0 1	1 0	0 1
1 0	1 1	0 1
1 1	0 0	0 1
0 0	1 0	1 0
0 1	1 1	1 0
1 0	0 0	1 0
1 1	0 1	1 0
0 0	1 1	1 1
0 1	0 0	1 1
1 0	0 1	1 1
1 1	1 0	1 1

the signal constellation diagram. Researchers have found binary, nonlinear codes and nonbinary, linear codes that give total phase-invariant properties [44,47,63,65].

7.3 MULTIDIMENSIONAL LATTICE TRELLIS-CODED MODULATION

In the 2-D TCM schemes, we have seen that a 2-D constellation of 2^γ points is used to send $(\gamma - 1)$ information bits per signaling interval using a rate-$(n - 1)/n$ convolutional code. The 2-D constellation is partitioned into 2^n 2-D subsets with increased intrasubset minimum Euclidean distance. $(n - 1)$ of the $(\gamma - 1)$ information bits per signaling interval enter a rate-$(n - 1)/n$ convolutional encoder, and the n coded bits specify which 2-D subset is to be used. The remaining $\gamma - n$ uncoded information bits specify which point from the selected 2-D subset is used for transmission.

Example 7.6

We can use a rate-2/3 convolutional code with 32-PSK signals to send four bits of information per signaling interval. In this case, $n = 3$ and $\gamma = 5$. The 2-D 32-PSK constellation is partitioned into eight 2-D subsets. Two of the four information bits per signaling interval enter a rate-2/3 convolutional encoder and the three coded bits specify which 2-D subset is to be used. The remaining two uncoded information bits specify which point from the selected 2-D subset is used for transmission.

To improve the performance of the 2-D TCM schemes, more powerful convolutional codes are required, but the coding gain increases more slowly as the number of encoder states increase. Is there any other alternative to improve the performance, say, with multi-D TCM schemes? The answer is yes. As the number of dimensions increases, more space is available for signal design. A simple way to generate a multi-D TCM signal is by time division. If we add a redundant bit per signaling interval and send the 2-D TCM signals N times, a 2N-dimensional signal can be obtained. The 2N-dimensional signal can be regarded as a point in a 2N-dimensional Euclidean vector space with 2N axes. The 2N axes are orthogonal (at a right angle) to each other. A 2N-component real vector can, therefore, be used to pinpoint the signal in the 2N-dimensional Euclidean vector space. The elements in the 2N-component real vector are the orthogonal projections of the 2N-dimensional signal to the 2N axes of the 2N-dimensional Euclidean vector space. A 2-D TCM scheme can, therefore, be extended to multi-D TCM scheme [24,32–34,45,49,62].

Instead of adding one redundant bit per signaling interval, a more effective way is to add a redundant bit every N intervals. This multi-D TCM scheme construction method, due to Wei [24], offers a number of advantages over the 2-D TCM schemes. As we shall see in the following sections, the mapping between the coded bits and the $2N$-dimensional signals in this construction method can be converted to N constituent 2-D mappings and the expansion in the constituent 2-D constellations are not double. The next three sections will show how to construct and partition multi-D constellations from multi-D lattices, the construction of phase-invariance convolutional codes, the mapping rules, and the Viterbi decoding method for multi-D lattice TCM schemes.

7.3.1 Partitioning of Multidimensional Lattices

What is a lattice? How do we partition a lattice? An N-dimensional lattice is simply a periodically arranged set of points in an N-dimensional vector space. Figure 7.20 shows an infinite 2-D square lattice with *minimum squared Euclidean distance* (MSED) d_0^2. It can be seen that each point lies at the intersections of an infinitely large checkerboard.

The partitioning of a $2N$-dimensional lattice is based on the partitioning of the constituent N-dimensional lattices, which is, in turn, based on the partitioning of the constituent $N/2$-dimensional lattices. As a result, the partitioning of a $2N$-dimensional lattice is finally based on the partitioning of the constituent 2-D lattices. The approach simplifies both the construction of multi-D lattice TCM schemes and the decoding procedures. The size of the constituent 2-D lattices and the peak-to-average signal power ratio can also be reduced, which is desirable for practical data transmission systems. Two examples are given to show the concept of partitioning *four-dimensional* (4-D) and *eight-dimensional* (8-D) lattices with MSED d_0^2. The partitioning of an infinite 2-D square lattice with MSED d_0^2 into four sublattices (subsets), A, B, C, and D, with MSED $4d_0^2$, as shown in Figure 7.21, is taken as the constituent 2-D lattice for Examples 7.7 and 7.8.

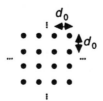

Figure 7.20 An infinite 2-D square lattice.

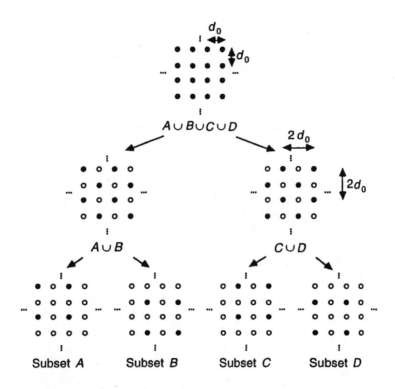

Figure 7.21 Partitioning of an infinite 2-D square lattice.

Example 7.7

Figure 7.22 shows the partitioning of a 4-D lattice with MSED d_0^2 into two 4-D family lattices with MSED $2d_0^2$ and eight 4-D sublattices with MSED $4d_0^2$. The partitioning of the 4-D lattice is based on the partitioning of two constituent 2-D lattices, as shown in Figure 7.23. The first constituent 2-D lattice with MSED d_0^2 is first partitioned into two 2-D families $A \cup B$ and $C \cup D$ with MSED $2d_0^2$ (see Figure 7.21), where $U \cup V$ denotes the union of U and V. The 2-D families are further partitioned into four 2-D sublattices A, B, C, and D with MSED $4d_0^2$. Similarly, the second constituent 2-D lattice with MSED d_0^2 is first partitioned into two 2-D families $A \cup B$ and $C \cup D$ with MSED $2d_0^2$. The 2-D families are further partitioned into four 2-D sublattices A, B, C, and D with MSED $4d_0^2$.

To obtain the 4-D sublattices, we first form sixteen 4-D "types" by concatenation of a pair of 2-D sublattices, denoted as $(A \times A)$, $(A \times B)$, . . . , $(A \times D)$,

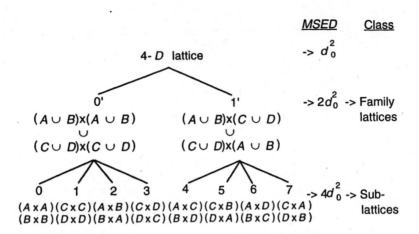

Figure 7.22 Partitioning of 4-D lattice.

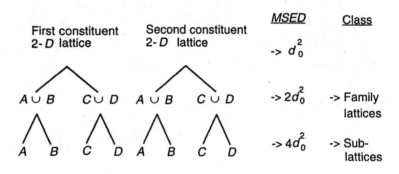

Figure 7.23 Partitioning of constituent 2-D lattices.

$(B \times A)$, $(B \times B)$, . . . , $(B \times D)$, . . . , $(D \times A)$, $(D \times B)$, . . . , $(D \times D)$, where $U \times V$ denotes the Cartesian product of sets U and V. The MSED of each 4-D type is $4d_0^2$, same as the 2-D sublattices. The sixteen 4-D types are grouped into eight 4-D sublattices, denoted as 0, 1, . . . , 7. The MSED of each 4-D sublattice is maintained at $4d_0^2$ and can be verified as follows. The two first constituent 2-D sublattices associated with the two 4-D types in each 4-D sublattice span a 2-D family of $A \cup B$ or $C \cup D$. Also, the two second constituent 2-D sublattices associated with the two 4-D types in each 4-D sublattice span a 2-D family of $A \cup B$ or $C \cup D$. Each 2-D family has MSED of $2d_0^2$. Therefore, a 4-D sublattice has MSED of $2d_0^2 + 2d_0^2 = 4d_0^2$ (same MSED as the 4-D types).

The two 4-D family lattices may be obtained from the constituent 2-D family lattices using the same approach. Therefore, we concatenate a pair of 2-D family lattices to form four 4-D types, denoted as $(A \cup B) \times (A \cup B)$, $(A \cup B) \times (C \cup D)$, $(C \cup D) \times (A \cup B)$, and $(C \cup D) \times (C \cup D)$. Each of those four 4-D types has MSED of $2d_0^2$. The 4-D types are grouped into two 4-D family lattices, denoted as $0'$ and $1'$. The lattice $[(A \cup B) \times (A \cup B)] \cup [(C \cup D) \times (C \cup D)]$ belongs to the 4-D family lattice $0'$. The MSED of each 4-D family lattice is maintained at $2d_0^2$. It is left as an exercise for the reader to verify that the MSED of each 4-D family lattice is $2d_0^2$.

Example 7.8

Figure 7.24 shows the partitioning of an 8-D lattice with MSED d_0^2 into two 8-D family lattices with MSED $2d_0^2$ and sixteen 8-D sublattices with MSED $4d_0^2$. The partitioning of the 8-D lattice is based on the partitioning of two constituent 4-D lattices as shown in Figure 7.25.

To obtain the 8-D sublattices, we form sixty-four 8-D types by concatenation of a pair of 4-D sublattices, denoted as $(0,0)$, $(0,1)$, . . . , $(0,7)$, $(1,0)$, $(1,1)$, . . . , $(1,7)$, . . . , $(7,0)$, $(7,1)$, . . . , $(7,7)$. The MSED of each 8-D type is $4d_0^2$, the same as the 4-D sublattices. The sixty-four 8-D types are grouped into sixteen 8-D sublattices, denoted as 0^*, 1^*, . . . , 15^*. The MSED of each 8-D sublattice is also maintained at $4d_0^2$.

Other ways to partition the 8-D lattice into sixteen 8-D sublattices to give the same distance properties are possible, but they do not give phase-invariant property.

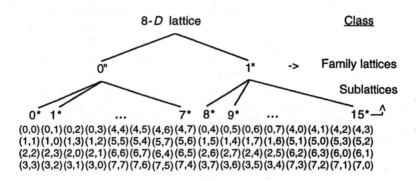

Figure 7.24 Partitioning of 8-D lattice.

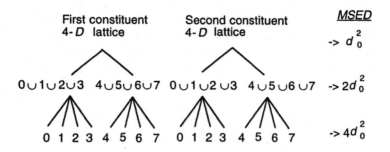

Figure 7.25 Partitioning of constituent 4-D lattices.

The general picture of partitioning a $2N$-dimensional lattice is shown in Figure 7.26.

The partitioning of a $2N$-dimensional lattice into families, subfamilies, and sublattices with increasing MSED (a factor of 2) is done by

1. Partitioning its constituent N-dimensional lattices into families, subfamilies, and sublattices with the same increasing degree of MSED;
2. Forming $2N$-dimensional types (a concatenation of a pair of N-dimensional sublattices);
3. Grouping the $2N$-dimensional types into $2N$-dimensional sublattices with the same MSED as the constituent N-dimensional sublattices.

$2N$-dimensional subfamilies or families can be obtained from N-dimensional subfamilies or families of same MSED by the same principle. Also, the partitioning of the lattice is done so that each sublattice is phase-invariant to as many phase ambiguities as possible. Then, the construction of phase-invariant convolutional code using those $2N$-dimensional sublattices does not need to consider the phase ambiguities, and the code is much easier to construct. Of course, one can concatenate N 2-D sublattices to form all the $2N$-dimensional subtypes, as shown in Figure 7.26. In that case, the $2N$-dimensional lattices are partitioned to the lowest level. No grouping is now needed. However, the construction of the convolutional code becomes difficult, and the complexity of the maximum-likelihood decoding would be impractical to implement.

In the 2-D TCM schemes, a 2-D constellation of 2^γ points is used to send $(\gamma - 1)$ information bits per signaling interval using a rate-$(n - 1)/n$ convolutional code. The 2-D constellation is partitioned into 2^n 2-D subsets with increased intrasubset minimum Euclidean distance. $(n - 1)$ of the $(\gamma - 1)$ information bits per signaling interval enter the rate-$(n - 1)/n$ convolutional encoder, and the n coded bits specify which 2-D subset is to be used. The remaining

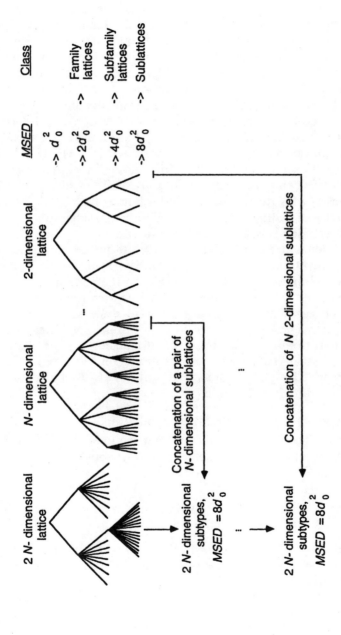

Figure 7.26 Partitioning of a 2N-dimensional lattice.

$\gamma - n$ uncoded information bits specify which point from the chosen 2-D subset is used for transmission. The 2-D coded scheme of 2^γ points is compared with the corresponding 2-D uncoded scheme of $2^{(\gamma-1)}$ points at the same information bits per signaling interval. (We encountered such a scheme in Example 7.6.)

In the $2N$-dimensional lattice TCM schemes, where N is a power of 2, a $2N$-dimensional constellation of $2^{N(\gamma-1)+1}$ points is used to send $(\gamma - 1)$ information bits per signaling interval using a rate-$(n - 1)/n$ convolutional code. The $2N$-dimensional constellation is partitioned into 2^n $2N$-dimensional subsets with increased intrasubset minimum Euclidean distance. $(n - 1)$ of the $N(\gamma - 1)$ information bits arriving in each block of N signaling intervals enter the rate-$(n - 1)/n$ convolutional encoder, and the n coded bits specify which $2N$-dimensional subset is to be used. The remaining $N(\gamma - 1) - (n - 1)$ uncoded information bits, with the help of a $2N$-dimensional block encoder and a bit converter, specify which point from the chosen $2N$-dimensional subset is used for transmission. The $2N$-dimensional coded scheme of $2^{N(\gamma-1)+1}$ points is compared with the corresponding $2N$-dimensional uncoded scheme of $2^{N(\gamma-1)}$ points at the same information bits per signaling interval.

The $2N$-dimensional constellation with finite points can be constructed from an infinite $2N$-dimensional lattice if we bear in mind that the set partitioning of the $2N$-dimensional lattice is based on the constituent 2-D lattices. For example, we can take a finite number of points from the infinite 2-D square lattice shown in Figure 7.21 to form a finite 2-D constellation with same number of points. In general, the partitioning of the infinite $2N$-dimensional lattice underlies the partitioning of the finite $2N$-dimensional constellation. From now on, we shall use "sublattice" and "subset" on partitioning lattice and constellation, respectively. The construction of the $2N$-dimensional constellation of $2^{N(\gamma-1)+1}$ points is as follows:

1. Obtain or select a constituent 2-D constellation.
2. Divide the 2-D constellation into an inner group of $2^{(\gamma-1)}$ points (the same number of points used in the constituent 2-D constellations of the corresponding $2N$-dimensional uncoded scheme) and an outer group of $2^{(\gamma-1)}/N$ points.
3. Concatenate N such 2-D constellations and excluding those $2N$-dimensional points that were formed from more than one 2-D outer point.

As a result, the inner group is used $2N - 1$ times as often as the outer group, and the peak-to-average signal power ratio of the $2N$-dimensional constellation becomes minimum.

Note that in step 2 the concatenation of N 2-dimensional inner points gives $2^{N(\gamma-1)}$ $2N$-dimensional points in the $2N$-dimensional uncoded scheme. The $2N$-dimensional coded scheme of $2^{N(\gamma-1)+1}$ points is compared with the corresponding $2N$-dimensional uncoded scheme of $2^{N(\gamma-1)}$ points at the same information bits per signaling interval.

Example 7.9

A 24-point constituent 2-D constellation with $(\gamma - 1) = 4$ and $N = 2$.

There are $2^{(\gamma-1)} = 16$ inner points and $2^{(\gamma-1)}/N = 8$ outer points. There are $2^{N(\gamma-1)+1} = 512$ points in the 4-D constellation.

7.3.2 Signal Mapping Rules and Phase-Invariant Code Construction

We are now ready to show the construction of a rate-$(n - 1)/n$ convolutional code, the mapping method of the n convolutionally encoded and $N(\gamma - 1) - (n - 1)$ uncoded bits into a $2N$-dimensional constellation. In fact, the $2N$-dimensional constellation mapping is converted to N constituent 2-D constellation mappings with the assistance of a bit converter and a $2N$-dimensional block encoder. The technique is best described by an example. A rate-2/3, 16-state convolutional code with a 4-D constellation of $2^9 = 512$ points and partitioned 24-point constituent 2-D constellations are shown in Figures 7.27 and 7.28, respectively. The 24-point 2-D constellation is called a 24-CR

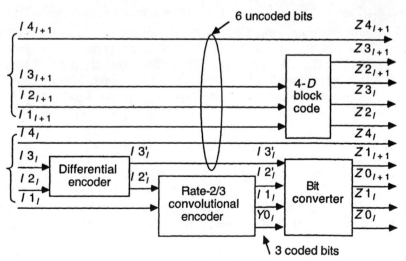

Figure 7.27 Sixteen-state code with 4-D constellation.

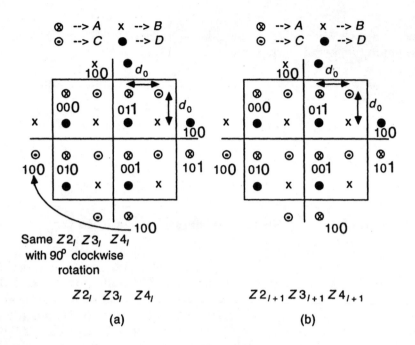

Figure 7.28 (a) First constituent and (b) second constituent 24-point 2-D signals partitioned into four subsets.

(CRoss) 2-D constellation. Each of the 24-point constituent constellations with MSED d_0^2 is partitioned into four subsets with MSED $4d_0^2$. In this 4-D TCM coding scheme, $N = 2$, $n = 3$, and $(\gamma - 1) = 4$. Mapping is performed on the nine bits $Y0_l$, $I1_l$, $I2'_l$, $I3'_l$, $I4_l$, $I1_{l+1}$, $I2_{l+1}$, $I3_{l+1}$, and $I4_{l+1}$. The bit converter and the 4-D block encoder take the three encoded bits, $Y0_l$, $I1_l$ and $I2'_l$, and the six remaining uncoded bits, $I3'_l$, $I4_l$, $I1_{l+1}$, $I2_{l+1}$, $I3_{l+1}$, and $I4_{l+1}$, and produce two groups of five selection bits, $Z0_l\, Z1_l\, Z2_l\, Z3_l\, Z4_l$ and $Z0_{l+1}\, Z1_{l+1}\, Z2_{l+1}\, Z3_{l+1}\, Z4_{l+1}$, each.

Three convolutionally encoded bits, $Y0_l$, $I1_l$, and $I2'_l$, specify a 4-D sublattice (subset) from the set $\{0, 1, \ldots, 7\}$ in Table 7.6. Each 4-D sublattice (subset) has two 4-D types. The uncoded bit $I3'_l$ specifies a 4-D type within the specified 4-D sublattice (subset).

To obtain a first constituent 2-D point, the bit converter output bit pair $Z0_l\, Z1_l$ selects a 2-D subset from the 2-D set $\{A, B, C, D\}$ according to Table 7.7.

The 4-D block encoder output bit pair $Z2_l\, Z3_l$ selects the inner ($Z2_l\, Z3_l = 00$ or 01) or outer group ($Z2_l\, Z3_l = 10$) of the selected 2-D subset according to Table 7.8. The inner group is split into two. If $Z2_l\, Z3_l = 00$, one-half of the

Table 7.6
Eight-Sublattice Partitioning of 4-D Lattice

4-D Sublattices (Subsets)[a]	$Y0_l I1_l I2'_l I3'_l$	4-D Types[b]	$Z0_l Z1_l$	$Z0_{l+1} Z1_{l+1}$
0	0 0 0 0	$(A \times A)$	0 0	0 0
0	0 0 0 1	$(B \times B)$	0 1	0 1
1	0 0 1 0	$(C \times C)$	1 0	1 0
1	0 0 1 1	$(D \times D)$	1 1	1 1
2	0 1 0 0	$(A \times B)$	0 0	0 1
2	0 1 0 1	$(B \times A)$	0 1	0 0
3	0 1 1 0	$(C \times D)$	1 0	1 1
3	0 1 1 1	$(D \times C)$	1 1	1 0
4	1 0 0 0	$(A \times C)$	0 0	1 0
4	1 0 0 1	$(B \times D)$	0 1	1 1
5	1 0 1 0	$(C \times B)$	1 0	0 1
5	1 0 1 1	$(D \times A)$	1 1	0 0
6	1 1 0 0	$(A \times D)$	0 0	1 1
6	1 1 0 1	$(B \times C)$	0 1	1 0
7	1 1 1 0	$(C \times A)$	1 0	0 0
7	1 1 1 1	$(D \times B)$	1 1	0 1

[a]4-D sublattices 0, 1, 4, and 5 are 180° invariant to sublattices 2, 3, 6, and 7, respectively. The phase rotation corresponds to the bit inversion of $I1_l$.
[b]Rotating 4-D type $(A \times A)$ clockwise by 90°, 180°, and 270° gives 4-D types $(B \times B)$, $(C \times C)$, and $(D \times D)$, respectively. The phase rotation of 0°, 90°, 180°, and 270° corresponds to $I2'_l I3'_l$ = 00, 01, 10, and 11, respectively.

Table 7.7
Mapping Between $Z0_l Z1_l$, $Z0_{l+1} Z1_{l+1}$ and Two Constituent 2-D Subsets

First Constituent 2-D subset	$Z0_l Z1_l$	Second Constituent 2-D Subset	$Z0_{l+1} Z1_{l+1}$
A	0 0	A	0 0
B	0 1	B	0 1
C	1 0	C	1 0
D	1 1	D	1 1

Table 7.8
4-D Block Encoder

$I1_{l+1} I2_{l+1} I3_{l+1}$	$Z2_l Z3_l$	$Z2_{l+1} Z3_{l+1}$
0 0 0	0 0	0 0
0 0 1	0 0	0 1
0 1 0	0 0	1 0
0 1 1	0 1	1 0
1 0 0	1 0	0 0
1 0 1	1 0	0 1
1 1 0	0 1	0 0
1 1 1	0 1	0 1

inner group is selected; if $Z2_l$ $Z3_l$ = 01, the other half of the inner group is selected. Table 7.8 shows the encoding process of the 4-D block encoder.

Finally, the uncoded bit $Z4_l = I4_l$ selects a 2-D point from the selected inner or outer group according to Figure 7.28.

To obtain a second constituent 2-D point, we replace $Z0_l$ $Z1_l$ $Z2_l$ $Z3_l$ $Z4_l$ with $Z0_{l+1}$ $Z1_{l+1}$ $Z2_{l+1}$ $Z3_{l+1}$ $Z4_{l+1}$ and use the bit converter and the 4-D block encoder to select the point. Finally, the 4-D point corresponding to the concatenation of the two selected constituent 2-D points is the one selected for transmission.

In practice, we employ a 2-D modulator of 2^5 = 32-QAM constellation to transmit the first constituent 2-D point. The modulator takes $Z0_l$ $Z1_l$ $Z2_l$ $Z3_l$ $Z4_l$ and maps to a signal point. Only 24 points are used, and the remaining eight points in the 32-QAM constellation are not used at all. To transmit the second constituent 2-D point, the same principle is used, and the mapping is performed on $Z0_{l+1}$ $Z1_{l+1}$ $Z2_{l+1}$ $Z3_{l+1}$ $Z4_{l+1}$.

In a 2-D TCM scheme, it can be seen that the 2-D TCM scheme expands from $2^{(\gamma-1)}$ points in the uncoded case to 2^γ points in the coded case. All 2^γ points are used by the 2-D modulator. However, in the 2N-dimensional lattice TCM scheme, the expansion in the constituent 2-D constellation is not double. For transmission and implementation purposes, the 2-D modulator uses the constituent 2-D constellation of 2^γ points (double the number of points used in the constituent 2-D constellation of the corresponding 2N-dimensional uncoded scheme), but the 2-D modulator does not use all 2^γ points per signaling interval for transmission.

What about the phase-invariant problem? From Table 7.6, we can see that the design of the bit converter ensures that the 4-D types are invariant to 90 deg, 180 deg, and 270 deg rotations. When a 4-D type is rotated clockwise by 0 deg, 90 deg, 180 deg, and 270 deg, another 4-D type is obtained. The phase rotation of 0 deg, 90 deg, 180 deg, and 270 deg corresponds to $I2'_l I3'_l = 00, 01, 10$, and 11, respectively. The 4-D subsets, specified by $Y0_l I1_l I2'_l$, are invariant to 180 deg rotation. That corresponds to the bit inversion of $I1_l$. For example, the 4-D subsets 0, 1, 4, and 5 are 180 deg invariant to subsets 2, 3, 6, and 7, respectively. Thus, the construction of phase-invariant convolutional code using those 4-D sublattices does not need to consider 180 deg phase rotation. To make the 4-D subsets under 90 deg phase-invariant, we need to assign the 4-D subsets to the trellis path in a certain manner. The rules are stated as follows:

1. The 4-D subsets associated with the transitions leading from or entering a state are different from each other, but they must belong to the same 4-D family $0'$ or $1'$, as shown in our early example of partitioning a 4-D lattice to eight 4-D sublattices.

2. The free MSED between two sequences corresponding to two distinct trellis paths is larger than $4d_0^2$.

3. Denote U as the 4-D subset associated with the transition from a present trellis state $S1_l S2_l S3_l S4_l$ to a next state $S1_{l+2} S2_{l+2} S3_{l+2} S4_{l+2}$ and V as a 90 deg clockwise-rotated version of U. Then V is associated with the transition from the present trellis state $\overline{S1}_l S2_l \overline{S3}_l S4_l$ to the next state $\overline{S1}_{l+2} S2_{l+2} \overline{S3}_{l+2} S4_{l+2}$, where an overbar denotes inversion. For example, if $U = 0$ is associated with the transition from the present state 0000 to the next state 0000, then $V = 1$ is associated with the transition from the present state 1010 to the next state 1010, as shown in Figure 7.29.

The assigned trellis diagram and the encoder circuit are shown in Figures 7.29 and 7.30, respectively.

The second rule can be satisfied with the following assignment to the trellis. If the 4-D subset V is associated with the transition from a present trellis state $S1_l S2_l S3_l S4_l$ to an even-numbered (or odd-numbered) next state, then V is also associated with the transition from a present trellis state $S1_l S2_l \overline{S3}_l S4_l$ to an odd-numbered (or even-numbered) next state. For example, if $V = 1$ is associated with the transition from the present state 1010 to the next state 1010, then $V = 1$ is also associated with the transition from the present state 1000 to the next state 0011, as shown in Figure 7.29.

Furthermore, we can see that the first bit converter output bit pair $Z0_l Z1_l$ select only one subset from the first constituent 2-D subsets A, B, C, and D, and the second bit converter output bit pairs $Z0_{l+1} Z1_{l+1}$ also select only one subset from the second constituent 2-D subsets A, B, C, and D. Therefore, we can assign the same bit pattern $Z2_{p'} Z3_{p'} Z4_{p'}$, $p' = 0$ or 1, with each point of the four 2-D subsets obtained after 90 deg, 180 deg, and 270 deg clockwise

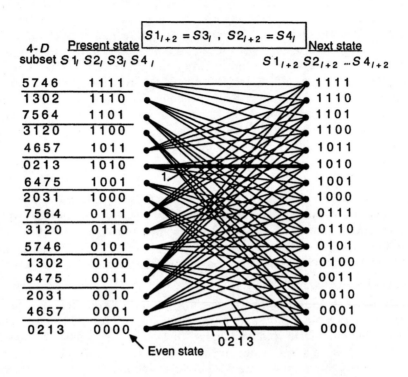

Figure 7.29 Trellis diagram of 16-state, rate-2/3 convolutional encoder of Figure 7.27.

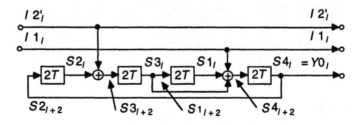

Figure 7.30 Sixteen-state, rate-2/3 convolutional encoder. Note: T = signaling interval.

rotations. The $2N$-dimensional TCM scheme now becomes phase-invariant to all rotations. Differential encoding and decoding on the bit pair $I2_l$ $I3_l$ can be employed. That is carried out with modulo-$4_{base\,2}$ operation.

In summary, three convolutionally-encoded bits, $Y0_l$, $I1_l$, and $I2'_l$, specify a 4-D subset, and the uncoded bit $I3'_l$ specify a 4-D type within a 4-D subset. The bit converter output bit pairs $Z0_l$ $Z1_l$ and $Z0_{l+1}$ $Z1_{l+1}$ specify the first and second constituent 2-D subsets, respectively. The 4-D block encoder output bit pair $Z2_l$ $Z3_l$ selects the inner or outer group of the selected first constituent 2-D subset, and the remaining block encoder output bit pair $Z2_{l+1}$ $Z3_{l+1}$ selects the inner or outer group of the selected second constituent 2-D subset according to Table 7.8. Finally, the uncoded bits $Z4_l$ and $Z4_{l+1}$ select two constituent 2-D points from the chosen group within the previously selected two constituent 2-D subsets. The pair of 2-D points specifies the 4-D point for transmission.

The ACG of the multi-D TCM coded scheme over the corresponding multi-D uncoded scheme is $10 \log_{10}[(d_{\text{fed}}^2/P_{\text{av}})_{\text{coded}}/(d_{\text{fed}}^2/P_{\text{av}})_{\text{uncoded}}]$, where d_{fed}^2 is the free MSED and P_{av} is the average signal power for the multi-D coded and the uncoded schemes.

7.3.3 Multidimensional Viterbi Algorithm Decoding

The operation of a multi-D Viterbi algorithm decoder is better explained by an example. Figure 7.31 shows the Viterbi decoding algorithm for the 4-D lattice TCM scheme in Figure 7.27 with 24-point constituent 2-D constellations of Figure 7.28.

The decoding operations are as follows:

1. Receive the first 2-D point R_1.
2. Find the closest 2-D point in each of the first constituent four 6-point 2-D subsets A, B, C, and D and calculate its associated 2-D subset metric MA, MB, MC, and MD, respectively.
3. Receive the second 2-D point R_2.
4. Find the closest 2-D point in each of the second constituent four 6-point 2-D subsets A, B, C, and D and calculate its associated 2-D subset metric MA, MB, MC, and MD, respectively.
5. Find the closest 4-D point in each of the sixteen 4-D types $(A \times A)$, $(A \times B)$, $\ldots$, $(A \times D)$, $(B \times A)$, $(B \times B)$, $\ldots$, $(B \times D)$, $\ldots$, $(D \times A)$, $(D \times B)$, $\ldots$, $(D \times D)$ and its associated 4-D type metric $MA + MA$, $MA + MB$, $\ldots$, $MA + MD$, $MB + MA$, $MB + MB$, $\ldots$, $MB + MD$, $\ldots$, $MD + MA$, $MD + MB$, $\ldots$, $MD + MD$, respectively.
6. Compare the two 4-D type metrics for the pair of 4-D types within each of the eight 4-D subsets 0, 1, $\ldots$, 7 (see Figure 7.22 and Table 7.6). The minimum metric in that pair of 4-D type is taken as the 4-D subset metric of each 4-D subset. Denote these eight 4-D subset metric as $M0$, $M1$, $\ldots$, $M7$.
7. The 4-D point associated with the smallest 4-D type metric corresponding to a 4-D subset is the 4-D point in that 4-D subset that is closest to the received 4-D point. For example, if $MB + MB$ is the smaller 4-D type

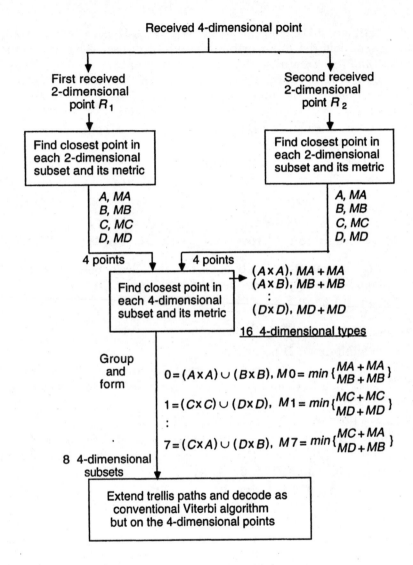

Figure 7.31 Viterbi decoding algorithm for 4-D TCM scheme.

metric, the 4-D point associated with the 4-D subset metric $M0$ correspond-ing to the 4-D subset 0 is the 4-D point in the 4-D subset 0 that is closest to the received 4-D point.

8. 4-D subset metrics $M0, M1, \ldots, M7$ are used to update the survivor path metrics in the trellis. The decoder then picks the path with minimum

metric and decodes a 4-D point with a decoding delay in the usual way. The metric update operation is shown in Figure 7.32.

In summary,

1. 2-D TCM
   a. Transmit $\gamma - 1$ information bits per signaling interval using a rate-$(n - 1)/n$ convolutional encoder.
   b. Use a 2-D constellation of 2^{γ} points.
   c. n coded bits specify a 2-D subset.
   d. $\gamma - n$ uncoded bits specify a point from the selected 2-D subset.
   e. γ bits (coded plus uncoded bits) map to a 2-D modulator. All 2^{γ} points are used for transmission.
   f. Comparison is made between the uncoded scheme of $2^{\gamma-1}$ points and the coded scheme of 2^{γ} points, that is, at the same information bits per signaling interval in both cases.

2. $2N$-dimensional lattice TCM
   a. Transmit $\gamma - 1$ information bits per signaling interval using a rate-$(n - 1)/n$ convolutional encoder.
   b. Use a $2N$-dimensional constellation of $2^{N(\gamma-1)+1}$ points.
   c. n coded bits specify a $2N$-dimensional subset.
   d. $[N(\gamma - 1) - (n - 1)]$ uncoded bits, with the help of a $2N$-dimensional block encoder and bit converter, specify a point from the selected $2N$-dimensional subset.
   e. $N\gamma$ bits (uncoded bits plus bits after $2N$-dimensional block encoding and bit conversion) map to a $2N$-dimensional modulator. This is done by mapping γ bits to a 2-D modulator per signaling interval N times. Not all 2^{γ} points per signaling interval are used by the 2-D modulator for transmission.

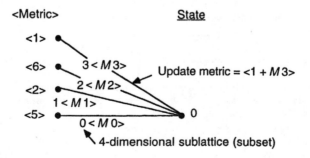

Figure 7.32 Viterbi decoding metric update for 4-D TCM scheme.

    f. Comparison is made between the $2N$-dimensional uncoded scheme of $2^{N(\gamma-1)}$ points and the $2N$-dimensional coded scheme of $2^{N(\gamma-1)+1}$ points, that is, at the same information bits per signaling interval in both cases.

7.3.4 Advantages of Using 2N-Dimensional Lattice TCM Scheme

$2N$-dimensional lattice TCM schemes have the following advantages.

- Phase invariance to all rotations is possible, and the convolutional code is usually a linear type of encoder.
- Peak-to-average signal power is at minimum due to the fact that the inner group is used $2N - 1$ times more often than the outer group.
- More coding gain (smaller constituent 2-D constellation resulting in more space in the $2N$-dimensional space with larger signal separation) is achievable with a trade-off against implementation complexity.
- Not all 2^γ points are used by the 2-D modulator for transmission during each signaling interval. Hence, a smaller constituent 2-D constellation (less than 2^γ) is used to generate the $2N$-dimensional lattice TCM scheme.
- It is easy to send a noninteger number of information bits per signaling interval.

    From Table 7.9, it can be seen that the multi-D lattice TCM scheme transmits an integer number of information bits per signaling interval. If we choose a 1,024-point 4-D constellation, we can actually transmit a noninteger number of information bits per signaling interval. An example is shown in Table 7.10.

    Due to the noninteger number of signal points in the constituent 2-D constellations, the construction of the 4-D coded scheme of $2^{10} = 1,024$ points

Table 7.9
Comparison Between 4-D Coded and Uncoded Schemes

4-D Coded Scheme	*4-D Uncoded Scheme*
$N = 2$	2
$(\gamma - 1) = 4$ bits per signaling interval	4 bits per signaling interval
$2^{N(\gamma-1)+1} = 512$ 4-D points	$2^{N(\gamma-1)} = 256$ 4-D points
$2^{\gamma-1} = 16$ 2-D inner points	—
$(2^{\gamma-1})/N = 8$ 2-D outer points	—
Constituent 24-point 2-D constellations	Constituent 16-point 2-D constellations
Uses **24-CR** 2-D constellation	Uses **16-QAM** 2-D constellation
Uses **32-QAM** 2-D modulator	Uses **16-QAM** 2-D modulator

Table 7.10
Comparison Between 4-D Coded and Uncoded Schemes

4-D Coded Scheme	4-D Uncoded Scheme
$N = 2$	2
$(\gamma - 1) = 4.5$ bits per signaling interval	4.5 bits per signaling interval
$2^{N(\gamma-1)+1} = 1{,}024$ 4-D points	$2^{N(\gamma-1)} = 512$ 4-D points
$2^{\gamma-1} = 22.63$ 2-D inner points	—
$(2^{\gamma-1})/N = 11.31$ 2-D outer points	—
Constituent 33.94-point 2-D constellations	Constituent 22.63-point 2-D constellations
Uses **33.94-ary** 2-D constellation	Uses **32-ary** 2-D constellation
Uses **64-QAM** 2-D modulator	Uses **32-QAM** 2-D modulator

seems to be impossible. In fact, a 2-D constellation of 32 points is first constructed, and the 4-D of 1,024 points is then formed by simply concatenating a pair of such 2-D constellations (resulting in a 1,024-point 4-D constellation). This is shown in Table 7.11.

7.4 MULTIDIMENSIONAL *M*-PSK TRELLIS-CODED MODULATION

So far, we have seen that the multi-D lattice TCM schemes, due to Wei [24], offer a number of advantages over the 2-D TCM schemes. What about multi-D *M*-PSK TCM schemes? This section examines the multi-D *M*-PSK and its constituent lower-dimensional *M*-PSK constellations, the set-partitioning methods, the construction of phase-invariant convolutional codes, the mapping rules, and the Viterbi decoding method for multidimensional *M*-PSK TCM schemes constructed by Wei [34]. Other multidimensional *M*-PSK TCM constructions can be found in [45] and [62].

Table 7.11
Comparison Between 2-D Coded and Uncoded Schemes

2-D Coded Scheme	2-D Uncoded Scheme
$N = 1$	1
$(\gamma - 1) = 4$ bits per signaling interval	4 bits per signaling interval
$2^{N(\gamma-1)+1} = 32$ 2-D points	$2^{N(\gamma-1)} = 16$ 2-D points
Uses **32-QAM** 2-D constellation	Uses **16-QAM** 2-D constellation
Uses **32-QAM** 2-D modulator	Uses **16-QAM** 2-D modulator

7.4.1 Partitioning of Multidimensional *M*-PSK Constellations

A simple way of generating a multi-D *M*-PSK signal is by time division. If N 2-D *M*-PSK signals are sent in N consecutive time intervals, a $2N$-dimensional *M*-PSK signal is obtained. The partitioning of a $2N$-dimensional *M*-PSK constellation is based on the partitioning of the constituent N-dimensional *M*-PSK constellations, which, in turn, is based on the partitioning of the constituent $N/2$-D *M*-PSK constellations. As a result, the partitioning of a $2N$-dimensional *M*-PSK constellation is finally based on the partitioning of the constituent 2-D *M*-PSK constellations. However, a simple concatenation of the constituent 2-D *M*-PSK constellations may appear to have difficulty achieving both high coding gains and full phase invariance at the same time [34]. The key to solving the problem is to delete some $2N$-dimensional *M*-PSK points, if necessary, formed from concatenation of the constituent 2-D *M*-PSK constellations. The approach, due to Wei [34], simplifies both the construction of multi-D *M*-PSK TCM schemes and the decoding procedures. However, the construction technique leads to many different arrangements of multi-D TCM schemes. To demonstrate the construction technique, we simply assume 4-D and 8-D 8-PSK signals for sending an integer and a noninteger number of information bits per signaling interval, respectively. Examples 7.10 and 7.11 show the concept of partitioning 4-D and 8-D *M*-PSK constellations.

Example 7.10

A $2^{2\beta+1}$-point 4-D $2^{\beta+1}$-PSK constellation, $\beta \geq 2$, for sending β integer number of information bits per signaling interval can be constructed by concatenating a pair of 2-D $2^{\beta+1}$-PSK constellations and deleting half of the 4-D points as follows: $[(A \cup B) \times (A \cup B)] \cup [(C \cup D) \times (C \cup D)]$, where $U \times V$ and $U \cup V$ denote the Cartesian product and union, respectively, of the sets U and V. Figures 7.33 and 7.34 show the 32-point 4-D 8-PSK constellation partitioned into a maximum of sixteen 4-D subsets and the two constituent 2-D 8-PSK constellations partitioned into four 2-D subsets, respectively.

The MSED of the 32-point 4-D 8-PSK constellation is 1.1716 and can be verified as follows. The first constituent 2-D 8-PSK constellation associated with the 4-D 8-PSK constellation spans a 2-D set of $A \cup B \cup C \cup D$. Also, the second constituent 2-D 8-PSK constellation associated with the 4-D 8-PSK constellation spans a 2-D set of $A \cup B \cup C \cup D$. Each 2-D 8-PSK constellation has MSED of 0.5858. Therefore, the 4-D 8-PSK constellation has MSED of 0.5858 + 0.5858 = 1.1716. For example, MSED between the 4-D points (0,0) and (1,1) in the 32-point 4-D 8-PSK constellation is 0.5858 + 0.5858 = 1.1716.

The 32-point 4-D 8-PSK constellation is partitioned into two 16-point 4-D subsets, $(A \cup B) \times (A \cup B)$ and $(C \cup D) \times (C \cup D)$, with an intrasubset MSED

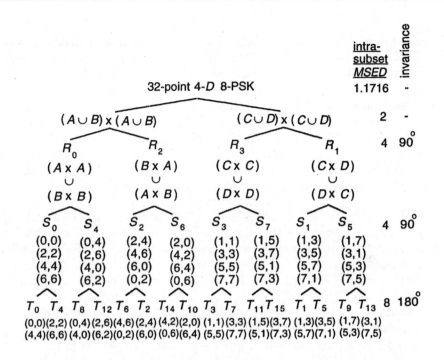

Figure 7.33 Partition of 32-point 4-D 8-PSK (*After:* [34]).

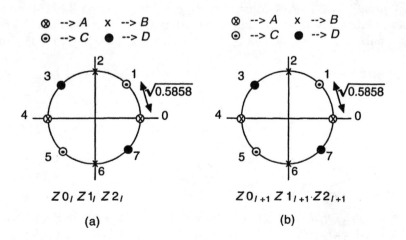

Figure 7.34 (a) First constituent and (b) second constituent 2-D 8-PSK signals partitioned into four subsets.

of 2 and can be verified as follows. The squared Euclidean distance between any 4-D points in each of the two 16-point 4-D subsets is at least 2. For example, the squared Euclidean distance between the 4-D points (0,0) and (0,6) in the 16-point 4-D subset $(A \cup B) \times (A \cup B)$ is $0 + 2 = 2$. Therefore, the two 16-point 4-D 8-PSK subsets have MSED of 2. These two subsets are, in turn, partitioned into four subsets R_i with an intrasubset MSED of 4. Those four subsets can, in turn, be partitioned into eight subsets S_i with the same intrasubset MSED of 4. The eight subsets S_i can be further partitioned into 16 subsets T_i with an intrasubset MSED of 8. Each subset R_i or S_i is invariant under a 90 deg phase rotation, and each T_i is invariant under 180 deg phase rotation.

Note that, in general, the MSED of the two subsets, $(A \cup B) \times (A \cup B)$ and $(C \cup D) \times (C \cup D)$, obtained after the first partition of the $2^{2\beta+1}$-point 4-D $2^{\beta+1}$-PSK constellation for $\beta \geq 2$ is the same as that of the 2-D 2^{β}-PSK constellation.

The construction of the $2^{2\beta+1}$-point 4-D $2^{\beta+1}$-PSK constellation for sending β integer number of information bits per signaling interval is as follows:

1. Obtain or select a constituent 2-D $2^{\beta+1}$-PSK constellation.
2. Concatenate two such 2-D $2^{\beta+1}$-PSK constellations to form a $2^{2(\beta+1)}$-point 4-D $2^{\beta+1}$-PSK constellation and delete half of the 4-D points. A $2^{2\beta+1}$-point 4-D $2^{\beta+1}$-PSK constellation is obtained.

Example 7.11

A $2^{4\beta+2}$-point 8-D $2^{\beta+1}$-PSK constellation, $\beta \geq 2$, for sending $\beta + (1/4)$ noninteger number of information bits per signaling interval can be constructed by concatenating a pair of $2^{2\beta+1}$-point 4-D $2^{\beta+1}$-PSK constellations. Figure 7.35 shows the

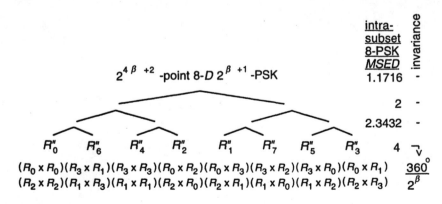

Figure 7.35 Partition of $2^{4\beta+2}$-point 8-D $2^{\beta+1}$-PSK, $\beta \geq 2$ (*After:* [34]).

$2^{4\beta+2}$-point 8-D $2^{\beta+1}$-PSK constellation partitioned into a maximum of eight 8-D subsets R''_i. The partition is based on the four-subset partitions of the $2^{2\beta+1}$-point 4-D $2^{\beta+1}$-PSK constellations, as shown in Figure 7.33. For $\beta = 2$, we have a 1,024-point 8-D 8-PSK constellation.

The MSED of the 1,024-point 8-D 8-PSK constellation is 1.1716 and can be verified as follows. The two, first and second constituent, 32-point 4-D 8-PSK constellations associated with the 8-D 8-PSK constellation span a 4-D 8-PSK constellation of $[(A \cup B) \times (A \cup B)] \cup [(C \cup D) \times (C \cup D)]$, which, in turn, spans a 2-D 8-PSK constellation of $A \cup B \cup C \cup D$ with MSED of 1.1716. The squared Euclidean distance between any 8-D points in the 1,024-point 8-D 8-PSK constellation is at least 1.1716. For example, the squared Euclidean distance between the 8-D points $(R_0 \times R_0)$ and $(R_0 \times R_1)$ is $0 + 1.1716 = 1.1716$, where the second constituent 4-D subsets R_0 and R_1 span a 2-D 8-PSK constellation of $A \cup B \cup C \cup D$ with MSED of 1.1716. Therefore, the 8-D 8-PSK constellation has MSED of 1.1716.

The 1,024-point 8-D 8-PSK constellation is partitioned into eight 8-D subsets. To obtain the 8-D subsets, we first form sixteen 8-D types by concatenation of a pair of 4-D subsets, denoted as $(R_0 \times R_0)$, $(R_0 \times R_1)$, ..., $(R_0 \times R_3)$, $(R_1 \times R_0)$, $(R_1 \times R_1)$, ..., $(R_1 \times R_3)$, ..., $(R_3 \times R_0)$, $(R_3 \times R_1)$, ..., $(R_3 \times R_3)$. The sixteen 8-D types are grouped into eight 8-D subsets, denoted as R''_0, R''_1, ..., R''_7. The MSED of each 8-D subset is 4 and can be verified as follows. The two, first constituent, 4-D 8-PSK types associated with the 8-D 8-PSK subset R''_i span a 2-D 8-PSK subset of $(A \cup B) \times (A \cup B)$ or $(C \cup D) \times (C \cup D)$ with MSED of 2. Also, the two, second constituent, 4-D 8-PSK types associated with the 8-D 8-PSK subset R''_i span a 2-D 8-PSK subset of $(A \cup B) \times (A \cup B)$ or $(C \cup D) \times (C \cup D)$ with MSED of 2. Therefore, the 8-D 8-PSK subset R''_i has MSED of 4. For example, the MSED between 4-D subsets $(R_0 \times R_0)$ and $(R_2 \times R_2)$ is $2 + 2 = 4$. Each 8-D subset R''_i is invariant under a $(1/2^\beta) \cdot 360$ deg phase rotation.

Note that, in general, the intrasubset MSED of the eight subsets, R''_i, obtained after the partitioning of the $2^{4\beta+2}$-point 8-D $2^{\beta+1}$-PSK constellation for $\beta \geq 2$ is twice as large as those of the 2-D 2^β-PSK constellations.

The construction of the $2^{4\beta+2}$-point 8-D $2^{\beta+1}$-PSK constellation for sending $\beta + (1/4)$ noninteger number of information bits per signaling interval is as follows:

1. Obtain or select a constituent $2^{2\beta+1}$-point 4-D $2^{\beta+1}$-PSK constellation.
2. Concatenate two such 4-D $2^{\beta+1}$-PSK constellations to form a $2^{4\beta+2}$-point 8-D $2^{\beta+1}$-PSK constellation.

To make the resulting multi-D M-PSK TCM scheme transparent to phase ambiguities of a multi-D M-PSK constellation, the partitioning of the constellation also is done so that each subset is phase-invariant to as many phase ambiguities as possible. Other phase ambiguities can then be taken care of by a convolutional encoder employed in the scheme. If the encoder can cope with all the remaining phase ambiguities not covered by the multi-D subsets, the encoder turns out to be linear; otherwise, the encoder becomes nonlinear.

In the 2-D TCM schemes, a 2-D constellation of 2^γ points is used to send $(\gamma - 1)$ information bits per signaling interval using a rate-$(n - 1)/n$ convolutional code. The 2-D constellation is partitioned into 2^n 2-D subsets with increased intrasubset minimum Euclidean distance. $(n - 1)$ of the $(\gamma - 1)$ information bits per signaling interval enter the rate-$(n - 1)/n$ convolutional encoder, and the n coded bits specify which 2-D subset is to be used. The remaining $\gamma - n$ uncoded information bits specify which point from the chosen 2-D subset is used for transmission. The 2-D coded scheme of 2^γ points is compared with the corresponding 2-D uncoded scheme of $2^{(\gamma-1)}$ points at the same information bits per signaling interval. (We encountered such a scheme in Section 7.2.)

In the $2^{2\beta+1}$-point 4-D $2^{\beta+1}$-PSK TCM schemes, a 4-D $2^{\beta+1}$-PSK constellation of $2^{2\beta+1}$ points is used to send β information bits per signaling interval using a rate-$(n - 1)/n$ convolutional code. The 4-D $2^{\beta+1}$-PSK constellation is partitioned into 4-D subsets with increased intrasubset minimum Euclidean distance. $(n - 1)$ of the 2β information bits arriving in each block of two signaling intervals enter the rate-$(n - 1)/n$ convolutional encoder, and the n coded bits specify which 4-D subset is to be used. The remaining $(2\beta + 1) - n$ uncoded information bits, with the help of a 4-D $2^{\beta+1}$-PSK mapper, specify which point from the chosen 4-D subset is used for transmission. The $2^{2\beta+1}$-point 4-D $2^{\beta+1}$-PSK TCM scheme is compared with the corresponding uncoded $2^{2\beta}$-point 4-D 2^β-PSK scheme at the same information bits per signaling interval and the same bandwidth.

In the $2^{4\beta+2}$-point 8-D $2^{\beta+1}$-PSK TCM schemes, an 8-D $2^{\beta+1}$-PSK constellation of $2^{4\beta+2}$ points is used to send $\beta + (1/4)$ information bits per signaling interval using a rate-$(n - 1)/n$ convolutional code. The 8-D $2^{\beta+1}$-PSK constellation is partitioned into 8-D subsets with increased intrasubset minimum Euclidean distance. $(n - 1)$ of the $4\beta + 1$ information bits arriving in each block of four signaling intervals enter the rate-$(n - 1)/n$ convolutional encoder, and the n coded bits specify which 8-D subset is to be used. The remaining $(4\beta + 2) - n$ uncoded information bits, with the help of an 8-D $2^{\beta+1}$-PSK mapper, specify which point from the chosen 8-D subset is used for transmission. The $2^{4\beta+2}$-point 8-D $2^{\beta+1}$-PSK TCM scheme is compared with the corresponding uncoded $2^{4\beta}$-point 8-D 2^β-PSK scheme at the same information bits per signaling interval but a different bandwidth. At the same information bits per signaling interval, it can be shown that the coded scheme requires less bandwidth by a factor of $4\beta/(4\beta + 1)$ [34].

7.4.2 Four-Dimensional *M*-PSK TCM: Signal Mapping Rules and Phase-Invariant Code Construction

We are now ready to show the construction of a rate-$(n - 1)/n$ convolutional code, the mapping of the n convolutionally encoded and $(2\beta + 1) - n$ uncoded bits onto a $2^{2\beta+1}$-point 4-D $2^{\beta+1}$-PSK constellation for sending β integer information bits per signaling interval. The technique is best described by an example. A rate-1/2, four-state convolutional code with a 32-point 4-D 8-PSK constellation in Figure 7.33 is shown in Figure 7.36. The two partitioned constituent 2-D 8-PSK constellations in Figure 7.34 are assumed. In this coding scheme, $\beta = 2$ and $n = 2$. To make the multi-D TCM scheme fully phase-invariant, (1) the convolutional encoder should be invariant to phase rotations, and (2) the differential encoder, the assignment of the encoded bits to the 4-D subsets, and the assignment of the remaining uncoded bits to the signal points in a selected 4-D subset should be jointly considered.

The four input information bits, Ii_l and Ii_{l+1}, $1 \le i \le (\beta = 2)$, gathered in two successive signaling intervals l and $l + 1$, are first differentially encoded. The differential encoder is a modulo-8 adder, as shown below:

$$I1'_{l+1}\ I2'_l\ I1'_l = (I1'_{l-1}\ I2'_{l-2}\ I1'_{l-2} + I1_{l+1}\ I2_l I1_l)\ \text{MOD-8}_{\text{base 2}} \qquad (7.5)$$

From Figure 7.33, we can see that the 4-D subsets R_j and S_j are invariant to 90 deg. The 4-D subsets T_j are invariant to 180 deg. To make the 4-D subsets under $\theta = 0$ deg and 45 deg phase invariant, we need to assign the subsets to the trellis path in a certain manner. The rules are as follows:

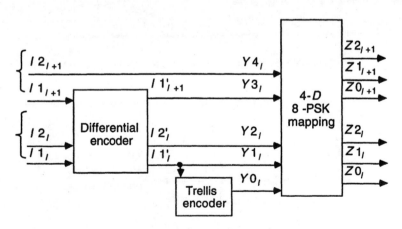

Figure 7.36 Phase-invariant TCM with 32-point 4-D 8-PSK signals ($\beta = 2$ information bits per signaling interval) (*After:* [34]).

1. The 4-D subsets associated with the transitions leading from or entering a state are different from each other, but they must belong to the same 4-D subset $(A \cup B) \times (A \cup B)$ or $(C \cup D) \times (C \cup D)$. For example, all even-numbered state are associated with 4-D subsets R_0 and R_2 belonging to the 4-D subset $(A \cup B) \times (A \cup B)$.

2. Denote U as the 4-D subset associated with the transition from a present trellis state $S1_l S2_l$ to a next state $S1_{l+2} S2_{l+2}$ and V as a 4-D subset obtained by rotating U with the phase angle θ. Then V is associated with the transition from the present trellis state $\overline{S1}_l \overline{S2}_l$ to the next state $\overline{S1}_{l+2} \overline{S2}_{l+2}$, where an overbar denotes inversion. For example, if $U = R_0$ is associated with the transition from the present state 00 to the next state 00, then $V = R_3$ is associated with the transition from the present state 11 to the next state 11, as shown in Figure 7.37.

The fully assigned trellis diagram and the encoder circuit are shown in Figures 7.37 and 7.38, respectively. The trellis encoder is linear because we

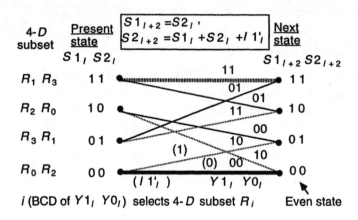

Figure 7.37 Trellis diagram of four-state, rate-1/2 convolutional encoder of Figure 7.36.

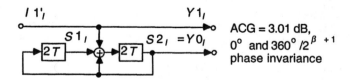

Figure 7.38 Four-state, rate-1/2 linear convolutional encoder with 4-D 8-PSK signals. Note: T = signaling interval.

have enough input information bits in each pair of signaling interval to cope with the number of phase ambiguities that were not covered by the invariance property of the 4-D subsets after partitioning of the 4-D 8-PSK constellation.

Two encoded bits, $Y1_l$ and $Y0_l$, are used to select a 4-D subset R_i, where the subscript is the *binary-coded-decimal* (BCD) value of $Y1_l Y0_l$. The assignment, therefore, is not carried out in a random manner. The three remaining uncoded bits, $Y2_l$, $Y3_l$, and $Y4_l$, further select a 4-D point from the selected 4-D subset via a 4-D 8-PSK mapper. The 4-D 8-PSK mapper takes the two encoded bits, $Y0_l$ and $Y1_l$, and the three remaining uncoded bits, $Y2_l$, $Y3_l$, and $Y4_l$, and produces two groups of three selection bits $Z0_l Z1_l Z2_l$ and $Z0_{l+1} Z1_{l+1} Z2_{l+1}$. $Z0_l Z1_l Z2_l$ and $Z0_{l+1} Z1_{l+1} Z2_{l+1}$ specify the first and second constituent 2-D points, respectively.

To obtain the first and second constituent 2-D points, the 4-D 8-PSK mapping device in Figure 7.36 can be implemented to maintain phase invariance by using the following procedure.

1. Use $Y1_l$ and $Y0_l$ to select a pair of 2-D points from the selected 4-D subset R_i according to Table 7.12.
2. To obtain the first constituent 2-D point, rotate both 2-D points by $(r/2^\beta)$ · 360 deg anticlockwise, where r is the BCD value of $Y3_l Y2_l$.
3. To obtain the second constituent 2-D point, rotate the second 2-D point of step 2 by $(s/2^{\beta-1})$ · 360 deg anticlockwise, where s is the BCD value of $Y4_l$.

It is important to note that the final selected pair of 2-D points is still in the chosen 4-D subset R_i.

The ACG of the multi-D TCM coded scheme over the corresponding multi-D uncoded scheme is $10 \log_{10}[(d_{\mathrm{fed}}^2/P_{\mathrm{av}})_{\mathrm{coded}}/(d_{\mathrm{fed}}^2/P_{\mathrm{av}})_{\mathrm{uncoded}}]$, where d_{fed}^2 is the free MSED and P_{av} is the average signal power for the multi-D coded and uncoded schemes at the same information bits per signaling interval and same bandwidth.

Table 7.12
4-D 8-PSK Constellation Mapping to Achieve Phase Invariance

$Y1_l Y0_l$	*First Constituent 2-D Point*	*Second Constituent 2-D Point*
00	0	0
01	1	3
10	2	4
11	1	1

7.4.3 Eight-Dimensional *M*-PSK TCM: Signal Mapping Rules and Phase-Invariant Code Construction

To show the construction of a rate-$(n-1)/n$ convolutional code and the mapping of the n convolutionally encoded and $(4\beta + 2) - n$ uncoded bits into a $2^{4\beta+2}$-point 8-D $2^{\beta+1}$-PSK constellation for sending $\beta + (1/4)$ noninteger information bits per signaling interval, we use a rate-2/3, eight-state convolutional code with the 1,024-point 8-D 8-PSK signal set partitioning in Figure 7.35 to describe the principles. The coding scheme is shown in Figure 7.39, where $\beta = 2$ and $n = 3$. To make the multi-D TCM scheme fully phase invariance, (1) the trellis encoder should be phase-invariant, and (2) the differential encoder, the assignment of the encoded bits to the 8-D subsets, and the assignment of the remaining uncoded bits to the signal points in a selected 8-D subset should also be jointly considered.

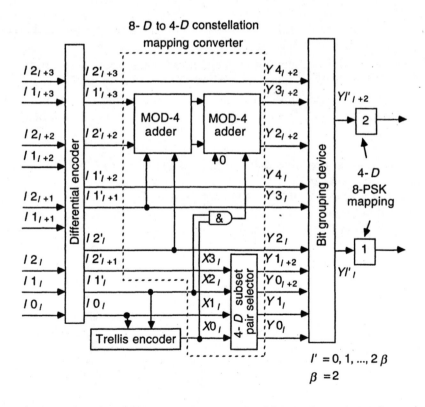

Figure 7.39 Phase-invariant TCM with 1,024-point 8-D 8-PSK signals (β + 1/4 information bits per signaling interval) (*After:* [34]).

The differential encoder of this scheme is the same as that in the last section, except that it now operates once every four signaling intervals. The eight input information bits, Ii_l, Ii_{l+1}, Ii_{l+2}, and Ii_{l+3}, $1 \le i \le (\beta = 2)$, gathered in four successive signaling intervals l, $l + 1$, $l + 1$, and $l + 3$ together with the extra information bit $I0_l$ are differentially encoded.

From Figure 7.35, we can see that the 8-D subsets R''_i are invariant to 90 deg. To make the 8-D subsets under $\theta = 0$ deg and 45 deg phase invariant, we need to assign the subsets to the trellis path in a certain manner. The rules are as follows:

1. The 8-D subsets associated with the transitions leading from or entering a state are different from each other, but they must belong to the same 8-D subset $(R''_0 \cup R''_2 \cup R''_4 \cup R''_6)$ or $(R''_1 \cup R''_3 \cup R''_5 \cup R''_7)$. For example, all even-numbered state are associated with 8-D subsets R''_0, R''_2, R''_4, and R''_6 belonging to the 8-D subset $(R''_0 \cup R''_2 \cup R''_4 \cup R''_6)$.

2. Denote U as the 8-D subset associated with the transition from a present trellis state $S1_l$ $S2_l$ $S3_l$ to a next state $S1_{l+4}$ $S2_{l+4}$ $S3_{l+4}$ and V as an 8-D subset obtained by rotating U with the phase angle θ. For each present state, the four possible next states are $S1_{l+4}$ $S2_{l+4}$ $S3_{l+4}$, where $S2_{l+4}$ $S3_{l+4} =$ 00, 01, 10, or 11. Then V is associated with transition from the present trellis state $\overline{S1}_l$ $\overline{S2}_l$ $\overline{S3}_l$ to the next state $\overline{S1}_{l+4}$ $\overline{S2}_{l+4}$ $\overline{S3}_{l+4}$, where an overbar denotes inversion. For example, if $U = R''_0$ is associated with the transition from the present state 000 to the next state 000, then $V = R''_7$ is associated with the transition from the present state 111 to the next state 111, as shown in Figure 7.40.

The fully assigned trellis diagram and the encoder circuit are shown in Figures 7.40 and 7.41, respectively. The trellis encoder is linear because we have enough input information bits in each four signaling intervals to cope with the number of phase ambiguities that were not covered by the invariance property of the 8-D subsets after partitioning of the 8-D 8-PSK constellation.

Three encoded bits, $X2_l$, $X1_l$, and $X0_l$, are used to select an 8-D subset R''_i, where the subscript is the BCD value of $X2_l$ $X1_l$ $X0_l$. The assignment, therefore, is not carried out in a random manner. The seven remaining uncoded bits $I1'_{l+1}$, $I1'_{l+2}$, $I1'_{l+3}$, $I2'_l$, $I2'_{l+1} = X3_l$, $I2'_{l+2}$, and $I2'_{l+3}$, further select an 8-D point from the selected 8-D subset.

A straightforward implementation of the 8-D mapping (see the 4-D example in Section 7.4.2) is possible, but the complexity is very high. Alternatively, we can simply convert the 8-D mapping into a pair of 4-D mappings. An uncoded bit $X3_l$ is used to select a 4-D subset pair $(R_j \times R_{j'})$ from the earlier selected 8-D subset R''_i, where j and j' are the BCD equivalents of $Y1_l Y0_l$ and $Y1_{l+2} Y0_{l+2}$,

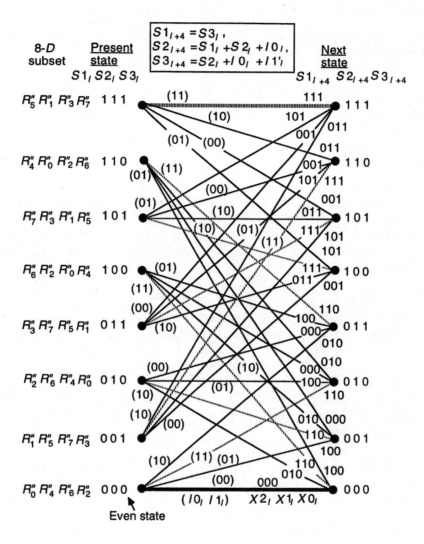

Figure 7.40 Trellis diagram of eight-state, rate-2/3 convolutional encoder of Figure 7.39.

respectively. If $X3_I = 0$, the first 4-D subset pair within the 8-D subset R''_i is selected; otherwise, the second pair is selected.

To maintain rotational invariance, some of the remaining uncoded bits are then modified by two modulo-4 adders in an 8-D to 4-D constellation mapping converter as follows:

$$C2\ C1 = (A2\ A1 + B2\ B1)\ \text{MOD-}4_{\text{base 2}} \qquad (7.6)$$

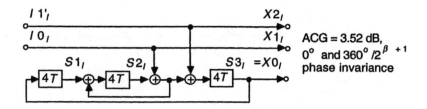

Figure 7.41 Eight-state, rate-2/3 linear convolutional encoder with 8-D 8-PSK signals. Note: T = signaling interval.

where Ai and Bi denote the ith modulo-4 adder input bits and Ci denotes the ith modulo-4 adder output bit for $1 \le i \le (\beta = 2)$. The MOD-4 adders are performing differential encoding within an 8-D point (i.e., in between the two 4-D points of the 8-D point), whereas the differential encoder before the mapping converter is doing differential encoding between successive 8-D points.

The 10 output bits of the 8-D to 4-D mapping converter are then grouped into two groups: $\{Y l'_n\}$ and $\{Y l'_{n+2}\}$, $0 \le l' \le 2\beta$. Each group addresses a 4-D 8-PSK mapper to get a pair of 2-D points for transmission. These 4-D 8-PSK mappers may be done with phase invariance by using the following procedure.

1. Use $Y1_l$ and $Y0_l$ to select a pair of 2-D points from the selected 4-D subset R_i according to Table 7.13.
2. To obtain the first constituent 2-D point, rotate both 2-D points by $(r/2^{\beta}) \cdot 360$ deg anticlockwise, where r is the BCD value of $Y3_l Y2_l$.
3. To obtain the second constituent 2-D point, rotate the second 2-D point of step 2 by $(s/2^{\beta-1}) \cdot 360$ deg anticlockwise, where s is the BCD value of $Y4_l$.
4. Use $Y1_{l+2}$ and $Y0_{l+2}$ to select a pair of 2-D points from the selected 4-D subset R_i according to Table 7.14.
5. To obtain the third constituent 2-D point, rotate both 2-D points by $(r/2^{\beta})$ $\cdot$ 360 deg anticlockwise, where r is the BCD value of $Y3_{l+2} Y2_{l+2}$.

Table 7.13
4-D 8-PSK Constellation Mapping to Achieve Phase Invariance

$Y1_l Y0_l$	*First Constituent 2-D Point*	*Second Constituent 2-D Point*
00	0	0
01	1	3
10	0	2
11	1	1

Table 7.14
4-D 8-PSK Constellation Mapping to Achieve Phase Invariance

$Y1_{l+2}\,Y0_{l+2}$	Third Constituent 2-D Point	Fourth Constituent 2-D Point
00	0	0
01	1	3
10	0	2
11	1	1

6. To obtain the fourth constituent 2-D point, rotate the second 2-D point of step 5 by $(s/2^{\beta-1}) \cdot 360$ deg anticlockwise, where s is the BCD value of $Y4_{l+2}$.

It is important to note that the final selected 8-D point, formed by the pair of 4-D points or four 2-D points, is still in the chosen 8-D subset R''_i. In summary, three encoded bits, $X2_l$, $X1_l$, and $X0_l$, select an 8-D subset, and the 8-D mapping is converted to a pair of 4-D mappings. An uncoded bit $X3_l$ is used to select a 4-D subset pair $(R_j \times R_{j'})$ from the earlier selected 8-D subset R''_i, where j and j' are the BCD equivalents of $Y1_l Y0_l$ and $Y1_{l+2} Y0_{l+2}$, respectively. If $X3_l = 0$, the first 4-D subset pair within the 8-D subset R''_i is selected; otherwise, the second pair is selected. All output bits of the 8-D to 4-D mapping converter is grouped into two groups. Each group addresses a 4-D 8-PSK mapper to get a pair of 2-D points for transmission.

The ACG of the multi-D TCM coded scheme over the corresponding multi-D uncoded scheme is $10 \log_{10}[(d^2_{\text{fed}}/P_{\text{av}})_{\text{coded}}/(d^2_{\text{fed}}/P_{\text{av}})_{\text{uncoded}}]$, where d^2_{fed} is the free MSED and P_{av} is the average signal power for the multi-D coded and uncoded schemes at the same information bits per signaling interval, but the coded schemes require less bandwidth at the same information rate.

7.4.4 Multidimensional Viterbi Algorithm Decoding

7.4.4.1 Four-Dimensional 8-PSK TCM Scheme

Referring to the example of the 4-D 8-PSK TCM scheme for sending $\beta = 2$ integer number of information bits per signaling interval, the block diagram of a 4-D TCM scheme with Viterbi algorithm decoder is shown in Figure 7.42.

The decoding operations are as follows:

1. Receive the first 2-D point.
2. Find the closest 2-D point in each of the four 2-point 2-D subsets, A, B, C, and D and calculates its associated 2-D subset metric, MA, MB, MC, and MD, respectively.

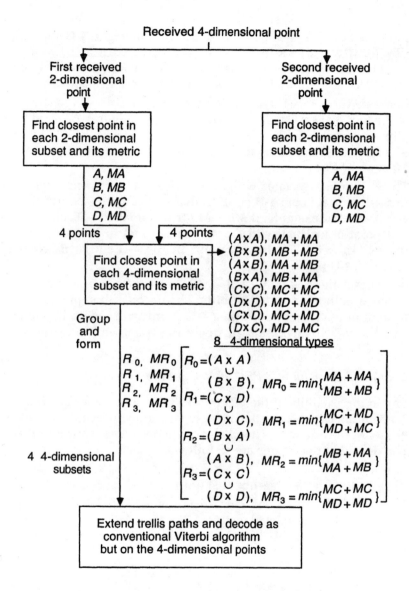

Figure 7.42 Viterbi decoding algorithm for 4-D *M*-PSK TCM scheme.

3. Receive the second 2-D point.

4. Find the closest 2-D point in each of the four 2-point 2-D subsets, *A*, *B*, *C*, and *D* and calculate its associated 2-D subset metric, *MA*, *MB*, *MC*, and *MD*, respectively.

5. Find the closest 4-D point in each of the eight 4-D types, $(A \times A)$, $(B \times B)$, $(B \times A)$, $(A \times B)$, $(C \times C)$, $(D \times D)$, $(C \times D)$ and $(D \times C)$, and its associated 4-D type metric, $MA + MA$, $MB + MB$, $MB + MA$, $MA + MB$, $MC + MC$, $MD + MD$, $MC + MD$, and $MD + MC$, respectively.

6. Compare the two 4-D type metrics for the pair of 4-D types within each of the four 4-D subsets R_0, R_1, R_2, and R_3 (see Figures 7.33 and 7.42). The minimum metric in that pair of 4-D type is taken as the 4-D subset metric of each 4-D subset. Denote those four 4-D subset metrics as MR_0, MR_1, MR_2, and MR_3.

7. The 4-D point associated with the smallest 4-D type metric corresponding to a 4-D subset is the 4-D point in that 4-D subset closest to the received 4-D point. For example, if $MB + MB$ is the smaller 4-D subset metric, the 4-D point associated with the 4-D subset metric MR_0 corresponding to the 4-D subset R_0 is the 4-D point in the 4-D subset R_0 closest to the received 4-D point.

8. 4-D subset metrics, MR_0, MR_1, MR_2, and MR_3, are used to update the survivor path metrics in the trellis. The decoder then picks the path with minimum metric and decodes a 4-D point with a decoding delay in the usual way. The metric update operation is shown in Figure 7.43.

7.4.4.2 Eight-Dimensional 8-PSK TCM Scheme

Referring to the example of the 8-D 8-PSK TCM scheme for sending $\beta + (1/4)$ noninteger number of information bits per signaling interval, the block diagram of an 8-D TCM scheme with Viterbi algorithm decoder is shown in Figure 7.44. The decoding operations are as follows:

1. Receive the first and second 2-D points.
2. Find the first and second closest points in each 4-D subset, R_0, R_1, R_2, and R_3, and its associated metric, MR_0, MR_1, MR_2, and MR_3, respectively (see the usual Viterbi algorithm decoding procedures for the 4-D 8-PSK

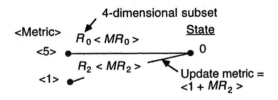

Figure 7.43 Viterbi decoding metric update for 4-D *M*-PSK TCM scheme.

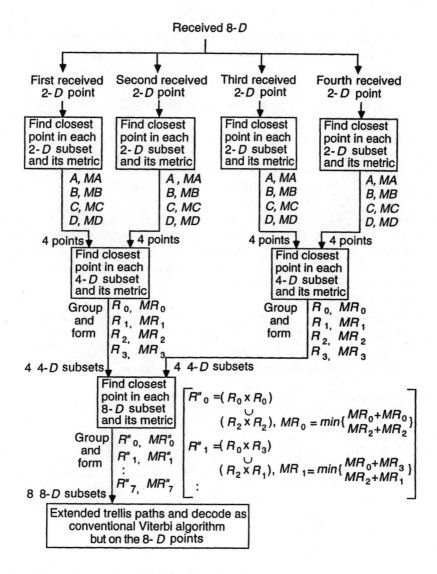

Figure 7.44 Viterbi decoding algorithm for 8-D *M*-PSK TCM scheme.

TCM scheme). There is a total of four 8-D subsets and four 8-D subset metrics.

3. Receive the third and fourth 2-D points.
4. Find the third and fourth closest points in each 4-D subset, R_0, R_1, R_2, and R_3, and its associated metric, MR_0, MR_1, MR_2, and MR_3, respectively

(see the usual Viterbi algorithm decoding procedures for the 4-D 8-PSK TCM scheme). There is a total of four 8-D subsets and four 8-D subset metrics.

5. Find the closest 8-D point in each of the sixteen 8-D types $(R_0 \times R_0)$, $(R_0 \times R_1), \ldots, (R_3 \times R_3)$, and its associated 8-D type metric $MR_0 + MR_0$, $MR_0 + MR_1, \ldots, MR_3 + MR_3$, respectively.

6. Compare the two 8-D type metrics for the pair of 8-D types within each of the eight 8-D subsets $R''_0, R''_1, \ldots, R''_7$ (see Figure 7.35). The minimum metric in that pair of 8-D type is taken as the 8-D subset metric of each 8-D subset. Denote those eight 8-D subset metric as MR''_0, $MR''_1, \ldots,$ MR''_7.

7. The 8-D point associated with the smallest 8-D type metric corresponding to an 8-D subset is the 8-D point in that 8-D subset closest to the received 8-D point. For example, if $MR_2 + MR_2$ is the smaller 8-D type metric, the 8-D point associated with the 8-D subset metric MR''_0 corresponding to the 8-D subset R''_0 is the 8-D point in the 8-D subset R''_0 closest to the received 8-D point.

8. 8-D subset metrics, $MR''_0, MR''_1, \ldots, MR''_7$, are used to update the survivor path metrics in the trellis. The decoder then picks the path with minimum metric and decodes an 8-D point with a decoding delay in the usual way. The metric update operation is shown in Figure 7.45.

In summary,

1. 2-D TCM
   a. Transmit $\gamma - 1$ information bits per signaling interval using a rate-$(n - 1)/n$ convolutional encoder.
   b. Use a 2-D constellation of 2^γ points.

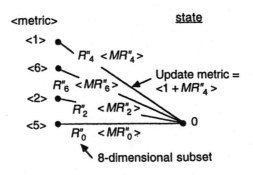

Figure 7.45 Viterbi decoding metric update for 8-D *M*-PSK TCM scheme.

    c. n coded bits specify a 2-D subset.

    d. $\gamma - n$ uncoded bits specify a point from the selected 2-D subset.

    e. γ bits (coded plus uncoded bits) map to a 2-D modulator.

    f. Comparison is made between the uncoded scheme of $2^{\gamma-1}$ points and the coded scheme of 2^{γ} points, that is, at the same information bits per signaling interval.

2. $2^{2\beta+1}$-point 4-D $2^{\beta+1}$-PSK TCM for sending β integer number of information bits per signaling interval.

    a. Transmit β information bits per signaling interval using a rate-$(n-1)/n$ convolutional encoder.

    b. Use a $2^{2\beta+1}$-point 4-D $2^{\beta+1}$-PSK constellation.

    c. n coded bits specify a 4-D subset.

    d. $(2\beta + 1) - n$ uncoded bits, with the help of a 4-D $2^{\beta+1}$-PSK mapper, specify a 4-D point from the selected 4-D subset.

    e. $2(\beta + 1)$ bits (bits after 4-D mapping) map to a 4-D modulator. That is done by mapping two groups of $\beta + 1$ bits to a 2-D modulator in two consecutive signaling intervals to get a pair of 2-D points for transmission.

    f. Comparison is made between the $2^{2\beta}$-point 4-D uncoded scheme and the $2^{2\beta+1}$-point 4-D coded scheme, that is, at the same information bits per signaling interval and same bandwidth.

3. $2^{4\beta+2}$-point 8-D $2^{\beta+1}$-PSK TCM for sending $\beta + (1/4)$ noninteger number of information bits per signaling interval.

    a. Transmit $\beta + (1/4)$ information bits per signaling interval using a rate-$(n-1)/n$ convolutional encoder.

    b. Use a $2^{4\beta+2}$-point 8-D $2^{\beta+1}$-PSK constellation.

    c. n coded bits specify an 8-D subset.

    d. $(4\beta + 2) - n$ uncoded bits, with the help of a 8-D $2^{\beta+1}$-PSK mapper, specify an 8-D point from the selected 8-D subset.

    e. $4\beta + 2$ bits (bits after 8-D mapping) map to an 8-D modulator. This can be done by transmitting a pair of 4-D points. The 8-D mapping is first converted to a pair of 4-D mappings. An uncoded bit is used to select a 4-D subset pair from the earlier selected 8-D subset. All output bits of the 8-D to 4-D mapping converter are then grouped into two groups of $2\beta + 1$ bits each. Each group addresses a 4-D $2^{\beta+1}$-PSK mapper to get a pair of 2-D points for transmission.

    f. Comparison is made between the $2^{4\beta}$-point 8-D uncoded scheme and the $2^{4\beta+2}$-point 8-D coded scheme, that is, same information bits per signaling interval. At the same information bits per signaling interval, the coded scheme requires less signal bandwidth by a factor of $4\beta/(4\beta + 1)$.

7.4.5 Advantages of Using Multidimensional *M*-PSK TCM Scheme

Multi-D *M*-PSK TCM schemes have the following advantages.

- Phase invariance to all rotations is possible, and the convolutional code is usually a linear type of encoder.
- More coding gain is achievable with a trade-off against implementation complexity.
- It is easy to send a noninteger number of information bits per signaling interval.

Tables 7.15 and 7.16 compare the 4-D and 8-D coded and uncoded schemes for sending integer and noninteger number of information bits per signaling interval. Rather than concatenating four constituent 2-D 8-PSK constellations, the construction of the 1,024-point 8-D coded 8-PSK TCM scheme can be implemented by concatenation of a pair of constituent 32-point 4-D 8-PSK constellations. The 32-point 4-D 8-PSK constellation employed in the 32-point 4-D TCM scheme is used to generate the 1,024-point 8-D 8-PSK constellation.

In satellite communications, a nonlinear *traveling-wave-tube amplifier* (TWTA) is often operated near its saturation region for maximum power effi-

Table 7.15
Comparison Between 4-D Coded and Uncoded Schemes

32-point 4-D 8-PSK Coded Scheme	*16-point 4-D 4-PSK Uncoded Scheme*
$\beta = 2$ bits per signaling interval	$\beta = 2$ bits per signaling interval
$8^2/2 = 32$ 4-D points	$4^2 = 16$ 4-D points
Constituent 8-point 2-D constellations	Constituent 4-point 2-D constellations
Uses **8-PSK** 2-D constellation	Uses **4-PSK** 2-D constellation
Uses **8-PSK** 2-D modulator	Uses **4-PSK** 2-D modulator

Table 7.16
Comparison Between 8-D Coded and Uncoded Schemes

1,024-Point 8-D 8-PSK Coded Scheme	*256-Point 8-D 4-PSK Uncoded Scheme*
$\beta + 1/4 = 2.25$ bits per signaling interval	$\beta = 2$ bits per signaling interval
$2^{10} = 1,024$ 8-D points	$4^4 = 256$ 8-D points
Constituent 8-point 2-D constellations	Constituent 4-point 2-D constellations
Uses **8-PSK** 2-D constellation	Uses **4-PSK** 2-D constellation
Uses **8-PSK** 2-D modulator	Uses **4-PSK** 2-D modulator

ciency. The levels of harmonic distortions generated by the amplifier are high. Constant-envelope modulation is required and is, in fact, commonly used for satellite communications. Because trellis-coded PSK modulation falls into the class of coded modulation schemes with constant-envelope modulation, coded PSK modulation may be the choice for the design of future satellite communication systems. On the other hand, modulation schemes with a lattice type of signal constellation belong to the class of nonconstant-envelope modulation. For satellite communications, it is possible to employ coded or uncoded nonconstant-envelope modulation schemes. However, the amplifier must be operated in the linear region.

Over the past decades, trellis-coded modulation has evolved as a combined coding and modulation technique to achieve good coding gains without bandwidth expansion or reduction of information rate. In particular, trellis-coded lattice modulation has found its practical applications in the bandwidth-limited region of voice-band data communications. Both 2-D and multi-D trellis-coded lattice modulation schemes are now widely used for high-speed data transmission over the general switched telephone network and on leased point-to-point telephone circuits [66–68]. Chapter 9 briefly describes several examples of high-speed modems employing TCM techniques for data transmission over voice-band channels.

References

[1] Anderson, J. B., and D. P. Taylor, "A Bandwidth-Efficient Class of Signal-Space Codes," *IEEE Trans. on Information Theory*, Vol. IT-24, No. 6, November 1978, pp. 703–712.

[2] Taylor, D. P., and H. C. Chan, "A Simulation Study of Two Bandwidth-Efficient Modulation Techniques," *IEEE Trans. on Communications*, Vol. COM-29, No. 3, March 1981, pp. 267–275.

[3] Borelli, W. C., H. F. Rashvand, and P. G. Farrell, "Convolutional Codes for Multi-Level Modems," *Elect. Lett.*, Vol. 17, No. 9, April 1981, pp. 331–333.

[4] Clark, A. P., and W. Ser, "Improvement in Tolerance to Noise through the Transmission of Multilevel Coded Signals," *IEE Conf. Proc.*, Vol. 49, April 1981, pp. 129–141.

[5] Ungerboeck, G., "Channel Coding With Multilevel/Phase Signals," *IEEE Trans. on Information Theory*, Vol. IT-28, No. 1, January 1982, pp. 55–55.

[6] Forney, G. D., Jr., et al., "Efficient Modulation for Band-Limited Channels," *IEEE J. Select. Areas Commun.*, Vol. SAC-2, No. 5, September 1984, pp. 632–646.

[7] Wei, L. F., "Rotationally Invariant Convolutional Channel Coding With Expanded Signal Space—Part I: 180°," *IEEE J. Select. Areas Commun.*, Vol. SAC-2, No. 5, September 1984, pp. 659–671.

[8] Wei, L. F., "Rotationally Invariant Convolutional Channel Coding With Expanded Signal Space—Part II: Nonlinear Codes," *IEEE J. Select. Areas Commun.*, Vol. SAC-2, No. 5, September 1984, pp. 672–686.

[9] Thapar, H. K., "Real-Time Application of Trellis Coding to High-Speed Voiceband Data Transmission," *IEEE J. Select. Areas Commun.*, Vol. SAC-2, No. 5, September 1984, pp. 648–658.

[10] Calderbank, A. R., and J. E. Mazo, "A New Description of Trellis Codes," *IEEE Trans. on Information Theory*, Vol. IT-30, No. 6, November 1984, pp. 784–791.

[11] Wilson, S. W., H. A. Sleeper, II, P. J. Schottler, and M. T. Lyons, "Rate 3/4 Convolutional Coding of 16-PSK: Code Design and Performance Study," *IEEE Trans. on Communications,* Vol. COM-32, No. 12, December 1984, pp. 1308–1315.

[12] Pizzi, S. V., and S. G. Wilson, "Convolutional Coding Combined With Continuous Phase Modulation," *IEEE Trans. on Communications,* Vol. COM-33, No. 1, January 1985, pp. 20–29.

[13] Calderbank, A. R., and N. J. A. Sloane, "Four-Dimensional Modulation With an Eight-State Trellis Code," *AT&T Tech. J.,* Vol. 64, No. 5, May-July 1985, pp. 1005–1018.

[14] Calderbank, A. R., and N. J. A. Sloane, "An Eight-Dimensional Trellis Code," *IEEE Proc.,* Vol. 74, No. 5, May 1986, pp. 757–759.

[15] Honig, M. L., "Optimization of Trellis Codes With Multilevel Amplitude Modulation With Respect to an Error Probability Criterion," *IEEE Trans. on Communications,* Vol. COM-34, No. 8, August 1986, pp. 821–825.

[16] Ungerboeck, G., "Trellis-Coded Modulation With Redundant Signal Sets—Part I: Introduction," *IEEE Commun. Mag.,* Vol. 25, No. 2, February 1987, pp. 5–11.

[17] Ungerboeck, G., "Trellis-Coded Modulation With Redundant Signal Sets—Part II: State of the Art," *IEEE Commun. Mag.,* Vol. 25, No. 2, February 1987, pp. 12–21.

[18] Divsalar, D., M. K. Simon, and J. H. Yuen, "Trellis Coding With Asymmetric Modulations," *IEEE Trans. on Communications,* Vol. COM-35, No. 2, February 1987, pp. 130–141.

[19] Zhu, Z. C., and A. P. Clark, "Rotationally Invariant Coded PSK Signals," *IEE Proc.,* Pt. F, Vol. 134, No. 1, February 1987, pp. 43–52.

[20] Calderbank, A. R., and N. J. A. Sloane, "New Trellis Codes Based on Lattices and Cosets," *IEEE Trans. on Information Theory,* Vol. IT-33, No. 2, March 1987, pp. 177–195.

[21] Zehavi, E., and J. K. Wolf, "On the Performance Evaluation of Trellis Codes," *IEEE Trans. on Information Theory,* Vol. IT-33, No. 2, March 1987, pp. 196–202.

[22] Collins, B. E., T. R. Fischer, S. A. Gronemeyer, and R. J. McGuire, "Application of Coded Modulation to 1.544-Mbit/s Data-in-Voice Modems for FDM FM and SSB Analog Radio Systems," *IEEE J. Select. Areas Commun.,* Vol. SAC-5, No. 5, April 1987, pp. 369–377.

[23] Padovani, R., and J. K. Wolf, "Coded Phase/Frequency Modulation," *IEEE Trans. on Communications,* Vol. COM-34, No. 5, May 1987, pp. 446–453.

[24] Wei, L. F., "Trellis-Coded Modulation With Multidimensional Constellations," *IEEE Trans. on Information Theory,* Vol. IT-33, No. 4, July 1987, pp. 483–501.

[25] Marsan, M. A., G. Albertengo, and S. Benedetto, "Performance Evaluation of Combined Coding and Modulation Schemes for Nonlinear Channels," *IEEE Trans. on Communications,* Vol. COM-35, No. 9, September 1987, pp. 969–972.

[26] Hong, M. L., "On Constructing Embedded Multilevel Trellis Codes," *IEEE Trans. on Communications,* Vol. 36, No. 2, February 1988, pp. 218–221.

[27] Benedetto, S., M. J. Marsan, G. Albertengo, and E. Giachin, "Combined Coding and Modulation: Theory and Applications," *IEEE Trans. on Information Theory,* Vol. IT-34, No. 2, March 1988, pp. 223–235.

[28] Driscoll, J. P., and N. Karia, "Detection Processes for V.32 Modem Using Trellis Coding," *IEE Proc.,* Pt. F., Vol. 135, No. 2, April 1988, pp. 143–154.

[29] Ungerboeck, G., "Codes for QPSK Modulation With Invariance Under 90° Rotation," *Mobile Satellite Conf. Proc.,* JPL Pub. 88-9, May 1988, pp. 277–282.

[30] Clark, A. P., "Detection of Coded and Distorted QAM Signals," *J. Inst. Elect. & Radio Eng.,* Vol. 58, No. 4, June 1988, pp. 187–196.

[31] Viterbi, A. J., J. K. Wolf, E. Zehavi, and R. Padovani, "A Pragmatic Approach to Trellis-Coded Modulation," *IEEE Commun. Mag.,* Vol. 27, No. 7, July 1989, pp. 11–19.

[32] Forney, G. D., Jr., and L. F. Wei, "Multidimensional Constellations—Part I: Introduction, Figures of Merit and Generalised Cross Constellations," *IEEE J. Sel. Areas Commun.,* Vol. SAC-7, No. 6, August 1989, pp. 877–892.

[33] Forney, G. D., Jr., "Multidimensional Constellations—Part II: Voroni Constellations," *IEEE J. Sel. Areas Commun.*, Vol. SAC-7, No. 6, August 1989, pp. 941–958.

[34] Wei, L. F., "Rotationally Invariant Trellis-Coded Modulations With Multidimensional M-PSK," *IEEE J. Sel. Areas Commun.*, Vol. SAC-7, No. 9, December 1989, pp. 1281–1295.

[35] Yuen, J. H., et al., "Modulation and Coding for Satellite and Space Communications," *IEEE Proc.*, Vol. 78, No. 7, July 1990, pp. 1250–1266.

[36] Divsalar, D., M. K. Simon, and M. Shahahahari, "The Performance of Trellis Coded M-DPSK With Multiple Symbol Detection," *IEEE Trans. on Communications*, Vol. COM-38, No. 9, September 1990, pp. 1391–1403.

[37] Turgeon, J. M., and P. J. McLane, "Minimal Transmitter Complexity Design of Analytically Described Trellis Codes," *IEEE Trans. on Communications*, Vol. COM-38, No. 9, September 1990, pp. 1352–1378.

[38] Mengali, U., A. Sandri, and A. Spalvieri, "Phase Ambiguity Resolution in Trellis-Coded Modulations," *IEEE Trans. on Communications*, Vol. COM-38, No. 12, December 1990, pp. 2087–2088.

[39] Fung, A., and P. J. McLane, "Phase Jitter Sensitivity of Rotationally Invariant 8 and 16 Point Trellis Codes," *IEE Proc.*, Pt. I, Vol. 138, No. 4, August 1991, pp. 247–255.

[40] Forney, G. D., Jr., "Geometrically Uniform Codes," *IEEE Trans. on Information Theory*, Vol. IT-37, No. 5, September 1991, pp. 1241–1260.

[41] Kato, S., M. Morikura, and S. Kubota, "Implementation of Coded Modems," *IEEE Commun. Mag.*, Vol. 129, No. 12, December 1991, pp. 88–97.

[42] Lee, L. H. C., K. W. W. Leung, Z. N. Lee, and M. L. Yau, "New Rate-1/3 Trellis Codes With 8-PSK Signals for Bandlimited AWGN Channels," *Elect. Lett.*, Vol. 28, No. 1, January 1992, pp. 24–26.

[43] Chouly, A., and H. Sari, "Six-Dimensional Trellis-Coding With QAM Signal Sets," *IEEE Trans. on Communications*, Vol. COM-40, No. 1, January 1992, pp. 24–33.

[44] Wu, J., and D. J. Costello, Jr., "New Multilevel Codes Over GF(q)," *IEEE Trans. on Information Theory*, Vol. IT-38, No. 3, May 1992, pp. 933–939.

[45] Benedetto, S., M. Mondin, G. Montorsi, and L. Mallard, "Geometrically Uniform Multidimensional PSK Trellis Codes," *Elect. Lett.*, Vol. 28, No. 14, July 1992, pp. 1286–1288.

[46] Calderbank, A. R., and G. J. Pottie, "Upper Bound for Small Trellis Codes," *IEEE Trans. on Information Theory*, Vol. IT-38, No. 6, November 1992, pp. 1791–1795.

[47] Lopez, F. J., R. A. Carrasco, and P. G. Farrell, "Ring-TCM Codes for QAM," *Elect. Lett.*, Vol. 28, No. 25, December 1992, pp. 2358–2359.

[48] Chung, H. Y., and S. G. Wilson, "Multimode Modulation and Coding of QAM," *IEEE Trans. on Communications*, Vol. COM-41, No. 1, January 1993, pp. 1–6.

[49] Pietrobon, S. S., and D. J. Costello, Jr., "Trellis Coding With Multidimensional QAM Signal Sets," *IEEE Trans. on Information Theory*, Vol. IT-39, No. 2, March 1993, pp. 325–336.

[50] Soleymani, M. R., and L. King, "TCM Schemes With Partially Overlapped Signal Constellations," *IEEE Trans. on Communications*, Vol. COM-41, No. 3, March 1993, pp. 435–438.

[51] Porath, J. E., and T. Aulin, "Algorithmic Construction of Trellis Codes," *IEEE Trans. on Communications*, Vol. COM-41, No. 5, May 1993, pp. 649–654.

[52] Fettweis, G., "Novel 6-PSK Trellis Codes," *Proc. Int. Conf. on Commun.*, Geneva, Switzerland, May 23–26, 1993, pp. 106–110.

[53] Eyuboglu, M. V., G. D. Forney, Jr., P. Dong, and G. Z. Long, "Advanced Modulation Techniques for V.fast," *European Trans. on Telecommun. and Related Technologies*, Vol. 4, No. 3, May-June 1993, pp. 243–256.

[54] Benedetto, S., R. Garello, M. Mondin, and G. Montorsi, "Geometrically Uniform Partitions of L × MPSK Constellations and Related Binary Trellis Codes," *IEEE Trans. on Information Theory*, Vol. IT-39, No. 6, November 1993, pp. 1773–1798.

[55] Benedetto, S., R. Garello, M. Mondin, and G. Montorsi, "Geometrically Uniform TCM Codes Over Groups Based on $L \times$ MPSK Constellations," *IEEE Trans. on Information Theory*, Vol. IT-40, No. 1, January 1994, pp. 137–152.

[56] Malladi, S. S., F. Q. Wang, D. J. Costello, Jr., and H. C. Ferreira, "Construction of Trellis Codes With a Good Distance Profile," *IEEE Trans. on Communications*, Vol. COM-42, No. 2/3/4, February/March/April 1994, pp. 290–298.

[57] Chen, C. J., T. Y. Chen, and H. A. Loeliger, "Construction of Ring Codes for 6PSK," *IEEE Trans. on Information Theory*, Vol. IT-40, No. 2, March 1994, pp. 563–566.

[58] Ugrelidze, N. A., and S. A. Shavgulidze, "Convolutional Codes Over Rings for CPFSK Signalling," *Elect. Lett.*, Vol., 30, No. 11, May 1994, pp. 832–834.

[59] Litzenburger, M., and W. Rupprecht, "Systematic Trellis-Coded Modulation," *Proc. 44th IEEE Vech. Technol. Conf.*, Stockholm, Sweden, June 7–10, 1994, pp. 972–976.

[60] Benedetto, S., M. Mondin, and G. Montorsi, "Performance Evaluation of Trellis-Coded Modulation Schemes," *IEEE Proc.*, Vol. 82, No. 6, June 1994., pp. 833–855.

[61] Szulakiewicz, P., and R. Kotrys, "New TCM Codes for 4PSK-2PSK Modulation," *Elect. Lett.*, Vol. 30, No. 13, June 1994, pp. 1032–1033.

[62] Vitetta, G. M., "Some New Rotationally Invariant TCM Schemes for Multi-Dimensional *M*-PSK," *IEE Proc. Commun.*, Vol. 141, No. 3, June 1994, pp. 143–150.

[63] Baldini, R., and P. G. Farrell, "Coded Modulation Based on Rings of Integers Modulo-q, Part 2: Convolutional Codes," *IEE Proc. Commun.*, Vol. 141, No. 3, June 1994, pp. 137–142.

[64] Pietrobon, S. S., "Comment: New TCM Codes for 4PSK-2PSK Modulation," *Elect. Lett.*, Vol. 30, No. 17, August 1994, pp. 1383–1384.

[65] Pietrobon, S. S., G. Ungerboeck, L. C. Perez, and D. J. Costello, Jr., "Rotationally Invariant Nonlinear Trellis Codes for Two-Dimensional Modulation," *IEEE Trans. on Information Theory*, Vol. IT-40, No. 6, November 1994, pp. 1773–1791.

[66] CCITT Study Group XVII, "Recommendation V.32 for a Family of 2-Wire, Duplex Modems Operating on the General Switched Telephone Network and on the Leased Telephone-Type Circuits," Document AP VIII-43-E, May 1984.

[67] CCITT Recommendation V.32 *bis*, "A Duplex Modem Operating at Data Signalling Rates of up to 14400 bit/s for Use on the General Switched Telephone Network and on Leased Point-to-Point 2-Wire Telephone-Type Circuit," February 1991.

[68] ITU-T Recommendation V.34, "A Modem Operating at Data Signalling Rates of up to 28800 bit/s for Use on the General Switched Telephone Network and on Leased Point-to-Point 2-Wire Telephone-Type Circuit," September 1994.

Combined Coding, Modulation, and Equalization

8.1 INTRODUCTION

In Chapter 7, we saw that TCM with Viterbi decoding can achieve significant coding gains on bandwidth-constrained channels and has been a fertile field of application for new concepts in communication theory. The coded modulation scheme carries the same number of information bits per signal symbol as the corresponding uncoded modulation scheme. Convolutional codes of total encoder memory K are optimally designed for free Euclidean distance rather than free Hamming distance of the code. An available coding gain of more than 2 dB can be achieved at very low error rates with simple codes for bandwidth-constrained AWGN channels. More powerful codes offer coding gains of up to 6 dB [1].

Recently coded and uncoded QAM schemes for ISI channels have been considered in [2–16]. In the presence of ISI, each transmitted signal will spread into adjacent signal intervals, and adjacent signals will interfere with each other. The process of removing interference from adjacent signals is referred to as equalization. This chapter assumes 1-D and 2-D modulation signals and begins with the theory of decision-feedback equalization for uncoded data-transmission systems over a linear channel with ISI and AWGN. It then considers the principles and combined design of channel coding, modulation, and equalization for ISI channels. The full-state and reduced-state combined trellises, drawn according to the generator matrix of the code and the signal symbols associated with the ISI terms at the input of the decoder, are considered. A (2, 1, 2) convolutional code with *4-ary amplitude-shifted keying modulation* (4-ASK) signals is studied.

Further, this chapter presents the simulated bit-error probability performance of a (2, 1, 2) linear convolutional code with 4-ASK signals and combined equalization and trellis decoding over an ISI channel with AWGN. The tolerances to AWGN of the combined equalization and trellis decoding systems are compared to the uncoded binary ASK system having the same signal symbol rate. Simulation tests have shown that the full-state and reduced-state combined equalization and trellis decoding systems achieve significant gains in noise margin. The code with reduced-state combined equalization and trellis decoding is attractive for operation on many practical linear ISI channels.

8.2 NONLINEAR (DECISION-FEEDBACK) EQUALIZER

In a typical uncoded data-transmission system over a linear channel with ISI and AWGN, a conventional nonlinear (decision-feedback) equalizer is often used at the receiver [17–19]. The equalizer is usually implemented as a linear feedforward transversal filter followed by a *decision-feedback equalizer* (DFE), shown in Figure 8.1. This is a synchronous serial system, such as could be used over the public switched telephone network. The components of the information sequence $\{X_l\}$, for $l \geq 0$, are statistically independent and equally likely binary digits, where

$$\mathbf{X}_l = [x_l^{(1)} x_l^{(2)} \cdots x_l^{(n-1)}] \tag{8.1}$$

Each $(n - 1)$-component information vector $\mathbf{X}_l$ is mapped onto a signal point in the 2-D signal constellation diagram. The mapping is one-to-one, such that

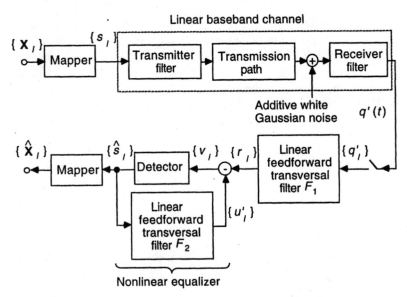

Figure 8.1 Model of an uncoded digital data-transmission system with nonlinear equalization.

each $\mathbf{X}_l$ maps uniquely onto a signal point in the signal space. The binary information sequence $\{\mathbf{X}_l\}$ to be transmitted, therefore, is carried by the signal symbols $\{s_l\}$, which have any one of the 2^{n-1} possible values, so that s_l has a mean-square value of unity. The signals symbols $\{s_l\}$ are spaced at regular time intervals.

The transmission path includes a 2^{n-1}-ary modulator at the transmitter, a bandpass transmission path such as a telephone circuit, and a coherent demodulator at the receiver. The transmitter filter, transmission path, and receiver filter together form a linear baseband channel. The receiver filter is a lowpass filter having a flat amplitude response and linear phase characteristic over the passband and a cut-off frequency (in hertz) at half the signal symbol rate. The output signal from the receiver filter is sampled once per signal waveform. The noise samples at the output of the sampler are statistically independent Gaussian random variables with zero mean and fixed variance σ^2 along each dimension. Samples at the output of the sampler are fed to the linear feedforward transversal filter F_1. The filter F_1 is here acting as an all-pass network that removes all phase distortion introduced by the channel into the received and sampled signal q_l' but does not change any amplitude distortion in this signal. It further processes the sampled impulse response of the linear baseband channel to be "minimum phase," which implies that the energy of a signal is concentrated as much as possible toward the first few samples. The resulting nonlinear equalizer gives the maximum signal-to-noise power spectral density ratio in the equalized signal, subject to exact equalization of the channel and with no change in signal level introduced by the filter F_1. Furthermore, the filter F_1 does not change the statistics of the noise samples [17,19], so they remain statistically independent Gaussian variables with zero means and variance σ^2 along each dimension. The receiver filter, sampler, and transversal filter F_1 together form a sample-whitened matched filter [17,19].

The sampled impulse response of the baseband channel, sampler, and transversal filter F_1 can be modeled by the $(\mu + 1)$-component complex vector

$$\mathbf{B} = [b_0 b_1 \cdots b_\mu] \tag{8.2}$$

which is such that $b_0 \neq 0$ and $b_i = 0$ for $i < 0$ and $i > \mu$, the delay in transmission being neglected. $b_1, b_2, \ldots, b_\mu$ correspond to the components in vector $\mathbf{B}$ that introduce ISI, and $\mathbf{B}$ is either time-invariant or else varies only slowly with time. Figure 8.2 shows the equivalent model of the uncoded system of Figure 8.1.

The complex-valued received signal sample at time l is

$$r_l = s_l b_0 + \sum_{h=1}^{\mu} s_{l-h} b_h + w_l \tag{8.3}$$

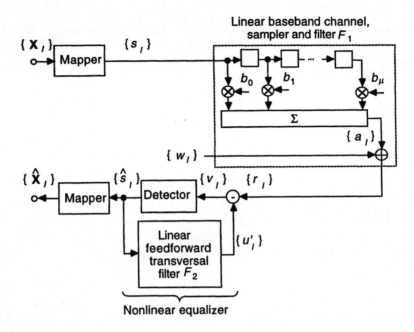

Figure 8.2 Equivalent model of Figure 8.1.

The summation term in (8.3) describes the ISI, and w_l is the AWGN component in r_l. The receiver is assumed to have prior knowledge of **B** and of the possible values of s_l. The detected value of s_l is designated $\hat{s}_l$. The linear feedforward transversal filter F_2 has μ taps, holding the detected signal symbols $\hat{s}_{l-1}$, $\hat{s}_{l-2}$, ..., $\hat{s}_{l-\mu}$, and associated with the tap gains b_1, b_2, ..., b_μ, respectively. This is shown in Figure 8.3. Thus, the output signal from the filter F_2 at time l is

$$u'_l = \sum_{h=1}^{\mu} \hat{s}_{l-h} b_h \qquad (8.4)$$

which is subtracted from r_l to give the equalized signal

$$v_l = r_l - u'_l \qquad (8.5)$$

at the input to the detector. With the correct detection of s_{l-1}, s_{l-2}, ..., $s_{l-\mu}$,

$$v_l = s_l b_0 + w_l \qquad (8.6)$$

Regardless of the detected values of s_{l-1}, s_{l-2}, ..., $s_{l-\mu}$, the detector takes $\hat{s}_l$ as the possible value of s_l such that $\hat{s}_l b_0$ is closest to v_l. With correct detection of

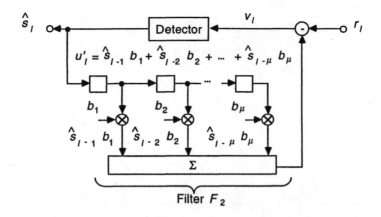

Figure 8.3 Detector and transversal filter F_2 from Figure 8.2.

$s_{l-1}, s_{l-2}, \ldots, s_{l-\mu}$, the nonlinear equalizer maximizes the signal-to-noise power spectral density ratio in the equalized signal subject to the exact equalization of the channel [17,19].

To achieve extra gain in noise margin over an ISI channel, a maximum-likelihood sequence detector can be used [2,4,18]. Further gains in noise margin can be achieved by applying error-correction codes. Section 8.3 discusses the principle and the design of combined channel coding, modulation, and equalization for ISI channels. 4-ASK modulation is assumed, but the technique is also applicable to M-ary PSK and QAM types of modulation signals.

8.3 CODED SYSTEM MODEL AND ASSUMPTIONS

The model of a coded synchronous serial digital data-transmission system is shown in Figure 8.4. The components of the information sequence $\{X_l\}$, for $l \geq 0$, are statistically independent and equally likely binary digits. These binary digits are coded by a rate-$(n-1)/n$ convolutional encoder, and the output sequence of the convolutional encoder is $\{Y_l\}$, where

$$\mathbf{Y}_l = [y_l^{(1)} y_l^{(2)} \cdots y_l^{(n)}] \tag{8.7}$$

with elements 0 and 1. The n-component vector $\mathbf{Y}_l$ is then mapped onto a signal point in the 2^n-ary signal constellation diagram. The average energy per signal symbol is unity.

In general, the design of rate-$(n-1)/n$ convolutional codes with 2^n-ary signals involves the concept of mapping by set partitioning, as described in Chapter 7. For example, the set partitioning for 4-ASK signals is shown in

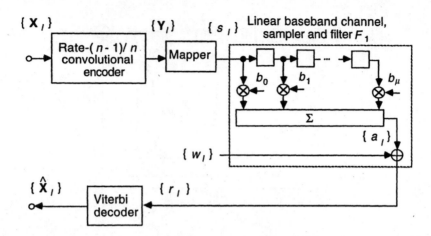

Figure 8.4 Model of a coded digital data-transmission system.

Figure 8.5; the signal points are labeled as 0, 1, 2, and 3. Figures 8.6 and 8.7 show a four-state rate-1/2 convolutional code and its assigned trellis diagram, respectively.

The sampled impulse response of the baseband channel, sampler, and transversal filter F_1 is again modeled by the $(\mu + 1)$-component complex vector

$$\mathbf{B} = [b_0 b_1 \cdots b_\mu] \tag{8.8}$$

which is such that $b_0 \neq 0$ and $b_i = 0$ for $i < 0$ and $i > \mu$, the delay in transmission being neglected. $\mathbf{B}$ is either time-invariant or else varies only slowly with time. With ideal timing and carrier-phase synchronization, the complex-valued received signal sample at time l is

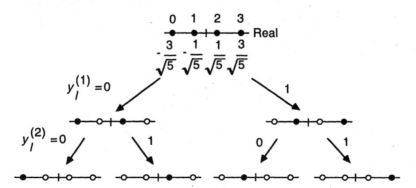

Figure 8.5 Set partitioning of 4-ASK signals.

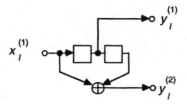

Figure 8.6 (2, 1, 2) convolutional encoder.

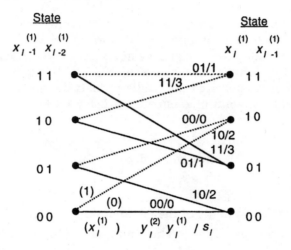

Figure 8.7 Assigned trellis diagram for the (2, 1, 2) convolutional encoder in Figure 8.6.

$$r_l = s_l b_0 + \sum_{h=1}^{\mu} s_{l-h} b_h + w_l \tag{8.9}$$

where w_l is a 2-D AWGN sample at time l with zero mean and variance $\sigma^2 = N_0/2$ along each dimension. At the receiving end, the soft-decision maximum-likelihood decoder is assumed to have prior knowledge of **B** and of the 2^n possible values of s_l. It uses that knowledge and the combined trellis (described in Section 8.4) to recover the transmitted information sequence. This maximum-likelihood decoder essentially performs the equalization and decoding of the TCM scheme simultaneously. The decoder can be implemented by means of the well-known Viterbi algorithm [20].

8.4 COMBINED TRELLIS DIAGRAM

Consider the encoder generator matrix $\mathbf{G}(D) = [D \ 1 + D^2]$ of a rate-1/2 convolutional code of encoder memory order $m = 2$ and constraint length $\nu = 3$. The encoder circuit diagram and the trellis diagram for the code are shown in Figures 8.6 and 8.7. In general, there are 2^K trellis states and $2^{(n-1)}$ paths leaving or entering a state for a rate-$(n-1)/n$ convolutional code of total encoder memory K.

8.4.1 Full-State Combined Trellis

In the presence of μ ISI terms, there are $(2^{n-1})^{\mu}$ ISI states associated with each encoder state of a 2^K-state rate-$(n-1)/n$ convolutional code with 2^n-ary modulation. The full-state combined trellis, drawn according to the generator matrix $\mathbf{G}(D)$ of the code and the signal symbols associated with all the ISI terms at the input of the decoder, has a total of $2^K \cdot (2^{n-1})^{\mu}$ states. There are 2^{n-1} transitions leaving or entering each trellis state. If the ith shift-register length of the $(n, n-1, m)$ convolutional encoder is L_i for $1 \leq i \leq (n-1)$, the length L_i is given by

$$L_i = \max_{1 \leq j \leq n} [\deg G_i^{(j)}(D)] \qquad (8.10)$$

where $G_i^{(j)}(D)$ are the elements of the generator matrix $\mathbf{G}(D)$ and $\deg G_i^{(j)}(D)$ is the degree of polynomial $G_i^{(j)}(D)$. The combined trellis state at time l can be represented as $(x_l^{(1)} x_l^{(2)} \cdots , x_l^{(n-1)} \ x_{l-1}^{(1)} x_{l-1}^{(2)} \cdots , x_{l-1}^{(n-1)} \ \cdots , x_{l-L_1+1}^{(1)} x_{l-L_2+1}^{(2)} \cdots$ $x_{l-L_{n-1}+1}^{(n-1)} \ s_l \ s_{l-1} \cdots \ s_{l-\mu+1})$, where $(s_l \ s_{l-1} \cdots s_{l-\mu+1})$ corresponds to a signal symbol path that takes the convolutional encoder from the encoder state $(x_{l-\mu}^{(1)} x_{l-\mu}^{(2)} \cdots x_{l-\mu}^{(n-1)} \ x_{l-1-\mu}^{(1)} x_{l-1-\mu}^{(2)} \cdots x_{l-1-\mu}^{(n-1)} \cdots x_{l-L_1+1-\mu}^{(1)} x_{l-L_2+1-\mu}^{(2)} \cdots$ $x_{l-L_{n-1}+1-\mu}^{(n-1)})$ to the encoder state $(x_l^{(1)} x_l^{(2)} \cdots x_l^{(n-1)} \ x_{l-1}^{(1)} x_{l-1}^{(2)} \cdots x_{l-1}^{(n-1)} \cdots$ $x_{l-L_1+1}^{(1)} x_{l-L_2+1}^{(2)} \cdots x_{l-L_{n-1}+1}^{(n-1)})$. It can be seen that the length of the trellis state vector is determined by n, L_i, and the number of ISI terms.

For a 2^K-state rate-1/2 convolutional code with 4-ASK signals, the full-state combined trellis has a total of $2^K \cdot (2)^{\mu}$ states. The state at time l can be represented as $(x_l^{(1)} x_{l-1}^{(1)} \cdots , x_{l-L_1+1}^{(1)} \ s_l \ s_{l-1} \cdots s_{l-\mu+1})$, where $(s_l \ s_{l-1} \cdots s_{l-\mu+1})$ corresponds to a signal symbol path that takes the convolutional encoder from the encoder state $(x_{l-\mu}^{(1)} x_{l-1-\mu}^{(1)} \cdots s_{l-L_1+1-\mu}^{(1)})$ to the encoder state $(x_l^{(1)} x_{l-1}^{(1)} \cdots$ $x_{l-L_1+1}^{(1)})$. Figure 8.8 shows the full-state combined trellis of the four-state rate-1/2 convolutional code associated with the three-component vector $\mathbf{B} = [b_0 \ b_1 \ b_2]$.

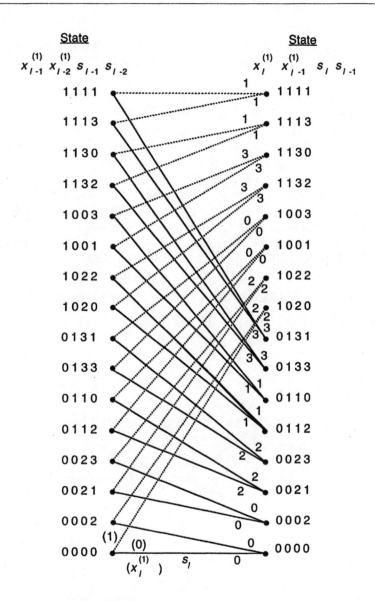

Figure 8.8 Full-state combined trellis diagram.

8.4.2 Reduced-State Combined Trellis

It can be seen that the number of combined trellis states become very large when there are a significant number of ISI terms presented in the system even the values of K and n are small. The complexity of a decoder for such a system becomes very high. A form of reduced-state combined trellis, due to Chevillat and Eleftheriou [8], is required. Here, the reduced-state combined trellis state at time l is expressed as $(x_l^{(1)} x_l^{(2)} \ldots x_l^{(n-1)} \; x_{l-1}^{(1)} x_{l-1}^{(2)} \ldots x_{l-1}^{(n-1)} \ldots$ $x_{l-L_1+1}^{(1)} x_{l-L_2+1}^{(2)} \ldots x_{l-L_{n-1}+1}^{(n-1)} \; s_l)$. For example, the reduced-state combined trellis of the four-state rate-1/2 convolutional encoder associated with the three-component vector $\mathbf{B} = [b_0 \; b_1 \; b_2]$ is shown in Figure 8.9. In general, the reduced-state combined trellis has $2^K \cdot (2^{n-1})$ states with 2^{n-1} transitions leaving or entering each trellis node for a 2^K-state rate-$(n-1)/n$ convolutional encoder with 2^n-ary modulation. The reduced-state combined trellis included only the signal symbol associated with the first ISI term at the input of the decoder; the signal symbols associated with the remaining ISI terms are not represented by the trellis. The latter can be estimated from the past history of the surviving paths in the decoder and are discussed in Section 8.5.

8.5 COMBINED EQUALIZATION AND TRELLIS DECODING

The combined equalization and trellis decoder is implemented using the Viterbi algorithm; the decoder operates directly on the full-state or the reduced-state

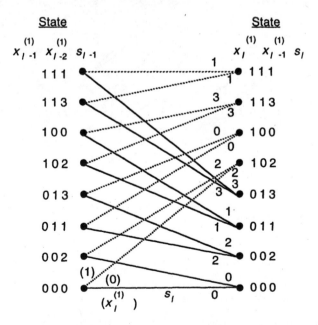

Figure 8.9 Reduced-state combined trellis diagram drawn with the signal symbol associated with the first ISI term at the input of the decoder.

combined trellis. The Viterbi decoding technique involves finding the shortest path through a weighted trellis. The decoder determines the signal sequence $\{\hat{s}_l\}$ closest in distance to the received sequence $\{r_l\}$. That is accomplished by the Viterbi algorithm, which recursively minimizes the metric

$$M_l(r_0/s_0, r_1/s_1, \cdots, r_l/s_l) = M_{l-1}(r_0/s_0, r_1/s_1, \cdots, r_{l-1}/s_{l-1})$$
$$+ |r_l - a_l|^2 \qquad (8.11)$$

over all signal sequences $\{s_l\}$, where

$$a_l = \hat{s}_l b_0 + \sum_{h=1}^{\mu} \hat{s}_{l-h} b_h \qquad (8.12)$$

To compute a_l, the estimated signal symbols $\hat{s}_{l-\mu}, \hat{s}_{l-\mu+1}, \ldots, \hat{s}_l$ are taken from the combined trellis and the associated surviving path histories held by the decoder.

The drawback of the ideal Viterbi algorithm decoder is the exponentially increasing number of operations and memory path histories to be stored. In practice, a decision is made when the decoder has searched approximately ψ segments into the trellis. We have chosen $\psi = 6\nu$ without significant degradation in error probability performance. That is exactly what a combined equalization and Viterbi trellis decoder does. For a rate-$(n-1)/n$ convolutional code of total encoder memory K with 2^n-ary signals, the decoder here holds $2^K(2^{n-1})^\mu$ surviving paths (for full-state combined trellis) or $2^K(2^{n-1})$ surviving paths (for reduced-state combined trellis), with fixed search length 6ν and operates iteratively on the combined trellis by means of the Viterbi algorithm. Associated with any path are the corresponding sequences $\{X_l\}$ and $\{s_l\}$ and the metric. On receipt of the sample r_l, the decoder computes the metrics of all the paths entering a node of the combined trellis. That is done by adding the $|r_l - a_l|^2$ term entering that node to the metric $M_{l-1}(r_0/s_0, r_1/s_1, \ldots, r_{l-1}/s_{l-1})$ of the associated path (surviving path) at time $l-1$. For each node, the decoder now selects the path with the minimum metric. The resultant $2^K(2^{n-1})^\mu$ surviving paths (for full-state combined trellis) or $2^K(2^{n-1})$ (for reduced-state combined trellis) are stored together with the associated metrics. The decoder then makes a firm decision and decodes the information bits associated with the path of minimum metric. The process repeats in this way with the receipt of the next sample r_{l+1}.

8.6 COMPUTER SIMULATION RESULTS

The variation of the bit error rate in the $\{X_l\}$ with E_s/N_0 ratio has been measured by computer simulation for the uncoded binary ASK system with nonlinear equalizer and the coded 4-ASK systems with combined equalization and trellis decoding described here. A four-state rate-1/2 trellis code has been used in the tests. The parameters of the code and the sampled impulse-responses of the channel are given in Tables 8.1 and 8.2, respectively. The channel is commonly called a partial-response channel. The channel introduces pure amplitude distortion and has minimum phase [19]. The vector **B** in Table 8.2 has unit length so that there is no signal gain or attenuation in transmission.

Perfect timing and carrier-phase synchronization are assumed throughout. In every test, random information data are sent, and the average signal energy to noise power spectral density ratio is expressed as E_s/N_0 in dB, that is,

$$10 \log_{10}(E_s/N_0) = 10 \log_{10}(E_s/2\sigma^2) \tag{8.13}$$

where E_s is the average energy per signal symbol and is set equal to unity. For all the tests, the search length (decoding delay) ψ is fixed to be six times the constraint length of the code. The results are shown in Figure 8.10.

Figure 8.10 shows the tolerances to noise of various coded and uncoded systems over AWGN channel and the partial-response channel, respectively. For the same symbol rate, the coded 4-ASK system with full-state and reduced-state combined decoding systems offer significant improvement in error probability performance to that of the uncoded binary ASK system with decision-feedback equalization over the partial-response channel. At an error rate of 1 in 10^3, the required E_s/N_0 ratios for the coded and uncoded system over the partial-response channel are summarized in Table 8.3. It can be seen that the best of systems tested is the full-state combined trellis decoding system. The

Table 8.1
Parameters of the (2, 1, 2) Convolutional Encoder With 4-ASK Signals

K	ν	$G(D)$	d_{fed}^2	Asymptotic coding gain in AWGN channel (dB)
2	3	$[D \ 1 + D^2]$	7.2	2.55

Table 8.2
Sampled Impulse Response of the Partial-Response Channel

Sampled Impulse Response $\mathbf{B} = [b_0 \ b_1 \ \dots \ b_\mu]$		
0.408	0.816	0.408

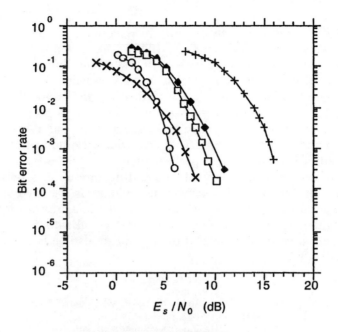

- ─+─ Uncoded binary ASK with DFE
- ─◆─ Coded 4-ASK with reduced-state trellis decoding
- ─□─ Coded 4-ASK with full-state trellis decoding
- ─✕─ Uncoded binary ASK (AWGN channel)
- ─○─ Coded 4-ASK (AWGN channel)

Figure 8.10 Performance of various coded and uncoded systems over AWGN channel and partial-response channel.

Table 8.3
E_s/N_0 (dB) for an Error Rate of 1 in 10^3 for Various Coded and Uncoded Systems Over the Partial-Response Channel

Uncoded Binary ASK With DFE	Coded 4-ASK With Reduced-State Decoding	Coded 4-ASK With Full-State Decoding
15.5	10.0	8.7

reduced-state combined trellis decoding degrades the performance relative to the full-state combined trellis decoding system.

In a practical implementation of the 2^n-ary TCM scheme for ISI channels, the decoding complexity relates to the parameters K and n of the code and the number of ISI terms μ. When the Viterbi decoder operates on the full-state combined trellis, the decoder stores $2^K \cdot (2^{n-1})^\mu$ ψ-component surviving vectors. Each surviving vector stores the information symbols along with the metric. In the presence of a large number of ISI terms or severe amplitude distortion, the implementation of the full-state equalization and trellis decoding system becomes impractical even for small values of K and n. A possible arrangement is to use a more powerful convolutional code and the reduced-state combined equalization and trellis decoding. That arrangement offers a trade-off between implementation complexity and performance.

More advanced topics on combined coding, modulation, and equalization using precoding for bandwidth-constrained channels are beyond the scope of this book. For more details, the reader should refer to a tutorial paper by Forney and Eyuboglu [21] on combined coding and equalization using precoding. Recent advances on the research of the topic can also be found in [22–25].

References

[1] Ungerboeck, G., "Channel Coding With Multilevel/Phase Signals," *IEEE Trans. on Information Theory*, Vol. IT-28, No. 1, January 1982, pp. 55–67.

[2] Forney, G. D., Jr., "Maximum-Likelihood Sequence Estimation of Digital Sequences in the Presence of Intersymbol Interference," *IEEE Trans. on Information Theory*, Vol. IT-18, No. 3, May 1972, pp. 363–378.

[3] Wesolowski, K., "Efficient Digital Receiver Structure for Trellis-Coded Signals Transmitted Through Channels With Intersymbol Interference," *Elect. Lett.*, Vol. 23, No. 24, November 1987, pp. 1265–1267.

[4] Eyuboglu, M. V., and S. U. H. Qureshi, "Reduced-State Sequence Estimation With Set Partitioning and Decision Feedback," *IEEE Trans. on Communications*, Vol. COM-36, No. 1, January 1988, pp. 13–40.

[5] Zou, G., and K. Wesolowski, "Comparison of Decoding Algorithm for Trellis Coded Modulation Using Viterbi Algorithm in the Presence of Intersymbol Interference," *Elect. Lett.*, Vol. 24, No. 9, April 1988, pp. 541–542.

[6] Eyuboglu, M. V., "Detection of Coded Modulation Signals on Linear Severely Distorted Channels Using Decision-Feedback Noise Prediction With Interleaving," *IEEE Trans. on Communications*, Vol. COM-36, No. 4, April 1988, pp. 401–409.

[7] Wong, L. N., and P. J. McLane, "Performance of Trellis Codes for a Class of Equalized ISI Channels," *IEEE Trans. on Communications*, Vol. COM-36, No. 12, December 1988, pp. 1330–1336.

[8] Chevillat, P. R., and E. Eleftheriou, "Decoding of Trellis-Encoded Signals in the Presence of Intersymbol Interference and Noise," *IEEE Trans. on Communications*, Vol. COM-37, No. 7, July 1989, pp. 669–676.

[9] Raghavan, S. A., J. K. Wolf, and L. B. Milstein, "On the Performance Evaluation of ISI Channels," *IEEE Trans. on Information Theory*, Vol. IT-39, No. 3, May 1993, pp. 957–965.

[10] Sheen, W. H., and G. L. Stuber, "Error Probability of Reduced-State Sequence Estimation of Trellis-Coded Modulation on Intersymbol Interference Channels," *IEEE Trans. on Communications*, Vol. COM-41, No. 9, September 1993, pp. 1265–1269.

[11] Simmons, S. J., "Alternative Trellis Decoding for Coded QAM in the Presence of ISI," *IEEE Trans. on Communications*, Vol. 42, No. 2/3/4, February/March/April 1994, pp. 1455–1459.

[12] Wolf, J. K., and G. Ungerboeck, "Trellis Coding for Partial-Response Channels," *IEEE Trans. on Communications*, Vol. COM-34, No. 8, August 1986, pp. 765–773.

[13] Zehavi, E., and J. K. Wolf, "On Saving Decoder States for Some Trellis Codes and Partial Response Channels," *IEEE Trans. on Communications*, Vol. COM-36, No. 2, February 1988, pp. 222–224.

[14] Immink, K. A. S., "Coding Techniques for Partial-Response Channels," *IEEE Trans. on Communications*, Vol. COM-36, No. 10, October 1988, pp. 1163–1165.

[15] Forney, G. D., Jr., and A. R. Calderbank, "Coset Codes for Partial Response Channels; or, Coset Codes With Spectral Nulls," *IEEE Trans. on Information Theory*, Vol. IT-35, No. 5, September 1989, pp. 925–943.

[16] Haeb, R., "A Modified Trellis Coding Technique for Partial Response Channels," *IEEE Trans. on Communications*, Vol. COM-40, No. 3, March 1992, pp. 513–520.

[17] Clark, A. P., *Equalisers for Digital Modems*, London: Pentech Press, 1985.

[18] Clark, A. P., L. H. Lee, and R. S. Marshall, "Developments of the Conventional Nonlinear Equalisers," *IEE Proc. F, Commun., Radar & Signal Process.*, Vol. 134, No. 2, April 1982, pp. 85–94.

[19] Clark, A. P., *Advanced Data-Transmission Systems*, London: Pentech Press, 1977.

[20] Viterbi, A. J., "Error Bounds for Convolutional Codes and an Asymptotically Optimum Decoding Algorithm," *IEEE Trans. on Information Theory*, Vol. IT-13, No. 2, April 1967, pp. 260–269.

[21] Forney, G. D., Jr., and M. V. Eyuboglu, "Combined Equalization and Coding Using Precoding," *IEEE Commun. Mag.*, Vol. 29, No. 12, December 1991, pp. 25–34.

[22] Eyuboglu, M. V., and G. D. Forney, Jr., "Trellis Precoding: Combined Coding, Precoding and Shaping for Intersymbol Interference Channels," *IEEE Trans. on Information Theory*, Vol. IT-38, No. 2, March 1992, pp. 301–314.

[23] Wei, L. F., "Precoding Technique for Partial-Response Channels With Applications to HDTV Transmission," *IEEE J. Sel. Areas Commun.*, Vol. SAC-11, No. 1, January 1993, pp. 127–135.

[24] Laroia, R., S. A. Tretter, and N. Farvardin, "A Simple and Effective Precoding Scheme for Noise Whitening on Intersymbol Interference Channels," *IEEE Trans. on Communications*, Vol. COM-41, No. 10, October 1993, pp. 1460–1463.

[25] Laroia, R., "Coding for Intersymbol Interference Channels-Combined Coding and Precoding," *IEEE Trans. on Information Theory*, Vol. IT-42, No. 4, July 1996, pp. 1053–1061.

Applications of Convolutional Codes

9.1 INTRODUCTION

Since Shannon's work in 1948 [1], error-control coding has been an active area for research and has found its applications in many practical systems. Most of the early work in error-control coding was mainly devoted to space communication systems, where power was limited and the bandwidth was not a major concern. The goal was simply to reduce the power requirement and achieve Shannon's channel capacity limit. Recently, error-control coding has found its applications in the bandwidth-limited region of satellite communications, mobile communications, and voice-band data communications. There, the goal is to reduce the power requirement and increase spectral efficiency. This chapter describes applications of error-control convolutional coding techniques to space communications, satellite communications, mobile communications, and voice-band data communications.

9.2 APPLICATIONS TO SPACE COMMUNICATIONS

In deep-space communications, the received signal power usually is weak at the earth station. Noise is additive white Gaussian, and the errors are random in nature. A large error-correcting capability is needed. Because the bandwidth is not restricted, it is possible to build a complex channel decoder. Therefore, low-rate, powerful, error-correcting codes with sequential decoding are often used. Code concatenation is also a possibility to improve system performance [2].

9.2.1 *Pioneer* Missions

The *Pioneer 9* solar orbit mission, launched in 1968, was the first deep-space mission employing an error-correcting convolutional code. A (2, 1, 20) systematic convolutional code found by Lin and Lyne was proposed for the mission [3]. The rate-1/2 convolutional code has an encoder memory order $m = 20$ and has a minimum Hamming distance $d_{min} = 10$. The code connection vectors are $G^{(1)} = (4000000)_8$ and $G^{(2)} = (7154737)_8$ in octal form. A modified version of the (2, 1 20) convolutional code with eight-level soft-decision sequential decoding, operating up to 521 bps, was actually employed in the mission [4]. The new rate-1/2 code was constructed by appending four zeros to each of the connection vectors. The modified rate-1/2 convolutional code has an encoder memory order $m = 24$ and has a larger minimum Hamming distance $d_{min} = 11$. Coding gain is about 3 dB when compared with the uncoded coherent BPSK signaling scheme.

In the later *Pioneer 10* mission for Jupiter launched in 1972 and the *Pioneer 11* mission for Saturn launched in 1973, a (2, 1, 31) nonsystematic quick-look-in convolutional code suggested by Massey and Costello [5] with eight-level soft-decision sequential decoding using the Fano algorithm was employed [6]. The code connection vectors are $G^{(1)} = (35565573735)_8$ and $G^{(2)} = (25565573735)_8$ in octal form and are right justified. The code has a minimum Hamming distance $d_{min} = 11$ and a free minimum Hamming distance of 23. The data rate is up to 2 Kbps for both coding systems. A bit-error probability of 10^{-5} can be achieved at $E_b/N_0 = 2.5$ dB.

9.2.2 *Voyager* Mission

In 1977, the *Voyager* spacecraft was launched to explore the outer planets. It reached the planets Jupiter and Saturn in 1979 and 1981, respectively. Pictures of those planets were sent back to earth stations. Two convolutional codes were designed at the Jet Propulsion Laboratory and employed for the mission: the (2, 1, 6) and (3, 1, 6) convolutional codes with free minimum Hamming distance of 10 and 15, respectively [7]. The connection vectors of the (2, 1, 6) convolutional code are $G^{(1)} = (171)_8$ and $G^{(2)} = (133)_8$; the connection vectors of the (3, 1, 6) convolutional code are $G^{(1)} = (133)_8$, $G^{(2)} = (171)_8$, and $G^{(3)} = (165)_8$ in octal form and are right justified.

Both convolutional codes with coherent BPSK signals can be decoded by an eight-level soft-decision Viterbi decoder [8], capable of very high speed, up to 100 Kbps. At a bit-error probability of 10^{-5}, the (2, 1, 6) and (3, 1, 6) convolutional codes give a coding gain of 5.1 dB and 5.6 dB, respectively, when compared with the uncoded coherent BPSK signaling scheme.

To improve system performance, the (2, 1, 6) convolutional code was used in concatenation with a nonbinary linear block code, a (255, 223) Reed-Solomon code over *Galois Field GF*($q = 2^8$) in the mission of the *Voyager* to Uranus in 1986. (The reader may wish to consult [9] for the theory of Reed-Solomon codes.) The block diagram of the concatenated coding system is shown in

Figure 9.1. In that communication system, the Reed-Solomon code is served as an outer code with block interleaving, and the convolutional code is used as an inner code as studied by Forney [2]. Interleaving is a process of rearranging the symbols in a sequence in a predefined manner.

For transmission, the Reed-Solomon q-ary coded sequence is first divided into λ sequences of $(q-1)$ symbols each. The block interleaver accepts a block of $\lambda(q-1)$ symbols and permutes the symbols. The permutation is accomplished by filling the rows of an λ-row by $(q-1)$-column array with symbols. λ is defined as the interleaving depth. Symbols are entered into the interleaver array by rows, and symbols are read out by columns. At the receiver, symbols are entered into the deinterleaver array by columns, and symbols are read out by rows. Figure 9.2 shows an interleaver with λ rows and $(q-1)$ columns. A block of $\lambda(q-1)$ symbols are input to the interleaver. It can be seen that any burst of less than λ symbol errors results in isolated errors at the deinterleaver output. A burst of length b is defined as the length of an error sequence that begins with an error and ends with an error. Isolated errors are separated by at least $(q-1)$ symbols. The total delay is $2\lambda(q-1)$ symbols. An interleaving depth of 5 is employed in the *Voyager* mission.

The system operated at about 30 Kbps. The inner convolutional code was decoded by an eight-level soft-decision Viterbi decoder, and the Reed-Solomon

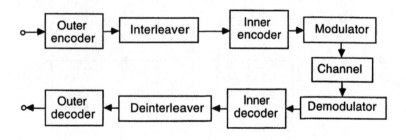

Figure 9.1 A concatenated coding system block diagram.

	$q-1$		
1	2	⋯	$q-1$
q	$q+1$	⋯	$2(q-1)$
⋮	⋮		⋮
$[\lambda(q-1)+2]-q$	$[\lambda(q-1)+3]-q$	⋯	$\lambda(q-1)$

Figure 9.2 A λ-by-$(q-1)$ block interleaver.

code was decoded by a Massey-Berlekamp hard-decision decoder [9]. As shown in Figure 9.3, with the (2, 1, 6) convolutional code alone, the scheme with AWGN can achieve an error rate of 10^{-5} with an E_b/N_0 ratio of about 4.5 dB, and the concatenated coding scheme with ideal interleaving and AWGN can achieve an error rate of 10^{-5} with an E_b/N_0 ratio of 2.6 dB.

9.2.3 *Galileo* Mission

A concatenated coding scheme with coherent BPSK signals is employed on the *Galileo* spacecraft launched in 1989. An inner (4, 1, 14) convolutional encoder used in concatenation with the (255, 223) Reed-Solomon code was designed

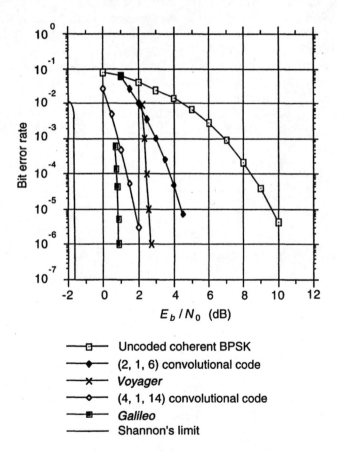

Figure 9.3 Performance of convolutional and concatenated coding systems with eight-level soft-decision Viterbi decoding on AWGN channels.

at the Jet Propulsion Laboratory [10]. The (4, 1, 14) convolutional code has a minimum free Hamming distance of 35, and the connection vectors of the code are $G^{(1)} = (46321)_8$, $G^{(2)} = (51271)_8$, $G^{(3)} = (63667)_8$, and $G^{(4)} = (70535)_8$ in octal form and are right justified. The first and third coded bits are inverted. The inversion of bits simply ensures sufficient symbol transitions in the code sequence for improved symbol synchronization. In terms of system performance, the new concatenated coding scheme was designed to provide an extra 2 dB of coding gain over the corresponding concatenated coding scheme employed in the *Voyager* mission.

Figure 9.3 also shows the bit-error performance of the inner convolutional coding and the concatenated coding schemes with AWGN. The inner convolutional code with eight-level soft-decision decoding can achieve an error rate of 10^{-5} with an E_b/N_0 ratio of about 1.75 dB and the concatenated coding scheme with an E_b/N_0 ratio of about 0.8 dB.

9.3 APPLICATIONS TO SATELLITE COMMUNICATIONS

In satellite communications, antenna size and power are restricted on board the satellite. Noise is again additive white Gaussian, and errors are random in nature. Powerful error-correcting codes should be employed. However, the available bandwidth is also limited, and high-rate codes are preferred. Many early satellite communication systems employed majority-logic convolutional codes for simplicity and high-speed operation. It can be seen that there is a trade-off between coding gain and bandwidth.

In 1969, an (8, 7, 146) systematic self-orthogonal convolutional code with threshold decoding was employed for the digital color television transmission system (DITEC) over the INTELSAT IV satellite link [11,12]. The DITEC system was built by the Communications Satellite Corporation and operated at a data rate of 33.6 Mbps. The generator matrix of the code is

$$G(D) = \begin{bmatrix} 1\ 0\ 0\ 0\ 0\ 0\ 0\ 1 + D^2 + D^8 + D^{32} + D^{88} + D^{142} \\ 0\ 1\ 0\ 0\ 0\ 0\ 0\ 1 + D^3 + D^{19} + D^{52} + D^{78} + D^{146} \\ 0\ 0\ 1\ 0\ 0\ 0\ 0\ 1 + D^{11} + D^{12} + D^{62} + D^{85} + D^{131} \\ 0\ 0\ 0\ 1\ 0\ 0\ 0\ 1 + D^{21} + D^{25} + D^{39} + D^{82} + D^{126} \\ 0\ 0\ 0\ 0\ 1\ 0\ 0\ 1 + D^5 + D^{20} + D^{47} + D^{84} + D^{144} \\ 0\ 0\ 0\ 0\ 0\ 1\ 0\ 1 + D^{58} + D^{96} + D^{106} + D^{113} + D^{141} \\ 0\ 0\ 0\ 0\ 0\ 0\ 1\ 1 + D^{41} + D^{77} + D^{108} + D^{117} + D^{130} \end{bmatrix} \qquad (9.1)$$

It has six orthogonal parity-check equations, has a minimum Hamming distance of 7, and can correct three errors. At $E_b/N_0 = 6.8$ dB, the system can achieve a bit-error-rate of 10^{-5}.

In 1975, an (8, 7, 47) systematic self-orthogonal convolutional code with threshold decoding was suggested by Wu [13] and employed by the INTELSAT single-channel-per-carrier system, operating at a data rate of 64 Kbps. The generator matrix of the code is

$$
\mathbf{G}(D) = \begin{bmatrix}
1\ 0\ 0\ 0\ 0\ 0\ 0\ 1 + D^3 + D^{19} + D^{43} \\
0\ 1\ 0\ 0\ 0\ 0\ 0\ 1 + D^{21} + D^{34} + D^{43} \\
0\ 0\ 1\ 0\ 0\ 0\ 0\ 1 + D^{29} + D^{33} + D^{47} \\
0\ 0\ 0\ 1\ 0\ 0\ 0\ 1 + D^{25} + D^{36} + D^{37} \\
0\ 0\ 0\ 0\ 1\ 0\ 0\ 1 + D^{15} + D^{20} + D^{46} \\
0\ 0\ 0\ 0\ 0\ 1\ 0\ 1 + D^2 + D^8 + D^{34} \\
0\ 0\ 0\ 0\ 0\ 0\ 1\ 1 + D^7 + D^{17} + D^{45}
\end{bmatrix}
\tag{9.2}
$$

It has four orthogonal parity-check equations, has a minimum Hamming distance of 5, and can correct two errors.

9.4 APPLICATIONS TO MOBILE COMMUNICATIONS

In mobile communications, the available power and bandwidth are very limited. The transmitted signal is subject to multipath fading, and the size of the mobile transceiver is also restricted. Recent design and development of mobile communication systems make extensive use of error-control coding techniques and cellular concepts. The concept of cellular mobile radio makes maximum use of the channel bandwidth by reusing the available frequencies in different cells and is well suited for the growing demand of efficient digital mobile transmission on bandlimited channels. As a result, cellular radio systems suffer from significant co-channel interference as well as adjacent channel interference and fading. Good error-correcting codes with interleaving and a less complex decoder are preferred.

9.4.1 GSM Digital Radio System

In the United Kingdom, the *total access communications system* (TACS) has been used for commercial mobile communications since 1985. The system is an analog system. Other incompatible analog systems are also employed on the Continent. The lack of capacity in the existing analog systems and the ever increasing number of users motivate the development of more efficient transmission systems. In 1982, the *Committee of European Post and Telecomms* (CEPT) formed the *Groupe Speciale Mobile* (GSM) Committee. Various multiple-access methods, transmission rates, coding and interleaving techniques, and modulation methods were studied. Field trials were also conducted. Based on the results of the trails, the GSM Committee has drawn up and agreed on standard and design specifications for a unified Pan-European digital cellular scheme in 1988, known as the full-rate GSM system, which operates in the 900 MHz band and at a gross coded speed of 22.8 Kbps [14,15].

The full-rate GSM digital mobile radio system is a *time-division multiple access* (TDMA) scheme with eight time slots per TDMA frame. It uses digitized speech along with digital signal processing techniques to give higher spectral efficiency and higher levels of integration. To combat burst errors, error-control coding with interleaving is employed. A model of the full-rate GSM system is shown in Figure 9.4.

Speech samples are analyzed and processed in 20-ms blocks by a *regular pulse excited linear predictive coder* (RPE-LPC) with long-term prediction [16]. The coder is operated at 13 Kbps, which corresponds to 260 bits per speech frame. It is known that the performance of the coder is sensitive to errors that degrade the speech quality. Thus, error-control coding is employed to improve the system performance. Digitized binary speech symbols $U = [u_0 \, u_1 \ldots u_{259}]$ are first arranged in descending order of importance. They are then divided into two classes (classes 1 and 3), where class 1 contains the first 182 bits and class 3 contains the remaining 78 bits. The first 50 critical bits are encoded by a (53, 50) systematic cyclic block code with generator polynomial $g(X) = X^3 + X + 1$. Three parity-check bits $P = [p_0 \, p_1 \, p_2]$ are generated and used for error detection and bad-frame indication at the receiver. One hundred eighty-two class 1 bits are split into two equal parts and reordered, and the three parity-check bits are then inserted into the middle of the two reordered parts as follows:

$$x_f = u_{2f} \qquad \text{for } f = 0, 1, \ldots, 90$$
$$x_{184-f} = u_{2f+1} \qquad \text{for } f = 0, 1, \ldots, 90$$
$$x_{91+f} = p_f \qquad \text{for } f = 0, 1, 2$$
$$x_f = 0 \qquad \text{for } f = 185, 186, 187, 188.$$

These 189 bits (182 class-1 bits plus three parity-check bits together with four tailing zeros) are encoded by a (2, 1, 4) convolutional code with generator matrix $G(D) = [1 + D^3 + D^4 \; 1 + D + D^3 + D^4]$ and total encoder memory $K = 4$. The four tailing zeros are used to properly terminate the encoder trellis for decoding. Finally, the 78 uncoded class-3 bits are appended to the 378 coded bits to give a total of 456 bits $Y = [y_0 \, y_1 \ldots y_{455}]$, where $[y_{378} \, y_{379} \ldots y_{455}] = [u_{182} \, u_{183} \ldots u_{259}]$. The 456 bits are reordered according to Table 9.1 and block diagonal interleaved over eight time slots, where f is the bit position of the corresponding subblock. Early system performance evaluation with various interleaving and reordering techniques pointed to this particular interleaving and reordering

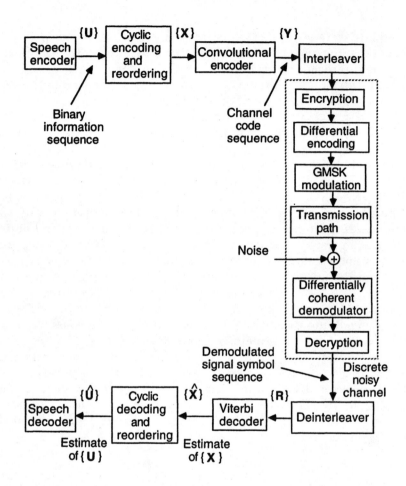

Figure 9.4 Model of the full-rate GSM digital communication system.

arrangement. The cyclic block encoding, reordering, and convolutional coding processes for each speech frame are shown in Figure 9.5; the structure of the interleaver is shown in Figure 9.6.

Each time slot is built with two subblocks belonging to two successive speech frames. The numbered bits of the first four current subblocks and the numbered bits of the last four previous subblocks are arranged in such a way that the result of the block diagonal interleaving is a redistribution of the 456 reordered bits. For example, the distribution of bits from current subblock B_3 and previous subblock B_7 onto a time slot is shown in Figure 9.7. Time slots from the current user and seven other users are grouped together in sets of eight consecutive time slots as one TDMA frame. Those frames are then grouped

Table 9.1
Reordering and Partitioning a 456-Bit Coded Frame Into Eight Subblocks

f	B_0	B_1	B_2	B_3	B_4	B_5	B_6	B_7
0	$i = 0$	57	114	171	228	285	342	399
1	64	121	178	235	292	349	406	7
2	128	185	242	299	356	413	14	71
3	192	249	306	363	420	21	78	135
4	256	313	370	427	28	85	142	199
5	320	377	434	35	92	149	206	263
6	384	441	42	99	156	213	270	327
7	448	49	106	163	220	277	334	391
8	56	113	170	227	284	341	398	455
9	120	177	234	291	348	405	6	63
10	184	241	298	355	412	13	70	127
11	248	305	362	419	20	77	134	191
12	312	369	426	27	84	141	198	255
13	376	433	34	91	148	205	262	319
14	440	41	98	155	212	269	326	383
15	48	105	162	219	276	333	390	447
16	112	169	226	283	340	397	454	55
17	176	233	290	347	404	5	62	119
18	240	297	354	411	12	69	126	183
19	304	361	418	19	76	133	190	247
20	368	425	26	83	140	197	254	311
21	432	33	90	147	204	261	318	375
22	40	97	154	211	268	325	382	439
23	104	161	218	275	332	389	446	47
24	168	225	282	339	396	453	54	111
25	232	289	346	403	4	61	118	175
26	296	353	410	11	68	125	182	239
27	360	417	18	75	132	189	246	303
28	424	25	82	139	196	253	310	367
29	32	89	146	203	260	317	374	431
30	96	153	210	267	324	381	438	39
31	160	217	274	331	388	445	46	103
32	224	281	338	395	452	53	110	167
33	288	345	402	3	60	117	174	231
34	352	409	10	67	124	181	238	295
35	416	17	74	131	188	245	302	359
36	24	81	138	195	252	309	366	423
37	88	145	202	259	316	373	430	31
38	152	209	266	323	380	437	38	95
39	216	273	330	387	444	45	102	159
40	280	337	394	451	52	109	166	223
41	344	401	2	59	116	173	230	287
42	408	9	66	123	180	237	294	351
43	16	73	130	187	244	301	358	415

Table 9.1 (continued)
Reordering and Partitioning a 456-Bit Coded Frame Into Eight Subblocks

f	B_0	B_1	B_2	B_3	B_4	B_5	B_6	B_7
44	80	137	194	251	308	365	422	23
45	144	201	258	315	372	429	30	87
46	208	265	322	379	436	37	94	151
47	272	329	386	443	44	101	158	215
48	336	393	450	51	108	165	222	279
49	400	1	58	115	172	229	286	343
50	8	65	122	179	236	293	350	407
51	72	129	186	243	300	357	414	15
52	136	193	250	307	364	421	22	79
53	200	257	314	371	428	29	86	143
54	264	321	378	435	36	93	150	207
55	328	385	442	43	100	157	214	271
56	392	449	50	107	164	221	278	335

to form one multiframe. The TDMA structure (not explored further here) and the grouping hierarchy of the full-rate GSM system is shown in Figure 9.8.

For each user, the 456 interleaved code symbols are encrypted, differentially encoded and sent to the modulator. *Gaussian minimum-shifted keying* (GMSK) modulation with a modulation index of 0.3 and differentially coherent demodulation are employed [17]. The encryption unit, differential encoder, and modulator together with the transmission path, the demodulator, and the decryption unit form a discrete noisy channel subject to Rayleigh fading and cochannel interference. At the receiving end, the received sequence is deinterleaved and reordered, and the eight-level soft-decision Viterbi algorithm decoder operates on the deinterleaved and reordered sequence and makes a firm decision at the end of each frame to recover the transmitted information sequence. The estimated information symbols are reordered, and the first 50 bits are used to compute a 3-bit syndrome vector $\mathbf{S} = [s_0 \ s_1 \ s_2]$. If the recomputed syndrome vector is zero, the decoded speech frame is declared as a good frame; otherwise, a bad frame is detected. Finally, the four tailing bits are extracted, and the 260 estimated information bits together with the bad frame indication are sent to the speech decoder for further processing.

The average bit-error rate performance of the full-rate GSM system has been measured by computer simulation. Six thousand speech frames were transmitted over the discrete noisy channel in each test. All tests were carried out under the conditions of frequency hopping, independent Rayleigh fading (fading between time slots is uncorrelated), a mobile unit traveling at 50 kph, and various cochannel interference conditions. The results of the simulation

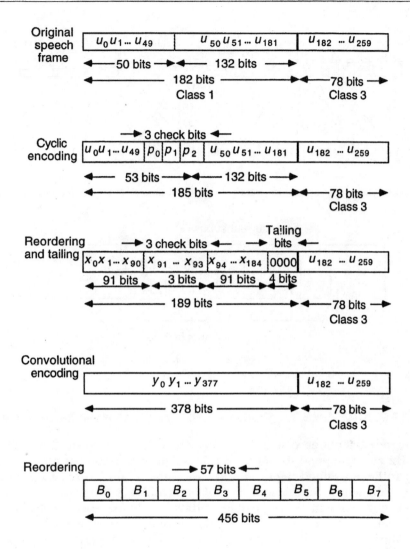

Figure 9.5 Channel coding and reordering of each speech frame in the full-rate GSM system.

tests, operating at the *carrier-to-cochannel interference ratios* (CIR) of 10 dB, 7 dB, and 4 dB, are shown in Figure 9.9. A CIR ratio of 10 dB corresponds to 50% cell coverage, 7 dB to 90% cell coverage (a location just inside a cell boundary), and 4 dB to a location just outside a cell boundary. Table 9.2 shows the average bit error rate in each class, operating at various CIR channel conditions. At CIR = 10 dB, the system can provide an acceptable bit-error rate performance for the transmission of speech signals.

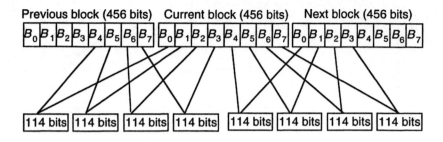

Figure 9.6 Diagonal interleaving structure over eight time slots for the full-rate GSM system.

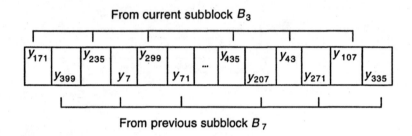

Figure 9.7 Distribution of bits within a typical time slot.

9.5 APPLICATIONS TO VOICE-BAND DATA COMMUNICATIONS

Voice-grade telephone channel bandwidth typically extends from 300 Hz to 3400 Hz and is a good example of a bandwidth-constrained channel. In the bandwidth-constrained region, multilevel modulation is used to increase the spectral efficiency. Since the early 1960s, significant progress has been made in the development of voice-band data modems. By the early 1980s, 2400-bps full-duplex dial-up data modems were common. Recently, one of the key advances in voice-band data modems development was the use of combined coding and multilevel modulation technique. Inspired by Massey [18], Unger-boeck [19] proposed a series of TCM schemes. A survey of modem development was later presented by Forney [20].

In 1982, an *International Telephone and Telegraph Consultative Commit-tee* (CCITT) study group was formed to standardize a family of voice-band data modems for use on the general switched telephone network and on leased point-to-point telephone circuits. During 1983, 1-D and 2-D TCM with QAM signaling schemes were considered. A 90 deg rotationally invariant eight-state nonlinear convolutional code proposed by Wei [21] was chosen as the CCITT Recommendation V.32 for two-wire 9.6 Kbps transmission [22]. With soft-

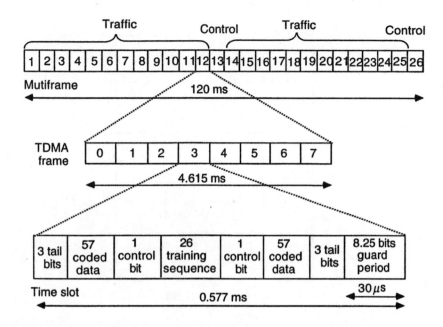

Figure 9.8 Traffic channel multiframe and time slot structure.

decision maximum-likelihood decoding, the code can achieve 4-dB coding gains when compared with an uncoded 16-QAM signal. Figure 9.10 shows the nonlinear convolutional encoder with differential encoding and the 32-CRoss signal constellation. A detailed block diagram of the coded system and implementation are shown in [23] and [24].

A modified version of the code with 128-CRoss signals was also considered by the CCITT Study Group XVII in 1985 [25] and adopted in the CCITT Recommendation V.32 *bis* in 1991 for four-wire transmission at rates up to 14.4 Kbps [26]. Figure 9.11 shows the nonlinear convolutional encoder with differential encoding and the 128-CRoss signal constellation.

In 1993, the *International Telecommunication Union—Telecommunications Standardization Sector* (ITU-T) Study Group 14 (formerly CCITT Study Group XVII) was developing a new high-speed modem recommendation (V.fast) for full-duplex four-wire data transmission over the leased point-to-point telephone circuits. Four-dimensional rotationally invariant systematic 16-state, 32-state, and 64-state convolutional codes due to Wei [27], Williams [28], and Wei [29] were proposed for the V.fast modem standard, respectively. These codes have up to about 1 dB more coding gain than the V.32 code and were adopted by the ITU-T Recommendation V.34 (formerly known as CCITT Recommendation) in 1994 for four-wire transmission at rates up to 28.8 Kbps [30].

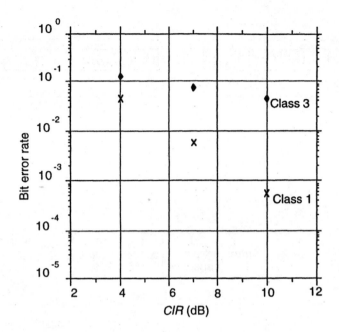

Figure 9.9 Performance of the full-rate GSM system.

Table 9.2
Bit Error Rate in Each Class for the Full-Rate GSM System

CIR (dB)	Class 1 Bit Error Rate	Class 3 Bit Error Rate
10	$5.38(10^{-4})$	$4.51(10^{-2})$
7	$5.97(10^{-3})$	$7.81(10^{-2})$
4	$4.32(10^{-2})$	0.126

Figures 9.12 and Figure 9.13 show the 4-D convolutional encoders and the one-quarter of the signal points in a 960-QAM super signal constellation adopted in the ITU-T V.34 standard. The 960-QAM super signal constellation is formed by adding the 0 deg, 90 deg, 180 deg, and 270 deg rotated versions of the signal constellation in Figure 9.13.

At such a high data transmission rate, V.34 features many advanced signal processing techniques. It employs nonlinear equalization at the transmitter using precoding to reduce equalizer noise enhancement caused by amplitude distortion [30,31]. To improve noise immunity, the 4-D signal constellation is shaped by imposing a nonuniform 2-D Gaussian probability distribution on the 2-D signal constellation [30,31]. A brief summary of the ITU-T V.32, V.32 *bis*, and V.34 standards is shown in Table 9.3.

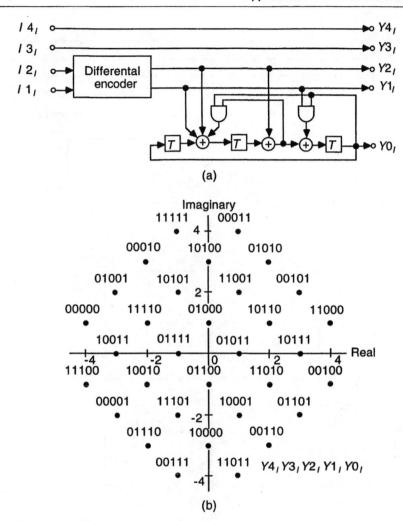

Figure 9.10 (a) Differential encoder and nonlinear convolutional encoder and (b) 32-Cross signal constellation adopted by the CCITT V.32 standard. Note: *T* = signaling interval.

With ever improving quality of the telephone channels, it is now possible to operate at a transmission rate of 33.6 Kbps, which is not far away from the channel capacity of the telephone lines. Recently, more powerful 4-D rotationally invariant systematic convolutional codes (128 and 256 states) were also found and proposed by Wang and Costello [32] for the V.34 *bis* modem standard.

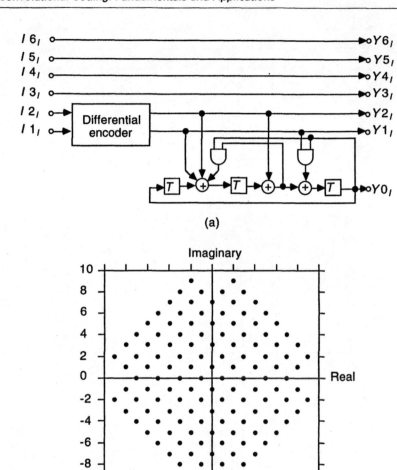

(a)

(b)

Figure 9.11 (a) Differential encoder and nonlinear convolutional encoder and (b) 128-Cross signal constellation adopted by the CCITT V.32 *bis* standard. Note: T = signaling interval.

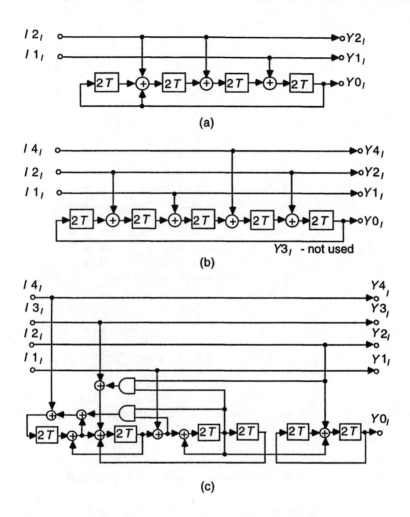

Figure 9.12 (a) 16-state convolutional encoder, (b) 32-state convolutional encoder, and (c) 64-state convolutional encoder adopted by the ITU-T V.34 standard. Note: T = signaling interval.

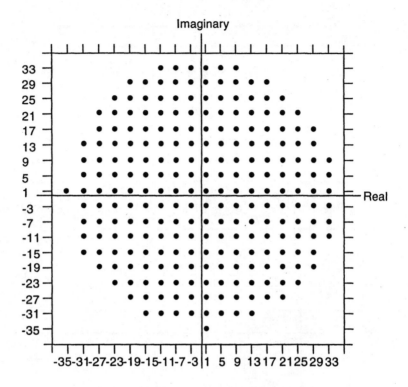

Figure 9.13 One-quarter of the signal points in a 960-QAM super signal constellation adopted by the ITU-T V.34 standard.

Table 9.3
ITU-T (CCITT) Standards for High-Speed Voice-Band Data Modems

ITU-T (CCITT)	*Bit Rate (bps)*	*Modulation Scheme*	*Wires/ Duplex*	*Synchronous/ Asynchronous*	*Type of Line (Dial-up/Leased)*
V.32	9,600	2-*D* TCM/32-CR	2/full	Synchronous	Dial-up
V.32 *bis*	14,400	2-*D* TCM/128-CR	4/full	Synchronous	Leased
V.34	28,800	4-*D* TCM/960-QAM	4/full	Synchronous	Leased

References

[1] Shannon, C. E., "A Mathematical Theory of Communication," *Bell Syst. Tech. J.*, Vol. 27, No. 3, July 1948 , pp. 379–423, and Vol. 27, No. 4, October 1948, pp. 623–656.

[2] Forney, G. D., Jr., *Concatenated Codes*, Cambridge: MIT Press, 1967.

[3] Lin, S., and H. Lyne, "Some Results on Binary Convolutional Code Generators," *IEEE Trans. on Information Theory*, Vol. IT-13, No. 1, January 1967, pp. 134–139.

[4] Forney, G. D., Jr., "Final Report on a Study of a Sample Sequential Decoder," Appendix A, Codex Corp., Watertown, Mass., U.S. Army Satellite Communication Agency Contract DAA B 07-68-C-0093, April 1968.

[5] Massey, J. L., and D. J. Costello, Jr., "Nonsystematic Convolutional Codes for Sequential Decoding in Space Applications," *IEEE Trans. on Communication Technology*, Vol. COM-19, No. 11, November 1971, pp. 806–813.

[6] Fano, R. M., "A Heuristic Discussion of Probabilistic Decoding, " *IEEE Trans. on Information Theory*, Vol. IT-9, No. 2, April 1963, pp. 64–74.

[7] Yuen, J. H., ed., *Deep Space Telecommunications Systems Engineering*, New York: Plenum Press, 1983.

[8] Viterbi, A. J., "Error Bounds for Convolutional Codes and an Asymptotically Optimum Decoding Algorithm," *IEEE Trans. on Information Theory*, Vol. IT-13, No. 2, April 1967, pp. 260–269.

[9] Lin, S., and D. J. Costello, Jr., *Error Control Coding: Fundamentals and Applications*, Prentice-Hall, 1983.

[10] Yuen, J. H., et al., "Modulation and Coding for Satellite and Space Communications," *IEEE Proc.*, Vol. 78, No. 7, July 1990, pp. 1250–1266.

[11] Wu, W. W., "New Convolutional Codes—Part I," *IEEE Trans. on Communications*, Vol. COM-23, No. 9, September 1975, pp. 942–956.

[12] Massey, J. L., *Threshold Decoding*, Cambridge: MIT Press, 1963.

[13] Wu, W. W., "New Convolutional Codes—Part II," *IEEE Trans. on Communications*, Vol. COM-24, No. 1, January 1976, pp. 19–33.

[14] GSM Recommendations 05.03, "Channel Coding," Draft version 3.4.0, November 1988.

[15] Hodges, M. R. L., "The GSM Radio Interface," *British Telecom Technol. J.*, Vol. 8, No. 1, January 1990, pp. 31–43.

[16] Helling, K., et al., "Speech Coder for the European Mobile Radio System," *Proc. ICASSP-89*, Glasgow, UK, 1989, pp. 1065–1069.

[17] Murota, K., and K. Hirade, "GMSK Modulation for Digital Mobile Radio," *IEEE Trans. on Communications*, Vol. COM-29, No. 7, July 1981, pp. 1044–1050.

[18] Massey, J. L., "Coding and Modulation in Digital Communications," *Proc. Int. Zurich Seminar on Digital Commun.*, Zurich, March 1974, pp. E2(1)–(4).

[19] Ungerboeck, G., "Channel Coding With Multilevel/Phase Signals," *IEEE Trans. on Information Theory*, Vol. IT-28, No. 1, January 1982, pp. 55–55.

[20] Forney, G. D., Jr., "Coded Modulation for Band-Limited Channels, " *IEEE Information Theory Society Newsletter*, Vol. 40, December 1990, pp. 1–7.

[21] Wei, L. F., "Rotationally Invariant Convolutional Channel Coding With Expanded Signal Space—Part II: Nonlinear Codes," *IEEE J. Select. Areas Commun.*, Vol. SAC-2, No. 5, September 1984, pp. 672–686.

[22] CCITT Study Group XVII, "Recommendation V.32 for a Family of 2-Wire, Duplex Modems Operating on the General Switched Telephone Network and on the Leased Telephone-Type Circuits," Document AP VIII-43-E, May 1984.

[23] Ahmed, H. M., and R. B. Kline, "Recent Advances in DSP Systems," *IEEE Commun. Mag.*, Vol. 29, No. 5, May 1991, pp. 32–45.

[24] Kato, S., M. Morikura, and S. Kubota, "Implementation of Coded Modems," *IEEE Commun. Mag.*, Vol. 29, No. 12, December 1991, pp. 88–97.

[25] CCITT Study Group XVII, "Draft Recommendation V.33 for 14400 Bits per Second Modem Standardized for Use on Point-to-Point 4-Wire Leased Telephone-Type Circuits," Circular No. 12, COM XVII/YS, Geneva, 17 May 1985.

[26] CCITT Recommendation V.32 *bis,* "A Duplex Modem Operating at Data Signalling Rates of up to 14400 bit/s for Use on the General Switched Telephone Network and on Leased Point-to-Point 2-Wire Telephone-Type Circuit," February 1991.

[27] Wei, L. F., "Trellis-Coded Modulation With Multidimensional Constellations," *IEEE Trans. on Information Theory*, Vol. IT-33, No. 4, July 1987, pp. 483–501.

[28] British Telecom, "Code Choice for V.fast," Contribution D9, CCITT Study Group 14, Geneva, August 1993.

[29] AT&T, "A New 4-D 64-State Rate 4/5 Trellis Code," Contribution D19, CCITT Study Group 14, Geneva, August 1993.

[30] ITU-T Recommendation V.34, "A Modem Operating at Data Signalling Rates of up to 28800 bit/s for Use on the General Switched Telephone Network and on Leased Point-to-Point 2-Wire Telephone-Type Circuit," September 1994.

[31] Eyuboglu, M. V., G. D. Forney, Jr., P. Dong, and G. Z. Long, "Advanced Modulation Techniques for V.fast," *European Trans. on Telecommun. and Related Technologies*, Vol. 4, No. 3, May-June 1993, pp. 243–256.

[32] Wang, F. Q., and D. J. Costello, Jr., "New Rotationally Invariant Four-Dimensional Trellis Codes," *IEEE Trans. on Information Theory*, Vol. IT-42, No. 1, January 1996, pp. 291–300.

Appendix A
Connection Vectors of Convolutional
Codes for Viterbi Decoding

This appendix presents a set of tables of good nonsystematic, noncatastrophic convolutional codes for Viterbi decoding. Tables A.1 and A.2 list the best rate-1/2 and rate-1/3 nonsystematic convolutional codes with maximal d_{free}, respectively. Those codes were found by Larsen [1]. Tables A.3, A.4, and A.5 list the best rate-2/3, 3/4, and 4/5 nonsystematic convolutional codes with maximal d_{free}, respectively. Those codes were found by Paaske and Daut et al. [2,3]. The connection vectors are given in octal notation and are right justified. For example, the connection vector $G^{(1)} = [11101]$ becomes $[011\ 101] \underline{\underline{\Delta}} (35)_8$ after the right justification. For each code of total encoder memory K, the constraint length ν, the minimum free Hamming distance d_{free}, and the weight spectra of all paths with weight d_{free} through $d_{free} + 4$ are given.

Table A.1
Connection Vectors (in Octal) and Weight Spectra of the Best Rate-1/2 Nonsystematic
Convolutional Codes With Maximal d_{free}

K	ν	$G^{(1)}, G^{(2)}$	d_{free}	$(a_d, d = d_{free}, d_{free} + 1, \ldots)$ $[c_d, d = d_{free}, d_{free} + 1, \ldots]$
2	3	5, 7	5	(1, 2, 4, 8, 16)
				[1, 4, 12, 32, 80]
3	4	15, 17	6	(1, 3, 5, 11, 25)
				[2, 7, 18, 49, 130]
4	5	23, 35	7	(2, 3, 4, 16, 37)
				[4, 12, 20, 72, 225]
5	6	53, 75	8	(1, 8, 7, 12, 48)
				[2, 36, 32, 62, 332]
6	7	133, 171	10	(11, 0, 38, 0, 193)
				[36, 0, 211, 0, 1404]
7	8	247, 371	10	(1, 6, 12, 26, 52)
				[2, 22, 60, 148, 340]

From: [1].

Table A.2
Connection Vectors (in Octal) and Weight Spectra of the Best Rate-1/3 Nonsystematic Convolutional Codes With Maximal d_{free}

K	ν	$G^{(1)}, G^{(2)}, G^{(3)}$	d_{free}	$(a_d, d = d_{\text{free}}, d_{\text{free}} + 1, \ldots)$ $[c_d, d = d_{\text{free}}, d_{\text{free}} + 1, \ldots]$
2	3	5, 7, 7	8	(2, 0, 5, 0, 13) [3, 0, 15, 0, 58]
3	4	13, 15, 17	10	(3, 0, 2, 0, 15) [6, 0, 6, 0, 58]
4	5	25, 33, 37	12	(5, 0, 3, 0, 13) [12, 0, 12, 0, 56]
5	6	47, 53, 75	13	(1, 3, 6, 4, 5) [1, 8, 26, 20, 19]
6	7	133, 165, 171	15	(3, 3, 6, 9, 4) [7, 8, 22, 44, 22]
7	8	225, 331, 367	16	(1, 0, 8, 0, 24) [1, 0, 24, 0, 113]

From: [1].

Table A.3
Connection Vectors (in Octal) and Weight Spectra of the Best Rate-2/3 Nonsystematic Convolutional Codes With Maximal d_{free}

K	ν	$G^{(1)}, G^{(2)}, G^{(3)}$	d_{free}	$(a_d, d = d_{\text{free}}, d_{\text{free}} + 1, \ldots)$ $[c_d, d = d_{\text{free}}, d_{\text{free}} + 1, \ldots]$
1	2	3, 6, 2	2	(1, 4, 5, 8, 13) [1, 8, 18, 38, 77]
2	2	17, 6, 15	3	(1, 4, 14, 40, 116) [2, 12, 57, 226, 833]
3	3	33, 15, 22	4	(1, 7, 19, 72, 262) [1, 16, 80, 420, 1902]
4	3	27, 75, 72	5	(5, 18, 58, 215, 792) [19, 87, 390, 1829, 7996]
5	4	177, 55, 112	6	(9, 19, 80, 276, 1122) [36, 99, 600, 2480, 11982]
6	4	236, 155, 337	7	(17, 53, 133, 569, 2327) [86, 360, 1148, 5767, 27277]
7	5	1225, 655, 1574	8	(47, 0, 543, 0, 8472) [265, 0, 5495, 0, 110834]

From: [2,3].

Table A.4
Connection Vectors (in Octal) and Weight Spectra of the Best Rate-3/4 Nonsystematic Convolutional Codes With Maximal d_{free}

K	ν	$G^{(1)}, G^{(2)}, \ldots, G^{(4)}$	d_{free}	$(a_d, d = d_{free}, d_{free} + 1, \ldots)$ $[c_d, d = d_{free}, d_{free} + 1, \ldots]$
1	2	13, 15, 2, 14	2	(2, 8, 17, 40, 96) [2, 28, 82, 228, 672]
2	2	36, 14, 32, 7	3	(6, 23, 80, 296, 1109) [17, 108, 544, 2608, 11902]
3	2	13, 25, 61, 47	4	(10, 46, 202, 949, 4444) [33, 273, 1773, 10565, 60423]
4	3	127, 45, 106, 172	4	(3, 27, 127, 582, 2836) [9, 125, 934, 5554, 32826]
5	3	45, 124, 216, 357	5	(9, 47, 222, 1123, 5839) [32, 292, 1897, 11946, 74581]
6	3	472, 215, 113, 764	6	(30, 112, 640, 3109, 16485) [188, 881, 7014, 39797, 252726]

From: [2,3].

Table A.5
Connection Vectors (in Octal) and Weight Spectra of the Best Rate-4/5 Nonsystematic Convolutional Codes With Maximal d_{free}

K	ν	$G^{(1)}, G^{(2)}, \ldots, G^{(5)}$	d_{free}	$(a_d, d = d_{free}, d_{free} + 1, \ldots)$ $[c_d, d = d_{free}, d_{free} + 1, \ldots]$
1	2	13, 4, 11, 26, 36	2	(4, 18, 47, 138, 414) [10, 60, 242, 940, 3462]
2	2	67, 15, 26, 52, 57	2	(1, 12, 54, 251, 1166) [4, 60, 396, 2387, 13687]
3	2	13, 23, 56, 132, 174	3	(1, 21, 143, 780, 4644) [3, 89, 1040, 8110, 61049]
4	2	237, 274, 156, 255, 337	3	(8, 43, 224, 1268, 7118) [44, 325, 2198, 15231, 101130]

From: [2,3].

References

[1] Larsen, K. J., "Short Convolutional Codes With Maximal Free Distance for Rates 1/2, 1/3, and 3/4," *IEEE Trans. on Information Theory*, Vol. IT-19, No. 3, May 1973, pp. 371–372.

[2] Paaske, E., "Short Binary Convolutional Codes With Maximal Free Distance for Rates 2/3 and 3/4," *IEEE Trans. on Information Theory*, Vol. IT-20, No. 5, September 1974, pp. 683–689.

[3] Daut, D. G., J. W. Modestino, and L. W. Wismer, "New Short Constraint Length Convolutional Code Constructions for Selected Rational Rate," *IEEE Trans. on Information Theory*, Vol. IT-28, No. 5, 1982, pp. 794–800.

Appendix B
Connection Vectors of Convolutional
Codes for Sequential Decoding

This appendix presents a set of tables of *optimum distance profile* (ODP) systematic and nonsystematic, noncatastrophic convolutional codes for sequential decoding. Tables B.1 and B.2 list the best rate-1/2 ODP systematic and nonsystematic convolutional codes, respectively. These codes were found by Johannesson and Paaske [1,2]. The connection vectors are given in octal notation and are right justified. For example, the connection vector $G^{(1)} = [11101]$ becomes $[011\ 101] \triangleq (35)_8$ after the right justification. For each code of encoder memory order m, the constraint length ν, the total encoder memory K, the Hamming distance d_m over one constraint length, and the minimum free Hamming distance d_{free} are given.

Table B.1
Rate-1/2 Optimum Distance Profile Systematic Convolutional Codes

m	ν	K	$G^{(1)}, G^{(2)}$	d_m	d_{free}
1	2	1	2, 3	3	3
2	3	2	4, 7	3	4
3	4	3	10, 15	4	4
4	5	4	20, 35	4	5
5	6	5	40, 73	5	6
6	7	6	100, 167	5	6
7	8	7	200, 345	6	6
8	9	8	400, 671	6	7
9	10	9	1000, 1633	6	8
10	11	10	2000, 3465	7	8
11	12	11	4000, 7153	7	9
12	13	12	10000, 15623	8	9
13	14	13	20000, 33445	8	9
14	15	14	40000, 67115	8	10
15	16	15	100000, 163117	8	10

Table B.1 (continued)
Rate-1/2 Optimum Distance Profile Systematic Convolutional Codes

m	ν	K	$G^{(1)}, G^{(2)}$	d_m	d_{free}
16	17	16	200000, 334473	9	12
17	18	17	400000, 671167	9	12
18	19	18	1000000, 1562313	9	12
19	20	19	2000000, 3462307	10	12
20	21	20	4000000, 7144761	10	12

From: [1,2].

Table B.2
Rate-1/2 Optimum Distance Profile Nonsystematic Convolutional Codes

m	ν	K	$G^{(1)}, G^{(2)}$	d_m	d_{free}
1	2	1	3, 2	3	3
2	3	2	7, 5	3	5
3	4	3	17, 13	4	6
4	5	4	31, 27	4	7
5	6	5	75, 55	5	8
6	7	6	147, 135	5	10
7	8	7	313, 275	6	10
8	9	8	751, 557	6	12
9	10	9	1755, 1363	6	12
10	11	10	3645, 2671	7	14
11	12	11	6643, 5175	7	14
12	13	12	14677, 11651	8	15
13	14	13	22555, 37457	8	16
14	15	14	65231, 43677	8	17
15	16	15	123741, 155027	8	18
16	17	16	347433, 251341	9	19
17	18	17	506477, 673711	9	20
18	19	18	1352755, 1771563	9	21
19	20	19	2451321, 3546713	10	22
20	21	20	6567413, 5322305	10	22

From: [1,2].

References

[1] Johannesson, R., "Robustly-Optimum Rate One-Half Binary Convolutional Codes," *IEEE Trans. on Information Theory*, Vol. IT-21, No. 4, July 1975, pp. 464–468.
[2] Johannesson, R., and E. Paaske, "Further Results on Binary Convolutional Code With an Optimum Distance Profile," *IEEE Trans. on Information Theory*, Vol. IT-24, No. 2, March 1978, pp. 264–268.

Appendix C
Puncturing Matrix for Punctured and Rate-Compatible Punctured Convolutional Codes

This appendix presents a set of tables of good punctured and RCPC codes for Viterbi decoding. These codes are obtained by puncturing a rate-$1/n$ mother code of total encoder memory K and $n = 2$. Tables C.1 to C.6 list the best rate-P/Q', $Q' = n \cdot P - \delta$, punctured convolutional codes with maximal d_{free} for $2 \leq P \leq 7$ and $\delta = (n - 1)P - 1$, where δ specifies the total number of punctured symbols. These punctured codes were found by Yasuda et al. [1]. Tables C.7 to C.11 list the best rate-P/Q' RCPC codes with maximal d_{free} for $3 \leq P \leq 7$ and $1 \leq \delta \leq (n - 1)P - 1$. These RCPC codes were found by Lee [2]. The connection vectors are given in octal notation and are right justified. For example, the connection vector $\mathbf{G}^{(1)} = [11101]$ becomes $[011\ 101] \triangleq (35)_8$ after the right justification. In both cases, the mother code and the punctured code have the same total encoder memory K. For each code of total encoder memory K, the n-by-P puncturing array $\mathbf{P}_\delta$, the punctured code rate-P/Q', the minimum free Hamming distance d_{free}, and the weight spectra of all paths with weight d_{free} through $d_{\text{free}} + 4$ are given.

Table C.1

Weight Spectra of Punctured Convolutional Codes Generated From Rate-1/2 Mother Code of Total Encoder Memory $2 \leq K \leq 6$ and Puncturing Period $P = 2$

Mother Code			Punctured Convolutional Code		
K	$G^{(1)}, G^{(2)}$	P_δ	Punctured Rate-P/Q'	d_{free}	$(a_d, d = d_{\text{free}}, d_{\text{free}} + 1, \ldots)$ $[c_d, d = d_{\text{free}}, d_{\text{free}} + 1, \ldots]$
2	5, 7	10	2/3	3	(1, 4, 14, 40, 116)
		11			[1, 10, 54, 226, 856]
3	15, 17	11	2/3	4	(3, 11, 35, 114, 378)
		01			[10, 43, 200, 826, 3314]
4	23, 35	11	2/3	4	(1, 0, 27, 0, 345)
		01			[1, 0, 124, 0, 2721]
5	53, 75	10	2/3	6	(19, 0, 220, 0, 3089)
		11			[96, 0, 1904, 0, 35936]
6	133, 171	11	2/3	6	(1, 16, 48, 158, 642)
		10			[3, 70, 285, 1276, 6160]

From: [1].

Table C.2

Weight Spectra of Punctured Convolutional Codes Generated From Rate-1/2 Mother Code of Total Encoder Memory $2 \leq K \leq 6$ and Puncturing Period $P = 3$

Mother Code			Punctured Convolutional Code		
K	$G^{(1)}, G^{(2)}$	P_δ	Punctured Rate-P/Q'	d_{free}	$(a_d, d = d_{\text{free}}, d_{\text{free}} + 1, \ldots)$ $[c_d, d = d_{\text{free}}, d_{\text{free}} + 1, \ldots]$
2	5, 7	101	3/4	3	(6, 23, 80, 290, 1050)
		110			[15, 104, 540, 2557, 11441]
3	15, 17	110	3/4	4	(29, 0, 532, 0, 10059)
		101			[124, 0, 4504, 0, 126049]
4	23, 35	101	3/4	3	(1, 2, 23, 124, 576)
		110			[1, 7, 125, 936, 5915]
5	53, 75	100	3/4	4	(1, 15, 65, 321, 1661)
		111			[3, 85, 490, 3198, 20557]
6	133, 171	110	3/4	5	(8, 31, 160, 892, 4512)
		101			[42, 201, 1492, 10469, 62935]

From: [1].

Table C.3
Weight Spectra of Punctured Convolutional Codes Generated From Rate-1/2 Mother Code of
Total Encoder Memory $2 \leq K \leq 6$ and Puncturing Period $P = 4$

Mother Code		Punctured Convolutional Code			
K	$G^{(1)}, G^{(2)}$	P_δ	Punctured Rate-P/Q'	d_{free}	$(a_d, d = d_{\text{free}}, d_{\text{free}} + 1, \ldots)$ $[c_d, d = d_{\text{free}}, d_{\text{free}} + 1, \ldots]$
2	5, 7	1011 1100	4/5	2	(1, 12, 53, 238, 1091) [1, 36, 309, 2060, 12320]
3	15, 17	1011 1100	4/5	3	(5, 36, 200, 1070, 5919) [14, 194, 1579, 11313, 77947]
4	23, 35	1010 1101	4/5	3	(3, 16, 103, 675, 3969) [11, 78, 753, 6901, 51737]
5	53, 75	1000 1111	4/5	4	(7, 54, 307, 2005, 12970) [40, 381, 3251, 27123, 213451]
6	133, 171	1111 1000	4/5	4	(3, 24, 172, 1158, 7409) [12, 188, 1732, 15256, 121372]

From: [1].

Table C.4
Weight Spectra of Punctured Convolutional Codes Generated From Rate-1/2 Mother Code of
Total Encoder Memory $2 \leq K \leq 6$ and Puncturing Period $P = 5$

Mother Code		Punctured Convolutional Code			
K	$G^{(1)}, G^{(2)}$	P_δ	Punctured Rate-P/Q'	d_{free}	$(a_d, d = d_{\text{free}}, d_{\text{free}} + 1, \ldots)$ $[c_d, d = d_{\text{free}}, d_{\text{free}} + 1, \ldots]$
2	5, 7	10111 11000	5/6	2	(2, 26, 129, 633, 3316) [2, 111, 974, 6857, 45555]
3	15, 17	10100 11011	5/6	3	(15, 96, 601, 3918, 25391) [63, 697, 6367, 53574, 426471]
4	23, 35	10111 11000	5/6	3	(5, 37, 309, 2282, 16614) [20, 265, 3248, 32328, 297825]
5	53, 75	10000 11111	5/6	4	(19, 171, 1251, 9573, 75167) [100, 1592, 17441, 166331, 1591841]
6	133, 171	11010 10101	5/6	4	(14, 69, 654, 4996, 39699) [92, 528, 8694, 79453, 792114]

From: [1].

Table C.5
Weight Spectra of Punctured Convolutional Codes Generated From Rate-1/2 Mother Code of
Total Encoder Memory $2 \leq K \leq 6$ and Puncturing Period $P = 6$

Mother Code			Punctured Convolutional Code			
K	$G^{(1)}, G^{(2)}$	P_δ	Punctured Rate-P/Q'	d_{free}	$(a_d, d = d_{\text{free}}, d_{\text{free}} + 1, \ldots)$ $[c_d, d = d_{\text{free}}, d_{\text{free}} + 1, \ldots]$	
2	5, 7	101111 110000	6/7	2	(4, 39, 221, 1330, 8190) [5, 186, 1942, 16642, 131415]	
3	15, 17	100011 111100	6/7	2	(1, 25, 188, 1416, 10757) [2, 134, 1696, 18284, 179989]	
4	23, 35	101010 110101	6/7	3	(14, 100, 828, 7198, 60847) [69, 779, 9770, 113537, 1203746]	
5	53, 75	110110 101001	6/7	3	(5, 55, 517, 4523, 40476) [25, 475, 6302, 73704, 823440]	
6	133, 171	111010 100101	6/7	3	(1, 20, 223, 1961, 18093) [5, 169, 2725, 32233, 370861]	

From: [1].

Table C.6
Weight Spectra of Punctured Convolutional Codes Generated From Rate-1/2 Mother Code of
Total Encoder Memory $2 \leq K \leq 6$ and Puncturing Period $P = 7$

Mother Code			Punctured Convolutional Code			
K	$G^{(1)}, G^{(2)}$	P_δ	Punctured Rate-P/Q'	d_{free}	$(a_d, d = d_{\text{free}}, d_{\text{free}} + 1, \ldots)$ $[c_d, d = d_{\text{free}}, d_{\text{free}} + 1, \ldots]$	
2	5, 7	1011111 1100000	7/8	2	(6, 66, 408, 2636, 17844) [8, 393, 4248, 38142, 325739]	
3	15, 17	1000010 1111101	7/8	2	(2, 38, 346, 2772, 23958) [4, 219, 3456, 38973, 437072]	
4	23, 35	1010011 1101100	7/8	3	(13, 145, 1471, 14473, 143110) [49, 1414, 21358, 284324, 3544716]	
5	53, 75	1011101 1100010	7/8	3	(9, 122, 1195, 12139, 123889) [60, 1360, 18971, 252751, 3165885]	
6	133, 171	1111010 1000101	7/8	3	(2, 46, 499, 5291, 56179) [9, 500, 7437, 105707, 1402743]	

From: [1].

Table C.7
Weight Spectra of RCPC Codes Generated From Rate-1/2 Mother Code of Total Encoder Memory
$2 \leq K \leq 6$ and Puncturing Period $P = 3$

Mother Code			RCPC Code		
K	$G^{(1)}, G^{(2)}$	P_δ	RCPC Code Rate-P/Q'	d_{free}	$(a_d, d = d_{\text{free}}, d_{\text{free}} + 1, \ldots)$ $[c_d, d = d_{\text{free}}, d_{\text{free}} + 1, \ldots]$
2	5, 7	110	3/5	4	(3, 12, 24, 56, 142)
		111			[4, 32, 104, 312, 961]
		110	3/4	3	(6, 23, 80, 284, 1027)
		101			[15, 104, 540, 2536, 11302]
3	15, 17	011	3/5	4	(1, 8, 14, 44, 135)
		111			[2, 26, 52, 234, 860]
		011	3/4	4	(29, 0, 532, 0, 10117)
		110			[124, 0, 4504, 0, 126471]
4	23, 35	111	3/5	5	(1, 10, 23, 66, 205)
		101			[1, 39, 104, 426, 1556]
		101	3/4	4	(29, 0, 532, 0, 11045)
		101			[164, 0, 5200, 0, 151211]
5	53, 75	101	3/5	6	(4, 14, 35, 107, 323)
		111			[20, 53, 188, 810, 2677]
		100	3/4	4	(1, 15, 65, 321, 1661)
		111			[3, 85, 490, 3198, 20557]
6	133, 171	111	3/5	7	(7, 20, 58, 146, 477)
		101			[25, 90, 358, 1080, 4287]
		110	3/4	5	(8, 31, 160, 892, 4512)
		101			[42, 201, 1492, 10469, 62935]

Source: [2]. Reprinted with permission. © 1994 IEEE.

Table C.8
Weight Spectra of RCPC Codes Generated From Rate-1/2 Mother Code of Total Encoder Memory
$2 \leq K \leq 6$ and Puncturing Period $P = 4$

Mother Code		RCPC Code			
K	$G^{(1)}, G^{(2)}$	P_δ	RCPC Code Rate-P/Q'	d_{free}	$(a_d, d = d_{free}, d_{free} + 1, \ldots)$ $[c_d, d = d_{free}, d_{free} + 1, \ldots]$
2	5, 7	1101	4/7	4	(3, 9, 21, 48, 111)
		1111			[4, 19, 72, 224, 651]
		1001	4/6	4	(23, 0, 182, 0, 1530)
		1111			[66, 0, 1108, 0, 13836]
		1001	4/5	2	(1, 15, 63, 262, 1136)
		1110			[3, 54, 387, 2299, 12679]
3	15, 17	1111	4/7	4	(1, 0, 27, 0, 170)
		1101			[2, 0, 80, 0, 903]
		1110	4/6	4	(6, 21, 66, 213, 716)
		1101			[16, 78, 368, 1495, 6064]
		1110	4/5	3	(8, 43, 224, 1212, 6521)
		1001			[31, 264, 1947, 13535, 89172]
4	23, 35	1111	4/7	5	(1, 9, 16, 37, 154)
		1101			[1, 31, 72, 175, 1003]
		1111	4/6	4	(2, 0, 54, 0, 691)
		0101			[2, 0, 248, 0, 5444]
		1111	4/5	3	(4, 20, 137, 844, 4946)
		0100			[21, 137, 1344, 10854, 77549]
5	53, 75	1011	4/7	6	(1, 15, 32, 60, 202)
		1111			[5, 59, 158, 360, 1524]
		1010	4/6	6	(38, 0, 440, 0, 6178)
		1111			[192, 0, 3808, 0, 71872]
		1000	4/5	4	(7, 54, 307, 2005, 12970)
		1111			[40, 381, 3251, 27123, 213451]
6	133, 171	1111	4/7	7	(2, 12, 43, 98, 244)
		1011			[6, 37, 193, 581, 1771]
		1111	4/6	6	(2, 32, 96, 316, 1284)
		1010			[6, 140, 570, 2552, 12320]
		1111	4/5	4	(3, 24, 172, 1158, 7409)
		1000			[12, 188, 1732, 15256, 121372]

Source: [2]. Reprinted with permission. © 1994 IEEE.

Table C.9
Weight Spectra of RCPC Codes Generated From Rate-1/2 Mother Code of Total Encoder Memory
$2 \leq K \leq 6$ and Puncturing Period $P = 5$

Mother Code			RCPC Code		
K	$G^{(1)}, G^{(2)}$	P_δ	RCPC Code Rate-P/Q'	d_{free}	$(a_d, d = d_{\text{free}}, d_{\text{free}} + 1, \ldots)$ $[c_d, d = d_{\text{free}}, d_{\text{free}} + 1, \ldots]$
2	5, 7	11011	5/9	4	(2, 11, 21, 47, 105)
		11111			[2, 21, 66, 205, 578]
		11001	5/8	4	(11, 25, 55, 165, 415)
		11111			[22, 85, 292, 1043, 3217]
		01001	5/7	3	(4, 25, 69, 277, 887)
		11111			[6, 92, 375, 2148, 8448]
		00001	5/6	2	(2, 26, 131, 657, 3423)
		11111			[6, 116, 1004, 7183, 47588]
3	15, 17	11111	5/9	5	(4, 15, 31, 74, 198)
		01111			[10, 37, 120, 368, 1164]
		10111	5/8	4	(2, 16, 40, 113, 340)
		01111			[5, 43, 171, 643, 2346]
		10110	5/7	3	(1, 14, 55, 199, 820)
		01111			[2, 45, 271, 1400, 7224]
		10010	5/6	3	(15, 96, 601, 3948, 25838)
		01111			[63, 697, 6367, 53925, 432521]
4	23, 35	11111	5/9	5	(1, 7, 20, 41, 121)
		11011			[6, 12, 91, 219, 728]
		11111	5/8	5	(8, 21, 61, 208, 649)
		01011			[28, 99, 353, 1534, 5729]
		11110	5/7	4	(4, 28, 104, 428, 1869)
		01011			[9, 143, 710, 3715, 20348]
		11110	5/6	3	(5, 37, 309, 2282, 16669)
		00011			[20, 265, 3248, 32343, 298571]
5	53, 75	11011	5/9	6	(1, 8, 31, 72, 150)
		11111			[2, 32, 130, 387, 1033]
		11011	5/8	6	(13, 42, 110, 335, 1181)
		01111			[53, 199, 737, 2645, 11000]
		11001	5/7	5	(16, 67, 269, 1185, 5276)
		01111			[75, 432, 2302, 12646, 66755]
		10001	5/6	3	(4, 35, 268, 1977, 15002)
		01111			[17, 257, 2899, 27961, 260839]
6	133, 171	11111	5/9	7	(1, 11, 42, 76, 178)
		11101			[3, 36, 167, 406, 1175]
		11111	5/8	6	(2, 20, 49, 149, 510)
		10101			[6, 85, 238, 987, 4280]
		11111	5/7	5	(4, 39, 177, 611, 2863)
		10001			[16, 226, 1545, 6399, 35360]
		11111	5/6	3	(1, 17, 136, 1143, 8717)
		10000			[3, 187, 1797, 19202, 180275]

Source: [2]. Reprinted with permission. © 1994 IEEE.

Table C.10
Weight Spectra of RCPC Codes Generated From Rate-1/2 Mother Code of Total Encoder Memory
$2 \le K \le 6$ and Puncturing Period $P = 6$

Mother Code		RCPC Code			
K	$G^{(1)}, G^{(2)}$	P_δ	RCPC Code Rate-P/Q'	d_{free}	$(a_d, d = d_{\text{free}}, d_{\text{free}} + 1, \ldots)$ $[c_d, d = d_{\text{free}}, d_{\text{free}} + 1, \ldots]$
2	5, 7	111011	6/11	4	(2, 11, 23, 47, 102)
		111111			[2, 19, 68, 191, 530]
		011011	6/10	4	(6, 24, 48, 112, 293)
		111111			[8, 64, 208, 624, 1946]
		011011	6/9	3	(2, 21, 41, 147, 363)
		101111			[2, 61, 170, 892, 2698]
		011011	6/8	3	(12, 46, 160, 604, 2330)
		101101			[30, 208, 1080, 5252, 24542]
		011011	6/7	2	(4, 46, 254, 1427, 8373)
		100101			[13, 252, 2308, 18083, 133171]
3	15, 17	111111	6/11	5	(3, 16, 33, 73, 187)
		011111			[7, 38, 115, 360, 1031]
		111110	6/10	4	(1, 14, 35, 86, 238)
		011111			[2, 36, 135, 455, 1501]
		111110	6/9	4	(8, 32, 96, 318, 1110)
		001111			[17, 122, 501, 2207, 9228]
		110110	6/8	3	(3, 35, 120, 604, 2541)
		001111			[7, 157, 776, 5346, 27346]
		110110	6/7	2	(1, 26, 192, 1402, 10412)
		001011			[4, 137, 1654, 17152, 163275]
4	23, 35	111111	6/11	6	(8, 18, 41, 117, 270)
		110111			[20, 64, 211, 663, 1833]
		111111	6/10	5	(2, 20, 46, 132, 410)
		110110			[2, 78, 208, 852, 3112]
		101111	6/9	4	(3, 11, 55, 196, 668)
		110110			[5, 49, 299, 1396, 6181]
		101111	6/8	3	(1, 9, 66, 300, 1416)
		110100			[1, 43, 412, 2630, 15964]
		001111	6/7	3	(17, 141, 1132, 9416, 78482)
		110100			[104, 1492, 16873, 178718, 1812273]
5	53, 75	111111	6/11	6	(2, 10, 31, 72, 152)
		111101			[7, 49, 117, 389, 1029]
		111111	6/10	5	(2, 8, 30, 82, 262)
		101101			[4, 38, 132, 450, 1888]
		111111	6/9	4	(1, 9, 47, 161, 489)
		101001			[2, 42, 275, 1197, 4438]
		111111	6/8	4	(6, 46, 214, 1094, 5449)
		001001			[28, 252, 1770, 11640, 69924]
		111111	6/7	3	(4, 112, 597, 7384, 54585)
		000001			[35, 1033, 8662, 131305, 1223436]

Table C.10 (continued)
Weight Spectra of RCPC Codes Generated From Rate-1/2 Mother Code of Total Encoder Memory
$2 \leq K \leq 6$ and Puncturing Period $P = 6$

Mother Code		RCPC Code			
K	$\mathbf{G}^{(1)}, \mathbf{G}^{(2)}$	$\mathbf{P}_\delta$	RCPC Code Rate-P/Q'	d_{free}	$(a_d, d = d_{\text{free}}, d_{\text{free}} + 1, \ldots)$ $[c_d, d = d_{\text{free}}, d_{\text{free}} + 1, \ldots]$
6	133, 171	111111	6/11	8	(8, 47, 71, 176, 451)
		110111			[24, 187, 350, 1126, 3329]
		011111	6/10	7	(11, 53, 99, 266, 983)
		110111			[43, 217, 556, 1924, 8185]
		011111	6/9	6	(17, 63, 148, 658, 2620)
		110011			[72, 325, 1056, 5933, 27173]
		011101	6/8	5	(16, 77, 355, 1830, 9617)
		110011			[74, 491, 3121, 20372, 128012]
		011101	6/7	3	(1, 20, 223, 1961, 18102)
		110010			[5, 169, 2725, 32233, 371012]

Source: [2]. Reprinted with permission. © 1994 IEEE.

Table C.11

Weight Spectra of RCPC Codes Generated From Rate-1/2 Mother Code of Total Encoder Memory $2 \leq K \leq 6$ and Puncturing Period $P = 7$

Mother Code			RCPC Code		
K	$G^{(1)}, G^{(2)}$	P_δ	RCPC Code Rate-P/Q'	d_{free}	$(a_d, d = d_{\text{free}}, d_{\text{free}} + 1, \ldots)$ $[c_d, d = d_{\text{free}}, d_{\text{free}} + 1, \ldots]$
2	5, 7	1110111	7/13	4	(2, 11, 25, 52, 105)
		1111111			[2, 17, 70, 206, 528]
		1110110	7/12	4	(6, 20, 43, 104, 246)
		1111111			[8, 48, 160, 522, 1504]
		1100110	7/11	4	(18, 45, 69, 288, 798)
		1111111			[36, 189, 340, 1866, 6416]
		1100100	7/10	3	(4, 38, 96, 244, 1064)
		1111111			[8, 130, 540, 1786, 9668]
		1100100	7/9	2	(2, 14, 100, 240, 1414)
		1111011			[4, 46, 540, 1838, 14334]
		1100100	7/8	2	(7, 72, 439, 2785, 18173)
		1011011			[28, 467, 4606, 39748, 323416]
3	15, 17	1111111	7/13	5	(2, 19, 36, 65, 193)
		1111101			[4, 46, 126, 301, 1039]
		1111111	7/12	5	(12, 35, 71, 188, 526)
		1111100			[28, 118, 325, 1111, 3587]
		1111111	7/11	4	(3, 31, 78, 185, 649)
		0111100			[5, 101, 362, 1191, 4900]
		1111111	7/10	3	(1, 16, 73, 217, 831)
		0111000			[1, 55, 342, 1483, 7030]
		1110111	7/9	3	(10, 60, 290, 1446, 7458)
		0111000			[39, 360, 2494, 16100, 100773]
		1100111	7/8	2	(2, 46, 370, 2968, 24722)
		0111000			[7, 297, 3820, 42654, 450025]
4	23, 35	1111111	7/13	5	(1, 6, 19, 39, 110)
		1101111			[3, 12, 65, 186, 579]
		1111111	7/12	5	(4, 15, 38, 107, 318)
		1101011			[8, 54, 172, 608, 2175]
		1111111	7/11	4	(1, 9, 35, 109, 327)
		0101011			[1, 27, 164, 657, 2438]
		1111110	7/10	4	(4, 30, 101, 412, 1692)
		0101011			[6, 145, 652, 3364, 17173]
		1111110	7/9	3	(2, 23, 141, 679, 3956)
		0100011			[2, 158, 1207, 7741, 57379]
		1111100	7/8	2	(1, 18, 193, 1835, 17906)
		0100011			[1, 131, 2122, 28710, 365844]
5	53, 75	1111111	7/13	6	(1, 9, 36, 75, 137)
		1111011			[2, 41, 153, 391, 881]
		1111111	7/12	6	(7, 36, 73, 185, 575)
		1101011			[29, 165, 417, 1294, 4693]
		1111111	7/11	5	(2, 30, 76, 226, 751)

Table C.11 (continued)
Weight Spectra of RCPC Codes Generated From Rate-1/2 Mother Code of Total Encoder Memory
$2 \le K \le 6$ and Puncturing Period $P = 7$

Mother Code			RCPC Code		
K	$G^{(1)}, G^{(2)}$	P_δ	RCPC Code Rate-P/Q'	d_{free}	$(a_d, d = d_{\text{free}}, d_{\text{free}} + 1, \ldots)$ $[c_d, d = d_{\text{free}}, d_{\text{free}} + 1, \ldots]$
		0101011			[9, 140, 409, 1737, 6618]
		1111101	7/10	4	(3, 19, 77, 316, 1318)
		0101011			[14, 102, 520, 2718, 14010]
		1111101	7/9	3	(1, 15, 90, 500, 2710)
		0100011			[7, 88, 655, 4915, 32974]
		1111101	7/8	2	(1, 11, 173, 1494, 15507)
		0100010			[7, 71, 1971, 24072, 321739]
6	133, 171	1111111	7/13	8	(6, 43, 80, 174, 423)
		1110111			[16, 152, 382, 1086, 3063]
		1111111	7/12	7	(4, 37, 102, 220, 622)
		1110110			[10, 141, 520, 1545, 5109]
		1111111	7/11	6	(4, 28, 94, 296, 957)
		1010110			[10, 119, 496, 2170, 8391]
		1111111	7/10	5	(4, 31, 131, 535, 2282)
		1000110			[14, 174, 889, 4915, 25538]
		1111111	7/9	4	(2, 38, 202, 1149, 6761)
		1000100			[5, 279, 1889, 13785, 100491]
		1111111	7/8	3	(2, 42, 468, 4939, 52821)
		1000000			[14, 389, 6792, 97243, 1317944]

Source: [2]. Reprinted with permission. © 1994 IEEE.

References

[1] Yasuda, Y., K. Kashiki, and Y. Hirata, "High-Rate Punctured Convolutional Codes for Soft-Decision Viterbi Decoding," *IEEE Trans. on Communications*, Vol. COM-32, No. 3, March 1984, pp. 315–318.

[2] Lee, L. H. C., "New Rate-Compatible Punctured Convolutional Codes for Viterbi Coding," *IEEE Trans. on Communications*, Vol. COM-42, No. 12, December 1994, pp. 3073–3079.

Appendix D
Generator Polynomials for
Self-Orthogonal Systematic
Convolutional Codes

This appendix presents a set of tables of good self-orthogonal systematic convolutional codes for majority-logic decoding. Tables D.1, D.2, and D.3 list the best rate-1/2, rate-2/3, and rate-3/4 self-orthogonal systematic convolutional codes, respectively. These codes were found by Bussgang and Robinson et al. [1,2]. For each code of error-correcting power t_{ML}, the encoder memory order m is given.

Table D.1
Generator Polynomials of the Best Rate-1/2 Self-Orthogonal Convolutional Codes

t_{ML}	m	$G_1^{(2)}(D)$
1	1	$1 + D$
2	6	$1 + D^2 + D^5 + D^6$
3	17	$1 + D^2 + D^7 + D^{13} + D^{16} + D^{17}$
4	35	$1 + D^7 + D^{10} + D^{16} + D^{18} + D^{30} + D^{31} + D^{35}$
5	55	$1 + D^2 + D^{14} + D^{21} + D^{29} + D^{32} + D^{45} + D^{49} + D^{54} + D^{55}$
6	85	$1 + D^2 + D^6 + D^{24} + D^{29} + D^{40} + D^{43} + D^{55} + D^{68} + D^{75} + D^{76} + D^{85}$

From: [1,2].

Table D.2

Generator Polynomials of the Best Rate-2/3 Self-Orthogonal Convolutional Codes

t_{ML}	m	$G_1^{(3)}(D)$	$G_2^{(3)}(D)$
1	2	$1 + D$	$1 + D^2$
2	13	$1 + D^8 + D^9 + D^{12}$	$1 + D^6 + D^{11} + D^{13}$
3	40	$1 + D^2 + D^6 + D^{24} + D^{29} + D^{40}$	$1 + D^3 + D^{15} + D^{28} + D^{35} + D^{36}$
4	86	$1 + D + D^{27} + D^{30} + D^{61} + D^{73}$ $+ D^{81} + D^{83}$	$1 + D^{18} + D^{23} + D^{37} + D^{58} + D^{62}$ $+ D^{75} + D^{86}$
5	130	$1 + D + D^6 + D^{25} + D^{32} + D^{72}$ $+ D^{100} + D^{108} + D^{120} + D^{130}$	$1 + D^{23} + D^{39} + D^{57} + D^{60} + D^{74}$ $+ D^{101} + D^{103} + D^{112} + D^{116}$
6	195	$1 + D^{17} + D^{46} + D^{50} + D^{52} + D^{66}$ $+ D^{88} + D^{125} + D^{150} + D^{165} + D^{168}$ $+ D^{195}$	$1 + D^{26} + D^{34} + D^{47} + D^{57} + D^{58}$ $+ D^{112} + D^{121} + D^{140} + D^{181} + D^{188}$ $+ D^{193}$

From: [1,2].

Table D.3

Generator Polynomials of the Best Rate-3/4 Self-Orthogonal Convolutional Codes

t_{ML}	m	$G_1^{(4)}(D)$	$G_2^{(4)}(D)$	$G_3^{(4)}(D)$
1	3	$1 + D$	$1 + D^2$	$1 + D^3$
2	19	$1 + D^3 + D^{15} + D^{19}$	$1 + D^8 + D^{17} + D^{18}$	$1 + D^6 + D^{11} + D^{13}$
3	67	$1 + D^5 + D^{15} + D^{34} +$ $D^{35} + D^{42}$	$1 + D^{31} + D^{33} + D^{44}$ $+ D^{47} + D^{56}$	$1 + D^{17} + D^{21} + D^{43}$ $+ D^{49} + D^{67}$
4	129	$1 + D^9 + D^{33} + D^{37} +$ $D^{38} + D^{97} + D^{122} + D^{129}$	$1 + D^{11} + D^{13} + D^{23}$ $+ D^{62} + D^{76} + D^{79} + D^{123}$	$1 + D^{19} + D^{35} + D^{50}$ $+ D^{71} + D^{77} + D^{117}$ $+ D^{125}$
5	202	$1 + D^7 + D^{27} + D^{76}$ $+ D^{113} + D^{137} + D^{155}$ $+ D^{156} + D^{170} + D^{202}$	$1 + D^8 + D^{38} + D^{48} +$ $D^{59} + D^{82} + D^{111} + D^{146}$ $+ D^{150} + D^{152}$	$1 + D^{12} + D^{25} + D^{26} +$ $D^{76} + D^{81} + D^{98} + D^{107}$ $+ D^{143} + D^{197}$

From: [1,2].

References

[1] Bussgang, J. J., "Some Properties of Binary Convolutional Code Generators," *IEEE Trans. on Information Theory*, Vol. IT-11, No. 1, January 1965, pp. 90–100.

[2] Robinson, J. P., and A. J. Bernstein, "A Class of Binary Recurrent Codes With Limited Error Propagation," *IEEE Trans. on Information Theory*, Vol. IT-13, No. 1, January 1967, pp. 106–113.

Appendix E
Generator Polynomial Matrix for
Two-Dimensional Linear Trellis Codes

This appendix presents a set of tables of good rate-$(n-1)/n$ 2-D linear trellis codes with coherent M-ary signals for bandlimited AWGN channels, where $M = 2^n$. Tables E.1 and E.2 list the best rate-1/2 and rate-2/3 linear trellis codes with coherent 4-PSK and 8-PSK signals, respectively. Table E.3 lists the best rate-3/4 linear trellis codes with coherent 16-QAM signals. Those codes were found by Ungerboeck [1,2]. The connection vectors are given in octal notation and are right justified. For example, the connection vector $\mathbf{G}^{(1)} = [11101]$ becomes $[011\ 101] \underset{=}{\Delta} (35)_8$ after the right justification. The elements of the 1-by-n parity-check polynomial matrix $\mathbf{H}(D) = [H_1^{(1)}(D)\ H_1^{(2)}(D) \ldots H_1^{(n)}(D)]$ are given in polynomial form. For each trellis code of total encoder memory K, the constraint length ν, the minimum squared free Euclidean distance d_{fed}^2, the ACG in decibels, and the number of nearest neighbors, N_{fed}, with distance d_{fed}^2 are given. The trellis codes with coherent M-PSK signals are compared with the uncoded coherent $M/2$-PSK signals. All the signal points lie on the unit circle, and the average symbol energy E_s is unity. The trellis codes with coherent 16-QAM signals are compared with the uncoded coherent 8-ary amplitude-phase-shifted keying (8-APSK) signals. The signal constellations of the 16-QAM and 8-APSK signals are shown in Figures E.1 and E.2, respectively. The performance of the rate-1/2, $K = 2$ and 3 trellis codes with coherent 4-PSK signals and unquantized Viterbi decoding in AWGN channels are shown in Figure E.3. For all cases, the decoding search length is set to six times the constraint length of the code.

Table E.1
Connection Vectors and Parity-Check Polynomials of the Best Rate-1/2 Linear Trellis Codes
With 4-PSK Signals

K	ν	$G^{(1)}, G^{(2)}$	$H_1^{(1)}(D), H_1^{(2)}(D)$	d_{fed}^2	N_{fed}	ACG (dB)
2	3	2, 5	$1 + D^2, D$	10	1	3.98
3	4	6, 15	$1 + D + D^3, D + D^2$	12	2	4.77
4	5	4, 31	$1 + D + D^4, D^2$	14	3	5.44
5	6	14, 61	$1 + D + D^5, D^2 + D^3$	16	5	6.02
6	7	42, 171	$1 + D + D^2 + D^3 + D^6,$ $D + D^5$	20	11	6.99

From: [1].

Table E.2
Connection Vectors and Parity-Check Polynomials of the Best Rate-2/3 Linear Trellis Codes
With 8-PSK Signals

K	ν	$G^{(1)}, G^{(2)}, G^{(3)}$	$H_1^{(1)}(D), H_1^{(2)}(D), H_1^{(3)}(D)$	d_{fed}^2	N_{fed}	ACG (dB)
2	3	4, 21, 10	$1 + D^2, D, 0$	4.0	1	3.01
3	3	4, 22, 11	$1 + D^3, D, D^2$	4.586	2	3.60
4	3	4, 76, 35	$1 + D + D^4, D^2, D + D^2 + D^3$	5.172	≈ 2.3	4.13
5	5	250, 1100, 602	$1 + D^2 + D^5, D + D^2 + D^3, D^2 +$ $D^3 + D^4$	5.758	4	4.59
6	4	24, 206, 131	$1 + D + D^6, D^3 + D^4, D + D^2 + D^4$ $+ D^5$	6.343	≈ 5.3	5.01

From: [2].

Table E.3
Connection Vectors and Parity-Check Polynomials of the Best Rate-3/4 Linear Trellis Codes
With 16-QAM Signals

K	ν	$G^{(1)}, G^{(2)}, \ldots, G^{(4)}$	$H_1^{(1)}(D), H_1^{(2)}(D), H_1^{(3)}(D), H_1^{(4)}(D)$	d_{fed}^2	N_{fed}	ACG (dB)
2	3	10, 101, 40, 20	$1 + D^2, D, 0, 0$	1.6	4	3.01
3	3	10, 104, 41, 20	$1 + D^3, D, D^2, 0$	2	16	3.98
4	3	10, 332, 231, 40	$1 + D + D^4, D^2, D + D^2 + D^3, 0$	2.4	56	4.77
5	4	100, 1104, 1441, 200	$1 + D^5, D + D^2, D^3, 0$	2.4	16	4.77
6	5	1510, 14111, 5441, 2000	$1 + D^6, D + D^2 + D^3, D^2 + D^4$ $+ D^5, 0$	2.8	56	5.44

From: [2].

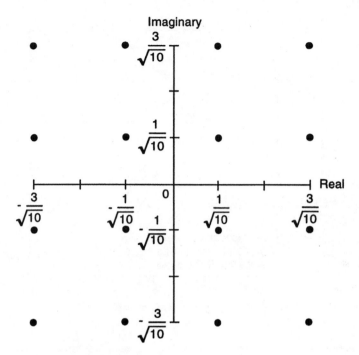

Figure E.1 16-QAM signal constellation.

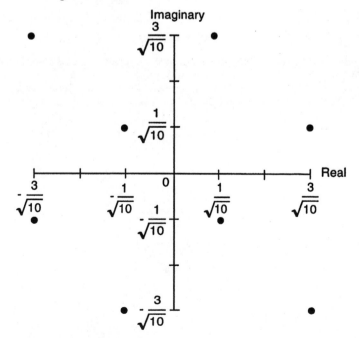

Figure E.2 8-APSK signal constellation.

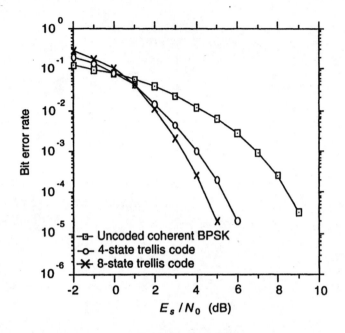

Figure E.3 Performance of rate-1/2 trellis codes with coherent 4-PSK signals and unquantized Viterbi decoding of search length 6ν in AWGN channels.

References

[1] Ungerboeck, G., "Codes for QPSK Modulation With Invariance Under 90° Rotation," *Mobile Satellite Conf. Proc.*, JPL Pub. 88-9, May 1988, pp. 277–282.

[2] Ungerboeck, G., "Trellis-Coded Modulation With Redundancy Signal Sets, Part 2: State of the Art," *IEEE Commun. Mag.*, Vol. 25, No. 2, February 1987, pp. 12–21.

This appendix contains a ANSI-standard C program called *conv_trel.c,* which generates the encoder trellis of an (*n*, *k*, *m*) linear binary systematic or non-systematic convolutional code and checks if the code is catastrophic or non-catastrophic. All the symbols are clearly defined in the program. They are not further discussed here.

The program reads the codeword length *nn*, the code dimension *kk*, the connection vector length *cvl*, and the connection vectors *cv* from the input file INCONV_TREL.DAT. An example of the input file is shown in Table F.1. During program execution, an output file RSCONV_TREL.DAT is generated. After execution of the program *conv_trel.c*, the codeword length *nn*, the code dimension *kk*, the code constraint length *vv*, the total number of trellis state *ts*, the connection vector length *cvl*, the connection vectors *cv*, the encoder trellis in a form of table, and the catastrophic flag are stored in the output file RSCONV_TREL.DAT. An example of the output file is shown in Table F.2.

F.1 ENCODER TRELLIS PROGRAM LISITING

```
/*
** FILE NAME    : conv_trel.c
**
** DESCRIPTION  : Generate encoder trellis of (nn, kk) linear binary
**                systematic or non-systematic convolutional code and
**                check if the code is catastrophic or non-catastrophic.
**
** DEPENDENCIES : INCONV_TREL.DAT
**
** REVISION     : Issue-1.0, date-28/08/1995
*/
```

```
/*====================================================================*/
/* FILE NAME : conv_trel.c                                            */
/*                                                                    */
/* DESCRIPTION :                                                      */
/*    This program reads data from file INCONV_TREL.DAT & generates   */
/*    the encoder trellis of an (nn, kk) linear binary systematic or  */
/*    non- systematic convolutional code.  It also checks if the code */
/*    is catastrophic or non-catastrophic.  Results are stored in     */
/*    file RSCONV_TREL.DAT.                                           */
/*                                                                    */
/* INTERFACE :                                                        */
/*    Input                                                           */
/*        data file INCONV_TREL.DAT                                   */
/*    Output                                                          */
/*        data file RSCONV_TREL.DAT                                   */
/*                                                                    */
/* REMARKS :                                                          */
/*    cvl must be divisible by kk.                                    */
/*                                                                    */
/*    The following parameters are delcared as global variables.      */
/*                                                                    */
/*    extern int catastrophic;          1 => catastrophic,            */
/*                                      0 => non-catastrophic         */
/*    extern int cvl;                   length of connection vectors  */
/*    extern int kk;                    code dimension                */
/*    extern int nn;                    codeword length               */
/*                                                                    */
/*    extern int cv[MAX_CV_ROW][MAX_CV_COL];                          */
/*                                      nn x cvl connection vectors   */
/*                                                                    */
/* REFERENCE :                                                        */
/*    [1] Lin, S., and Costello, D. J., Jr., Error-Control Coding :   */
/*        Fundamentals and Applications, Prentice-Hall, 1985.         */
/*====================================================================*/
#include <stdio.h>
#include <stdlib.h>
#include <math.h>

/* global definitions */
#define MAX_CV_COL      64      /* max. columns of cv */
#define MAX_CV_ROW      64      /* max. rows of cv */

/* local definitions */
#define MAX_ENC_SR      64      /* max. columns of enc_sr */
#define MAX_IVECTOR     64      /* max. length of ivector */
```

```
#define MAX_LOC           64     /* max. columns of location */
#define MAX_MAX_DEGREE    64     /* max. columns of max_degree */
#define MAX_PS_VECTOR     64     /* max. columns of ps_vector */
#define MAX_TREL_COL      20     /* max. columns of trel */
#define MAX_TREL_ROW      2048   /* max. rows of trel */
#define MAX_Y             64     /* max. columns of y */

/* global variables initialisations */
int catastrophic;   /* 1 => catastrophic, 0 => non-catastrophic */
int cvl;            /* length of connection vectors */
int kk;             /* code dimension */
int nn;             /* codeword length */


int cv[MAX_CV_ROW][MAX_CV_COL];    /* nn x cvl connection vectors */


FILE *fp_in_conv_trel, *fp_rs_conv_trel, *fopen();

main ()
{
    /* global variables declarations */
    extern int catastrophic;    /* 1 => catastrophic,
                                   0 => non-catastrophic */
    extern int cvl;             /* length of connection vectors */
    extern int kk;              /* code dimension */
    extern int nn;              /* codeword length */

    extern int cv[MAX_CV_ROW][MAX_CV_COL];
                                /* nn x cvl connection vectors */


    /* local variables declarations */
    int bcd;            /* bcd value of a vector */
    int blk;            /* = cvl / kk */
    int col;            /* column pointer */
    int i, j, ii, jj;   /* general purpose variables */
    int ivalue;         /* general purpose variable */
    int next_st;        /* trellis next state in bcd */
    int pow_of_kk;      /* = 2 ** kk */
    int pres_st;        /* trellis present state in bcd */
    int row;            /* row pointer */
    int tot_enc_m;      /* total encoder memory */
    int ts;             /* total no. of trellis states */
    int vv;             /* code constraint length */
    int x_bcd;          /* bcd value of uncoded word */
    int wt;             /* codeword weight */
```

```
int enc_sr[MAX_ENC_SR];              /* encoder single shift-register */
int ivector[MAX_IVECTOR];            /* general purpose vector */
int location[MAX_LOC];               /* state locations in enc_sr */
int max_degree[MAX_MAX_DEGREE];      /* max. degree of a polynomial */
int ps_vector[MAX_PS_VECTOR];        /* present state binary vector */
int trel[MAX_TREL_ROW][MAX_TREL_COL];   /* encoder trellis table */
int y[MAX_Y];                        /* binary codeword */

fp_in_conv_trel = fopen("INCONV_TREL.DAT", "r");
fp_rs_conv_trel = fopen("RSCONV_TREL.DAT", "w");
rewind(fp_in_conv_trel);
rewind(fp_rs_conv_trel);
/*------------------------*/
/*  Read nn, kk, cvl & cv  */
/*------------------------*/
fscanf(fp_in_conv_trel, "%d %d %d ", &nn, &kk, &cvl);
for (i = 0; i < nn; i++) {
   for (j = 0; j < cvl; j++) {
      fscanf(fp_in_conv_trel, "%d ", &ivalue);
      cv[i][j] = ivalue;
   }
}
/*------------------------------------------------------------------*/
/*  Find the maximum degree of each generator polynomial from cv  */
/*------------------------------------------------------------------*/
/* divide cv into blocks */
blk = cvl / kk;
/* find max. degree among all max_degree[ii], 0 < ii < kk */
for (ii = 0; ii < kk; ii++) {
   /* for each ii, reset max_degree[ii] & column pointer for cv */
   max_degree[ii] = 0;
   col = ii + kk;
   for (j = 1; j < blk; j++) {
      /* for j-th block of cv, update max_degree if cv has a 1 */
      for (i = 0; i < nn; i++) {
         if (cv[i][col] != 0) {
            max_degree[ii] = j;
         }
         else {
            ;
         }
      }
      /* increment pointer to next block */
      col = col + kk;
   }
```

```
}
/*--------------------------------------------------------*/
/*  Find code constraint length, total encoder memory,  */
/*  ts & pow_of_kk                                       */
/*--------------------------------------------------------*/
vv = 0;
for (i = 0; i < kk; i++) {
   if (max_degree[i] > vv) {
      vv = max_degree[i];
   }
   else {
      ;
   }
}
vv = vv + 1;

tot_enc_m = 0;
for (i = 0; i < kk; i++) {
   tot_enc_m = tot_enc_m + max_degree[i];
}
ts = power(2, tot_enc_m);
pow_of_kk = power(2, kk);
/*-------------------------------------------*/
/*  Find state locations in enc_sr from cv  */
/*-------------------------------------------*/
/* divide cv into blocks */
blk = cvl / kk;
/* find right most 1 position in cv associated with max_degree[ii] */
for (ii = 0; ii < kk; ii++) {
   /* for each ii, reset ivector[ii] & column pointer for cv */
   ivector[ii] = 0;
   col = ii + kk;
   for (j = 1; j < blk; j++) {
      /* for j-th block, update ivector if column of cv has a 1 */
      for (i = 0; i < nn; i++) {
         if (cv[i][col] != 0) {
            ivector[ii] = col;
         }
         else {
            ;
         }
      }
      /* increment pointer to next block */
      col = col + kk;
   }
```

```
   }

   /* use ivector to find state locations */
   blk = cvl / kk;
   ii = 0;
   for (i = 0; i < kk; i++) {
      jj = i;
      col = i;
      if (ivector[i] != 0) {
         for (j = 0; j < blk; j++) {
            if (col != ivector[jj] != 0) {
               /* store state location */
               location[ii] = col;
               ii = ii + 1;
               col = col + kk;
            }
            else {
               ;
            }
         }
      }
      else {
         ;
      }
   }
   /*--------------------------------*/
   /*  Compute trellis table & store  */
   /*--------------------------------*/
   row = 0;
   for (pres_st = 0; pres_st < ts; pres_st++) {
      /* convert present state from bcd to binary vector */
      bcd_to_binary(pres_st, tot_enc_m, ps_vector);

      for (x_bcd = 0; x_bcd < pow_of_kk; x_bcd++) {
         /* convert uncoded bits from bcd to binary vector */
         bcd_to_binary(x_bcd, kk, ivector);

         /* clear encoder single shift-register */
         for (i = 0; i < cvl; i++) {
            enc_sr[i] = 0;
         }

         /* put ps_vector into state locations in enc_sr */
         for (i = 0; i < tot_enc_m; i++) {
            col = location[i];
```

```
      enc_sr[col] = ps_vector[i];
}

/* shift enc_sr kk bits to the right */
for (i = 0; i < (cvl - kk); i++) {
    enc_sr[cvl - 1 - i] = enc_sr[cvl - 1 - i - kk];
}

/* store bcd of present state in trel */
trel[row][0] = pres_st;

/* store uncoded binary bits in trel */
for (i = 0; i < kk; i++) {
    trel[row][2 + i] = ivector[i];
}

/* put uncoded binary bits into enc_sr */
for (i = 0; i < kk; i++) {
    enc_sr[i] = ivector[i];
}

/* read next state binary bits from enc_sr state locations */
for (i = 0; i < tot_enc_m; i++) {
    col = location[i];
    ivector[i] = enc_sr[col];
}

/* convert next state vector (binary) to bcd & store in trel */
next_st = binary_to_bcd(tot_enc_m, ivector);
trel[row][1] = next_st;

/* find encoder output binary bits & store in trel */
for (i = 0; i < nn; i++) {
    y[i] = 0;
    for (j = 0; j < cvl; j++) {
        if (cv[i][j] != 0) {
            y[i] = y[i] + enc_sr[j];
            y[i] = y[i] % 2;
        }
        else {
            ;
        }
    }
    trel[row][2 + kk + i] = y[i];
}
```

```
        /* increment trel row pointer */
        row = row + 1;
    }
}
/*----------------------------------------------------------*/
/*  Re-arrange trellis in ascending order of next state  */
/*----------------------------------------------------------*/
ii = 0;
for (i = 0; i < ts; i++) {
    for (j = 0; j < (ts * pow_of_kk); j++) {
        if (trel[j][1] == i) {
            for (jj = 0; jj < (2 + kk + nn); jj++) {
                ivector[jj] = trel[ii][jj];
                trel[ii][jj] = trel[j][jj];
                trel[j][jj] = ivector[jj];
            }
            ii = ii + 1;
        }
        else {
            ;
        }
    }
}
/*-------------------------------------------------------------*/
/*  Check catastrophic code : self-looping state with 0 weight  */
/*-------------------------------------------------------------*/
catastrophic = 0;
for (i = 0; i < (pow_of_kk * ts); i++) {
    if (trel[i][0] == trel[i][1]) {
        /* pres_st equals next_st */
        if ((trel[i][0] == 0) && (trel[i][1] == 0)) {
            /* prest_st = 0 and equals next_st = 0 */
            ;
        }
        else {
            /* prest_st > 0 and equals next_st > 0 */
            /* find codeword weight */
            wt = 0;
            for (j = 0; j < nn; j++) {
                if (trel[i][2 + kk + j] != 0) {
                    wt = wt + 1;
                }
                else {
                    ;
                }
```

```
         }

         /* set catastrophic flag if wt = 0 */
         if (wt == 0) {
            catastrophic = 1;
         }
         else {
            ;
         }
      }
   }
   else {
      /* pres_st is not equal to next_st */
      ;
   }
}
/*-----------------*/
/*  Print results  */
/*-----------------*/
fprintf(fp_rs_conv_trel, "%3d %3d %3d %4d \n", nn, kk, vv, ts);
fprintf(fp_rs_conv_trel, "\n");

fprintf(fp_rs_conv_trel, "%3d \n", cvl);
for (i = 0; i < nn; i++) {
   for (j = 0; j < cvl; j++) {
      fprintf(fp_rs_conv_trel, "%3d ", cv[i][j]);
      }
   fprintf(fp_rs_conv_trel, "\n");
}
fprintf(fp_rs_conv_trel, "\n");

row = pow_of_kk * ts;
for (i = 0; i < row; i++) {
   for (j = 0; j < (2 + kk + nn); j++) {
      fprintf(fp_rs_conv_trel, "%3d ", trel[i][j]);
      }
      fprintf(fp_rs_conv_trel, "\n");
}
fprintf(fp_rs_conv_trel, "\n");
fprintf(fp_rs_conv_trel, "%3d \n", catastrophic);
fprintf(fp_rs_conv_trel, "----------------------------------- \n");
fprintf(fp_rs_conv_trel, "RSCONV_TREL.DAT is read by codect.c \n");
fprintf(fp_rs_conv_trel, "and the data format is \n");
fprintf(fp_rs_conv_trel, "\n");
fprintf(fp_rs_conv_trel, "nn kk vv ts \n");
```

```
    fprintf(fp_rs_conv_trel, "\n");
    fprintf(fp_rs_conv_trel, "cvl \n");
    fprintf(fp_rs_conv_trel, "cv[0;     0, 1, ..., cvl - 1] \n");
    fprintf(fp_rs_conv_trel, "cv[1;     0, 1, ..., cvl - 1] \n");
    fprintf(fp_rs_conv_trel, ": \n");
    fprintf(fp_rs_conv_trel, "cv[nn - 1; 0, 1, ..., cvl - 1] \n");
    fprintf(fp_rs_conv_trel, "\n");
    fprintf(fp_rs_conv_trel, "pres_st next_st ");
    fprintf(fp_rs_conv_trel, "x[0 ... kk - 1] y[0 ... nn - 1] \n");
    fprintf(fp_rs_conv_trel, ":        : \n");
    fprintf(fp_rs_conv_trel, "\n");
    fprintf(fp_rs_conv_trel, "catastrophic \n");
    fprintf(fp_rs_conv_trel, "\n");
    fclose(fp_in_conv_trel);
    fclose(fp_rs_conv_trel);
}




/*====================================================================*/
/* FUNCTION NAME : binary_to_bcd(length, vector)                      */
/*                                                                    */
/* DESCRIPTION :                                                      */
/*    Find binary-coded-decimal value of a binary vector of length    */
/*    length, where vector[0] = highest order.                        */
/*                                                                    */
/* INTERFACE :                                                        */
/*    Input                                                           */
/*        int length;                    length of binary vector      */
/*        int vector[];                   binary vector               */
/*    Output                                                          */
/*        int return(bcd);               bcd value of binary vector   */
/*====================================================================*/
int binary_to_bcd(length, vector)
int length;             /* length of vector */

int vector[];           /* binary vector */

{
    /* local variables declarations */
    int bcd;            /* bcd value of vector */
    int i;              /* general purpose variable */

    bcd = 0;
    for (i = 1; i <= length; i++) {
```

```
      if (vector[length - i] == 0)
         ;
      else
         bcd = power(2, i - 1) + bcd;
   }
   return(bcd);
}




/*=====================================================================*/
/* FUNCTION NAME : power(x, y)                                       */
/*                                                                   */
/* DESCRIPTION :                                                     */
/*     Find the value of x to the power of y.                        */
/*                                                                   */
/* INTERFACE :                                                       */
/*     Input                                                         */
/*         int x;                  an integer                        */
/*         int y;                  a positive integer                */
/*     Output                                                        */
/*         int return(p);          value of x to the power of y      */
/*=====================================================================*/
int power(x, y)
int x;      /* an integer */
int y;      /* a positive integer */

{
   /* local variables declarations */
   int i;   /* general purpose variables */
   int p;   /* value of x to the power of y */

   p = 1;
   for (i = 1; i <= y; i++) {
      p = p * x;
   }
   return(p);
}




/*=====================================================================*/
/* FUNCTION NAME : bcd_to_binary(bcd, length, vector)               */
/*                                                                   */
/* DESCRIPTION :                                                     */
/*     Given binary-coded-decimal value and binary vector length, find */
```

```
/*     the binary vector, where vector[0] = highest order.          */
/*                                                                  */
/* INTERFACE :                                                      */
/*     Input                                                        */
/*         int bcd;                      bcd value of binary vector */
/*         int length;                   length of binary vector    */
/*     Output                                                       */
/*         int vector[];                 binary vector              */
/*================================================================*/
int bcd_to_binary(bcd, length, vector)
int bcd;          /* bcd of vector */
int length;       /* length of vector */

int vector[];     /* binary vector */


{
    /* local variables declarations */
    int i;          /* general purpose variable */
    int qq;         /* quotient of qq / 2 */
    int remain;     /* remainder of qq / 2 */

    /* find binary vector of length 'length' */
    qq = bcd;
    for (i = 0; i < length; i++) {
        remain = qq % 2;
        qq = qq / 2;
        vector[length - 1 - i] = remain;
    }
    return;
}
```

Table F.1
Input File INCONV_TREL.DAT

---

2 1 3

1 0 1
1 1 1

INCONV_TREL.DAT is read by conv_trel.c
and the data format is

nn kk cvl

cv[0;   0, 1, ..., cvl - 1]
cv[1;   0, 1, ..., cvl - 1]
:
cv[nn - 1; 0, 1, ..., cvl - 1]

Table F.2
Output File RSCONV_TREL.DAT

```
2   1   3   4

3
1   0   1
1   1   1

0   0   0   0   0
1   0   0   1   1
2   1   0   0   1
3   1   0   1   0
0   2   1   1   1
1   2   1   0   0
2   3   1   1   0
3   3   1   0   1

0
```

RSCONV_TREL.DAT is read by codect.c
and the data format is

nn kk vv ts

cvl
cv[0;   0, 1, ..., cvl - 1]
cv[1;   0, 1, ..., cvl - 1]
:
cv[nn - 1; 0, 1, ..., cvl - 1]

pres_st next_st x[0 ... kk - 1] y[0 ... nn - 1]
:   :

catastrophic

Appendix G
Viterbi Codec Programs

This appendix contains a codec test program, *codect.c*; a convolutional encoding function, *conv_enc.c*; and a Viterbi decoding function, *vit_dec.c*. The program and functions are written in ANSI-standard C. All the symbols are clearly defined in the functions and the program. They are not further discussed here.

The codec test program, *codect.c*, reads the codeword length *nn*, the code dimension *kk*, the code constraint length *vv*, the total number of trellis states *ts*, the connection vector length *cvl*, the connection vectors *cv*, and the encoder trellis table from the file RSCONV_TREL.DAT (see Appendix F, Table F.2). It then reads the initial random number generator seed, *start*; the number of transmission frames, *x_tot*; the Gaussian noise, *mean*; the Gaussian noise standard deviation, *sd*; the lower limit of the value of *sd*, *limit*,; the decremental value of *sd*, *step*; and the decoding mode, *hard*, from the input file IN_CODECT.DAT. An example of the input file IN_CODECT.DAT is shown in Table G.1.

During program execution, an output file RS_CODECT.DAT is generated. The information symbol counter *x_cnt*, the error counter *xec*, and the uncoded delay line *xline* are initialized to 0. The information symbol counter *x_cnt* is incremented by *kk* after each transmission. An uncoded pattern is generated, stored in a vector *x* of length *kk*, and the delay line *xline*. Encoding process is then performed by calling the encoding function lin_bin_conv_enc(*x*, *y*). After the encoding, an encoded vector *y* of length *nn* is generated. Elements of *y* are BPSK modulated and stored in the vector *tx* of length *nn*. Gaussian noise samples are generated by calling the function g05ddf(*mean*, *sd*). Those noise samples are added to the transmitted vector *tx*. The received vector, *rx* = *tx* + *noise*, is hard-quantized and stored in the vector *rx_h* of length *nn*. Hard- or soft-decision decoding process is then performed by calling the decoding function viterbi_dec(*rx_s*, *ex*). After the decoding, the decoded information vector *ex* is returned. The decoded vector *ex* is compared with the uncoded information in the delay line *xline*. If *ex* is not equal to the contents in *xline*, the error counter *xec* is incremented accordingly. The information symbol count *x_cnt* is checked. If *x_cnt* is not equal to the number of transmission *x_tot*, the next information symbols are transmitted, and *x_cnt* is incremented; otherwise, the bit error rate is printed. *sd = sd − step*. If the standard deviation of the noise is less than the limit set by the user, stop; otherwise, transmit *x_tot* number of information symbols again with the new value of *sd*. After execution of the program *codect.c*, the Gaussian noise standard deviation, *sd*, the E_b/N_0 ratio in decibels, and the bit error rate are stored in the output file RS_CODECT.DAT. An example of the output file is shown in Table G.2.

G.1 CODEC TEST PROGRAM LISITING

```
/*
** FILE NAME    : codect.c
**
** DESCRIPTION  : Perform bit error rate simulation of (nn, kk) linear
**                binary systematic or non-systematic convolutional code
**                with BPSK signals and hard-decision/soft-decision
**                distance Viterbi trellis decoding over AWGN channel
**
** DEPENDENCIES : RSCONV_TREL.DAT, IN_CODECT.DAT,
**                conv_enc.c, vit_dec.c
**
** REVISION     : Issue-1.0, date-28/08/1995
*/


/*====================================================================*/
/* FILE NAME : codect.c                                              */
/*                                                                    */
/* DESCRIPTION :                                                      */
/*    The program reads parameters from files IN_CODECT.DAT & RSCONV_ */
/*    TREL.DAT and performs bit error rate simulation of (nn, kk)     */
/*    linear binary systematic or non-systematic convolutional code   */
/*    with BPSK signals and hard-decision/soft-decision distance      */
/*    Viterbi trellis decoding over AWGN channel.  Results are stored */
/*    in file RS_CODECT.DAT.                                          */
/*                                                                    */
/*    To perform bit error rate simulation, choose a +ve starting     */
/*    seed for random number,  choose no. of transmitted uncoded      */
/*    symbols x_tot, set noise mean = 0.0, choose a +ve value for     */
/*    noise standard deviation sd, set the lower limit of sd to       */
/*    limit, set the decremental step of sd to step and the decoding  */
/*    mode to 1 for hard or 0 for soft (infinite quantisation).       */
/*    Simulated bit error rate results are stored in file             */
```

```
/*      RS_CODECT.DAT.                                                    */
/*                                                                        */
/* INTERFACE :                                                            */
/*      Input                                                             */
/*          data file RSCONV_TREL.DAT                                     */
/*          data file IN_CODECT.DAT                                       */
/*      Output                                                            */
/*          data file RS_CODECT.DAT                                       */
/*                                                                        */
/* REMARKS :                                                              */
/*      The following parameters must be delcared as global variables.    */
/*                                                                        */
/*      extern int cvl;          length of connection vectors            */
/*      extern int dd;           decoding depth                          */
/*      extern int kk;           code dimension                          */
/*      extern int nn;           codeword length                         */
/*      extern int pow_of_kk;    = 2 ** kk                               */
/*      extern int ts;           total no. of trellis state              */
/*                                                                        */
/*      extern long seed;        running seed for random number generator */
/*                                                                        */
/*      extern double bra_dist[MAX_BRA_DIST];      branch distance        */
/*      extern double per_dist[MAX_PER_DIST];      permanent distance     */
/*      extern double run_dist[MAX_RUN_DIST];      running distance       */
/*                                                                        */
/*      extern int cv[MAX_CV_ROW][MAX_CV_COL];     connection vectors     */
/*      extern int enc_sr[MAX_ENC_SR];    encoder single shift-register   */
/*      extern int trel[MAX_TREL_ROW][MAX_TREL_COL];                      */
/*                                         encoder trellis table          */
/*      extern int xbin[MAX_XBIN_ROW][MAX_XBIN_COL];                      */
/*                                      temporary uncoded symbol storage  */
/*      extern int xper[MAX_XPER_ROW][MAX_XPER_COL];                      */
/*                                      permanent uncoded symbol storage  */
/*======================================================================*/
#include <stdio.h>
#include <stdlib.h>
#include <math.h>
#include "conv_enc.c"
#include "vit_dec.c"

/* global definitions */
#define MAX_BRA_DIST   256      /* max. length of bra_dist */
#define MAX_CV_COL     64       /* max. columns of cv */
#define MAX_CV_ROW     64       /* max. rows of cv */
#define MAX_ENC_SR     64       /* max. columns of enc_sr */
```

```
#define MAX_PER_DIST    256     /* max. length of per_dist */
#define MAX_RUN_DIST    256     /* max. length of run_dist */
#define MAX_TREL_COL    10      /* max. columns of trel */
#define MAX_TREL_ROW    2048    /* max. rows of trel */
#define MAX_XBIN_COL    256     /* max. columns of xbin */
#define MAX_XBIN_ROW    256     /* max. rows of xbin */
#define MAX_XPER_COL    256     /* max. columns of xper */
#define MAX_XPER_ROW    256     /* max. rows of xper */

/* local definitions */
#define MAX_EX      64      /* max. length of ex */
#define MAX_NOISE   64      /* max. length of noise */
#define MAX_RX      64      /* max. length of rx */
#define MAX_RX_H    64      /* max. length of rx_h */
#define MAX_TX      64      /* max. length of tx */
#define MAX_X       64      /* max. length of x */
#define MAX_XLINE   2048    /* max. length of xline */
#define MAX_Y       64      /* max. length of y */

/* global variables initialisations */
int cvl;          /* length of connection vectors */
int dd;           /* decoding depth */
int kk;           /* code dimension */
int nn;           /* codeword length */
int pow_of_kk;    /* = 2 ** kk */
int ts;           /* total no. of trellis states */

long seed;        /* running seed for random number generator */

double bra_dist[MAX_BRA_DIST];    /* branch distance */
double per_dist[MAX_PER_DIST];    /* permanent distance */
double run_dist[MAX_RUN_DIST];    /* running distance */

int cv[MAX_CV_ROW][MAX_CV_COL];    /* connection vectors */
int enc_sr[MAX_ENC_SR];            /* encoder single shift-register */
int trel[MAX_TREL_ROW][MAX_TREL_COL];
                                   /* encoder trellis table */
int xbin[MAX_XBIN_ROW][MAX_XBIN_COL];
                                   /* temporary uncoded symbol storage */
int xper[MAX_XPER_ROW][MAX_XPER_COL];
                                   /* permanent uncoded symbol storage */

FILE *fp_rs_conv_trel, *fp_in_codect, *fp_rs_codect, *fopen();

main ()
```

```
{
    /* global variables declarations */
    extern int cvl;          /* length of connection vectors */
    extern int dd;           /* decoding depth */
    extern int kk;           /* code dimension */
    extern int nn;           /* codeword length */
    extern int pow_of_kk;    /* = 2 ** kk */
    extern int ts;           /* total no. of trellis states */

    extern long seed;     /* running seed for random number generator */

    extern double bra_dist[MAX_BRA_DIST];    /* branch distance */
    extern double per_dist[MAX_PER_DIST];    /* permanent distance */
    extern double run_dist[MAX_RUN_DIST];    /* running distance */

    extern int cv[MAX_CV_ROW][MAX_CV_COL];    /* connection vectors */
    extern int enc_sr[MAX_ENC_SR];
                                    /* encoder single shift-register */
    extern int trel[MAX_TREL_ROW][MAX_TREL_COL];
                                    /* encoder trellis table */
    extern int xbin[MAX_XBIN_ROW][MAX_XBIN_COL];
                                    /* temporary uncoded symbol storage */
    extern int xper[MAX_XPER_ROW][MAX_XPER_COL];
                                    /* permanent uncoded symbol storage */

    /* local variables declarations */
    double epb;              /* energy per bit */
    double ebno;            /* Eb/No ratio */
    double g05caf();        /* 0.0 <= random no. generator <= 1.0 */
    double g05ddf();        /* Gaussian noise generator */
    double rn;              /* uniformly distributed random number */

    float ebno_db;          /* Eb/No ratio in dB */
    float limit;            /* lower limit for sd */
    float mean;             /* mean of additive Gaussian noise */
    float sd;               /* standard deviation of Gaussian noise */
    float step;             /* decremental step for sd */
    float xpe;              /* bit error rate */

    int hard;               /* hard-decision = 1, soft-decision = 0 */
    int i, j;               /* general purpose variables */
    int ivalue;             /* general purpose variable */
    int start;              /* user defined seed for random generator */
    int vv;                 /* code constraint length */
    int x_cnt;              /* transmitted information symbol counter */
```

```
int x_tot;                /* total no. of tx information symbols */
int xec;                  /* total no. of decoded bit errors */

long g05cbf();            /* return seed = start + 1 for even start */
                          /* or seed = start for odd start */
long newseed();           /* new seed for random generator */

double noise[MAX_NOISE];  /* Gaussian noise vector of length nn */
double rx[MAX_RX];        /* unquantised received vector, length nn */
double rx_h[MAX_RX_H];    /* hard received vector of length nn */
double tx[MAX_TX];        /* tx BPSK signal vector, length nn */

int ex[MAX_EX];           /* decoded information of length kk */
int x[MAX_X];             /* uncoded information of length kk */
int xline[MAX_XLINE];     /* uncoded information delay line */
int y[MAX_Y];             /* codeword of length nn */
fp_rs_conv_trel = fopen("RSCONV_TREL.DAT", "r");
fp_in_codect = fopen("IN_CODECT.DAT", "r");
fp_rs_codect = fopen("RS_CODECT.DAT", "w");
rewind(fp_rs_conv_trel);
rewind(fp_in_codect);
rewind(fp_rs_codect);
/*-----------------------------------------------------------*/
/*  Read codec parameters - nn, kk, vv, ts, cvl, cv, trel   */
/*-----------------------------------------------------------*/
fscanf(fp_rs_conv_trel, "%d %d %d %d ", &nn, &kk, &vv, &ts);
fscanf(fp_rs_conv_trel, "%d ", &cvl);
for (i = 0; i < nn; i++) {
   for (j = 0; j < cvl; j++) {
      fscanf(fp_rs_conv_trel, "%d ", &ivalue);
      cv[i][j] = ivalue;
   }
}

/* find pow_of kk & read trel */
pow_of_kk = 1;
for (i = 1; i <= kk; i++) {
   pow_of_kk = pow_of_kk * 2;
}
for (i = 0; i < (ts * pow_of_kk); i++) {
   for (j = 0; j < (2 + kk + nn); j++) {
      fscanf(fp_rs_conv_trel, "%d ", &ivalue);
      trel[i][j] = ivalue;
   }
}
```

```
/*------------------------------------------------------*/
/*  Read start, x_tot, mean, sd, limit, step & hard  */
/*------------------------------------------------------*/
fscanf(fp_in_codect, "%d %d %f %f %f %f %d ",
       &start, &x_tot, &mean, &sd, &limit, &step, &hard);
/*----------------------------------*/
/*  Perform bit error rate test  */
/*----------------------------------*/
fprintf(fp_rs_codect, "Bit error rate test results : \n");
fprintf(fp_rs_codect, " sd     Eb/No(dB)   BER \n");
/*-------------------*/
/*  Initialisation  */
/*-------------------*/
/*  find a seed for function g05caf & compute energy per bit  */
seed = g05cbf(start);
epb = 1.0 * ((double) nn / (kk + 0.0));
/* set decoding depth = six times the code constraint length */
dd = 6 * vv;

/*  For every sd, clear x_cnt & xec before transmission  */
line_1000:
x_cnt = 0;
xec = 0;

/*  Initialise uncoded delay line = 0 */
for (i = 0; i < (kk * dd); i++) {
   xline[i] = 0;
}

/*  Initialise encoder : set enc_sr to 0 */
for (i = 0; i < cvl; i++) {
   enc_sr[i] = 0;
}

/* Initialise decoder : */
/* set uncoded symbols in all survive paths to 0 */
for (i = 0; i < ts; i++) {
   for (j = 0; j < (kk * dd); j++) {
      xbin[i][j] = 0;
      xper[i][j] = 0;
   }
}
/* Initialise decoder : assign first running distance to 0.0 */
per_dist[0] = 0.0;
run_dist[0] = 0.0;
```

```
/* Initialise decoder : assign other running distances to infinity */
for (i = 1; i < ts; i++) {
   per_dist[i] = 100.0;
   run_dist[i] = 100.0;
}
/* Initialise decoder : clear all branch distances */
for (i = 0; i < pow_of_kk; i++) {
   bra_dist[i] = 0.0;
}
/* begin transmission */
line_1100: x_cnt = x_cnt + kk;
/*--------------------*/
/*  Tx kk information  */
/*--------------------*/
for (i = 0; i < kk; i++) {
   seed = newseed();
   rn = g05caf();
   if (rn <= 0.5)
      x[i] = 0;
   else
      x[i] = 1;
}
/* put x into r.h.s. of xline */
for (i = 0; i < kk; i++) {
   xline[(dd - 1) * kk + i] = x[i];
}
/*--------------------*/
/*  Perform encoding  */
/*--------------------*/
lin_bin_conv_enc(x, y);
/*--------------------------*/
/*  Perform BPSK modulation  */
/*--------------------------*/
for (i = 0; i < nn; i++) {
   if (y[i] == 0)
      tx[i] = -1.0;
   else
      tx[i] = 1.0;
}
/*--------------------*/
/*  Add channel noise  */
/*--------------------*/
/*  read AWG noise data  */
for (i = 0; i < nn; i++) {
   noise[i] = g05ddf(mean, sd);
```

```
   rx[i] = tx[i] + noise[i];
}
/*--------------------*/
/*  Hard quantisation  */
/*--------------------*/
for (i = 0; i < nn; i++) {
   if (rx[i] < 0.0)
      rx_h[i] = -1.0;
   else
      rx_h[i] = 1.0;
}
/*-------------------------------------*/
/*  Perform hard- or soft-decision     */
/*  (infinite quantisation) decoding   */
/*-------------------------------------*/
if (hard == 0) {
   viterbi_decoder(rx, ex);
}
else {
   viterbi_decoder(rx_h, ex);
}
/*---------------*/
/*  Error count  */
/*---------------*/
for (i = 0; i < kk; i++) {
   if (ex[i] == xline[i])
      ;
   else
      xec = xec + 1;
}
/*------------------------*/
/*  Shift xline left once  */
/*------------------------*/
/* shift xline left once */
for (i = 0; i < ((dd - 1) * kk); i++) {
   xline[i] = xline[i + kk];
}

/*-------------------------------------------------*/
/*  If x_cnt < x_tot, continue to transmit for  */
/*  the current value of sd                      */
/*-------------------------------------------------*/
if (x_cnt != x_tot)
   goto line_1100;
else
   ;
```

```
/*--------------------------*/
/*  Print error rate results  */
/*--------------------------*/
xpe = (double) xec / (x_tot + 0.0);
ebno = (double) epb / (2.0 * sd * sd);
ebno_db = 10.0 * log10(ebno);
fprintf(fp_rs_codect, "%5.2f %7.2f %10.3f", sd, ebno_db, xpe);
fprintf(fp_rs_codect, "\n");
/*--------------------------------------------------------*/
/*  Decrement sd for another bit error rate simulation  */
/*--------------------------------------------------------*/
sd = sd - step;
if (sd >= limit)
   goto line_1000;
else
   ;

fclose(fp_rs_conv_trel);
fclose(fp_in_codect);
fclose(fp_rs_codect);
}




/*======================================================================*/
/* FUNCTION NAME : g05cbf(start)                                      */
/*                                                                    */
/* DESCRIPTION :                                                      */
/*    Given start, the user defined seed, modify & return a new seed. */
/*    For even start, loc_seed = start + 1 otherwise loc_seed =       */
/*    start.                                                          */
/*                                                                    */
/* INTERFACE :                                                        */
/*    Input                                                           */
/*       int start;           user defined seed for random generator */
/*    Output                                                          */
/*       long return (loc_seed); new seed for random number generator */
/*                                                                    */
/* REMARKS :                                                          */
/*    Nil.                                                            */
/*======================================================================*/
long g05cbf(start)
int start;           /* user defined seed for random generator */
{
   long loc_seed;    /* local seed */
```

```
   if ((start % 2) == 0)
      loc_seed = start + 1;
   else
      loc_seed = start;

   if (loc_seed < 0 )
      loc_seed = -loc_seed;

   loc_seed = loc_seed % 1048576;
   return (loc_seed);
}




/*=====================================================================*/
/* FUNCTION NAME : newseed()                                           */
/*                                                                     */
/* DESCRIPTION :                                                       */
/*    Use running seed to find new seed before calling random no.     */
/*    generator function g05caf.                                       */
/*                                                                     */
/* INTERFACE :                                                         */
/*    Input                                                            */
/*        extern long seed;   running seed for random number generator */
/*    Output                                                           */
/*        long return (loc_seed); new seed for random number generator */
/*                                                                     */
/* REMARKS :                                                           */
/*    The following parameter must be delcared as global variable.    */
/*                                                                     */
/*    extern long seed;       running seed for random number generator */
/*=====================================================================*/
long newseed()
{
   /* global variable declaration */
   extern long seed;   /* running seed for random number generator */

   /* local variable declaration */
   long loc_seed;       /* local seed */

   loc_seed = (double) ((seed * 1029 + 221591) % 1048576);
   return(loc_seed);
}
```

```
/*=====================================================================*/
/* FUNCTION NAME : g05caf()                                            */
/*                                                                     */
/* DESCRIPTION :                                                       */
/*    Use the seed value of function newseed() to generate a           */
/*    uniformly distributed random number rn, where 0.0 <= rn <= 1.0.  */
/*                                                                     */
/* INTERFACE :                                                         */
/*    Input                                                            */
/*       long seed;          running seed for random number generator  */
/*    Output                                                           */
/*       double return(rn);  uniformly distributed random number       */
/*                                                                     */
/* REMARKS :                                                           */
/*    The following parameter must be delcared as global variable.     */
/*                                                                     */
/*    extern long seed;      running seed for random number generator  */
/*=====================================================================*/
double g05caf()
{
   /* global variable declaration */
   extern long seed;   /* running seed for random number generator */

   /* local variable declaration */
   double rn;              /* uniformly distributed random number */

   /* generate a uniformly distributed random number */
   rn = (double)seed / 1048576.0;
   return (rn);
}




/*=====================================================================*/
/* FUNCTION NAME : g05ddf()                                            */
/*                                                                     */
/* DESCRIPTION :                                                       */
/*    Given mean, sd & return a Gaussian random number by calling      */
/*    functions newseed() and g05caf().                                */
/*                                                                     */
/* INTERFACE :                                                         */
/*    Input                                                            */
/*       float mean;              mean of additive Gaussian noise      */
/*       float sd;                standard deviation of Gaussian noise */
/*    Output                                                           */
```

```
/*          double return (gauss_rn);    Gaussian random number           */
/*                                                                         */
/* REMARKS :                                                               */
/*    The following parameter must be declared as global variable.        */
/*                                                                         */
/*    extern long seed;         running seed for random no. generator */
/*=======================================================================*/
double g05ddf(mean, sd)
float mean;               /* mean of additive Gaussian noise */
float sd;                 /* standard deviation of Gaussian noise */
{
   /* global variable declaration */
   extern long seed;    /* running seed for random number generator */

   /* local variables declarations */
   int i;                 /* general purpose variable */
   int num;               /* total no. of rn to generate gauss_rn */

   long newseed();        /* new seed for random generator */

   double g05caf();       /* 0.0 <= random no. generator <= 1.0 */
   double gauss_rn;       /* Gaussian random number */
   double rn;             /* uniform distributed random number */
   double sum;            /* sum of rn */

   /* reset sum, set num to 12, compute sum of 12 rn & gauss_rn */
   sum = 0.0;
   num = 12;
   for (i = 0; i < num; i++) {
      seed = newseed();
      rn = g05caf();
      sum = sum + rn;
   }
   gauss_rn = sd * (sum - 6.0) * sqrt((double) ((double) num / 12.0)) +
              mean;
   return (gauss_rn);
}
```

G.2 CONVOLUTIONAL ENCODER PROGRAM LISITING

```
/*
** FILE NAME     : conv_enc.c
**
** DESCRIPTION   : Perform encoding of (nn, kk) linear binary systematic
```

```
**                or non-systematic convolutional code
**
** DEPENDENCIES : None
**
** REVISION    : Issue-1.0, date-28/08/1995
*/


/*===================================================================*/
/* FUNCTION NAME : lin_bin_conv_enc(x, y)                            */
/*                                                                   */
/* DESCRIPTION :                                                     */
/*    Perform encoding of (nn, kk) linear binary systematic or non-  */
/*    systematic convolutional code.  Given uncoded information      */
/*    length kk, codeword length nn, connection vectors length cvl,  */
/*    connection vectors cv, encoder single shift-register of length */
/*    cvl, and uncoded information x, compute codeword y.            */
/*                                                                   */
/* INTERFACE :                                                       */
/*    Input                                                          */
/*       int x[];                      uncoded information           */
/*    Output                                                         */
/*       int y[];                      codeword of length nn         */
/*                                                                   */
/* REMARKS :                                                         */
/*    The following parameters must be delcared as global variables. */
/*                                                                   */
/*    extern int cvl;                  length of cv                  */
/*    extern int kk;                   code dimension                */
/*    extern int nn;                   codeword length               */
/*                                                                   */
/*    extern int cv[MAX_CV_ROW][MAX_CV_COL];   connection vectors    */
/*    extern int enc_sr[MAX_ENC_SR];   encoder single shift-register */
/*                                                                   */
/*    Encoder register enc_sr MUST be clear before your first        */
/*    function call.                                                 */
/*                                                                   */
/* REFERENCE:                                                        */
/*    [1]  Lin, S. and  Costello, D. J., Jr.,  Error Control Coding: */
/*         Fundamentals and Applications, Prentice-Hall, Inc., 1983  */
/*===================================================================*/
/* global definitions */
#define MAX_CV_COL   64   /* max. columns of cv */
#define MAX_CV_ROW   64   /* max. rows of cv */
#define MAX_ENC_SR   64   /* max. columns of enc_sr */
```

```c
int lin_bin_conv_enc(x, y)
int x[];                    /* uncoded information of length kk */
int y[];                    /* codeword of length nn */

{
    /* global variables declarations */
    extern int cvl;                         /* length of cv */
    extern int kk;                          /* code dimension */
    extern int nn;                          /* codeword length */

    extern int cv[MAX_CV_ROW][MAX_CV_COL];    /* connection vectors */
    extern int enc_sr[MAX_ENC_SR];    /* encoder single shift-register */

    /* local variables declarations */
    int blk;      /* no. of blocks = cvl / kk in cv & rem (cvl / kk) = 0 */
    int i, j;   /* general purpose variables */
    /*--------------------------------*/
    /*  Perform convolutional encoding  */
    /*--------------------------------*/
    /* right shift enc_sr kk-bit per block if blk > 1 */
    blk = cvl / kk;
    if (blk > 1) {
        for (i = 0; i < (cvl - kk); i++) {
            enc_sr[(cvl - 1) - i] = enc_sr[(cvl - 1 - kk) - i];
        }
    }
    else {
        ;
    }
     /* put uncoded information bits into l.h.s. of enc_sr */
    for (i = 0; i < kk; i++) {
        enc_sr[i] = x[i];
    }

    /* clear y */
    for (i = 0; i < nn; i++) {
        y[i] = 0;
    }
    /* find encoded channel bits and store in y */
    for (i = 0; i < nn; i++) {
        for (j = 0; j < cvl; j++) {
            if (cv[i][j] != 0) {
                y[i] = y[i] + enc_sr[j];
                if (y[i] == 2) {
                    y[i] = 0;
```

```
            }
            else {
                ;
            }
        }
        else {
            ;
        }
    }
}
return;
}
```

G.3 VITERBI DECODER PROGRAM LISITING

```
/*
** FILE NAME    : vit_dec.c
**
** DESCRIPTION  : Perform minimum hard-decision or soft-decision
**                (infinite quantisation) distance Viterbi trellis
**                decoding of (nn, kk)linear binary systematic or
**                non-systematic convolutional code with coherent
**                BPSK signals
**
** DEPENDENCIES : None
**
** REVISION     : Issue-1.0, date-28/08/1995
*/


/*====================================================================*/
/* FUNCTION NAME : viterbi_decoder(rx_s, ex)                          */
/*                                                                    */
/* DESCRIPTION :                                                      */
/*    Perform minimum hard-decision or soft-decision (infinite       */
/*    quantisation) distance Viterbi trellis decoding of (nn, kk)     */
/*    linear binary systematic or non-systematic convolutional code  */
/*    with coherent binary phase-shift- keying (BPSK) signals.  Given */
/*    uncoded information length kk, codeword length nn, total number */
/*    of trellis states ts, convolutional trellis table trel,         */
/*    decoding depth dd, & the received data rx_s; find the closest   */
/*    codeword ey & uncoded information ex.  For each trellis state,  */
/*    compute branch distances and pick a minimum distance path.  For */
/*    all states, find the minimum distance path.  The decoded        */
/*    information is ex.  For hard-decision decoding, rx_s = 1.0 or   */
```

```
/*     -1.0.                                                           */
/*                                                                     */
/* INTERFACE :                                                         */
/*    Input                                                            */
/*        double rx_s[];                          received word        */
/*    Output                                                           */
/*        int ex[];                               decoded information  */
/*                                                                     */
/* REMARKS :                                                           */
/*    The following parameters must be declared as global variables.  */
/*                                                                     */
/*    extern int dd;          decoding depth                          */
/*    extern int kk;          code dimension                          */
/*    extern int nn;          codeword length                         */
/*    extern int pow_of_kk;   = 2 ** kk                               */
/*    extern int ts;          total no. of trellis states             */
/*                                                                     */
/*    extern long seed;       running seed for random number generator */
/*                                                                     */
/*    extern double bra_dist[MAX_BRA_DIST];       branch distance      */
/*    extern double per_dist[MAX_PER_DIST];       permanent distance   */
/*    extern double run_dist[MAX_RUN_DIST];       running distance     */
/*                                                                     */
/*    extern int trel[MAX_TREL_ROW][MAX_TREL_COL];                     */
/*                                encoder trellis table                */
/*    extern int xbin[MAX_XBIN_ROW][MAX_XBIN_COL];                     */
/*                                temporary uncoded symbol storage     */
/*    extern int xper[MAX_XPER_ROW][MAX_XPER_COL];                     */
/*                                permanent uncoded symbol storage     */
/*                                                                     */
/*    xbin, xper, per_dist[0], run_dist[0] MUST be clear before your   */
/*    first function call.  Also, rest of per_dist & run_dist are set  */
/*    to 100.0.                                                        */
/*                                                                     */
/* REFERENCE:                                                          */
/*    [1] Forney, G. D., Jr., "The Viterbi Algorithm", Proc. IEEE,     */
/*        vol. 61, pp. 268-278, 1973.                                  */
/*===================================================================*/
/* global definitions */
#define MAX_BRA_DIST    256    /* max. length of bra_dist */
#define MAX_PER_DIST    256    /* max. length of per_dist */
#define MAX_RUN_DIST    256    /* max. length of run_dist */
#define MAX_TREL_COL    10     /* max. columns of trel */
#define MAX_TREL_ROW    2048   /* max. rows of trel */
#define MAX_XBIN_COL    256    /* max. columns of xbin */
```

```
#define MAX_XBIN_ROW    256     /* max. rows of xbin */
#define MAX_XPER_COL    256     /* max. columns of xper */
#define MAX_XPER_ROW    256     /* max. rows of xper */

viterbi_decoder(rx_s, ex)
double rx_s[];     /* received word */
int ex[];          /* decoded information */

{
    /* global variables declarations */
    extern int dd;           /* decoding depth */
    extern int kk;           /* code dimension */
    extern int nn;           /* codeword length */
    extern int pow_of_kk;    /* = 2 ** kk */
    extern int ts;           /* total no. of trellis states */

    extern long seed;     /* running seed for random number generator */

    extern double bra_dist[MAX_BRA_DIST];     /* branch distance */
    extern double per_dist[MAX_PER_DIST];     /* permanent distance */
    extern double run_dist[MAX_RUN_DIST];     /* running distance */
    extern int trel[MAX_TREL_ROW][MAX_TREL_COL];
                              /* encoder trellis table */
    extern int xbin[MAX_XBIN_ROW][MAX_XBIN_COL];
                              /* temporary uncoded symbol storage */
    extern int xper[MAX_XPER_ROW][MAX_XPER_COL];
                              /* permanent uncoded symbol storage */

    /* local variables declarations */
    double dist;         /* Euclidean distance between 2 signal points */
    double min_dist;     /* minimum distance at a trellis stage */

    int col;             /* column pointer */
    int i, j, ii;        /* general purpose variables */
    int index;           /* an index pointer */
    int past_st;         /* trellis past state = present state in trel */
    int path;            /* no. of paths before calling mindex */
    int state;           /* = next state in trel */
    int row;             /* trellis table row pointer */
    /*-----------------------------------------------------------*/
    /*  For all states, shift xper left once & transfer to xbin  */
    /*-----------------------------------------------------------*/
    for (i = 0; i < ts; i++) {
        for (j = 0; j < ((dd - 1) * kk); j++) {
            xper[i][j] = xper[i][j + kk];
```

```
   }
   for (j = ((dd - 1) * kk); j < (dd * kk); j++) {
      xper[i][j] = 0;
   }
}
/* transfer xper to xbin */
for (i = 0; i < ts; i++) {
   for (j = 0; j < (dd * kk); j++) {
      xbin[i][j] = xper[i][j];
   }
}
/*----------------------------------------------------*/
/*  For all states, transfer per_dist to run_dist  */
/*----------------------------------------------------*/
for (i = 0; i < ts; i++) {
   run_dist[i] = per_dist[i];
}
/*--------------------------------------------------------------------*/
/*  For all states, find branch distances & pick min. path/state  */
/*--------------------------------------------------------------------*/
for (state = 0; state < ts; state++) {
   row = state * pow_of_kk;

   /*---------------------------------------------*/
   /*  At a state, compute all branch distances  */
   /*---------------------------------------------*/
   for (i = 0; i < pow_of_kk; i++) {
      /* for a path entering that node (state), */
      /* find metric between 2 vectors rx_s & trel */
      dist = 0.0;
      for (j = 0; j < nn; j++) {
         if (trel[row][2 + kk + j] == 0) {
            dist = (rx_s[j] + 1.0) * (rx_s[j] + 1.0) + dist;
         }
         else {
            dist = (rx_s[j] - 1.0) * (rx_s[j] - 1.0) + dist;
          }
      }

      /* check past state from trellis table */
      past_st = trel[row][0];
      /* update branch distance by adding dist to running distance */
      bra_dist[i] = run_dist[past_st] + dist;
      /* increment row which points to next row of trellis table */
      row = row + 1;
```

```
   }
   /*----------------------------------------------------------------*/
   /*  At a state find index of minimun bra_dist & pick that path   */
   /*----------------------------------------------------------------*/
   path = pow_of_kk;
   index = mindex(bra_dist, path);
   /* use index & find the row location in trellis table */
   row = state * pow_of_kk + index;
   /*----------------------------------------------------*/
   /*  At a state transfer xbin (pointed by past_st)   */
   /*  to xper (pointed by state)                      */
   /*----------------------------------------------------*/
   past_st = trel[row][0];
   for (j = 0; j < ((dd - 1) * kk); j++) {
      xper[state][j] = xbin[past_st][j];
   }
   /*----------------------------------------------------------------*/
   /*  At a state, transfer trellis information symbol to right  */
   /*  most side of xper & transfer branch distance to per_dist  */
   /*----------------------------------------------------------------*/
   for (j = 0; j < kk; j++) {
      xper[state][(dd - 1) * kk + j] = trel[row][2 + j];
   }

   /* transfer bra_dist to per_dist */
   per_dist[state] = bra_dist[index];
}

/*----------------------------------------------------------------*/
/*  For all states, select one min. distance for normalisation  */
/*----------------------------------------------------------------*/
path = ts;
index = mindex(per_dist, path);
/* per_dist normalisation */
min_dist = per_dist[index];
for (i = 0; i < ts; i++) {
   per_dist[i] = per_dist[i] - min_dist;
}
/*--------------------------------------------*/
/*  Select min. distance path & decode  */
/*--------------------------------------------*/
for (i = 0; i < kk; i++) {
   ex[i] = xper[index][i];
}
return;
```

```
}



/*===================================================================*/
/* FUNCTION NAME : mindex(sed, no_of_element)                        */
/*                                                                   */
/* DESCRIPTION :                                                     */
/*    Find location of the smallest element in sed.                  */
/*                                                                   */
/* INTERFACE :                                                       */
/*    Input                                                          */
/*        int no_of_element;      total no. of elements in sed       */
/*        double sed[];           a set of soft Euclidean distances  */
/*    Output                                                         */
/*        int return (index);     location of the min. element in sed */
/*                                                                   */
/* REMARKS :                                                         */
/*    The following parameter must be delcared as global variable.   */
/*                                                                   */
/*    extern long seed;           running seed for random no. generator */
/*===================================================================*/
int mindex(sed, no_of_element)
int no_of_element;     /* total no. of elements in sed */

double sed[];          /* a set of soft Euclidean distances */
 {
   /* global variable declaration */
   extern long seed;    /* running seed for random number generator */

   /* local variables declarations */
   double g05caf();       /* 0.0 <= random no. generator <= 1.0 */
   double running_sed;    /* running minimum sed */
   int i;                 /* general purpose variable */
   int index;             /* location of the min. element in sed */
   long newseed();        /* new seed for random generator */

   /* initialise running_sed & index */
   index = 0;
   running_sed = sed[0];
   /* find location of the min. element in sed */
   for (i = 1; i < no_of_element; i++) {
      if (running_sed < sed[i]) {
         /* no action */
         ;
```

```
        }
        else {
            if (running_sed == sed[i]) {
                /* toss a coin */
                seed = newseed();
                if (g05caf(seed) <= 0.5) {
                    /* no action */
                    ;
                }
                else {
                    /* update running_sed & index */
                    running_sed = sed[i];
                    index = i;
                }
            }
            else {
                /* update running_sed & index */
                running_sed = sed[i];
                index = i;
            }
        }
    }
    return(index);
}
```

Table G.1
Input File IN_CODECT.DAT

15	10000	0.0	1.0	0.1	0.1	0

IN_CODECT.DAT is read by codect.c
and the data format is :

start x_tot mean sd limit step hard

Table G.2
Output File RS_CODECT.DAT

Bit error rate test results:

sd	E_b/N_0(dB)	BER
1.00	0.00	0.099
0.90	0.92	0.048
0.80	1.94	0.016
0.70	3.10	0.002
0.60	4.44	0.000
0.50	6.02	0.000
0.40	7.96	0.000
0.30	10.46	0.000
0.20	13.98	0.000

About the Author

L. H. Charles Lee received a B.Sc. degree in electrical and electronic engineering from Loughborough University, England, in 1979; an M.Sc. degree from the University of Manchester Institute of Science and Technology, Manchester, England, in 1985; and a Ph.D. degree in electrical engineering from the University of Manchester in 1987.

From 1979 to 1984, Dr. Lee was with Marconi Communication Systems Ltd., Chelmsford, England, where he was engaged in the design and development of frequency hopping radios. In 1987 and 1988, he was appointed lecturer at Hong Kong Polytechnic. From 1989 to 1991, he was a staff member of the Communications Research Group, Department of Electrical Engineering, University of Manchester, where he was involved in the design of channel coding and interleaving for the Pan European GSM digital mobile radio system. Currently, Dr. Lee is with the School of Mathematics, Physics, Computing and Electronics, Macquarie University, Sydney, Australia. He has been working on the channel coding and modulation design for a 100-Mbps, 60-GHz indoor wireless LAN system. He has also served as a consultant for various companies in Australia and Asia.

Dr. Lee is a Chartered Engineer, a member of the Institution of Electrical Engineers, and a senior member of the Institute of Electrical and Electronics Engineers. His current research interests include error-control coding theory and digital communications.

Index

The Artech House Telecommunications Library
Vinton G. Cerf, Series Editor

Toll-Free Services: A Complete Guide to Design, Implementation, and Management, Robert A. Gable

Transmission Networking: SONET and the SDH, Mike Sexton and Andy Reid

Troposcatter Radio Links, G. Roda

Understanding Emerging Network Services, Pricing, and Regulation, Leo A. Wrobel and Eddie M. Pope

Understanding GPS: Principles and Applications, Elliot D. Kaplan, editor

Understanding Networking Technology: Concepts, Terms and Trends, Mark Norris

UNIX Internetworking, Second edition, Uday O. Pabrai

Videoconferencing and Videotelephony: Technology and Standards, Richard Schaphorst

Wireless Access and the Local Telephone Network, George Calhoun

Wireless Communications in Developing Countries: Cellular and Satellite Systems, Rachael E. Schwartz

Wireless Communications for Intelligent Transportation Systems, Scott D. Elliot and Daniel J. Dailey

Wireless Data Networking, Nathan J. Muller

Wireless LAN Systems, A. Santamaría and F. J. López-Hernández

Wireless: The Revolution in Personal Telecommunications, Ira Brodsky

Writing Disaster Recovery Plans for Telecommunications Networks and LANs, Leo A. Wrobel

X Window System User's Guide, Uday O. Pabrai

For further information on these and other Artech House titles, contact:

Artech House
685 Canton Street
Norwood, MA 02062
617-769-9750
Fax: 617-769-6334
Telex: 951-659
email: artech@artech-house.com

Artech House
Portland House, Stag Place
London SW1E 5XA England
+44 (0) 171-973-8077
Fax: +44 (0) 171-630-0166
Telex: 951-659
email: artech-uk@artech-house.com

WWW: http://www.artech-house.com